# Anthology of Medieval Spanish Poetry

European Masterpieces
Cervantes & Co. Spanish Classics N° 43

General Editor: TOM LATHROP
*Cervantes Society of America*

# Anthology of Medieval Spanish Poetry

Edited by

ANNETTE G. CASH
*and*
JAMES C. MURRAY

*Georgia State University*

FIRST EDITION



LinguaText, Ltd.
270 Indian Road
Newark, Delaware 19711
(302) 453-8695
Fax: (302) 453-8601

MANUFACTURED IN THE UNITED STATES OF AMERICA

ISBN: 978-1-58977-065-2

# Table of Contents

# Acknowledgments

WE ARE VERY GRATEFUL for the suggestions made as to content and the resolution of certain difficult lexical problems by Alan Deyermond. Our book is much improved because of his interest and advice. We are alsovery grateful to David Burton, editor of the companion volume, *Anthology of Medieval Spanish Prose* (Newark, DE: Cervantes & Co., 2005), who allowed us to use much of the information in the linguistic introduction to his volume.

We would also like to acknowledge Alexander McNair's edition of the *Poema de Mio Cid* (Cervantes&Co., 2008), Menéndez Pidal's edition of the "Gesta y Crónicas de los Siete Infantes en el siglo XIV" found in his *Reliquias de la Poesía Épica Española* (Madrid: Espasa-Calpe, 1951), Steve Kirby from whose edition of the *Libro de buen amor* (Cervantes & Co., 2007) we established our selections and Isidoro Janeiro, whose edition of Juan de Mena's *Trecientas* we used (Newark, DE: Juan de la Cuesta, 2008). We also consulted Manuel Alvar's *Poesía española medieval* (Barcelona: Planeta, 1969), Fernando Gómez Redondo's *Poesía española. Edad Media: juglaría, clerecía y romancero* (Barcelona: Crítica, 1996), and Dennis P. Seniff's *Antología de la literatura hispánica medieval* (Madrid: Gredos, 1992).

Tom Lathrop, editor of the series, kindly provided us with many of these texts in electronic form which made our work so much easier and also adjusted electronic texts that we had downloaded so that we could gloss them. The amount of time saved and fewer errors from our having to input texts manually were due to his help.

This anthology was class tested during the Spring of 2010 at Georgia State University in a senior level course in Spanish Medieval Literature. It was revised following our students' helpful comments and corrections.

Lingering errors are ours for which we take responsibility.

# Introduction to Students

THIS ANTHOLOGY OF MEDIEVAL Spanish poetry represents a range of works, many anonymous, produced in Spain between the 11th and the 15th centuries. While excellent critical and scholarly editions of many of these works exist, few advanced undergraduates have experience reading texts in Old Spanish. Forms and vocabulary no longer in use become a barrier to understanding and enjoying these wonderful texts. There do exist, however, anthologies in modern Spanish. We, on the other hand, have retained as much of the original language as possible, thereby maintaining the flavor of the Old Spanish.

John E. Keller chose most of the texts. They represent his abiding interest in and appreciation of the poetry of the Spanish 11th-15th centuries. His dedication to the work of Alfonso X, el Sabio, and to Gonzalo de Berceo led to his books in the Twayne World Authors series on these two giants of the Spanish Middle Ages. We also have used Nicholson B. Adams and John E. Keller's introductions to the centuries found in *A Brief Survey of Spanish Literature* (Paterson, N.J.: Littlefield, Adams, 1962).

Our anthology includes the earliest known poetry, lyric in nature, from the 11th century and continues with each century being divided into lyric, narrative, minstrel, scholar and dramatic poetry, if an example of drama exists. It was impossible to give complete works in most cases because some of the narrative poems extend to several thousand lines. Therefore we include selections of the most popular and critically studied segments of these poems. The chronology of medieval literature is not always agreed upon by all scholars, so some of these pieces may appear in different chronological order in histories and other anthologies. To make you aware of the works which we have included but which your instructor may not include, we have often repeated what was said in the general introduction to the century but in a more detailed fashion in the introduction before each selection. The general introductions offer a historical background and summary of the works in each century.

## LINGUISTIC INTRODUCTION

In order to understand much of what you are going to read, you must first be aware of the language that Spaniards spoke and wrote in the years 1200-1500.

### *Pronunciation*

Pronunciation is key in understanding some forms. Among the most essential sounds were the sibilants, those fricatives that make a hissing sound in the dental, alveolar, and palatal regions of the mouth. Each of these sounds had a voiced and an un-voiced equivalent. Beginning in the 16th and going into the early 17th century these sounds became confused. To avoid that confusion, the sounds underwent changes. The voiced sibilants unvoiced with the result that two sounds melded into one. In addition, the dental and alveolar sibilants became alveolar (along with the creation of the interdental [θ] in Castile) while the palatal sibilants moved to the velar region. A chart will illustrate this.

| GRAPH | PHONETIC LETTER | DESCRIPTION |
|---|---|---|
| ç | [ts] | voiceless dental fricative (ba**ts**) |
| z | [dz] | voiced dental fricative (a**dze**) |
| ss | [s] | voiceless alveolar fricative (**s**ome) |
| s | [z] | voiced alveolar fricative (ma**z**e) |
| x | [š] | voiceless palatal fricative (**sh**ip) |
| g (+ e,i), j | [ž] | voiced palatal fricative (**j**am) |

CHANGES:

| | | |
|---|---|---|
| c, s, ss, z | [s] | voiceless alveolar fricative (Ca**s**tigo, vali**ess**e) |

c (+e,i), z [θ] voiceless interdental fricative (in Castile) (**th**ink)

g, j [x] voiceless velar fricative (Sp. Jor**ge**)

In Old Spanish, we can consider two major categories of language: those that deal with forms, and those that deal with vocabulary.

*Forms*

Spelling, or orthography, was not standardized. Several distinct forms continued to be used well into the 16th and 17th centuries in Spain.

Originally, there were no written accent marks; these were added a few centuries later. We have added most of the accent marks.

The letters **v, u, b** all represented the same sound: the voiced bilabial [b] (**b**oy).

Bien sé que de uoluntat la oyrán
aquellos que a Dios amarán (*Santa María Egipciaca*)
I know that those who love God will hear it gladly

ha vestir e calçar
y bestias en que caualga (*Elena y María*)
he has clothes and shoes
and animals to ride

Vien se cuidó el monge seer despedazado (*Milagros*)
Indeed the monk thought he would be torn apart

A grandes bozes dixo: "Tiratme allá esse pecado." (*Mocedades*)
He said shouting, "Get this devil away from me."

Some Latin words that began with **f-** kept it into Old

Spanish. Today those words begin with **h-**.

El siglo va a zaga;
ya non sé qué me faga. (*Reyes Magos*)
the world is going backward,
I no longer know what will become of me

Dexemos al rey Carlos fablemos de ale (*Roncesvalles*)
Let us leave King Charles, let us speak of something else.

¡escarniremos las fijas del Canpeador! (*Mio Cid*)
Let us scorn the daughters of the Campeador!

e yendo por el camino una eglesia falló
e entró en ella a fazer su oración (*Siete infantes*)
and going along the road he found a church
and entered there to pray

The initial **rr-** reflects its pronunciation (trilled **r**). In some of the selections, this spelling has been has been kept or simplified depending on the edition we used.

fablarvos he por trovas e cuento rrimado (*Buen amor*)
I will speak to you in verse and rhymed story

la Virgen Santa Maria, por ende yo Juan Rroíz (*Buen amor*)
the Virgin Mary, therefore, I Juan Ruiz

Words that began with **qua-** also reflect their Latin roots. Today we spell them **cua-**.

quando qual quanto quatro qualquier

Words that ended in **-t**, today end in **-d**.

| | | | | |
|---|---|---|---|---|
| bondat | maldat | abbat | çibdat | piedat |
| vezindat | hedat | verdat | vanidat | grant |

The **ç**, called "c with *cedilla*," represented the voiceless alveolar affricate [ts]. Its voiced equivalent was [dz], written **z**.

| | | | | |
|---|---|---|---|---|
| preçiar | açúcar | entonçe | caçar | carçel |
| fazer | fizieron | dezir | razón | tredze |

The medial **-ss-** represented the voiceless alveolar fricative [s]. The **-s-** was its voiced equivalent [z].

«¡Dios, qué buen va**ss**alo! ¡Si oviesse buen señor!» (*Mio Cid*)
"God, what a good vassal! If he only had a good lord!"

por aprender corte**s**ía (*Razón de amor*)
to learn courtly behavior

non podieron los moros por los puertos passar (*Fernán González*)
the Moors could not go through the passes

çien donzellas fermosas que fuessen por casar (*Fernán González*)
one hundred beautiful maidens who were ready to marry

The initial **l-** of the verb **levar** (*llevar*) has not yet been palatalized by the diphthongization of the medial **-e-** in the present tense. It was conjugated: **lievo, lievas, lieva, levamos, levades, lievan**. This also happens with some other words: e.g. **luvia**

en su compaña .lx. pendones levava (*Mio Cid*)
in his company he had sixty knights

Non quiero más dezir: lieva dend', ve tu vía. (*Fernán González*)
I don't want to say any more, get up from there and go on your way.

a fonsario sagrado non te pudo levar (*Apolonio*)
he could not carry you to a sacred burial place

Fixa, sí Dios vos lieve a la su sancta gloria (*Santa Oria*)
My child, may God carry you to His holy glory

Often the medial **-n-** is used instead of **-m-** before **b** and **p**.

| sienpre | lunbre | tronpa | conprar | tienpo |
|---|---|---|---|---|
| nonbre | sonbra | linpia | canpos | costunbre |

The medial sequence **-sc-** sometimes had not yet simplified to **-c-**.

Hyas tornó pora Valençia | el que en buen ora nasçió. (*Mio Cid)*
Now he turned back to Valencia, the one born at a good time

a Dios mucho lo agradesçió (*Egipciaca)*
she thanked God for it very much

luego le van obedesçer (*Elena y María*)
they are going to obey him immediately

mejor me paresçe esto que non que vos enfamedes (*Buen amor*)
this seems better to me so that you are not defamed

The vowels **o** and **i** very often had not changed to **u** and **e**, respectively. Likewise, these two vowels had not yet become the diphthongs as we know them today. It is also likely that within the same selection you will notice that in one word these vowels have changed and in others they have not.

| | |
|---|---|
| veniendo / viniendo | quesiese / quisiese |
| quesiere / quisiere | dezía / dizía |
| mesmo / mismo | poseste / pusiste |
| feziese / fiziese | deligentemente / diligentemente |

Verb forms could be more varied in Old Spanish than they are today.

The Present Tense was basically the same as today. One exception is the verb **seer** (*ser*), whose **yo** form was **so**.

The Imperfect Tense for **-er** and **-ir** verbs had two different, yet interchangeable forms: one in **-ía** and another in **-íe** or **-ié**. It is very common to see both forms used in the same selection.

Fazían muy grand gozo que mayor non podían (*Fernán Gonz.*)
They made a great rejoicing, they could not rejoice more

Abrazáronse ambas commo façían en vida (*Santa Oria*)
They embraced each other as they did in life

Vidían que murmuraba, mas non la entendíen (*Santa Oria*)
They saw that she was murmuring but they did not understand her.

Peroque en sus piedes non se podíe tener (*Milagros*)
Although he was not able to stand on his feet

Non se temié del bispo nin de su cofradría (*Milagros*)
She was not afraid of the bishop or his company

Both the Future and the Conditional Tenses were in a state of flux. The forms that we know today existed alongside another, older form. The Latin Future was replaced early on with a periphrastic construction formed by the Infinitive plus the Present Indicative of **aver** (*haber*). Since Latin had no Conditional Tense, it was formed by the Infinitive plus the Imperfect of **aver**. This periphrastic construction occurred when object pronouns—whether direct, indirect, or both—were involved. The pronoun was attached (called a 'clitic' in linguistic terminology) to the Infinitive with the ending, derived from **aver**, written apart.

ca en yermo o en poblado | poder nos han alcançar (*Mio Cid*)
because they will be able to reach us in uninhabited places or towns

Ca es muy buen omne, e dart ha buen castigo. (*Milagros*)
Because he is a good man and he will give you a good penance.

el Campeador dexar las ha en vuestra mano (*Mio Cid*)
the Campeador will leave them in your care (hands)

si pudiéssemos matar el moro Avengalvón
quanta riquiza tiene aver la iemos nos (*Mio Cid*)

if we could kill the Moor Abengalbon,
we would have as much wealth as he has

Conbidar le ien de grado mas ninguno non osava (*Mio Cid*)
They would invite him willingly, but they did not dare

Until the 17th Century, there was only one form of the Imperfect Subjunctive, reflecting Latin. This form ended in **-sse-** or **-se-**.

Aquí dize de cómo el Açipreste rogó a Dios
que le diese graçia que podiese fazer este libro (*Buen amor*)
Here it says how the Archpriest begged God
to give him grace so that he might make this book

Non ha auer que le valiesse. (*Reys d'Orient*)
He had no wealth that might help him.

Ante que empezasse a sobir ennas gradas (*Milagros*)
Before he began to climb the steps

enbiara atreguar los condes, que non temiessen de daño.
(*Mocedades*)
he sent to arrange a truce with the counts so that they
would not fear any harm

como si ffuessen en pargamino (*Egipciaca*)
as if they were on parchment

What we know today as the **-ra** form of the imperfect subjunctive was, until the 17th century, the pluperfect indicative (*had gone, had written*, etc.)

como lo houiera por companyón (*Egipciaca*)
how she **had had** him as a companion

Nin lo que li dixiera Garçía su marido (*Santa Oria*)
Nor what her husband **had said** to her

mejor non albergara    después que fue nasçido. (*Fernán González*)
he **had not had** a better lodging since he was born

Non li çeló un punto de quanto que pasara. (*Milagros*)
He did not hide a single thing of all that **had happened**.

There was also a Future Subjunctive that disappeared in the 17th Century. It was formed like the Pluperfect with the final **-a** replaced with an **-e**.

Si nos fuéremos majadas abiltaredes a vos (*Mio Cid)*
If we are beaten, you will be shamed

que cuando esta calentura ovieres, que te sea menbrado,
cuantas cosas comenzares arrematarl'as con tu mano."
(*Mocedades*)
So that whenever you may have this fever you will be reminded that however many things you may begin you will complete them with your hand

E dize Dios que los que de agua fueren bautisados
fillos de Dios serán clamados,
e llos que de agua non fueren bautisados,
fillos de Dios non serán clamados. (*Razón de amor*)
And God says that those who were baptized with water
Will be called the children of God
And those that were not baptized with water
Will not be called the children of God

Seven verbs (**veer, seer, estar, dezir, fazer, aver,** and **tener**) had forms very different from today.

**Veer**, derived from the Latin verb *vidēre*, has the following irregularities:

| | | |
|---|---|---|
| PRESENT: | tú vees vos veedes | |
| PRETERIT: | él vido | |
| PRESENT PARTICIPLE: | veyendo | |

**Seer**, derived from the Latin *sedēre*, has these irregular forms:

| | | |
|---|---|---|
| PRESENT: | yo so | vos sodes |
| IMPERFECT: | yo seye | |
| PRESENT PARTICIPLE: | seyendo | |

**Estar** was rather regular, except for

| | |
|---|---|
| PRETERIT: | él estudo/ él estido |
| | ellos estudieron / ellos estidieron |
| PLUPERFECT: | estidiera |

The verb *andar* had similar forms in the Preterit: andudo/andido andudieron

**Fazer**, from the Latin *facere*, was highly irregular:

| | | | | |
|---|---|---|---|---|
| PRESENT: | fago | él faze [vos] fazedes | | |
| IMPERFECT: | fazía or fazíe | | | |
| PRETERIT : | fize | él fizo | fizides | fizieron |
| PLUPERFECT: | fiziera | | | |
| IMPERFECT SUBJ.: | fiziese or fiziesse | | | |
| FUTURE SUBJ.: | fiziere | | | |

**Dezir** (Latin *dicere*):

| | | | |
|---|---|---|---|
| *PRESENT*: | dizes | dize | dezides |
| IMPREFECT: | dezía, dezíe or dizía | | |
| PRETERIT: | dixe | dixo | dixieron |
| PLUPERFECT: | dixiera | | |
| IMPERFECT SUBJUNCTIVE: | dixiese or dixiesse | | |
| FUTURE SUBJUNCTIVE: | dixiere | | |

Notice that *dixieron*, and the forms derived from it, often contain an **-i-** that has not been absorbed by the **-x-**. The same holds true for the Preterit of the verb **traer**: **traxieron, traxiesse, traxiere.**

**Aver** (Latin *habēre*):

| | |
|---|---|
| PRESENT: | e as a avemos avedes an |
| IMPERFECT: | avíe or auía |
| PRETERIT: | ove ovo ovieron |
| PLUPERFECT: | oviera |
| PRESENT SUBJUNCTIVE: | aya |
| IMPERFECT SUBJ.: | oviese or oviesse |
| FUTURE SUBJUNCTIVE: | oviere |

**Tener** (Latin *tenēre*) was interchangeable with *aver* as an auxiliary.

| | |
|---|---|
| IMPERFECT: | tenie or tenía |
| PRETERIT: | tove tovo tovieron |
| PLUPERFECT: | toviera |
| IMPERFECT SUBJUNCTIVE: | toviese or toviesse |
| FUTURE SUBJUNCTIVE: | toviere |

**Aver** and **tener** were used interchangeably, as were **ser** and **estar**. To form a compound tense *ser* could be used with some past participles, **aver** with others. Sometimes the past participle agrees in number and gender with the subject.

**Plazer** had the following irregular forms:

| | |
|---|---|
| PRESENT: | plasco or plazo, plaze |
| IMPREFECT: | plazía or plazíe |
| PRETERIT: | plugo |
| PLUPERFECT: | pluguiera |
| IMPERFECT SUBJUNCTIVE: | pluguiese or pluguiesse |
| FUTURE SUBJUNCTIVE: | pluguiere |

Two other verbs deserve comment on forms.

**Vivir**

| | |
|---|---|
| IMPERFECT SUBJUNCTIVE: | yo visquiese |
| FUTURE SUBJUNCTIVE: | yo visquiere |

**Prender**

| | |
|---|---|
| PRETERIT: | yo prise |
| | ellos prisieron /presieron |

There were more contractions with **de** than Spanish has today.

dello deste della dallí daquel

Certain pronouns require clarification.

**Nos** could be either subject or object pronoun.

Mas en esto culpados nos seer non debemos (*Santa Oria*)
but in this we ought not to be blamed

Dixieron los fieles: | «Esto oímos nos.» (*Mio Cid*)
The faithful said: we heard this.

oy nos partiremos | e dexadas seredes de nos (*Mio Cid*)
today we will leave and you will be free of us

a nacer acá entre nos (*Coplas por la muerte de su padre*)
to be born here among us

**Vos** was a singular, and sometimes plural, term of respect for *you*. It used the second person plural form, ending in **-ades** or **-edes.**

Tanto buen amigo vos me solíades ganare (*Roncesvalles*)
You used to win so many good friends for me

E pues que vós dezides que es el daño fecho (*Buen amor*)
And since you say that the harm is already done

vos, señora doña Juana,
sois la más gentil criatura (Santillana, *Serranillas*)
you, lady doña Juana,
are the most noble being

Plural example:

HERODES: ¿Qué decides, dó ides? ¿A quién ides buscar?
¿De cuál tierra venides, o queredes andar? (*Reyes Magos*)
HEROD: What are you saying, where are you going?

Whom are you looking for? From what land do you come, where do you wish to go?

**Quien** could be either singular or plural.

¿Quieres saber quien trae esta mensajería? (*Fernán González*)
Do you want to know who brings this message?

con aquestas mis dueñas de quien so yo servida (*Mio Cid*)
with these ladies by whom I am served

Object pronouns were often attached to conjugated verb forms. The indirect object pronoun **le** and **se** were attached and dropped the final -**e**. The double objects could be written **ge lo, gelo,** or **selo**.

conquistó tod' el mundo, metiól' so su mano (*Alexandre*)
he conquered the whole world, he put it under his power

Mas valiól la Gloriosa reyna coronada. (*Milagros*)
But the Glorious Crowned Queen helped him.

e plango e quéxome de su crueza (Santillana, *Sonetos*)
and I weep and complain of her cruelty

Havíagelo la madre todo, bien razonado (*Santa Oria*)
her mother had told it to him completely and very well

Mas él non gelas quiso a ella ofreçer. (*Milagros*)
But he refused to offer them to her.

aconpáñanlo caualleros(*Elena y María*)
knights accompany him

Quísolo el diablo durament espantar,
Mas la Madre gloriosa sópogelo vedar. (*Milagros*)

The devil wanted to really frighten him
But the Glorious Mother knew how to prevent him from it.

In a prepositional phrase that included an infinitive, the object pronouns often come between the preposition and the infinitive:

que veníe en España pora gela ganar (*Fernán González*)
that he was coming to Spain to win it from him

Por non vos detener en otras ledanías (*Fernán González*)
In order not to detain you with other stories

Diz: «Por las verdades se pierden los amigos,
e por las non dezir se fazen desamigos» (*Buen amor*)
He says, because of the truth friends are lost
and for not saying it, enemies are made

e nos de vos partir nos hemos en vida (*Mio Cid*)
and we have to part from you in life

Word order can be confusing at times. In many cases, we have provided a footnote to clarify the order.

The gender of some words is not what it is today, and some nouns could be found in both masculine and feminine form such as **el color** and **la color** and **el mar** and **la mar**.

## MEDIEVAL SPANISH PROSODY

### *Scanning verses*

To scan a line of poetry in Spanish, the line is first divided into syllables. If the word ends in a stressed penultimate (second to last) vowel, you simply count the number of syllables. For example in the line:

Quien hubiera tal ventura

| Quien | hu | bie | ra | tal | ven | tu | ra |
|---|---|---|---|---|---|---|---|
| 1 | 2 | 3 | 4 | 5 | 6 | 7 | 8 |

there are 8 syllables.

If the word ends in a stressed vowel, you must add a syllable to the count.

Sobre las aguas del mar

| So | bre | la | s a | guas | del | mar | |
|---|---|---|---|---|---|---|---|
| 1 | 2 | 3 | 4 | 5 | 6 | 7 | [7 + 1 = 8] |

If the word ends in a vowel stressed on the antepenultimate (next to next to the last) syllable, one syllable is subtracted from the line.

Verdes riberas erráticas

| Ver | des | ri | be | ra | s e | rrá | ti | cas | |
|---|---|---|---|---|---|---|---|---|---|
| 1 | 2 | 3 | 4 | 5 | 6 | 7 | 8 | 9 | [9 – 1= 8] |

Sometimes poets need to have one less syllable in a line and elide two words into one syllable using the last vowel of one word and the first of the next. This is called synalepha, as in **aEu ro pa.**

Hiatus is the pronunciation of two successive vowels in adjacent words in different syllables: the opposite of synalepha. **Arte e industria**

Syneresis, on the other hand, is the union of two vowels in the same word, which are usually pronounced as two separate syllables: **poe ta, leal tad**

Dieresis, the opposite of syneresis is the dividing of two vowels normally pronounced as one syllable, i.e. a diphthong. For example: **sü a ve** and **rü i do**

*Metrical Forms*

Spanish Medieval Poetry is based on the syllable count of each line, the most common being the assonant rhyme, meaning that the rhyme is vocalic—last accented vowel and the last vowel of the word are repeated at the end of every verse, referred to as **llano** rhyme. If the word ends in a stressed syllable ending in a consonant, only the final vowels will rhyme every line, which is referred to as **agudo** rhyme. Here, as an example, are the first lines of the romance "Abenámar, Abenámar, moro de la morería."

Abenámar, Abenámar,
moro de la morería
el día que tú naciste,
grandes señales había.

On occasion one observes minstrel poetry in assonant rhyme of 16-syllable lines. These are really two 8 syllable lines with a cæsura, or break, after the eighth syllable or sometimes after the seventh or the ninth.

De los sos ojos tan fuerte mientre lorando
tornava la cabeça y estava los catando.
Vio puertas abiertas e uços sin cañados,
alcandaras vazias sin pielles e sin mantos
e sin falcones e sin adtores mudados.
Sospiro mio Çid ca mucho avie grandes cuidados.
fablo mio Çid bien e tan mesurado:
«¡Grado a ti, señor, padre que estas en alto!
¡Esto me an buelto mios enemigos malos!»

Here is an example of some **agudo** lines in accented **o** from the *Poema de Mio Cid.*

Exien lo ver | mugieres e varones,
burgeses e burgesas por las finiestras son,
plorando de los ojos tanto avien el dolor.

De las sus bocas todos dizían ʿuna razón:
«¡Dios, qué buen vassalo! ¡Si oviesse buen señor!»

There is, of course, full rhyme, meaning that the last accented vowel and the rest of the line are the same as in this first stanza from the fourteenth sonnet of the Marqués de Santillana.

| | |
|---|---|
| Cuando yo soy delante aquella dona | A |
| a cuyo mando me sojuzgó Amor, | B |
| cuido ser uno de los que en Tabor | B |
| vieron la gran claror que se razona, | A |

The letters at the end of the line indicate the rhyme scheme. Verses of 11-syllable lines, such as these, are called **arte mayor.** Very simply, lines longer than 8 syllables are known as **arte mayor**, and verses of 8 syllables or fewer are referred to as **arte menor**.

Some verse forms in addition to the romance are:

Sonnets of 14 lines usually made up of two quatrains and two tercets.

**Pie quebrado** which consists of two lines of 8 syllables followed by a four-syllable line as in these first lines of Jorge Manrique's *Coplas.*

Recuerde el alma dormida,
Avive el seso y despierte
contemplando
cómo se pasa la vida,
cómo se viene la muerte
tan callando,
cuán presto se va el placer,
cómo, después de acordado,
da dolor;
cómo, a nuestro parecer,
cualquiera tiempo pasado
fue mejor.

The common **mester de clerecía** is a verse form of 14 syllable lines in monorhymed quatrains also known as **cuaderna vía**. It is Gonzalo de Berceo's commonest verse form. Here is the last quatrain of "Milagro 21."

582. A la Virgo gloriosa todos graçias rendamos,
De qui tantos miraclos leemos e probamos;
Ella nos dé su gratia que servirla podamos,
E nos guíe fer cosas por ond salvos seamos. Amén.

The Paragogic **e**
This is a phenomenon in Spanish Medieval poetry which adds a non-etymological **e** to the last word of the line of poetry to assist in versification. Here are some lines from *Roncesvalles* that illustrate the paragogic **e**:

Levémosle a su tierra a Flanderes la ciudade!»
El enperador andaba 'catando por la mortaldade;

vido en la plaça Oliveros o yaze

el escudo crebantado por medio del braçale,
non vio sano en éll cuanto un dinero cabe;
tornado a orient como lo puso Roldane.

El buen enperador mandó la cabeza alçare

que le linpiasen la cara del polvo e de la sangre.

Como si fuese vivo començólo de preguntare:
«Digádesme, don Oliveros, caballero naturale,

dó dexastes a Roldán?, digádesme la verdade.

VOCABULARY

Like forms, vocabulary in the Spanish middle ages can be an obstacle to understanding a text. Some words no longer have the same meaning; some have merely gone through a spelling change; others no longer exist. You will quickly learn words and phrases that appear repeatedly. Here are some common ones:

| | |
|---|---|
| **agora** *adv* . | now |
| **aína** *adv.* | quickly, rapidly |
| **ál** *n.* | other, another thing |
| **asmar, cuedar, cuidar** | to think |
| **ca** *conj.* | because |
| **catar** | to look |
| **castigar** | to advise |
| **conbrir** | to eat |
| **defender** | to prohibit |
| **do, o, onde** *adv.* | where |
| **e, et** *conj.* | and |
| **estonçe** *adv.* | then |
| **fallar** | to find |
| **fasta** *prep.* | until |
| **fixa** *n.* | daughter |
| **guisa** *n.* | manner |
| **maguer** *conj.* | although |
| **muger, muggier** *n.* | woman |
| **non** | no |
| **ome, omne, ombre** *n.* | man |
| **pagarse de** | to be pleased with |
| **poridat** *n* . | secret |
| **y** *adv.* | there |

# *XI and XII Centuries: Introduction*

## HISTORICAL BACKGROUND

IT WAS DURING THE 10th century that Castile became an independent *condado* under the rule of the famous count Fernán González. In the 11th century Ferdinand I was crowed the first king of Castile. When he became heir of the kingdom of Leon, he became the first king of the two kingdoms. On his death the kingdoms suffered great confusion because his sons and daughters claimed the respective parts of the realm bequeathed them in Ferdinand's will. Castile went to Sancho; Galicia to García; Leon to Alfonso; and the cities of Toro and Zamora to the daughters Elvira and Urraca. Sancho II tried to seize all the territory for himself, but was murdered at Zamora during the siege, and Alfonso VI gained the power and unified the divided realm.

The 11th century saw the fall of Toledo (1085) to Alfonso's troops, the capture of Valencia by the Cid, and the continuation of the Reconquest which would not end until 1492 with the fall of Granada to Ferdinand and Isabella. The Cid, Ruy Díaz de Vivar, stands as the great hero of the age.

During the 11th century the monks of Cluny entered Spain, bringing the learning for which they were famous. Important also was the fall of the Caliphate of Cordoba to the Almorávides. Moorish Spain had reached the peak of its culture and magnificence under the Caliphs of Cordoba.

## *LYRIC POETRY*

At least as early as the mid-eleventh century there existed a kind of early Spanish lyric poetry in Andalusia, and probably in other parts of Spain. Proof of this lies in the *jarchas*. Jewish and Arabic poets wrote a kind of poetry called *muashaha* in either five or six stanzas of Arabic or Hebrew dealing with themes traditional to semitic poetry. They were in the habit of including a final, short stanza in Mozarabic Spanish called a *jarcha.* These *jarchas* were early Spanish folk poetry of a type later called *villancicos.* The fact that the Hispano-Romance words were written in Hebrew or in Arabic characters concealed the true nature of the *jarchas* for many years. A modern example of Hispano-Romance might be Tex-Mex or Spanglish. In 1948 Samuel M. Stern found twenty-four such compositions in a synagogue in Cairo, Egypt. Later Emilio García Gómez added to this number bringing their total to as many as fifty such poems, many of true lyric freshness, proving conclusively that Spain had a lyric poetry long before the times of Gonzalo de Berceo (1196?-1255?) who had previously been said to be the first lyric poet in Spanish, even before the schools of Galician-Portuguese poets (late 12th century to early 14th century). These *jarchas* may well be the oldest extant lyric poetry in medieval Europe, for they antedate the poems of William IX, Duke of Acquitaine (or William VII of Poitiers, as he is sometimes called, 1071-1126), called the first of the troubadours.

NARRATIVE POETRY

Narrative folk poetry, particularly of the sort that is found in the heroic poems of the Germanic peoples, may have existed among the Visigoths who overran Spain in the early fifth century. Such popular poetry probably survived, especially in areas not under Moorish control, but none has survived from a period earlier than the twelfth century.

## *Jarchas romances*[1]

It should be remembered that the *jarchas* were written in Arabic or Romance (the early Spanish of the XI and XII centuries), that

[1] The texts are from Emilio García Gómez. *Las jarchas romances de la serie árabe en su marco.* Madrid: Sociedad de Estudios y Publicaciones, 1965. All *jarchas* are taken from this edition, pps. 95, 144, 151, 187, 195, 287, 343.

they were love poems put into the mouths of women, although the poems were written by men, and that they are similar in form and manner of presentation to the early *villancicos* (folk songs) and *estribillos.* The *estribillo,* consisting of a few lines of poetry, began the lyric composition and was repeated at the end of each verse. Indeed, Spanish *coplas* sung to this day bear a close resemblance to the early *jarchas.*

VIIa
Ben, ya sahhara;
*¡Ven, oh hechicero!* ° — enchanter
Alba q'está kon bel fogore
*Un alba* ° *que tiene tan hermoso fulgor,* ° — dawn, brilliance
kand bene bid' amore.
*Cuando viene pide amor.*

XIV
¡Mamma, 'ay habibe!
*¡Madre, qué amigo!*
So l-yummella saqrella
*¡Bajo la 'guedejuela rubita* ° — long blond hair
el-quwello albo
*el 'cuello albo* ° — white neck
e bokella harmella
*y la "boquita coloradita* ° — dear red mouth

XV
No se kedó ni me kyéred gariré
*No 'se quedó,* ° *ni me quiere decir* — stay
kelma
*palabra*
No zey kon seno masuto dormire,
*No sé con el 'seno abrasado* ° *dormir,* — heart aflame
*no puedo,*
Mamma
*madre*

XX
Si 'os báis, ya sidi,
*Si os vais dueño ° mío* lord
k'ante besar-os-e
*mirad que antes ' 'he de ° besaros* I have to
la bokella hamra,
*la boquita roja*
fermelya ka-l-wars'.
bermeja° como la cúrcuma° red, saffron

XXI a
Ya mamma, me-w l-habibe
*Madre, mi amigo*
bais' e no mas tomarade.
*se va y no tornará ° más.* will return
Gar ké faréyo, ya mamma;
*Dime qué haré, madre;*
¿no un bezyello lesarade?
*¿no me dejará [siquiera] ° un besito?* even

XXIX
¡Ya qorazoni, ke keres bon' amar!
*¡Ay, corazón mío, que quieres ' buen amar! °* wonderful love
A liyorar
*Para llorar*
laita -ni 'obiese weliyos de mar.
*ojalá tuviese ' los ojos del mar! °* sea of tears

XXXV
Bokella 'al-'iqdi,
*Boquita de collar °* white pearls
dolze com as-suhdi,
*dulce como la miel °* honey
ben, bézame.
*Ven, bésame.*
Habibi, yi'indi.

*¡Amigo mío, ven a mí!*
adunam; amande
*¡únete a mí,!° amante* merge with me
Ke huyome.
*que me huyó.*

Yehuda Halevi (1075?-1141?), a Spanish Jewish physician, philosopher and poet, was born in Tudela, Navarre and died in Jerusalem. His poetry is both secular and religious with his secular themes being joyous, carefree youth and a delight in life. He is credited with the invention of the *sionida,* poems that expressed a longing for distant Jerusalem.

Ven, cidi, veni,
*Ven, señor mío, ven,*
el querer es tanto bieni
*¡el querer es tan grande bien*
d'est al-zameni,
*de este tiempo!*
con filyod d' Ibn al-Dayyeni.
*con el hijo de Ibn al-Dayyen.*

Des cuand mio Cidiello viénid
*Cuando mi señor viene,*
¡tan buona albischara!
*¡qué buenas albricias!°* news
com rayo de sol éxid
*como un rayo de sol sale*
en Wadalachyara
*en Guadalajara.*

Garid vos, ay yermaniellas,
*Decid vosotras, ¡hermanillas!*
cómo contener a mieu mali!
*¡Cómo soportar° mis males!°* endure, sufferings
sin el habib non vivréyu,

*Sin el amigo no podré vivir;*
advolarei demandari
*volaré ° en su busca. °* I will fly, search

Non me tancas, ya habibi,
*No me toques, ° oh amigo mío,* touch
fincad y en esu,
*permanece ° quieto ahí.* stay
al-yalala rujsatu,
*La majestad es toda indulgencia*
baste tu permisu.
*baste tu permiso.*

Vaise mio corayon de mib;
*Váse mi corazón de mí,*
ya Rab, ¿si se me tornarád?
*¡oh Señor! ¿acaso tornará?*
¡tan mal mio doler li-l-habib!
*¡Es tan grande mi dolor por el amigo!*
enfermo yed ¿cuánd sanarád?
*Está enfermo, ¿cuándo sanará?*

Abraham ben Ezra (1092-1167), born in Tudela, Navarre was an outstanding Jewish intellectual and author whose writings include works on philosophy, grammar, kabala, medicine, mathematics and astronomy. He was also a poet whose themes were both profane and religious and is recognized for his beautiful Hebrew verse. He died in Calahorra.

Gar qué farayyu
*Di, ¿qué haré yo?*
cómo vivrayu.
*¿cómo viviré yo?*
Est Alhabib espero
*Espero a mi amado.*

por él morrayu.
*Por él moriré yo.*

*Cantigas de amigo* and *villancicos* are most probably circulating orally in the eleventh through the twelfth centuries while the earliest extant texts of the *cantigas de amigo* are from the thirteenth century. The extant texts of the *villancicos* are of the late fifteenth century.

## *XII Century*

### HISTORICAL BACKGROUND

The 12$^{th}$ century was not a period conducive to literature. The Kingdoms of Castile and Leon, divided by Ferdinand among his children, were the source of war and confusion. Alfonso VI and Alfonso VII continued the endless Reconquest—the 700-odd years when Christians took back lands on the Iberian Peninsula that Moorish tribes took over —starting in 711—, and out of the warfare between Muslim and Christian came the famous epic *Poema de Mio Cid*, the great literary masterpiece of the century.
During this period the warrior monks of Islam, known as the Almoravides, defeated Alfonso VI and founded a strong realm in southern Spain. The Kingdom of Castile, in spite of defeat, continued to expand.
Spain's great military orders, founded to protect pilgrims and to wage war against the Muslims, came into being in the 12$^{th}$ century: Calatrava (1158), Alcántara (1166), Santiago (1175). Portugal's independence from Leon was recognized in 1143.

### LYRIC POETRY

No Castilian lyric poetry, as distinct from the *jarchas* of Southern Spain, has survived from the 12$^{th}$ century. The Mozarabs, Spaniards living under Moorish rule, probably continued the popular poetry they had been using in the 11$^{th}$ century. In the northwest, Galician-Portuguese poetry, some probably from folk tradition and some modeled upon the poetry of the troubadours of Provence, was beginning to flower, but it was not to reach the peak of its development for another century. It is quite possible, too, that in the north, native and popular poetry of some sort existed beside the poetry borrowed from the troubadours.

## NARRATIVE POETRY

*Poesía y recitación juglaresca.* The poetry of the minstrels, itinerate entertainers, was used for epics as well as for other narrative poems in the XIII century but in the XII century was exclusively epic. This form of poetry was characterized by lines of irregular length, averaging 16 syllables (although some had as many as 20) broken in the middle by a caesura, or pause. There was assonance (vowel) rather than full consonantal rhyme. All this poetry in the XII century is anonymous, even though narrative poetry reached its peak in this period.

The *Poema de Mio Cid*, most famous of the Spanish epics, was composed around 1140 (perhaps somewhat later), but the sole surviving manuscript, the date of which is in question, was copied by a scribe named Per Abbat. The *Poema* has 3700 lines.

## *POEMA DE MIO CID*

Based upon the life of Rodrigo Díaz de Vivar, who died in 1099, the poem is realistic, although it incorporates certain fictitious elements. In tone, presentation, and subject matter, the *Poema* differs greatly from the highly imaginative French epic, the *chanson de geste*. It is divided into three cantos; in Cantar I the Cid (the Arabic *Sidi* means 'lord'), so named by his allies among the Muslims, is exiled by Alfonso VI, and marches east with a conquering army through Moorish Spain; Cantar II tells of the Cid's capture of Moorish Valencia (historically accurate) and of the marriage of his daughters (legendary) to the Infantes de Carrión, who turn out to be great cowards; Cantar III deals with the affront to the Cid's daughters by their husbands and of the trial by combat between the husbands and the Cid's champions. The style of the *Poema* is terse, but the story moves along and sustains interest. The Cid was a hero of the people; his story is told realistically and simply by someone who lived during, or not long after, those times.

Here are some sections from Cantares I and III. The first folio—one page front and back—is missing, but it starts at a pretty intense moment, with the Cid in tears looking at the closed gates of Burgos, from where he has been exiled.

*In Cantar I the Cid has been exiled by the King Alfonso VI of Leon because some of the Cid's enemies have accused him of withholding tribute money that he had collected from the Moors for the king. The Cid observes his desolate house in Vivar and promises to return triumphant. He leaves his wife Doña Ximena and his two small daughters, Elvira and Sol in the care of the abbot of the monastery of San Pedro de Cardeña and hurries to leave the realm of Alfonso VI before the mandated deadline. On his way, many soldiers who want to serve him and enrich themselves join his army. There are many battles and victories for the Cid and his men.*

## *Poema de Mio Çid*

Cantar del destierro° — exile

| | | |
|---|---|---|
| De los sos° ojos | tan fuerte mientre lorando° | **=sus**, **=llorando** |
| tornava la cabeça | y estava los catando.° | looking |
| Vio puertas abiertas | e uços° sin cañados,° | doors, locks |
| Alcándaras° vazías | sin pielles° e sin mantos° | hooks, skins, cloaks |
| e sin falcones e sin | adtores mudados.° | molting hawks |
| Sospiró mío Çid | ca mucho avie grandes cuidados. | |
| Ffabló mío Çid | bien e tan mesurado:° | prudently |
| «¡Grado a ti, señor, | padre que estás en alto! | |
| ¡Esto me an vuelto° | míos enemigos malos!» | done |
| Allí pienssan de aguijar,° | allí sueltan las riendas. | spur on |
| A la exida de° Bivar | ovieron la corneja° diestra° | on leaving, crow, right |
| y entrando a Burgos | ovieron la siniestra.° | on the left |
| Meçió° mío Çid los ombros | y engrameó° la tiesta: | shrugged, shook |
| «¡Albriçia,° Álbar Ffáñez, | ca echados° somos de tierra!» | rejoice, thrown out |
| Mío Çid Ruy Díaz | por Burgos entrava, | |
| en su compaña | .lx. pendones° levava.° | knights, **=llevaba** |

| | |
|---|---|
| Exien° lo ver   mugieres e varones,° | came out, men |
| burgeses e burgesas   por las finiestras° son, | windows |
| plorando° de los ojos   tanto avien el dolor. | **=llorando** |
| De las sus bocas   todos dizían 'una razón:° | the same thing |
| «¡Dios, qué buen vassalo!°   ¡Si oviesse buen señor!» | **=vasallo** |
| | |
| Conbidar° le ien 'de grado°   mas ninguno non osava;° | invite, willingly, dare |
| el rey don Alfonsso   tanto avie la grand saña,° | anger |
| antes de la noche   en Burgos dél entró su carta° | decree |
| con grand recabdo°   e fuerte mientre sellada,° | warning, sealed |
| que a mío Çid Ruy Diaz   que nadi°  nol diesse(n) posada,° | **=nadie**, lodging |
| e aquel que gela diesse   sopiesse—vera palabra— | |
| que perderie los averes°   e más los ojos de la cara | possessions |
| e 'aun demás°   los cuerpos e las almas. | in addition |
| Grande duelo avien   las yentes° christianas; | **=gentes** |
| Asconden° se de mío Çid   ca nol osan dezir nada. | hide |
| El Campeador   adeliño° a su posada; | went directly |
| así commo legó a la puerta   falóla° bien çerrada | **=hallóla** |
| por miedo del rey Alfonsso   que assí lo avien parado° | arranged |
| que si non la quebrantas° por fuerça | break |
|   que non gela abriese nadi. | |
| Los de mío Çid   a altas vozes laman, | |
| los de dentro   non les querien tornar palabra. | |
| Aguijó mío Çid,   a la puerta se legava, | |
| sacó el pie del estribera,°   una feridal° dava; | stirrup, kick |
| non se abre la puerta   ca bien era çerrada. | |
| Una niña de nuef° años 'a ojo se parava:° | **=nueve**, appeared |
| «¡Ya Campeador   en buen ora çinxiestes° espada! | girded on |
| El rey lo ha vedado,°   anoch dél entró su carta | forbidden |
| con grant recabdo   e fuerte mientre sellada. | |
| Non vos osariemos° abrir   nin coger° por nada; | dare, welcome |
| si non, perderiemos   los averes e las casas | |
| e demás   los ojos de las caras. | |
| Çid, en el nuestro mal   vos non ganades nada; | |
| mas ¡el Criador vos vala°   con todas sus vertudes santas!» | help |
| Esto la niña dixo   e tornós pora su casa. | |

Ya lo vee el Çid    que del rey non avie graçia.
Partiós de la puerta,    por Burgos aguijava,
legó a Santa María,    luego descavalga,°    got off his horse
'fincó los inojos,°    de coraçón rogava.°    knelt down, prayed
La oraçión fecha    luego cavalgava;°    rode
salió por la puerta    e (en) Arlançón p[a]sava.    river of Burgos
Cabo° essa villa    en la glera° posava,    next, sandy area
fincava la tienda    e luego descavalgava.
Mío Çid Ruy Díaz    el que en buen ora çinxó espada
posó en la glera    quando nol coge nadi en casa,
derredor dél    una buena conpaña.
Assí posó mio Çid    commo si fuesse en montaña.
Vedada l'an compra    dentro en Burgos la casa
de todas cosas    quantas son de vianda;°    meat
non le osarien vender    'al menos dinarada.°    not the least amount
Martín Antolínez    el burgalés° complido°    from Burgos, excellent
a mío Çid e a los suyos    abástales° de pan e de vino;    supplies them
non lo conpra, ca él selo avie consigo;
de todo conducho°    bien los ovo bastidos.°    provisions, supplied

Pagós° mío Çid    el Campeador [conplido]    was pleased
e todos los otros    que van a so çervicio.
Fabló Martín Antolínez,    odredes° la que a dicho:    you will hear
«¡Ya Canpeador    en buen ora fuestes naçido!
Esta noch y[a]gamos°    e vay[a]mos nos al matino,°    let us rest, morning
ca acusado seré    de lo que vos he servido;
en ira del rey Alfonsso    yo seré metido.
Si 'con vusco°    escapo sano o vivo    with you
aun çerca o tarde    el rey querer me ha por amigo;
si non, quanto dexo    '¡no lo preçio un figo!»°    does not matter to me
Fabló mío Çid    el que en buen ora çinxó espada:
«¡Martín Antolínez    sodes ardida° lança!°    brave, warrior
Si yo bivo doblar vos he la soldada.°    wages
'Espeso e° el oro    e toda la plata;    I have spent
bien lo vedes    que yo no trayo° [nada],    **=traigo**
e 'huebos me serie°    pora toda mi compaña;    I would need it

fer lo he amidos, de grado non avrie nada.[2]
Con vuestro consejo° bastir quiero dos archas;° help, chests
Incamos° las d'arena° ca bien serán pesadas, we will fill, sand
cubiertas de guadalmeçi° e bien enclaveadas.° tooled leather, shu
Los guadameçis bermejos° e los clavos bien dorados.° red, gilded
Por Rachel e Vidas vayades me privado;° in a hurry
quando en Burgos me vedaron compra
y el rey me a airado,
non puedo traer el aver ca mucho es pesado,
enpeñar° gelo he por lo que fuere guisado.° pawn, just
De noche lo lieven que non lo vean christianos;
vealo el Criador con todos los sos santos,
yo más non puedo e amidos lo fago.»

Martín Antolínez non lo detar[da]va,° delay
por Rachel e Vidas a priessa demandava.
Passó por Burgos, al castiello° entrava, fortified part of ci
por Rachel e Vidas a priessa demandava.
Rachel e Vidas 'en uno° estavan amos together
en cuenta de sus averes, de los que avien ganados.
Legó Martín Antolínez a guisa de menbrado:
«¿O° sodes, Rachel e Vidas, los míos amigos caros? where
En poridad° fablar querría con amos.» secret
Non lo detardan, todos tres se apartaron:
«Rachel e Vidas: amos me dat las manos
que non me descubrades° a moros nin a christianos; tell anyone
por siempre vos faré ricos, que non seades menguados.° in need
El Campeador por las parias° fue entrado, tributes
grandes averes priso e mucho sobejanos;° abundant
retovo dellos 'quanto que fue algo,° all that had value
'por en vino a aquesto° por que fue acusado. for this reason
Tiene dos arcas lennas° de oro esmerado.° **=llenas**, precious
Ya lo vedes que el rey le a airado.
Dexado ha heredades e casas e palaçios;
aquelas non las puede levar, si non, ser ien ventadas;° discovered

[2] **Fer lo he…** *I will have to get it unwillingly since they will not give it to me.*

el Campeador dexar las ha     en vuestra mano,
e prestalde° de aver     lo que sea guisado.     lend him
Prended las archas     e meted las en vuestro salvo;°     care
con grand jura°     meted i las fes° amos     oath, word
que non las catedes     en todo aqueste año.»
Rachel e Vidas     seyen se consejando:°     consulting
«Nos huebos avemos     en todo de ganar algo.
Bien lo sabemos     que él algo gañó,°     earned
quando a tierra de moros entró     que grant aver sacó;
non duerme sin sospecha     qui aver trae monedado.°     money
Estas archas     prendamos las amas,
en logar las metamos     que non sean ventadas.
Mas dezid nos del Çid:     ¿de qué será pagado,
o qué ganançia nos dará     por todo aqueste año?»
Respuso Martín Antolínez     a guisa de menbrado:
«Mío Çid querrá lo que ssea aguisado,
pedir vos a poco     por dexar so aver en salvo;
acogen sele omnes     de todas partes menguados;
'a menester°     seis çientos marcos.»     he needs
Dixo Rachel e Vidas:     «Dar gelos [hemos] de grado.»
«Ya vedes que entra la noch,     el Cid es presurado;°     in a hurry
huebos avemos     que nos dedes los marchos.»°     silver marks
Dixo Rachel e Vidas:     «Non se faze assí el mercado.°     business
si non primero prendiendo     e después dando.»
Dixo Martín Antolínez:     «Yo desso me pago.
Amos tred°     al Campeador contado,     go
e nos vos ayudaremos     que assí es aguisado
por aduzir° las archas     e meter las en vuestro salvo,     bring
que non lo sepan     moros nin christianos.»
Dixo Rachel e Vidas:     «Nos desto nos pagamos;
las archas aduchas,     prendet seyes° çientos marcos.»     **=seis**

Martín Antolínez     cavalgó privado
con Rachel e Vidas     de voluntad e de grado.
Non viene a la pueent     ca° por 'el agua a pasado°     but, ford
que gelo non venta(n)ssen     de Burgos omne nado.

Afevos° los a la tienda del Campeador contado: behold
assí commo entraron al Çid besaron le las manos,
sonrrisós° mío Çid, estávalos fablando: smiled
«¡Ya don Rachel e Vidas avedes me olbidado!° forgotten
Ya me exco de tierra ca del rey so airado;
a lo quem semeja° de lo mío avredes algo, seems
mientras que vivades non seredes menguados.»
Don Rachel e Vidas a mío Çid besaron le las manos.
Martín Antolínez el pleito° a parado contract
que sobre aquelas archas dar le ien .vi. çientos marcos
e bien gelas guardarien fasta cabo del año;
ca assíl dieran la fe e gelo avien jurado
que si antes las catassen que fuessen perjurados,° perjured
non les diesse mío Çid de la ganançia un dinero malo.
Dixo Martín Antolínez: «Cargen las archas privado.
Levaldas, Rachel e Vidas, poned las en vuestro salvo;
yo iré con vus[c]o que adugamos° los marcos, bring
ca a mover a mío Çid ante que cante el gallo.»° rooster
Al cargar de las archas veriedes gozo tanto:
non las podien 'poner en somo° mager eran esforçados.° lift, strong
Gradan se Rachel e Vidas con averes monedados,
ca mientra que visquiessen° refechos° eran amos. lived, enriched
Rachel a mío Çid la manol ba besar:
«¡Ya Campeador en buen ora çinxiestes espada!
De Castiella vos ides pora las yentes estrañas;
assí es vuestra ventura,° grandes son vuestras ganançias, fortune
una piel° vermeja morisca e ondrada surcoat
Çid, beso vuestra mano 'en don° que la yo aya.» as a gift
«Plazme», dixo el Çid, «D'aquí sea mandada;
si vos la aduxier d'allá; si non, contalda sobre las arcas.»
En medio del palaçio tendieron un almofalla,° carpet
sobr'ella una savana° de rançal° e muy blanca; sheet, linen
'a tod el primer colpe° .iii.ccc marcos de plata echa[va]n, immediately
Notólos don Martino, sin peso los tomava;
los otros .ccc. en oro gelos pagavan.
Çinco escuderos tiene don Martino, a todos los cargava.

Quando esto ovo fecho    odredes lo que fablava:
«Ya don Rachel e Vidas    en vuestras manos son las arcas;
yo, que esto vos gané,    bien mereçía calças.»°    trousers
Entre Rachel e Vidas    aparte ixieron amos:
«Demos le buen don    ca él no'° lo ha buscado.    from us
Martín Antolínez    un burgalés contado
vos lo mereçedes,    darvos queremos buen dado°    gift
de que fagades calças    e rica piel e buen manto;
damos vos en don    a vos .xxx. marchos.
Mereçer no' lo hedes,    ca esto es aguisado,
Atorgar° nos hedes    esto que avemos parado.»    granted
Gradeçiólo don Martino    e reçibió los marchos;
Gradó° exir de la posada    y espidiós° de amos.    he was glad, **=se** despi-**dio**
Exido es de Burgos    e Arlançón a passado,
vino pora la tienda    del que en buen ora nasco;°    was born
reçibiólo el Çid    abiertos amos los braços:
«¿Venides, Martín Antolínez,    el mío fiel vassalo?
¡Aun vea el día    que de mí ayades algo!»
«Vengo, Campeador,    con todo buen recabdo;
vos .vi. çientos    e yo .xxx. he ganados.
Mandad coger° la tienda    e vayamos privado,    strike
en San Pero de Cardeña    i nos cante el gallo;
veremos vuestra mugier    menbrada 'fija dalgo;°    noble woman
mesuraremos° la posada    e quitaremos el reinado,    cut short
mucho es huebos    ca çerca viene el plazo.»°    deadline
Estas palabras dichas,    la tienda es cogida,
Mío Çid e sus conpañas    cavalgan tan aína.°    quickly
La cara del cavallo    tornó a Santa María,
alçó su mano diestra,    la cara se santigua:°    raised, made the sign OF the cross
«¡A ti lo gradesco, Dios,    que çielo e tierra guías!
¡Valan me tus vertudes    gloriosa Santa María!
D'aquí quito Castiella    pues que el rey he en ira;
non sé si entraré i más    en todos los míos días.
¡Vuestra vertud me vala    Gloriosa, en mi exida,
e me ayude é(l) me acorra    de noch e de día!
Si vos assí lo fiziéredes    e la ventura me fuere complida

| | |
|---|---|
| mando al vuestro altar   buenas donas e ricas; | |
| esto 'é yo en debdo °   que faga i cantar mill missas.» | I make a promise |
| Spidiós el caboso °   de cuer e de veluntad. | perfect one |
| Sueltan las riendas   e pienssan de aguijar. | |
| Dixo Martín Antolínez: | |
| «Veré a la mugier a todo mío solaz, ° | ease |
| Castigar ° los he   cómmo 'abrán a far. ° | advise, are to act |
| Si el rey melo quisiere tomar   '¡a mí non m'inchal! ° | I don't care |
| Antes seré con vusco   que el sol quiera rayar.» | |
| Tornavas Martín Antolínez a Burgos   e mío Çid aguij[ó] | |
| pora San Pero de Cardeña   quanto pudo 'a espol[ón] ° | spur on |
| con estos cavalleros   quel sirven a so sabor. | |
| A priessa cantan los gallos   e quieren 'quebrar albores ° | dawn is breaking |
| quando legó a San Pero   el buen Campeador. | |
| El abbat don Sancho   christiano del Criador | |
| rezava los matines °   'abuelta de los albores; ° | matins, at dawn |
| i estava doña Ximena   con çinco dueñas 'de pro ° | noble |
| rogando a San Pero   e al Criador: | |
| «¡Tú que a todos guías   val a mío Çid el Campeador!» | |
| | |
| Lamavan a la puerta,   i sopieron el mandado; | |
| ¡Dios, qué alegre fue   el abbat don Sancho! | |
| Con lumbres ° e con candelas   al corral 'dieron salto, ° | torches, rushed out |
| con tan grant gozo reçiben   al que en buen ora nasco: | |
| «¡Gradesco lo a Dios, mío Çid!»   dixo el abbat don Sancho; | |
| «Pues que aquí vos veo   prendet de mí ospedado.» ° | hospitality |
| Dixo el Çid: «Graçias, don abbat,   e so vuestro pagado. ° | grateful one |
| Yo adobaré ° conducho   pora mí e pora mis vassallos; | will prepare |
| mas por que me vo de tierra   dovos .l. marchos, | |
| si yo algún día visquier   servos han doblados. | |
| Non quiero fazer en el monesterio   un dinero de daño; | |
| evades ° aquí pora doña Ximena   dovos .c. marchos, | behold, |
| a ella e a sus fijas e a sus dueñas   sírvades las est año. | |
| Dues fijas dexo niñas   e 'prendet las ° en los braços, | take them |
| aquellas vos acomiendo a vos,   abbat don Sancho; | |
| dellas e de mi mugier   'fagades todo recabdo. ° | take good care |

Si essa despenssa vos falleçiere[3] o 'vos menguare° algo, — you need
bien 'las abastad,° 'yo assí vos lo mando;° — provide for them, I order you; each mark you spend
por 'un marco que despendades° al monesterio
dar yo quatro».
Otorgado gelo avíe[4] el abbat 'de grado.° — willingly
Afévos doña Ximena con sus fijas do va legando,
'señas dueñas° las traen e aduzen° las adelant.° — two ladies. lead, forward
Ant'el Campeador doña Ximena fincó los inojos amos,
Lorava de los ojos, quísol besar las manos:
«¡Merçed, Campeador, en ora buena 'fuestes nado!° — **=naciste**
Por 'malos mestureros° de tierra sodes° echado. — evil slanderers, **=sois**
¡Merçed, ya° Çid, 'barba tan complida!° — oh, perfect beard (epithet)
Fem° ante vos yo e vuestras fijas — **=me tienes**
—infantes° son e 'de días chicas—° — girls, very young
con aquestas mis dueñas de quien so° yo servida. — **=soy**
Yo lo veo que 'estades vos en ida° — prepared to leave
e nos de vos 'partir nos hemos° en vida: — **=tenemos que partir**
¡Da(n)d° nos consejo por amor de Santa María!» — **=dad**
a las sus fijas en braço' las prendía,
lególas° al coraçón ca mucho las quería. — he lifted them
Lora de los ojos, tan 'fuerte mientre° sospira: — **=fuertemente**
«¡Ya doña Ximena la mi mugier tan complida,
commo a la mi alma yo tanto vos quería!
Ya lo vedes° que partir nos emos en vida, — **=veis**
yo iré e 'vos fincaredes remanida.° — you will stay
¡Plega° a Dios e a Santa María — May it please
que aun con mis manos case estas mis fijas,
'o que de ventura e algunos días vida° — if I am lucky and live a while; **=honrada**,
e vos, mugier ondrada,° de mí seades° servida!» — **=seáis**; banquet
Grand yantar° le fazen al buen Campeador.
Tañen° las campanas en San Pero a clamor. — ring
Por Castiella oyendo van los pregones° — call to arms
commo se va de tierra mío Çid el Campeador;
unos dexan casas e otros onores,° — property

[3] **Si essa...** *if this amount is not enough*
[4] **Ortogado gelo... =gelo avíe otorgado** *had granted it to him*

en aques día a la puent de Arlançón
çiento quinze cavalleros todos juntados son;
todos demandan por mío Çid el Campeador.
Martín Antolínez con ellos cojó;° went
vansse pora San Pero do está el que en buen punto naçió.
Quando lo sopo mío Çid el de Bivar
quel creçe compaña por que más valdrá,
a priessa cavalga, reçebir los sal(i)e,
tornós a sonrisar, legan le todos, la manol ban besar.
Fabló mío Çid de toda voluntad:
«Yo ruego a Dios e al Padre spirital,
vos, que por mi dexades casas y heredades,
enantes° que yo muera algún bien vos pueda far, before
lo que perdedes doblado vos lo cobrar.»° pay
Plogo a mío Çid por que creçió en la yantar,° his company
plogo a los otros omnes todos quantos con él están.
Los .vi. días de plazo passados los an,
tres an por troçir° sepades que non más. left
Mandó el rey a mío Çid (a) aguardar,° watch
que si después del plazo en su tierral pudies tomar
por oro nin por plata non podrie escapar.
El día es exido, la noch querie entrar,
a sus cavalleros mandólos todos juntar:
«¡Oíd, varones, 'non vos caya en pesar!° don't worry
Poco aver trayo, dar vos quiero vuestra part.
Sed membrados commo lo devedes far;
a la mañana quando los gallos cantarán
non vos tardedes, mandedes ensellar;° saddle up
en San Pero a matines tandrá el buen abbat, will ring
la missa nos dirá, esta será de 'Santa Trinidad;° votive mass
la missa dicha, penssemos de cavalgar,
ca el plazo viene açerca, mucho avemos de andar.»
Cuemo° lo mandó mío Çid assí lo an todos ha far. **=como**
Passando va la noch, viniendo la man;° morning
'a los mediados gallos° pienssan de [ensellar]. 3:00 AM
'Tañen a matines 'a una priessa tan grand;

mío Çid e su mugier    a la eglesia van.
Echós° doña Ximena    en los grados° delant'el altar    she threw herself, steps
rogando al Criador    'quanto ella mejor sabe°    the best she knew how
que a mío Çid el Campeador    que Dios le curias° de mal:    keep him
«¡Ya Señor glorioso,    Padre que en çielo estás!
Fezist° çielo e tierra,    'el terçero° el mar    **=hiciste, =el tercer día**
fezist estrelas e luna    y el sol pora escalentar;°    **=calentar**
'prisist encarnación°    en Santa María madre,    became incarnate
en Belleem° apareçist    commo fue tu veluntad;°    **=Belén, =voluntad**
pastores te glorifficaron,    ovieron te a laudare,°    to praise
tres reyes de Arabia    te vinieron adorar
—Melchior    e Gaspar e Baltasar—
oro e tus° e mirra    te offreçieron commo fue tu veluntad;    incense
[salvest] a Jonás°    quando cayó en la mar,    Jonah
salvest a Daniel    con los leones en la mala cárçel,°    prison (lion's den)
salvest dentro en Roma    al señor San Sabastián,°    Roman martyr
salvest a Santa Susana[5]    del falso criminal;
por tierra andidiste° .xxxii. años,    Señor spirital,    **=anduviste**
mostrando los miraclos    por en avemos que fablar:
del agua fezist vino    e de la piedra pan,
resuçitest a Lázaro°    ca fue tu voluntad;    Lazarus
a los judíos te dexeste prender;    do dizen monte Calvario°    Calvary
pusieron te en cruz    por nombre en Golgotá,°    Golgotha
dos ladrones contigo,    estos de señas partes,
el uno es en paraíso    ca el otro non entró alá;
estando en la cruz    vertud fezist muy grant:
Longinos° era çiego    que nunquas vio alguandre,    Lance    Longinus
diot con la lança en el costado    dont ixió la sangre,    that pierces Jesus
corrió la sangre por el astil° ayuso,    shaft
    las manos se ovo de untar,°    wet
alçólas° arriba,    lególas a la faz,    raised them
abrió sus ojos,    cató a todas partes,
en ti crovo° al ora°    por end es salvo de mal;    he believed, immediately
en el monumento    resuçitest,

[5] Santa Susana was falsely accused of adultery and rescued by Daniel. Cf. Daniel 13.

wife prays to God husband be safe

fust° a los infiernos    commo fue tu voluntad,    **=fuiste**
quebrantaste las puertas    e saqueste los santos padres.
Tú eres rey de los reyes    e de tod el mundo padre,
a ti adoro e creo    de toda voluntad,
e ruego a San Peydro    que me ayude a rogar
por mío Çid el Campeador    que Dios le curie de mal,
¡quando oy nos partimos    en vida nos faz juntar!»
La oración fecha,    la missa acabada la an,
salieron de la eglesia,    ya quieren cavalgar.
El Çid a doña Ximena    iva la abraçar,
doña Ximena al Çid    la manol va besar,
lorando de los oios    que non sabe qué se far.
Y él a las niñas    tornó las a catar:
«A Dios vos acomiendo, fijas,    e a la mugier e al
Padre spirital;
agora nos partimos,    Dios sabe el ajuntar.»°    when we will meet aga
Lorando de los ojos    que non viestes atal,
asís parten unos d'otros    commo la uña° de la carne.°    nail, flesh
Mío Çid con los sos vassallos    penssó de cavalgar;
a todos esperando    la cabeça tornando va.
A tan grand sabor    fabló Minaya Álbar Fáñez:
«Çid ¿do son vuestros esfuerços?    ¡En buen ora
nasquiestes de madre!
Pensemos de ir nuestra vía,    esto 'sea de vagar.°    must be left for now
Aun todos estos duelos    en gozo se tornarán;
Dios que nos dio las almas    consejo nos dará.»
Al abbat don Sancho    tornan de castigar°    instruct
commo sirva a doña Ximena    e a la[s] fijas que ha,
e a todas sus dueñas    que con ellas están;
bien sepa el abbat    qué buen galardón dello prendrá.    reward
Tornado es don Sancho    e fabló Álbar Fáñez:
«Si viéredes yentes venir 'por connusco° ir, abbat,    with us
dezildes que prendan el rastro°    e pienssen de andar,    trail
ca en yermo° o en poblado    poder nos han alcançar.»    unpopulated place
Soltaron las riendas,    pienssan de andar;
çerca viene el plazo    por el reino quitar.

Wife finishes speech
Only God knows when
they'll be reunite

Vino mío Çid yazer a 'Spinaz de Can;° "unknown place"
grandes yentes sele acogen essa noch de todas partes.
Otro día mañana pienssa de cavalgar.
Ixiéndos va de tierra el Campeador leal;
de siniestro Sant Estevan —una buena çipdad—
de diestro Alilón las torres que moros las han,
passó por Alcobiella que de Castiella fin es ya,
la Calçada de Quinea iva la traspassar, sobre Navas
de Palos el Duero° va pasar, "river in Spain"
a la Figeruela mío Çid iva posar.
Vánssele acogiendo yentes de todas partes.
I 'se echava° mío Çid después que fue çenado.° lay down, eaten
Un sueñol priso dulçe, tan bien se adurmió.
El ángel Gabriel a él vino en [visión]:
«Cavalgad, Çid, el buen Campeador,
ca nunqua en tan buen punto cavalgó varón;
mientra que visquiéredes bien se fará lo to.»° =tuyo
Quando despertó el Çid la cara se santigó;
sinava° la cara, a Dios se acomendó. made the sign of the cross
Mucho era pagado del sueño que a soñado.
Otro día mañana pienssan de cavalgar;
es día a de plazo, sepades que non más.

Sees Gabriel in a vision

II

CANTAR DE LAS BODAS

*In this cantar El Cid is reconciled with King Alfonso and the King arranges the marriage of the Cid's daughters to the infantes (princes) of Carrión believing that these marriages will ennoble the Cid and his family. However, the infantes are really cowardly and noble only in rank but not in actions.*

III

CANTAR DE LA AFRENTA DE CORPES

*In this cantar we see the true nature of the* infantes *who abandon the battlefield and are made fun of by the Cid's men. They decide to take vengeance on their wives and ask that they be allowed to return to Carrión on the pretext of showing their wives the lands that are their dowry. They beat and abandon their wives in Corpes but one of the Cid's cousins suspects their treachery and rescues Elvira and Sol. The Cid demands justice for this insult from King Alfonso and the fate of the* infantes *is determined by a duel. Messengers from the kings of Navarre and Aragon arrive at the court and request the hands of the Cid's daughters in marriage for their sovereigns' sons. The death of the Cid occurs on the feast of Pentecost.*

| | |
|---|---|
| En Valençia seye mío Çid    con todos sus vassallos, | |
| con él amos° sus yernos°    los ifantes de Carrión. | **=ambos**, sons-in-law |
| Yazies en un escaño,°    durmie el Campeador; | bench |
| mala sobrevienta°    sabed que les cuntió:° | surprise, happened |
| saliós de la red°    e desatós° el león. | cage, got loose |
| En grant miedo se vieron    por medio de la cort; | |
| enbraçan° los mantos    los del Campeador | seize |
| e cercan° el escaño    e fincan° sobre so señor. | surround, lean |
| Ferrán Gonçález non vio allí dos alçasse,°    nin cámara abierta nin torre, | to hide |
| Metiós° so'l escaño    tanto ovo° el pavor;° | put himself, had, fear |
| Diego Gonçález    por la puerta salió | |
| diziendo de la boca:    «¡Non veré Carrión!» | |
| Tras una 'viga lagar°    metiós con grant pavor, | wine press |
| el manto y el brial°    todo suzio lo sacó | tunic. |
| En esto despertó    el que en buen ora naçió, | |
| vio çercado el escaño    de sus buenos varones: | |
| «¿Qués esto, mesnadas,°    o qué queredes vos?» | my men |
| «¡Hya señor ondrado    rebata° nos dio el león!» | fright |
| Mío Çid fincó el cobdo,°    en pie se levantó, | elbow |
| el manto trae al cuello    e adeliñó° pora[l] león; | went straight |
| el león quando lo vio    assí envergonçó° | became abashed |
| ante mío Çid la cabeça premió°    y el rostro fincó; | lowered |
| mío Çid don Rodrigo    al cuello lo tomó | |
| e lieva lo adestrando,°    en la red le metió. | leading |
| A maravilla lo han    quantos que i son | |
| e tornaron se al (a)palaçio    pora la cort. | |

Cid is in the palace the Infantes
& goes & challenges Lion & tame

Mío Çid por sos yernos demandó e no los falló,
Mager° los están lamando ninguno non responde. although
Quando los fallaron assí vinieron sin color;
¡non viestes tal juego° commo iva por la cort! fun made
Mandólo vedar° mío Çid el Campeador. stopped
Muchos tovieron por enbaídos° los ifantes de Carrión; shamed
'fiera cosa° les pesa desto que les cuntió. very badly
Ellos en esto estando don avien grant pesar,
fuerças de Marruecos Valençia vienen çercar;° lay siege
çinquaenta mill tiendas fincadas ha de las cabdales,° largest
aqueste era el rey Búcar, sil oyestes contar.
Alegravas el Çid e todos sus varones
que les creçe la ganançia ¡grado al Criador!
Mas, sabed, 'de cuer° les pesa a los ifantes de Carrión truly
ca veyen tantas tiendas de moros de que non avien sabor.
Amos hermanos apart salidos son:
«Catamos la ganançia e la perdida no;
ya en esta batalla a entrar abremos nos,
¡esto es aguisado° por non ver Carrión, certain
bibdas° remandrán° fijas del Campeador!» widows, will be
Oyó la poridad aquel Muño Gustioz,
vino con estas nuevas a mío Çid Ruy Díaz el Campeador:
«¡Evades qué pavor han vuestros yernos: tan osados son,
por entrar en batalla desean Carrión!
Hid los conortar,° ¡si vos vala el Criador! comfort
Que sean en paz e non ayan i raçión,° part
¡nos con vusco la vençremos e valer nos ha el Criador!»
Mío Çid don Rodrigo sonrrisando salió:
«¡Dios vos salve, yernos, ifantes de Carrión!
¡En braços tenedes mis fijas tan blancas commo el sol
Hyo desseo lides° e vos a Carrión; battles
en Valençia folgad° a todo vuestro sabor take your ease
ca d'aquelos moros yo so sabidor:
arrancar° melos trevo° con la merçed del Criador.» defeat, dare
. . . . . . . . . . . . . . . .
. . . . . . . . . . . . . . . .

There is a page missing here that probably has some fifty lines. In the Chronicle the infantes, shamed by the Cid's words, assure him of their decision to fight. King Búcar sends a message to the Cid ordering him to abandon Valencia which the Cid scornfully rejects. At the beginning of the battle, Fernán González asks the Cid for the honor of delivering the first blows but when he is confronted by one of the Moorish warriors, he turns his horse and flees. Pedro Bermúdez, in order to save everyone's honor, kills the Moor and gives his horse to Fernando encouraging him to take credit for this feat and promising him to keep it secret. In line 2338 Fernando finishes giving thanks to Pedro Bermúdez.

. . . . . . . . . . . . . . . .
. . . . . . . . . . . . . . . .
«¡Aun vea el ora que vos meresca dos tanto!»
En una conpaña tornados son amos;
assí lo otorga don Pero cuemo se alaba Ferrando.
Plogo a mío Çid e a todos sos vassallos:
«¡Aun si Dios quisiere y el Padre que está en alto
amos los míos yernos buenos serán en campo!»° — battlefield
Esto van diziendo e las yentes se alegando,
en la ueste° de los moros los atamores° sonando; — host, drums
a marav[i]lla lo avien muchos dessos christianos
ca nunqua lo vieran, ca nuevos son legados.
Más se maravillan entre Diego e Ferando,
por la su voluntad non serien allí legados.
Oíd lo que fabló el que en buen ora nasco:
«¡Alá, Pero Vermúez, el mío sobrino caro!
Curies me a Diego e curies me a don Fernando
míos yernos amos a dos, las cosas que mucho amo,
ca los moros—con Dios— non fincarán en canpo.»
«Yo vos digo, Çid, por toda caridad,
que oy los ifantes a mí por amo° non abrán; — protector
¡cúrielos 'qui quier,° ca dellos poco m'incal! — whoever
Hyo con los míos ferir quiero delant,
vos con los vuestros firme mientre a la çaga° tengades; — rearguard

si cueta° fuere    bien me podredes huviar.»°    tight spot, help
Aquí legó    Minaya Álbar Fáñez:
«¡Oíd, ya Çid    Canpeador leal!
Esta batalla    el Criador la ferá,
e vos tan dinno°    que con él avedes part.°    worthy, place
Mandad no'los ferir    de qual part vos semejar;°    seems best
el debdo° que a cada uno    a conplir° será.    duty, fulfill
¡Verlo hemos con Dios    e con la vuestra auze!»°    good luck
Dixo mío Çid:    «Ayamos más de vagar.»°    calm
Afevos el obispo don Jherónimo    muy bien armado,
paravas delant al Campeador    siempre con la buen auze:
«Oy vos dix la missa    de Santa Trinidade,
por esso salí de mi tierra    e vin vos buscar
por sabor que avía    de algún moro matar.
Mi orden e mis manos    querría las ondrar°    honor
e a estas feridas    yo quiero ir delant;
Pendón° trayo a corças°    e armas 'de señal°    pennant, coat of
si plogiesse a Dios    querría las ensayar,°    arms, ; emblazoned;
mío coraçón    que pudiesse folgar    try them
e vos, mío Çid,    de mí más vos pagar.
Si este amor non feches    yo de vos me quiero quitar.»
Essora dixo mío Çid:    «Lo que vos queredes plaz me.
Afé los moros a ojo, id los ensayar;°    attack
¡nos d'aquent° veremos    commo lidia el abbat!»    from here
El obispo don Jherónimo    'priso a espolonada°    began the attack
e iva los ferir    a cabo del albergada:°    encampment
por la su ventura    e Dios quel amava
a los primeros colpes°    dos moros matava de la lança;    blows
el astil a quebrado    e metió mano al espada,
ensayavas el obispo,    ¡Dios, qué bien lidiava!
Dos mató con lança    e .v. con el espada;
los moros son muchos,    derredor le çercavan,
davan le grandes colpes    mas nol falssan° las armas.    penetrate
El que en buen ora nasco    los ojos le fincava,
enbraçó el escudo°    e abaxó el asta,°    shield, lance
aguijó a Bavieca    el cavallo que bien anda,

hiva los ferir de coraçón e de alma;
en las azes° primeras el Campeador entrava, — lines
abatió° a .vii. e a .iiii. matava. — struck down
Plogo a Dios aquesta fue el arrancada.° — rout
Mío Çid con los suyos 'cae en alcança:° — chase them
veriedes quebrar tantas cuerdas° e arrancar se las estacas° — cords, stakes
e acostar se los tendales,° con huebras° eran tantas. — tents, adornments
Los de mío Çid a los de Búcar de las tiendas los sacan.
Sacan los de las tiendas, 'caen los en alcaz;° — pursue them
tanto braço con loriga° veriedes caer apart, — mail armor cover
tantas cabeças con yelmos° que por el campo caen, — helmets
cavallos sin dueños salir a todas partes;
.vii. migeros° conplidos duró el segudar.° — miles, pursuit
Mío Çid al rey Búcar cayól en alcaz:
«¡Acá torna, Búcar! Venist d'alent mar,
verte as con el Çid el de la barba grant,
¡saludar nos hemos amos e tajaremos° amista[d]!» — strike up
Respuso Búcar al Çid: «¡Cofonda Dios tal amistad!

El espada tienes desnuda en la mano e veot aguijar,
así commo semeja en mí la quieres ensayar;
mas si el cavallo non estropieça° o comigo non caye — trip
¡non te juntarás° comigo fata° dentro en la mar!» — join up, =**hasta**
Aquí respuso mío Çid: «¡Esto non será verdad!»
Buen cavallo tiene Búcar e grandes saltos faz
mas Bavieca el de mio Çid alcançando lo va.
Alcançolo el Çid a Búcar a tres braças° del mar, — measurement
arriba alçó Colada,° un grant golpe dadol ha, — the Cid's sword
las carbonclas° del yelmo tollidas gela[s] ha, — red gemstones
cortól el yelmo e—librado todo lo hal°— — all the rest
fata la çintura° el espada legado ha. — waist
Mató a Búcar al rey de alen mar
e ganó a Tizón° que mill marcos d'oro val. — "Bucar's sword"
Vençió la batalla maravillosa e grant.
Aquís ondró mío Çid e quantos con él son.

*The infantes ask to take their wives to see their inheritance in Carrión.*

Pidamos nuestras mugieres al Çid Campeador;
digamos que las levaremos a tierras de Carrión,
enseñar las hemos do las heredades son
sacar las hemos de Valençia, de poder del Campeador,
después en la carrera° feremos nuestro sabor — way
ante que nos retrayan° lo que cuntió del león. — reproach
¡Nos de natura° somos de condes de Carrión! — lineage
Averes levaremos grandes que valen grant valor;
¡escarniremos las fijas del Canpeador!»
«D'aquestos averes sienpre seremos ricos omnes,
podremos casar con fijas de reyes o de enperadores
¡ca de natura somos de condes de Carrión!
Assí las escarniremos a las fijas del Campeador
antes que nos retrayan lo que fue del león.»
Con aqueste consejo° amos tornados son. — decision
Fabló Ferán Gonçález e fizo callar la cort:
«¡Si vos vala el Criador, Çid Campeador!
Que plega a doña Ximena e primero a vos
e a Minaya Álbar Fáñez e a quantos aquí son:
dad nos nuestras mugieres que avemos a bendiçiones,
levar las hemos a nuestras tierras de Carrión,
meter las hemos en las villas
que les diemos por arras° e por onores; — marriage gift of groom
verán vuestras fijas lo que avemos nos,
los fijos que oviéremos en que avrán partiçión.»
Dixo el Campeador: «Darvos he mis
fijas e algo de lo mío.»
El Çid que nos curiava° de assí ser afontado:° — suspect, offended
«Vos les diestes villas por arras en tierras de Carrión;
hyo quiero les dar axuvar° .iii. mill marcos de [valor], — dowry
darvos e mulas e palafrés° muy 'gruessos de sazón,° — palfreys, excellent condition; war horses, swift
'cavallos pora en diestro° fuertes e corredores°
e muchas vestiduras de paños e de çiclatones;° — silk
dar vos he dos espadas, a Colada e a Tizón,

Infantes claim they're going to take the wives
to see their inheritance

| | |
|---|---|
| bien lo sabedes vos que las gané a guisa de varón. | |
| Míos fijos sodes amos quando mis fijas vos do; | |
| allá me levades las telas° del coraçón. | strings |
| ¡Qué lo sepan en Gallizia° y en Castiella y en León | **=Galicia** |
| con qué riqueza enbío° míos yernos amos a dos!° | **=envío**, both |
| A mis fijas sirvades, que vuestras mugieres son; | |
| si bien las servides yo vos rendré° buen galardón.»° | give, reward |
| 'Atorgado lo han° esto los iffantes de Carrión. | agreed to |
| Aquí reçiben las fijas del Campeador, | |
| Conpieçan° a reçebir lo que el Çid mandó. | **=comienzan** |
| Quando son 'pagados a todo so sabor° | satisfied completely |
| hya° mandavan cargar° iffantes de Carrión. | **=ya**, loaded |
| Grandes son las nuevas° por Valençia 'la mayor,° | news, the Great |
| todos prenden armas e cavalgan a vigor° | quickly |
| por que escurren° sus fijas del Campeador a tierras de Carrión. | escort |
| Hya quieren cavalgar, 'en espidimiento son.° | they are taking their leave |
| Amas hermanas don Elvira e doña Sol | |
| fincaron los inojos ant'el Çid Campeador: | |
| «¡Merçed vos pedimos, padre! ¡Sí vos vala° el Criador! | protect |
| Vos nos engendrastes,° nuestra madre nos parió;° | sired, gave birth |
| delant sodes amos, señora e señor. | |
| Agora nos enviades a tierras de Carrión, | |
| debdo nos es a cunplir lo que mandaredes vos. | |
| Assí vos pedimos merçed nos amas a dos | |
| que 'ayades vuestros mensajes° en tierras de Carrión.» | send your news |
| Abraçólas mío Çid e saludólas° amas a dos. | kissed |
| Él fizo aquesto, la madre lo doblava:° | did the same |
| «¡Andad, fijas, d'aquí el Criador vos vala! | |
| De mí e de vuestro padre bien avedes nuestra graçia.° | blessing |
| Hid a Carrión do sodes heredadas | |
| assí commo yo tengo° bien vos he casadas.» | see it |
| Al padre e a la madre las manos les besavan; | |
| amos las bendixieron° e dieron les su graçia. | **=bendijeron** |
| Mío Çid e los otros de cavalgar penssavan | |
| 'a grandes guarnimientos,° a cavallos e armas. | with much armor |

leave them naked in the woods & treat them terribly

Hya salien los ifantes de Valençia 'la clara° — the shining
esp[id]iéndos de las dueñas e de todas sus compañas;° — **=compañeras**
por la huerta° de Valençia teniendo° salíen armas. — orchard, brandishing
alegre va mío Çid con todas sus compañas.
Violo en los avueros el que en buen ora çinxó espada
que estos casamientos non serien sin alguna tacha;° — stain
nos puede repentir, que casadas las ha amas.
«¿O eres, mío sobrino, tú, Félez Muñoz?
Primo eres de mis fijas amas d'alma e de coraçón.
Mandot que vayas con ellas fata dentro en Carrión,
verás las heredades que a mis fijas dadas son;
con aquestas nuevas vernás° al Campeador.» — you will come
Dixo Félez Muñoz: «Plazme d'alma e de coraçón.»

Minaya Álbar Fáñez ante mío Çid se paró:
«Tornemos nos, Çid a Valençia la mayor,
que si a Dios ploguiere e al Padre Criador
hir las hemos ver a tierras de Carrión.»
«A Dios vos acomendamos don Elvira e doña Sol;
atales cosas fed° que en plazer caya a nos.» — do
Respondien los yernos: «¡Assí lo mande Dios!»
Grandes fueron los duelos a la departiçión;
el padre con las fijas loran de coraçón
assí fazían los cavalleros del Campeador.
«¡Oyas, sobrino, tú, Félez Muñoz!

Por Molina iredes, i yazredes una noch,
saludad a mío amigo el moro Avengalvón;
reçiba a míos yernos commo él pudier mejor.
Dil que enbío mis fijas a tierras de Carrión.
De lo que ovieren huebos sirvan las a so sabor,
desí escurra las fasta Medina por la mi amor;
de quanto él fiziere yol dar[é] por ello buen galardón.»
Cuemo la uña de la carne ellos partidos son.
Hyas tornó pora Valençia el que en buen ora nasçió.
Pienssan se de ir los ifantes de Carrión;

por Santa María d'Alvarrazín fazían la posada,
aguijan quanto pueden ifantes de Carrión;
felos en Molina con el moro Avengalvón.
El moro quando lo sopo plógol de coraçón,
saliólos reçebir con grandes avorozes;° celebrations
¡Dios, qué bien los sirvió a todo so sabor!
Otro día mañana con ellos cavalgó,
con dozientos cavalleros escurrir los mandó;
hivan troçir° los montes los que dizen de Luzón. cross
A las fijas del Çid el moro sus donas dio,
buenos seños cavallos a los ifantes de Carrión.
Troçieron Arbuxuelo e legaron a Salón,
o dizen el Anssarera ellos posados son.
Tod esto les fizo el moro por el amor del Çid Campeador.
Ellos veyen la riqueza que el moro sacó,
entramos hermanos conssejaron traçión:
«Hya pues que a dexar avemos fijas del Campeador
si pudiéssemos matar el moro Avengalvón
quanta riquiza tiene aver la iemos nos.
Tan en salvo lo abremos commo lo de Carrión,
nunqua avrie derecho de nos el Çid Campeador.»
Quando esta falssedad dizien los de Carrión
un moro latinado° bien gelo entendió; Spanish-speaking
non tiene poridad, díxolo [a] Avengalvón:
«Acayaz,° cúriate destos, ca eres mío señor; title of respect
tu muert oí conssejer° a los ifantes de Carrión.» plot

El moro Avengalvón mucho era buen barragán,° valient
con dozientos que tiene iva cavalgar.
Armas iva teniendo, parós ante los ifantes;
de lo que el moro dixo a los ifantes non plaze:
«Dezid me: ¿qué vos fiz ifantes de Carrión?
¡Hyo sirviendo vos 'sin art° e vos conssejastes loyally
pora mi muert!
Si no lo dexas por mío Çid el de Bivar
tal cosa vos faría que por el mundo sonas

e luego levaría sus fijas    al Campeador leal;
¡vos nunqua en Carrión    entrariedes jamás!

| | |
|---|---|
| Aquím parto de vos    commo de malos e de traidores. | |
| Hiré con vuestra graçia,    don Elvira e doña Sol; | |
| ¡poco preçio° las nuevas    de los de Carrión! | value |
| Dios lo quiera e lo mande,    que de tod el mundo es señor, | |
| d'aqueste casamiento    que[s] grade el Campeador.» | |
| Esto les ha dicho    y el moro se tornó; | |
| teniendo ivan armas    al troçir de Salón, | |
| cuemmo de buen seso    a Molina se tornó. | |
| Ya 'movieron del° Anssarera[6]    los ifantes de Carrión; | left |
| 'acojen se a andar°    de día e de noch, | they traveled |
| a siniestro dexan Ati[en]za°    una peña° muy fuert, | fortification |
| la sierra de Miedes    passaron la estoz,° | **=entonces** |
| por los Montes Claros    aguijan a espolón, | |
| a ssiniestro dexan a Griza    que Álamos[7] pobló° | populated |
| —allí son caños°    do a Elpha ençerró°— | caves, enclosed |
| a diestro dexan a Sant Estevan,    'más cae aluen;° | further on |
| entrados son los ifantes    al 'robredo° de Corpes, | oak grove |
| los montes son altos,    las ramas° pujan° con las nues,° | branches, touch, **=nubes** |
| e las bestias fieras°    que andan aderredor.° | wild, **=alrededor** |
| Falaron° un vergel°    con una limpia° fuent, | **=hallaron**, clearing, clear |
| mandan fincar° la tienda    ifantes de Carrión; | set up |
| con quantos que ellos traen    'i yazen° essa noch. | sleep there |
| Con sus mugieres en braços    demuestran les amor: | |
| '¡mal gelo cumplieron°    quando salíe el sol! | they did not keep their |
| Mandaron cargar las azemilas°    con grandes averes; | word; pack mules |
| cogida° han la tienda    do albergaron° de noch, | taken down, spent |
| adelant eran idos    'los de criazón.° | servants |

[6] Ansarera, Atienza, Sierra de Miedes (present day Sierra de Pela), Montes Claros (mistakenly placed to the north of Sierra de Pela, but is really south of it), Griza, Sant Estevan (de Gormaz). These are all place names albeit not geographically exact with regard to the route to Carrión from Valencia. However, use of geographic names adds to the realism of the poem.

[7] Alamos is a man's name and Elpha is a woman's name and both form part of a legend of the area.

Assí lo mandaron    los ifantes de Carrión
que non i fincás ninguno,    mugier nin varón,
'si non° amas sus mugieres    doña Elvira e doña Sol;    except for
Deportar° se quieren con ellas    a todo su sabor.    sport
Todos eran idos,    ellos .iiii. solos son.
'Tanto mal comidieron°    los ifantes de Carrión:    planned so much evil
«'Bien lo creades°    don Elvira e doña Sol:    believe it
aquí seredes° escarnidas    en estos fieros montes;    **=seréis**
oy nos partiremos    e dexadas seredes de nos,
non abredes° part    en tierras de Carrión.    **=tendréis**
Hirán aquestos mandados°    al Çid Campeador;    news
¡nos vengaremos° aquesta    por la del león!»    we will be avenged
Allí les tuellen°    los mantos e los pelliçones,°    snatch off, furs
'paran las° en cuerpos    y en 'camisas y en çiclatones.°    leave them, undergar-
'Espuelas tienen calçadas°    los malos traidores,    ments; they have the
en mano prenden las çinchas°    fuertes e duradores.°    spurs on; cinch belts
Quando esto vieron las dueñas    fablava doña Sol:    sturdy
«¡Por Dios vos rogamos don Diego e don Ferando!
Dos espadas tenedes    fuertes e tajadores°    sharp
—al una dizen Colada    e al otra Tizón—
¡cortandos las cabeças,    mártires seremos nos!
Moros e christianos    'departirán desta razón,°    will speak about this
'que por lo que nos mereçemos    no lo prendemos nos;[8]
¡atan malos enssienplos    non fagades sobre nos!
Si nos fuéremos majadas°    abiltaredes° a vos,    beaten, shamed
retraer vos lo an    en vistas o en cortes.»

Lo que ruegan las dueñas    non les ha ningún pro.°    advantage
Essora les conpieçan a dar    los ifantes de Carrión,
con las çinchas corredizas    majan° las tan sin sabor,    beat
con las espuelas agudas    don ellas an mal sabor
rompien las camisas e las carnes    a ellas amas a dos;
linpia salie la sangre    sobre los çiclatones.
Ya lo sienten ellas    en los sos coraçones.
¡Quál ventura serie esta    si ploguiesse al Criador

[8] We have done nothing to receive this treatment.

Infantes leave them alone, Cousin [illegible] following them

que assomasse essora    el Çid Campeador!
Tanto las majaron    que sin cosimente° son,    unconscious
Sangrientas° en las camisas    e todos los çiclatones.    bloody
Canssados son de ferir    ellos amos a dos
ensayándos amos    quál dará mejores colpes.
Hya non pueden fablar    don Elvira e doña Sol,
por muertas las dexaron    en el robredo de Corpes.
Levaron les los mantos    e las pieles armiñas°    ermine
mas dexan las maridas°    en briales° y en camisas    afflicted, underclothes
e a las aves del monte    e a las bestias de la fiera guisa.
Por muertas la[s] dexaron    sabed, que non por bivas.
¡Quál ventura serie    si assomas essora el Çid Campeador!
Los ifantes de Carrión    en el robredo de Corpes
por muertas las dexaron,
que el una al otra    nol 'torna recabdo.°    offer help
Por los montes do ivan    ellos ivan se alabando:
«De nuestros casamientos    agora somos vengados;
non las deviemos    tomar por barraganas°    concubines
si non fuéssemos    rogados,
pues nuestras parejas    'non eran pora en braços.°    legitimate wives
¡La desondra del león    assís irá vengando!»

Alabandos ivan    los ifantes de Carrión.
Mas yo vos diré    d'aquel Félez Muñoz,
sobrino era    del Çid Campeador:
mandaron le ir adelante    mas de su grado non fue.
En la carrera do iva    doliol el coraçón;
de todos los otros    aparte se salió,
en un monte espesso    Félez Muñoz se metió
fasta que viesse venir    sus primas amas a dos
o qué an fecho    los ifantes de Carrión.
Violos venir    e oyó una razón,
ellos nol vien    ni dend sabien raçión;
sabet bien que si ellos le viessen    non escapara de muert.
Vansse los ifantes,    aguijan a espolón.
Por el rastro    tornós Félez Muñoz,

Primo find w/ blood on shirts

falló sus primas amorteçidas° amas a dos; — fainted away
lamando «¡Primas, primas!» luego descavalgó,
arrendó° el cavallo, a ellas adeliñó: — reined in
«¡Ya primas, las mis primas don Elvira e doña Sol!
¡Mal se ensayaron los ifantes de Carrión!
¡A Dios plega e a Santa María que dent prendan
ellos mal galardón!»
Valas tornando a ellas amas a dos;
'tanto son de traspuestas° que non pueden dezir nada. — weakened
Partieron se le las tellas de dentro del coraçón,
lamando «¡Primas, primas don Elvira e doñ[a] Sol!
¡Despertedes, primas por amor del Criador!
Mientra es el día, ante que entre la noch,
¡los ganados fieros non nos coman en aqueste mont!»° — forest
Van recordando don Elvira e doña Sol,
abrieron los ojos e vieron a Félez Muñoz.
«¡Esforçad vos, primas, por amor del Criador!
De que non me fallaren los ifantes de Carrión
a grant priessa seré buscado yo;
si Dios non nos vale aquí morremos nos.»
Tan a grant duelo fablava doña Sol:
«¡Si vos lo meresca, mío primo, nuestro padre el Campeador!
¡Dandos del agua, sí vos vala el Criador!»
Con un sombrero que tiene Félez Muñoz
—nuevo era e fresco, que de Valençial sacó—
cogió del agua en él e a sus primas dio;
mucho son lazradas e amas las fartó.° — sated
Tanto las rogó fata que las assentó;° — he sat them up
valas conortando° e 'metiendo coraçón° — comforting, encouragi[ng]
fata que esfuerçan, e amas las tomó
e privado° en el cavallo las cavalgó; — quickly
con el so manto a amas las cubrió,
el cavallo priso por la rienda e luego dent° las part[ió]. — from there
Todos tres señeros° por los robredos de Corpes — individually
entre noch e dia salieron de los montes;
a las aguas de Duero ellos arribados son,

a la torre de don Urraca    elle las dexó.
A sant Estevan    vino Félez Muñoz,
falló a Diego Téllez    el que de Álbar Fáñez fue;
quando él lo oyó    pesól de coraçón,
priso bestias    e vestidos de pro, hiva
reçebir    a don Elvira e a doña Sol:
en Sant Estevan    dentro las metió,
quanto el mejor puede    allí las ondró.
Los de Sant Estevan    siempre mesurados son;
quando sabien esto    pesóles de coraçón
a llas fijas del Çid    dan les esfuerço;
allí sovieron° ellas    fata que sanas son.    were
Alabándos seyan    los ifantes de Carrion.
De cuer pesó esto    al buen rey don Alfonsso.
Van aquestos mandados    a Valençia la mayor;
quando gelo dizen    a mío Çid el Campeador
una grand ora    penssó e comidió;°    considered
alçó la su mano,    a la barba se tomó:
«¡Grado a Christus    que del mundo es señor
quando tal ondra me an dada    los ifantes de Carrión!
¡Par aquesta barba    que nadi non messó°    pulled
non la lograrán    los ifantes de Carrión,
que a mis fijas    bien las casaré yo!»

*The duel takes place between the Cid's champions and the infantes who are defeated.*

Los dos han arrancado;    dirévos de Muño Gustioz
con Assur Gonçález    commo se adobó:
firienssen en los escudos    unos tan grandes colpes;
Assur Gonçález    furçudo° e de valor    strong
firió en el escudo    a don Muño Gustioz,
tras el escudo    falssó° ge la guarnizón,°    broke, armor
'en vazío° fue la lança    ca en carne nol tomó.    missed the mark
Este colpe fecho    otro dio Muño Gustioz,
(tras el escudo    falssó ge la guarnizón)

por medio de la bloca° (d)el escudol quebrantó, center of the shield
nol pudo guarir, falssó ge la guarnizón,
apart le priso, que non cab el coraçón;
metiól por la carne adentro la lança con el pendón,
de la otra part una braça gela echó,
con él dio una tuerta, de la siella lo encamó,° unhorsed
al tirar de la lança en tierra lo echó;
vermejo salió el astil e la lança y el pendón.
Todos se cuedan que ferido es de muert.
La lança recombró° e sobr'él se paró; recovered
dixo Gonçalo Assúrez: «¡Nol firgades,° por Dios! strike
¡Vençudo es el campo quando esto se acabó!»
Dixieron los fieles: «Esto oímos nos.»
Mandó librar° el canpo el buen rey don Alfonsso, cleared
las armas que i rastaron° él selas tomó. were left
Por ondrados se parten los del buen Campeador,
vençieron esta lid ¡grado al Criador!
Grandes son los pesares por tierras de Carrión.

El rey a los de mío Çid de noche los enbió
que no les 'diessen salto° nin oviessen pavor. assault
A guisa de menbrados andan días e noches,
felos en Valençia con mío Çid el Campeador;
por malos los dexaron a los ifantes de Carrión,
conplido han el debdo que les mandó so señor;
alegre ffue d'aquesto mío Çid el Campeador.
Grant es la biltança° de ifantes de Carrion: humilliation
qui buena dueña escarneçe e la dexa después
¡atal le contesca o si quier peor!
Dexemos nos de pleitos° de ifantes de Carrión; demands
de lo que an preso mucho an mal sabor.
Fablemos nos d'aqueste que en buen ora naçió:
grandes son los gozos en Valençia la mayor
por que tan ondrados fueron los del Campeador.
Prísos a la barba Ruy Díaz so señor:
«¡Grado al rey del çielo, mis fijas vengadas son!

¡Agora las ayan quitas heredades de Carrión!
Sin verguença las casaré o a qui pese o a qui non.»
Andidieron en pleitos los de Navarra e de Aragón,
ovieron su ajunta con Alfonsso el de León;
fizieron sus casamientos con don Elvira e con doña Sol.
Los primeros fueron grandes mas aquestos son mijores;
a mayor ondra las casa que lo que primero fue:
¡ved quál ondra creçe al que en buen ora naçió
quando señoras son sus fijas de Navarra e de Aragón!
Oy los reyes d'España sos parientes son;
a todos alcança ondra por el que en buen ora naçió.
Passado es deste sieglo el día de çinquaesma:° Pentecost
¡de Christus haya perdón!
¡Assí ffagamos nos todos, justos e peccadores!
Estas son las nuevas de mío Çid el Campeador;
en este logar se acaba esta razón.
Quien escrivió este libro ¡dél Dios paraíso, amén!

PER ABBAT le escrivió en el mes de mayo
en era[9] de mill e .cc x lv. años.

## *Drama*

No survival of drama before the late twelfth or early thirteenth century has come down to us. Both lay and church drama, however, are known to have existed in France, and in thirteenth century Spain laws were written to regulate theatrical productions. These laws were found in the *Siete Partidas* of King Alfonso X.

### *AUTO DE LOS REYES MAGOS*

The *Auto de los Reyes Magos*, a short drama preserved in an incomplete manuscript of 147 lines, probably from the late twelfth century, is the only surviving play from this period. It belongs to the well-known Nativity Cycle, and relates the travels

[9] The **era** was 39 years earlier than the Gregorian calendar year.

of the Magi, their meeting, their arrival at the court of Herod, and the concern of the king of the Hebrews over the news of the birth of the Savior. The little play is filled with action and dramatic force, and there are touches of humor and some good characterization.
The text of the auto is based on an early manuscript of the Auto de los Reyes Magos. The five scenes presented here are the only fragment left to us, not just of this piece, but from all of medieval Spanish theater.[10]

GASPAR, rey
BALTASAR, rey
MELCHOR, rey
HERODES, rey
MAYORDOMO
SABIOS
Dos RABÍES

*Escena I*

GASPAR: Dios criador, ¡cuál° maravilla! — what
¡No sé cuál es aquesta estrella!
Agora primas la he veída[11].
'Poco tiempo ha° que es nacida. — short time ago
¿Nacido es el Criador
que es de las gentes señor?
Non es verdad, no sé qué digo.
Todo esto non vale un figo.[12]
Otra noche me lo cataré° — look at
Si es verdad, bien lo sabré.
¿Bien es verdad lo que yo digo?
'En todo, en todo° lo prohío° — completely, I believe
¿Non puede ser otra señal?° — sign
Aquesto es y non es al;° — anything else
nacido es Dios, 'por ver,° de hembra° — truly, woman

[10] The text is taken from that edited by Ramón Menéndez Pidal and published by him in the *Revista de Archivos, Bibliotecas y Museos* (Madrid, 1900). The text was re-edited in electronic form in 1996 by Vern Williamsen.
[11] **Agora primas...** *this is the first time I have seen it*
[12] **Non vale...** *not worth anything*

en aqueste mes de diciembre.
Allá iré '[d]o que fuere,° adorarlo he, — whereever he may be
por Dios de todos lo tendré.
BALTASAR: Esta estrella non sé dónd° viene, — **=de dónde**
quién la trae o quién la tiene.
¿Por qué es aquesta señal?
En mis días non vi a tal.
Ciertas° nacido es en tierras — **=ciertamente**
aquel que en pace° y en guerra — **=paz**
señor ha de ser de oriente,
de todos hasta en occidente.
Por tres noches me lo veré
y más de vero lo sabré.
¿En todo, en todo es nacido?
Non sé si algo he veído;
iré, lo adoraré
y pregaré° y rogaré. — pray
MELCHOR: Val, Criador, a tal facienda° — event
¿fue nunca alguandre° fallada — ever
o en escritura trovada?° — told
Tal estrella non es en cielo,
de esto soy yo buen estrellero;° — astrologer
bien lo veo sin escarno° — doubt
que un hombre es nacido de carne
que es señor de todo el mundo.
Así como el cielo es redondo;
de todas gentes señor será
y todo siglo° juzgará. — the world
¿Es? ¿Non es?
Cudo° que verdad es. — I believe
veer lo he otra vegada,° — time
si es verdad o si es nada.
Nacido es el Criador
de todas las gentes mayor;° — ruler
bien lo veo que es verdad,
iré allá, por caridad.

*Escena II*
(A Baltasar)
GASPAR: 'Dios vos salve°, señor; ¿sodes vos estrellero? — may God keep you
Decidme la verdad, de vos saberlo quiero.
¿Vedes tal maravilla?
Nacida es una estrella.
BALTASAR: Nacido es el Criador,
que de las gentes es señor.
Iré, lo adoraré.
GASPAR: Yo otrosí° rogar° lo he. — also, pray
(A los otros dos)
MELCHOR: Señores, ¿a cuál tierra queredes andar?
¿Queredes ir conmigo al Criador rogar?
¿Habedes° lo veído? Yo lo voy [a] adorar. — **=habéis**
GASPAR: Nos imos° otrosí, si le podremos fallar. — we are going
Andemos tras la estrella, veremos el lugar.
MELCHOR: ¿Cómo podremos probar si es hombre mortal
o si es rey de tierra o si celestial?
BALTASAR: ¿Queredes bien saber cómo lo sabremos?
Oro, mirra, incienso a él ofreceremos;
si fuere rey de tierra, el oro querrá;
si fuere hombre mortal, la mirra tomará;
si rey celestial, estos dos dejará,
tomará el incienso quel'° pertenecerá. — **=que le**
[los dos]: Andemos y así lo fagamos.

*Escena III*
(Gaspar y los otros dos reyes a Herodes)
[LOS TRES]: Sálvate el Criador, Dios te curie de mal,
un poco te diremos, non te queremos al,° — anything
Dios te dé longa vida y te curie de mal;
Imos° en romería aquel rey [a] adorar — **=vamos**
que es nacido en tierra, nol' podemos fallar.° — **=hallar**
HERODES: ¿Qué decides, [d]ó ides? ¿A quién ides buscar?
¿De cuál tierra venides, o queredes andar?
Decidme vuestros nombres, 'nom' los querades celar.° — don't hide them from

Herodes King
worried that there are other
kings that

GASPAR: A mí dicen Gaspar; me  
este otro, Melchor; a aquéste, Baltasar.  
Rey, un rey es nacido que es señor de tierra,  
que mandará el siglo en gran paz, sin guerra.  
HERODES: ¿Es así por verdad?  
GASPAR: Sí, rey, por caridad.  
HERODES: ¿Y cómo lo sabedes?  
¿Ya 'probado lo habedes?° **=lo habéis probado**  
GASPAR: Rey, verdad te diremos,  
que probado lo habemos.  
MELCHOR: Esto es gran maravilla,  
una estrella es nacida.  
BALTASAR: Señal face que es nacido  
y en carne humana venido.  
HERODES: ¿Cuánto 'i ha° que la visteis **=allí hace**  
y qué la percibisteis?  
GASPAR: Trece días ha,  
y más non habrá  
que la habemos veída  
y bien percibida.  
HERODES: Pues andad y buscad,  
y a él adorad,  
y por aquí tornad.  
Yo allá iré,  
y adorarlo he.

*Escena IV*  
HERODES: ¿Quién vio nunca tal mal?  
¡Sobre rey otro tal!  
¡Aún non soy yo muerto  
ni so° la tierra puesto! debajo de  
¿Rey otro sobre mí?  
¡Nunca a tal non vi!  
El siglo va 'a zaga;° backwards  
ya non sé qué 'me faga.° will become of me  
Por verdad no lo creo

hasta que yo lo veo.
Venga mío mayordoma
que míos 'haberes toma.° cares for my wealt
*(Sale el Mayordomo)*
Idme por míos abades,° abbots
y por mis podestades,° magistrates
y por míos escribanos,
y por míos gramtagos,° grammarians
y por míos estrelleros,
y por míos retóricos;° rhetoricians
decirme han la verdad, si yace° en escrito, is
o si lo saben ellos, o si lo han sabido.

*Escena V*
(Salen los Sabios de la corte)
[LOS SABIOS]: Rey, ¿qué te place? Henos venidos.
HERODES: ¿Y traedes vuestros escritos?
Los Sabios: Rey, sí traemos,
los mejores que nos habemos.
HERODES: Pues catad,
decidme la verdad,
si es aquel hombre nacido
que estos tres reyes me han dicho.
Di, Rabí, la verdad, si tú lo has sabido.
Rabí 1: 'Por veras° vos lo digo truly
que no lo fallo escrito.
"RABÍ 2: ¡Hamihalá!° '¡Cómo eres enartado!° "expresses anger,
¿Por qué eres rabí llamado? ceived
Non entiendes las profecías,
las que nos dijo Jeremías.
Por mi ley, ¡nos somos errados!° mistaken
¿Por qué non somos acordados?
¿Por qué non decimos verdad?
RABÍ 1: Yo non la sé por caridad.
RABÍ 2: Porque no la habemos usada,
ni en nuestras bocas es fallada.

# *XIII Century*

HISTORICAL BACKGROUND

This was an important century for Spain. The two great kingdoms of Castile and Leon were united under Ferdinand III, called "el Santo." Moorish Spain was greatly reduced by this monarch. Cordoba, Seville, Murcia fell to his armies, and by and large, the power of the Moors was broken, for only in the Kingdom of Granada did they hold firm. Ferdinand had the *Forum Judicum*, a compilation of Visigothic law, rendered into Spanish as the *Fuero Juzgo*.

His son, Alfonso X, called "el Sabio," although not so much a warrior and a politician as Ferdinand, was nevertheless in many ways even more important. He is remembered for his patronage of the arts and sciences, of music and literature, and for his efforts to have the extant knowledge of the realm translated into Spanish for all his subjects to use. His school of translators translated much from Arabic. Spanish learning in the century centered around the court of this king. Spanish law to this day owes its being to his code of laws (the *Siete Partidas*). Under his patronage Spain had her first important histories in Spanish, and Spanish music owes much of its early development to his support. His rule has been regarded as a kind of thirteenth-century renaissance.

King Alfonso's unsuccessful efforts to have himself elected Emperor of the Holy Roman Empire and his troubles with rebellious nobles and with his son, Sancho IV, "el Bravo," are more than compensated by his contributions to his country's culture and knowledge.

## *Lyric Poetry*

GALICIAN-PORTUGUESE LYRIC

It is quite likely that the lyric tradition represented by the *jarchas* survived and flourished in all parts of the Peninsula, but the bulk of poems which have actually survived in written form come from Galician-Portuguese territory. Most of these poems were modeled on those of the Provençal troubadours, and most are aristocratic rather than popular in inspiration. Even Castilian poets wrote their lyrics in Galician-Portuguese down to the 15th century. More than 2000 such songs composed by 200 named poets—kings, noblemen, and a few commoners--survive in three great song books, now referred to as *Cancioneiro da Ajuda*, *Cancioneiro portugués da Vaticana*, and *Cancioneiro Colocci-Brancuti*. Of the three classes of songs composed, the *cantigas de escarnio* are songs of insult and abuse, often quite scurrilous; the *cantigas de amor*, the *cantigas de amigo*, put in the mouth of the lovelorn lass and by far the most attractive of the group, often with real lyric freshness may come from popular origins. The Galician-Portuguese school of poets lasted for about a century and a half after 1200. It is never to be forgotten that all these early poems were written to be performed and not for reading.

CANTIGAS DE MARTÍN CODAX

1 Ondas do mar de Vigo

Ondas do mar de Vigo,
se vistes meu amigo?
E ai Deus!, se verra cedo?

Ondas do mar levado,
se vistes meu amado?
E ai Deus!, se verra cedo?

Se vistes meu amigo,
o por que eu sospiro?
E ai Deus!, se verra cedo?

Se vistes meu amado,
por que ei gran coidado?
E ai Deus!, se verra cedo?

Olas° del mar de Vigo° — waves, city of Galicia

Olas del mar de Vigo,
¿Visteis a mi amigo?
¡Ay Dios! ¿vendrá pronto?

Olas del mar agitado,°
¿Visteis a mi amado?
¡Ay Dios! ¿Vendrá pronto?

¿Visteis a mi amigo,
aquél por quien yo suspiro?
¡Ay Dios! ¿Vendrá pronto?

¿Visteis a mi amado,
quien me tiene tan preocupada?
¡Ay Dios! ¿Vendrá pronto?

2 Mandad'ei comigo
Mandad'ei comigo,
ca ven meu amigo.
E irei, madr' a Vigo

Comigo'ei mandado,
ca ven meu amado.
E irei, madr' a Vigo

Ca ven meu amigo
e ven san' e vivo.
E irei, madr' a Vigo

Ca ven meu amado
e ven viv' e sano.
E irei, madr' a Vigo

Ca ven san' e vivo
e d'el rei amigo
E irei, madr' a Vigo

° stormy

Ca ven viv' e sano
e d'el rei privado.
E irei, madr' a Vigo

Un mensaje he recibido
Un mensaje he recibido,
que viene mi amigo.
E iré, madre, a Vigo

Conmigo tengo un mensaje,
que viene mi amado.
E iré, madre, a Vigo

Que viene mi amigo
y viene sano y vivo.
E iré, madre, a Vigo

Que viene mi amado
y viene vivo y sano.
E iré, madre, a Vigo

Que viene sano y vivo
y del rey amigo.
E iré, madre, a Vigo

Que viene vivo y sano
y del rey favorito.
E iré, madre, a Vigo

3 Mia irmana fremosa
Mia irmana fremosa, treides comigo
a la ygreia de Vigo, u e o mar salido.
E miraremos las ondas.

Mia irmana fremosa, treides de grado

a la ygreia de Vigo, u e o mar levado.
E miraremos las ondas.

A la ygreia de Vigo, u e o mar salido,
e verra i mia madre e o meu amigo.
E miraremos las ondas

A la ygreia de Vigo, u e o mar levado,
e verra i mia madre o meu amado
E miraremos las ondas.

Hermosa hermana mía
Hermosa hermana mía, vente conmigo
a la iglesia de Vigo, donde está el mar agitado.
Y miraremos las olas.

Hermosa hermana mía, vente 'de buen grado ° — very willingly
a la iglesia de Vigo, donde está el mar enfurecido.
Y miraremos las olas.

A la iglesia de Vigo, donde está el mar agitado,
allí vendrá, madre, mi amigo
Y miraremos las olas.

A la iglesia de Vigo, donde está el mar enfurecido,
allí vendrá, madre, mi amado
Y miraremos las olas

4 Quantas sabedes amar amigo
Quantas sabedes amar amigo
treides comig' a lo mar de Vigo.
E bannar nos emos nas ondas!

Quantas sabedes amor amado,
treides comig' a lo mar levado.
E bannar nos emos nas ondas!

Treides comig' a lo mar de Vigo
e veeremos lo meu amigo.
E bannar nos emos nas ondas!

Treides comig' a lo mar levado
e veeremo' lo meu amado.
E bannar nos emos nas ondas!

Cuantas sabéis amar a un amigo
Cuantas sabéis amar a un amigo
venid conmigo al mar de Vigo.
¡Y nos bañaremos en las olas!

Cuantas sabéis de amor amado,
venid conmigo al mar agitado.
¡Y nos bañaremos en las olas!

Venid conmigo al mar de Vigo
y veremos a mi amigo.
¡Y nos bañaremos en las olas!

Venid conmigo al mar agitado
y veremos a mi amado.
¡Y nos bañaremos en las olas!

5 Eno sagrado, en Vigo

Eno sagrado, en Vigo,
baylava corpo velido.
Amor ei.

En Vigo, no sagrado,
baylava corpo delgado.
Amor ei.

Baylava corpo delgado

que nunca ouver' amado.
Amor ei.

Baylava corpo velido,
que nunca ouver' amigo.
Amor ei.

Que nunca ouver' amigo,
ergas no sagrad', en Vigo
Amor ei.

Que nunca ouver amado,
ergas en Vigo, no sagrado
Amor ei.

En lo sagrado,° en Vigo — shrine
En lo sagrado, en Vigo,
bailaba un cuerpo garrido.° — elegant
Amor tendré.

En Vigo, en lo sagrado,
bailaba un cuerpo delgado.
Amor tendré.

Bailaba un cuerpo delgado
que nunca tuviera un amado.
Amor tendré.

Bailaba un cuerpo garrido,
que nunca tuviera un amigo.
Amor tendré.

Que nunca tuviera un amigo,
Salvo° en lo sagrado, en Vigo. — except
Amor tendré.

Que nunca tuviera un amado,
salvo en Vigo, en lo sagrado.
Amor tendré.

6 Ay ondas que eu vin veer

Ay ondas que eu vin veer,
se me saberedes dizer
por que tarda meu amigo sen min.
Ay ondas que eu vin mirar,
se me saberedes contar
por que tarda meu amigo sen min.

Ay olas que vine a ver

Ay, olas que vine a ver,
si me supierais decir
¿Por qué tarda mi amigo, lejos de mí?

Ay, olas que vine a mirar,
si me supiérais contar
¿Por qué tarda mi amigo, lejos de mí?

## *Castilian Lyric*

Only a few poems of lyric nature might be traced from the 13th century, although there is a strong probability that much folk poetry existed. An example of this poetry is the *Eya velar*, a watchman's song that appears in Gonzalo de Berceo's narrative poem, *Duelo de la virgin*. The people who wrote books of poetry were the educated and they preferred Galician-Portuguese verse to Castilian.

### EYA VELAR

This is a song by a watchman at Christ's tomb inserted by Gonzalo de Berceo in his "Lamentation of the Virgin." It is most probably of folkloristic origin.

'¡Eya velar,° eya velar, eya velar! be watchful

| | |
|---|---|
| Velat aljama° de judíos, | quarter |
| eya velar, | |
| que non vos furten° el su dios, | steal |
| eya velar. | |
| Ca furtárvoslo querrán, eya velar, | |
| Andrés e Peidro e Johán, eya velar. | |
| No sabedes tanto d'escanto,° eya velar, | magic |
| que ixcades° de so el canto,° eya velar. | get you out, stone |
| Vuestra lengua tan palabrera,° eya velar, | talkative |
| ha vos dado mala carrera,° eya velar. | path |
| Vuestra lengua tan sin recabdo,° eya velar, | caution |
| por mal cabo° vos ha echado,° eya velar. | end, brought |
| Todos son homnes ladronciellos, eya velar, | |
| que asechan° por los pestiellos,° eya velar. | lurk, door lock |
| Todos son homnes plegadizos,° eya velar, | beggars |
| 'rioaduchos mescladizos,° eya velar. | mixture of flotsam |
| Non sabedes tanto d'engaño,° eya velar, | tricks |
| que ixcades end est un año, eya velar. | |
| Non sabedes tanta razón,° eya velar, | tales |
| que ixcades de la presón,° eya velar. | prison |
| El discípulo lo° vendió, eya velar, | Him |
| el maestro no·l entendió,° eya velar. | did not know |
| Don Tomaseio e Mateo, eya velar, | |
| de furtarlo han grant deseo, eya velar. | |
| Don Filipo, Simón e Judás, eya velar, | |
| por furtarlo buscan ayudas, eya velar. | |
| Si lo quieren acometer,° eya velar, | accomplish |
| hoy es día 'de parescer,° eya velar». | it seems |

## *Lament poetry*

*¡Ay Jherusalem!* deals with the Muslim siege of the defenders of Jerusalem and the profanation of the Holy Sepulcher in 1244. It was written to recruit crusaders, principally Spanish, to participate in the reconquest of Jerusalem. This is a crusade song with epic formulas as well as a lament, with clerecía elements, for the

defeat of Christian forces and the city of Jerusalem in 1244.

¡AY JHERUSALEM!
A los que adoran en la vera cruz,
salud e graçia de la vera luz,
que envió sin arte° — deceit
el maestre d'Acre[13]

5 a Jherusalem.
Bien querría más convusco plañir,° — lament
llorar noches e días, gemir° e non dormir, — moan
que contarvos prosas° — here poems
de nuevas° llorosas° — news, sad

10 de Jherusalem.
Creo que pecado me sería callar;° — to be silent
lloros e suspiros non me dan vagar° — respite
de escrebir el planto° — lament
en el Conçilio santo[14]

15 de Jherusalem.
De Jherusalem vos querría contar,
del Sepulcro Santo que es allende° el mar: — beyond
moros los çercaron° — lay seige
e 'lo derribaron,° — destroyed it

20 a Jherusalem.
Estos moros perros a la casa santa
siete años e medio la tienen çercada;
non dubdan° morir — were not afraid

---

[13] **Maestre d'Acre** is Guillaume de Châteauneuf, the Master of the Order of Knights Hospitalers (a military religious order) who helped pilgrims on their journey to Jerusalem. He wrote a letter describing the horrors stemming from the loss of the Holy City.
[14] **Conçilio santo** may refer to the first Papal Council in Lyon in 1245 or the second one in 1274.

por la conquerir

25 a Jherusalem.
Fazen ayuntamiento° los de Babilonia — meeting
con los africanos para los de Etiopia,
para los…
tártaros° e miros° — Tartars, possibly Moors

30 por Jherusalem.
Grandes afincanças° ponen con sus lanças — effort
por ir° a cristianos como a perdonanças.° — attack, earn pardon for sins;
'Llena por ençima° — overflowing
vençe morería° — Moorish armies

35 en Jherusalem.
Aunque los cristianos non pueden sofrir,° — endure
han pocas viandas° e mucho ferir.° — food, wounding
Non les viene acorro° — help
del su Consistorio° — papal court

40 en Jherusalem.
Ya todos acuerdan con el Patriarca.° — highest bishop of the area;
Para el 'Padre Santo° escriven una carta — Pope
con letras de sangre,
que mueren de fanbre° — **=hambre**

45 en Jherusalem.
Ca los muy amargos moros cuantos son[15]
tiénenlo çerrado° al altar de Sión° — surrounded, Zion
Non dubdan morir
por la conquerir

50 a Jherusalem.
Léyese° la carta en el Conçilio santo: — **se lee**
papa e cardenales fazían gran llanto,

[15] **Ca los…** Because the many Moors cause suffering

ronpen° sus vestidos, — tear
'dan grandes gemidos° — showing great grie

55 por Jherusalem.
Mandan dar pregones por la cristiandad,[16]
alçan sus pendones,° llaman° Trinidad. — banners, call on
"¡Valed,° los cristianos, — help
a vuestros hermanos

60 en Jherusalem!"
Non les da buen viaje la sagrada mar:
los vientos an contrarios, non les dexa andar.
Cuando están en calma
'esflaquéçeles el alma,° — their determin weakens

65 en Jherusalem.
Ora° es venida, por nuestros pecados, — time
de tan negro día moros esforçados.° — determined
Llena por encima vençe morería

70 en Jherusalem.
Pocos son cristianos, menos que ovejas.
Muchos son los moros, más que las estrellas.
Non dubdan morir por la conquerir

75 a Jherusalem.
'¡Cuánta grand batalla° fuera en aquel día! — what a great battle
Con los cavalleros es la clerezía,° — religious order of
'por tomar pasión° — willing to die
por la defensión° — =**defensa**

80 de Jherusalem.
Revenden° cristianos muy bien° la su sangre: — =**venden**, dearly
por muerte de uno° cient moros 'van delante.° — Christian, die (Mo
'de todo por ençima° — in spite of everyth

[16] **Mandan dar...** They order proclamations sent throughout Christendom

vençe morería

85 en Jherusalem.
Sacerdotes e fraires° en cadenas presos;° =**frailes**, prisoners
tienen a los abades en 'cepos de maderos.° stocks
afán° e armargura° affliction, sadness
hanlo° 'por folgura° consider it, as ease

90 en Jherusalem.
Tienen las doncellas° que eran delicadas° maidens, thin
en cadenas presas e muy atormentadas.
Afán e quebranto,° fazían grande llanto suffering

95. en Jherusalem.
Veen los cristianos a sus fijos asar,° burning
veen a sus mugeres bivas destetar;° having their breasts cut off
vanse por los caminos
cortos pies e manos

100. en Jherusalem.
De las vestimentas° fazían cubiertas;° church vestments, horse blankets; stable
del Sepulcro Santo fazían establo;°
de las cruzes santas
fazían estacas° stakes

105. en Jherusalem.
Quien este canto non quiere oír,
'non tiene mientes° de a Dios servir does not intend
'nin poner un canto° to help
en Conçilio santo

## *Narrative Minstrel Poetry*

### EPIC

*Roncesvalles*, written in the 1230's, shows the influence of the *chanson de geste*. Only 100 lines have survived, but it is apparent that these once belonged to a longer poem. In moving and vivid realism this fragment tells of the extreme grief of Charlemagne upon seeing the remains of his slaughtered army at the battle of Roncesvalles in 778, when Saracens (actually Basques) ambushed and destroyed the French host as it was returning from the siege of Saragossa. Of high emotional quality is the king's sorrow on finding the bodies of Roland (Charlemagne's nephew) and Oliver (one of the twelve peers and Roland's friend).

The lost epics of the thirteenth century, the existence of which is indicated in the Spanish prose chronicles of the thirteenth century, are of some importance, at least in subject matter: (1) *Rodrigo el Godo*, the story of the last king of the Visigoths, who lost his realm to the Moslems; (2) *Bernardo del Carpio*, the story of a fictitious Leonese hero of the eighth century; and (3) *El Cerco de Zamora*, which reports the events of the siege of Zamora by Sancho II and of this king's murder by Bellido Dolfos.

*CANTAR DE RONCESVALLES*

Roncesvalles is a 100-line fragment of an epic poem in the minstrel style. The fragment was found in Pamplona in 1916 and first published by Menéndez Pidal in 1917. It relates the story of the death of the twelve peers of France during the reign of Charlemagne who were ambushed as they were returning to France from battles in Spain. Roland, Charlemagne's nephew, was leading the rearguard at the time of the attack. The event occurs in the mountain pass in the Pyrenees near Roncesvalles.

In this fragment Charlemagne, who has returned to the battlefield, is addressing the dead warriors he has found and begins with Archbishop Turpin, then he comes across the body of Oliver, Roland's best friend and finally Roland. You will notice that some of the lines have been lost and parts of some lines are incomplete.

'Raçonóse con ella,° como si fuese vivo: — he spoke to it (head)
«Bueno pora° las armas, 'mejor pora ante° Jesuchristo; — =**para**, better serving

| | |
|---|---|
| consejador° de pecadores e dar... tanto... da... | counselor |
| el cuerpo 'priso martirio° por que le... | was martyred |
| Mas quién aconseyará° este viejo mesquino,[17] | will advise |
| que 'finca en grant cuita° con moros en periglo?»[18] | is in such sorrow, |
| Aquí clamó° sus escuderos Carlos el enperante:° | **=llamó**, **=emperador** |
| «Sacat° al arcebispo desta mortaldade!° | remove, slaughter |
| Levémosle° a su tierra a Flanderes la ciudade!» | **=llevémoslo** |
| El enperador andaba 'catando por° la mortaldade; | searching through |
| vido° en la plaça° Oliveros o° yaze | **=vio**, battlefield, |
| el escudo crebantado° por medio del braçale;[19] | **=donde**; **=quebran-** |
| non vio sano en éll cuanto un dinero cabe;[20] | **tado** |
| 'tornado a orient° como lo puso Roldane. | turned facing east |
| El buen enperador mandó la cabeza alçare° | lifted |
| que le linpiasen la cara del polvo° e de la sangre. | dust |
| Como si fuese vivo començólo de preguntare: | |
| «Digádesme,° don Oliveros, caballero naturale,° | **=decidme**, faithful |
| dó° dexastes° a Roldán? digádesme la verdade. | **=donde**, **=dejaste** |
| Cuando vos fiz° conpañeros déestesme tal homenaj[21] | **=hice** |
| por que nunca en vuestra vida non fuésedes partidos maes.[22] | |
| Dizímelo,° don Oliveros, dó lo iré buscare? | **=decídmelo** |
| Yo demandaba° por don Roldán, 'a la priesa tan grande.° | was looking, hurriedly |
| Ya mi sobrino ¿dónt° vos iré buscare?» | **=adónde** |
| Vio un colpe° que fizo don Roldane: | **=golpe** |
| «Esto fizo 'con cueyta° con grant dolor que habíae.°» | with difficulty, **=tenía** |
| Estonz alçó los ojos, cató 'cabo adelante° | looked, ahead |
| vido a don Roldán acostado a un pilare,° | large stone |
| como se acostó a la ora de finare.° | death |
| El rey cuando lo vido, oít° lo que faze: | **=oíd** |
| arriba alçó las manos por 'las barbas tirare,° | to pull out his beard |

[17] **Este viejo...** *this miserable old man.* Charlemagne is referring to himself in his grief.

[18] **Con moros...** *endangered by Moors*

[19] **Por medio...** *from the middle of the arm bracket*

[20] **No vio...** *He did not see a single part of his body uninjured.*

[21] **Diéstesme tal ...** *you gave me this promise.*

[22] **Por que...** *You would never part from each other.*

por las barbas floridas° bermeja° sallía la sangre; — white, red
'esa ora° el buen rey oít lo que dirade, — **=entonces**
diz: « Muerto es mío sobrino, el buen de don Roldane!
Aquí veo atal cosa que nunca vi tan grande;
Yo era pora morir e vos pora escapare.[23]
Tanto buen amigo vos me solíades ganare;[24]
'por vuestra amor arriba° muchos me solían amare; — because of your love
pues vos sodes muerto, sobrino, 'buscar me han° 'todo male.° — try to do, all kinds of evil;
Asaz° veo una cosa que sé que es verdade: — clearly
que la vuestra alma bien° sé que es en buen logare; — truly
mas atal viejo mesquino, agora que farade?° — will become (of me)
Hoy he perdido esfuerzo° con que solía ganare. — strength
¡Ay, mi sobrino, non me queredes fablare!
Non vos veo colpe nin lanzada° por que hobieses male,° — lance thrust, injury
por esso non vos creo que muerto sodes,° don Roldane. — **=sois**
Dexamos vos a zaga,° donde prisiestes male, — rear guard,
las mesnadas° e los pares° ambos van allae° — troops, peers, **=allá**
con vos, e amigo, por amor de vos guardare.
Sobrino, ¿por esso non me queredes fablare?
Pues sodes muerto, Francia poco vale.
Mío sobrino, ante que finásedes era yo pora morir maes.
Atal viejo mesquino, ¿quí° lo conseyarade?° — **=quién**, aconsejará
Cuando fui mancebo de la primera edade,
quis andar ganar precio° de Francia, de mi tierra natural; — honor
fuíme a Toledo a servir al rey Galafre[25]
que ganase a Durandarte[26] large;° — **=largo**
ganéla de moros cuando maté a Braymante,[27]
dila a vos, sobrino, con tal homenaje
que con vuestras manos non la diésedes a nadi;° — **=nadie**

---

[23] **Yo era …** *I should have died and you should have escaped.*

[24] **Tanto buen…** *you would win for me so many great friends*

[25] Galafre was the Emir of Toledo

[26] Name of Roland's sword

[27] Braymante was a powerful Moor who wanted to marry King Galafre's daughter, Galiana who married Charlemagne.

| | |
|---|---|
| saquéla de moros, vos tornástesla allae. | |
| ¡Dios vos perdone, que 'non podiestes maes!° | could not help it |
| Con vuestra rencura° el coraçón me quiere crebare. | suffering |
| Sallíme de Francia a tierras estrañas morare° | to live |
| por conquerir° Provincia° e demandar linaje; | **=conquistar**, Provence |
| acabé° a Galiana, a la muger leale. | I won |
| Naçiestes, mi sobrino; ha° XVII años de edade, | **=tenía** |
| fizvos caballero a un precio tan grande. | |
| 'Metím al camino,° pasé ata° la mare, | I set out, across |
| pasé Jerusalém, fasta la fuent° Jordane; | **=río** |
| corríemos° las tierras 'della e della parte.° | attack, on all sides |
| Con vos conquís Truquía° e Roma 'apriessa daba.° | **=Turquía**, I hurried |
| Con vuestro esfuerço arriba entramos en España, | |
| matastes los moros e las tierras ganabas, | |
| adobé° los caminos del apóstol Santiague; | I restored |
| non conquís a Çaragoça,° ont me ferió° tal lançada. | **=Zaragoza**, **=hirió** |
| ¡Con tal duelo° estó,° sobrino, agora non fues vivo! | grief, **=estoy** |
| ¡Agora ploguiés° al Criador, a mi señor Jesucristo | may it please |
| que finase en este logar, que me levase contigo! | |
| D'aquestos muertos que aquí tengo conmigo | |
| dizirme hías las nuevas, cada uno cómo fizo.»[28] | |
| El rey cuando esto dixo,'cayó esmortecido.° | he fainted |
| Dexemos al rey Carlos fablemos de ale° | someone else |
| digamos del duc Aymón, padre de don Rinalte.[29] | |
| Vido yazer su fijo entre las mortaldades;° | mortally wounded |
| Despeñós'° del caballo, tan grant duelo que faze, | dismounted |
| alçóli la cabeça, odredes° lo que dirade: | **=oiréis** |
| «Fijo, vuestras mañas,° ¿quí las podría contare? | virtues |
| que cuerpo tan caboso° homen° non vio otro tale. | perfect, no one |
| ¡Vos fuérades pora vivir, e yo pora morir maes! | |
| Mas atal viejo mesquino sienpre habrá male. | |

[28] **Dizirme hías...** *Tell me how each one died.*

[29] Duke Aymon of Dordogne and his son , Renalt of Montalban, did not participate in the battle of Roncesvalles even though the poem indicates that they did.

Por que más me conuerto porque perdoneste a Roldane.[30]
Finastes sobre moros, vuestra alma es en buen logare!
¿Quí levará los mandados° a vuestra
madre a las tierras de Montalbane?» news
El duc faziendo su duelo muit grande,
veníali el mandado que yazía esmortecido el enperante.
Mandó sacar el fijo de entre las mortaldades.
Venía el duc Aymón, e ese duc de Bretaña[31]
el caballero Belart, el fi de Terri d'Ardeña;[32]
vidieron al rey esmortecido estaba,
prenden agua fría, al rey con ella daban.

## *Debate poetry*

Disputes (Fr. *débats*), were popular in France, and were probably borrowed from that country by Spanish writers. These poems are usually in rhymed couplets and verses of eight syllables, although there is some irregularity in this respect. The *Razón de amor*, probably early 13th century, contains elements of Aragonese dialect. Its subject, the meeting of two lovers in a beautiful setting, follows to some degree the Galician variety of love poem and contains a good deal of symbolism and allegory. The versification is irregular and is based principally upon lines of eight and nine syllables. Attached to it appears a debate in verse entitled *Denuestos del agua y el vino* which is a dispute between water and wine, each of which argues its own virtues. The lines are irregular rhymed couplets. Still another poem of the same category is *Elena y María*. Elena's lover is a knight and María's is a cleric. Each girl states the virtues of her beloved. The rhymed couplets in octosyllabic verses are colored by Leonese dialect.

[30] **Por que...** *What consoles me is that you pardoned Roland. Possibly a reference to some dispute between them.*

[31] Solomon of Brittany

[32] **Belart, ...** is Berard de Mondidier, the son of Thierry d'Ardennes.

## RAZÓN DE AMOR CON LOS DENUESTOS DEL AGUA Y EL VINO

This early 13th century, most probably anonymous, lyric poem, although signed by a Lope de Moros who could be the author or the copyist, was found in a manuscript that also contained the debate poem *Denuestos del agua y el vino*. The *Razón de amor* is of the courtly love school. It recounts how the poet sees a lady place a silver glass in an orchard so that when her lover comes, he may refresh himself. Above the orchard the poet sees another glass filled with cool water. A *doncella* comes who complains of the sufferings of love after which she leaves at dawn and the poet remains disconsolate. At the end of the *Razón* a dove appears and pours water into the glass of wine which seems to connect the two poems and to introduce the debate which follows.

In the *Denuestos del agua y el vino* the water and the wine discuss their respective virtues and the other's vices trying to show the superiority of one over the other. The syllable count is irregular but the verse form is rhymed couplets.

*Sancti spiritus adsid nobis gratia amen.*[33]
Qui° triste tiene su corazón — whoever
venga oír esta razón.° — discourse
Odrá° razón acabada, — **=oirá**
Feita° d'amor e bien rimada. — **=hecha**
Un escolar la rimó
que siempre duenas° amó; — ladies
mas siempre ovo trianza° — courtships
en Alemania y en Françia;
moró° mucho en Lombardía° — lived, region in Italy
por aprender cortesía.° — courtly behavior
En el mes d'abril, depués yantar,° — eating
estava so° olivar.° — under, olive trees
Entre çimas° d'un mançanar° — top branches, apple grove
un vaso de plata vi estar;
pleno° era d'un claro vino, — **=lleno**

[33] ***Sancti spiritus...*** *May the grace of the Holy Spirit be with us. Amen.*

que era vermejo e fino;
cubierto era de tal mesura,
no lo tocás' la calentura.
Una duena lo ý° avi puesto, — there
que era senora del uerto,° — orchard
que cuan su amigo viniese,
d'aquel vino a beverle diesse.
Qui de tal vino oviesse
en la mana° cuan comiesse — morning
e d'ello oviesse cada día,
nuncas más enfermaría.
Ariba del mançanar
otro vaso vi estar;
pleno era d'un agua frida° — cold
que en el mançanar se naçía
Beviera d'ela de grado,
mas ovi miedo que era encantado.
Sobre un prado pus' mi tiesta,° — head
que no m' fiziese mal la siesta;[34]
partí de° mí las vistiduras, — I took off
que no m' fiziés' mal la calentura.
'Plegém' a° una fuente perenal,° — I drew near, perennial
nunca fue omne que vies' tal;
tan grant virtud en sí avía,
que de la fridor° que 'd'í ixía,° — cold, came out of it
çient pasadas° aderedor° — paces, from there
non sintriades° el calor. — feel
Todas yerbas que bien olíen
la fuent çerca sí las teníe:
ý es la salvia,° ý son as rosas, — sage
ý el lirio e las violas;
otras tantas yerbas ý avía
que sol° nombrar no las sabría. — even
Mas ell olor que d'í ixía

[34] **Que no...** so that the heat of the day might not harm me

a omne muerto resucitaría .
Pris'° del agua un bocado — I took
e fui todo esfriado.° — cooled off
En mi mano pris' una flor,
sabet, non toda la peyor'° — **=peor**
e quis' cantar de fin° amor. — courtly
Mas vi venir una doncela,° — maiden
pues naçí, non vi tan bella;
blanca era e bermeja,
cabelos cortos sobre'ell oreja,
fruente° blanca e loçana,° — **=frente**, smooth
cara fresca como maçana;° — **=manzana**
nariz egual° e dereita, — proportioned
nunca viesteis tan bien feita;
ojos negros e ridientes,° — smiling
boca 'a razón° e blancos dientes; — right size
labros vermejos, non muy delgados,
por verdat bien mesurados;
por la çentura° delgada, — waist
bien estant e mesurada.
El manto e su brial° — tunic
de xamet° era, que non 'd'ál;° — rich silk cloth, nothing else
un sombrero tien' en la tiesta,
que no l' fiziese mal la siesta;
unas luvas° tien' en la mano, — gloves
sabet, non gelas dio vilano.° — peasant
De las flores viene tomando,
en alta voz d'amor cantando.
E deçía: "¡Ay, meu amigo,
si me veré yamás° contigo! — **=jamás°**
Amet' sempre e amaré
cuanto que viva seré.
porque eres escolar,
quisquiere° te devría más amar. — everyone
nunca odí° de homne deçir — **=oí**

que 'tanta bona manera° ovo en sí. — so many good qualitie
Más amaría contigo estar,
que toda Espana mandar.
Mas d'una cosa só cuitada:
é° miedo de seder° enganada. — **=he, =ser**
Que dizen que otra dona
cortesa e bela e bona,
te quiere tan gran ben,
por ti pierde su sen.° — mind
E por esso é pavor
que a ésa quieras mejor.
Mas s'yo te vies' una vegada.° — time
'¡a plan° me queríes por amada!." — surely
Cuant 'la mía senor° esto dizía — my lady (courtly language); saw
sabet, a mí non vidía;°
pero° sé que no me conocía, — although
que de mí non foiría.° — **=huiría**
Yo non fiz'° aquí como vilano, — act
levém' e pris'la por la mano.
Juñiemos° 'amos en par° — joined, both of us
e posamos° so ell olivar. — rested
Dix'le yo: "Dezit, la mía senor,
si supiestes nunca d'amor."
Diz' ella: "A plan, con grant amor ando,
mas non coñozco mi amado;
pero dízem' un su mesajero
que es clérigo° e no cavelero,° — scholar, knight
sabe muio° de trobar, — a lot
de leyer e de cantar;
dizem' que es 'de buenas yentes,° — good family
mancebo barvapuñient° es." — young
"Por Dios, que digades, la mía senor,
¿qué donas° tenedes por la su amor?" — gifts
"Estas luvas y es° capiello,° — this, hat
est'° oral° y est' aniello° — this, veil, ring

envió a mí es meu amigo,
que por la su amor trayo comigo."
Yo conocí luego las alfayas,° — gifts
que yo ge las avía enviadas;
ela coñeció° una mi çinta 'man a mano,° — recognized, immediately
qu'ela la fiziera con la su mano.
Toliós' el manto de los hombros;
besóme la boca e por los ojos;
tan gran sabor° de mí avía, — pleasure
sol fablar non me podía.
"¡Dios Senor, a ti loado
cuant conozco meo amado!
Agora é tod bien comigo
cuant conozco meo amigo!"
Una grant pieça° alí estando, — while
de nuestro amor ementando,° — talking
ela m' dixo: "El mío Senor, ora m'sería de tornar
si a vos non fuese 'en pesar."° — displease
Yo l'dix': "It, la mia senor, pues que ir queredes,
mas de mi amor pensat, 'fe que devedes."° — by the faith you owe me
Ela m' dixo: "bien seguro seyt de mi amor,
no vos camiaría por un emperador."
La mía senor se va privado,° — quickly
dexa a m'i desconortado.° — disconsolate
Queque° la vi fuera del uerto, — as soon as
por poco non fui muerto.
Por verdat quisieram' adormir,
Mas una palomela° vi; — dove
tan blanca era como la niev del puerto,° — mountain pass
Volando viene por medio del uerto,
un cascavielo° dorado — bell
tray al pie atado.
En la fuent quiso entrar
mas cuando a mí vido estar,
entrós' en el vaso malgranar.° — pomegranate
Cuando en el vaso fue entrada

e fue toda bien esfriada,
ela que quiso exir festino,° quickly
vertios´°el agua sobr'el vino. spilled

DENUESTOS DEL AGUA Y EL VINO

Aquí s' copiençan° a denostar° **=comienzan,** ins
el vino y el agua, e a 'mal levar.° quarrel
El vino favló primero:
"¡Mucho m'es venido mal° companero! as a bad
Agua, as° 'mala mana,° you have, bad ma
non quería aver la tu compana;
que cuando te legas° a buen vino, **=llegas**
fázeslo feble° e mesquino."° weak, bad tasting
"Don vino, fe que devedes,
¿por cuáles bondades que vos avedes
a vos queredes alabar
e a mí queredes aviltar?° insult
¡Calat!° Yo e vos no nos denostemos, **=callad**
que vuestras mañas bien las sabemos;
bien sabemos qué recabdo° dades problems
en la cabeça do entrades.
Los buenos vos preçian poco,
que del sabio fazedes loco.
No es° homne tan senado,° there is, rational
que de ti 'se á fartado,° has his fill
que no haya perdío el sesso° y el recabdo."° judgment, prudenc
El vino con sana° pleno, anger
dixo: "¡Don agua, 'bierva vos veno!° you like to talk
¡Suzia, desberconçada,
salit buscar otra posada!° place to stay
Que podedes a Dios jurar
que nunca entrastes en tal lugar:
antes, amariella e astrosa,° vile
agora vermeja e fermosa."
Respondió el agua:
"Don vino, ¿qué ý ganades

| | |
|---|---|
| en villanías° que digades? | coarse remarks |
| Pero si vos ent° apagardes° | about this, you cool |
| digámoslos las verdades: | it |
| que no á homne que no lo sepa | |
| que fillo° sodes de la çepa,° | son, vine stalk |
| y por verdat vos digo | |
| 'que non sodes pora° comigo; | you should not get into |
| que grant tiempo á que vuestra madre seríe arduda° | it; burned |
| si non fusse por mi ayuda. | |
| Mas cuando veyo que le van cortar, | |
| Ploro e fágola vino° levar."° | wine, produce |
| Respondió el vino luego: | |
| "Agua, entiendo que lo dizes 'por juego.° | in jest |
| Por verdat, pláçem'° de coraçón | it pleases me |
| por que somos en esta razón; | |
| ca en esto que dizes puedes entender | |
| como es grant el mío poder. | |
| Ca veyes que no é manos ni piedes, | |
| Eio° a muchos valientes. | I knock down |
| E sí faría a cuantos en el mundo son, | |
| e si vivo fuese, Sansón.° | Samson |
| E dexemos todo lo ál: | |
| la mesa sin mí nada non val'." | |
| Ell agua yaze muerta ridiendo° | laughing |
| de lo qu'el vino está diziendo: | |
| "Don vino, sí vos dé Dios salud, | |
| que vos me fagades agora una virtud:° | test |
| fartad bien un villano, | |
| no lo prenda ninguno de la mano, | |
| e si antes d'una passada° no cayere en el lodo, | step |
| 'dios sodes de tod en todo. | |
| E si esto fazedes, | |
| otorgo que vençuda° m'avedes: | conquered |
| en una blanca paret | |
| çinco candelas ponet, | |
| e si el beudo° non dixiere que son çiento, | drunk |

de cuanto digo de todo miento."
"Par Dios, diz' el vino, mucho somos en buena razón
si comigo tuvieres entençión.° — case
¿Quieres que te diga agora una cosa?
No sé res tan lixosa:° — filthy
tú sueles cales° e calejas° mondar,° — streets, alley ways, clea
y por tantos de lixos° andar; — dirty places
por tantos de lugares
delegas° tus senalles,° — leave, signs
e sueles lavar pies e manos
e lavar muchos lixosos panos.
E sueles tanto andar con polvo mesclada
fasta que'en lodo eres tornada.
C'a mí siempre me tienen ornado,° — honored
de entro en buenas cubas° condesado.° — wine barrels, kept
E 'contart' é° otras mis manas,° — **=te contaré**, traits
mas temo que luego te asanas:° — get angry
yo fago al çiego veyer
y al coxo° corer — lame
y al mudo fabular° — speak
y al enfermo organar;° — sing
así com dize en el scripto,° — scriptures
de mí fazen el cuerpo de Jhesu Christo."
"¡Así, don vino, por caridad,
que tanta sabedes de divinidad!° — religion
Alauut,° yo y todo algo é en cristianismo, — my soul,
que de agua fazen el batismo.
E dize Dios que los que de agua fueren bautisados
fillos de Dios serán clamados,
e llos que de agua non fueren bautisados,
fillos de Dios non serán clamados."

Mi razón aquí la fino° — end
e mandatnos dar vino.

Qui me scripsit scribat,

semper cum domino bibat.
Lupus me feçit, de Moros.[35]

ELENA Y MARÍA

This anonymous debate takes place between two sisters who try to convince each other of the superiority of her lover: one lover being a cleric and the other a knight. This debate is not original and has many antecedents in Latin as well as vernacular languages. The debate part of the poem is found in verses 1-282. Since the two sisters are unable to solve their disagreement, they go to the court of King Oriol, famous for his great judgment in questions of love. The last lines tell of the arrival of the ladies at the court. The poem has come down to us without a beginning or an ending and is from the second half of the 13th century although some scholars have placed it in the first half of the century.

" . . . . . . . . . . Mesura
biue bien sin rancura;° — resentment
diz buenas palabras,
mas non sabe 'jogar las tabras° — joust
nin 'despende su ayer° — spend his money
en folía nin en 'mal sen»°. — foolishness
Elena la cató
de su palabra la sonsanó,° — rebuffed
grave mientre le respuso,° — answered
agora oyd cómo fabró:° — **=habló**
«Calla, María,
¿por qué dizes tal follía?
esa palabra que fabreste
al mío amigo denosteste,
mas se° lo bien catas — if
y por derecho lo asmas° — judge it reasonably
non eras tú pora° conmigo — equal

[35] **Qui me...** The one *who wrote me, let him write, let him always drink with the Lord. Lope de Moros made me. Feçit* should be the correct Latin *fecit.*

nin el tu amigo pora con el mío;
somos hermanas y fijas 'de algo,° noble
mays° yo amo 'el mays alto,° =**mas**, the better one
ca es cauallero armado,
de sus armas esforçado;° expert
el mío es defensor,
el tuyo es orador:° one who prays
quel mío defende tierras
y sufre° batallas y guerras, endures
ca el tuyo janta° y jaz° eats, lies down
y siempre está en paz».
María, 'atán por arte,° with great astuteness
respuso dela otra parte:° side
"¡Ve, loca trastornada,° silly fool
ca non sabes nada!"
¡Dizes que janta y jaz
porque está en paz!
Ca él biue bien onrrado
y sin todo cuydado;
ha comer e beuer
en buenos lechos jazer;
ha vestir e calçar° shoes
y bestias en que caualgar,° ride
vasallas y vasallos,
mulas y cauallos;
ha dineros y pannos
y otros aueres tantos.
De las armas non ha cura° worry
y otrosí° de lidiar, likewise
ca más val seso e mesura
que sienpre andar en locura,
commo el tu cauallero
que ha vidas de garçon.° lad
Quando al palaçio va,
sabemos vida quele dan:
el pan a raçión,° ration

| | |
|---|---|
| el vino 'sin sazón;° | not aged |
| sorie° mucho y come poco, | smiles |
| va cantando commo loco; | |
| commo tray° poco vestido, | wears |
| sienpre ha fanbre e frío. | |
| Come mal y jaze mal | |
| de noche en su ostal,° | lodging |
| ca quien anda en casa ajena | |
| nunca 'sal de pena.° | escapes suffering |
| Mientre él está allá, | |
| lazerades vos acá; | |
| parades mientes quando verná° | **=vendrá** |
| y cata le las manos qué adura,° | brings |
| y senon tray nada, | |
| luego es fría la posada». | |
| Elena con yra | |
| luego dixo: «esto es mentira. | |
| Enel palaçio anda mi amigo, | |
| mas non ha fanbre nin frío; | |
| anda vestido y calçado | |
| y bien encaualgado;° | mounted |
| aconpánanlo caualleros | |
| y síruenlo escuderos; | |
| dan le grandes soldadas° | income |
| y abasta° alas conpanas.° | supplies, soldiers |
| Quando al palaçio viene, | |
| apuesto° y muy bien,° | elegant, well mannered |
| con armas y con cauallos | |
| y con escuderos e con vasallos, | |
| sienpre trae açores° | hawks |
| y con falcones de los mejores; | |
| quando vien riberando° | hunting along the river y |
| las aves matando, | bank |
| butores° y abtardas° | vultures and buzzards |
| y otras aues tantas; | |
| quando al palaçio llega, | |

Dios, que bien semeja° — looks
açores gritando,
cauallos reninchando,° — neighing
alegre vien y cantando,
palabras 'de cortes° fabrando.° — courtly
A mí tien onrrada,
vestida y calçada;
viste me de çendal° — fine silk
e de ál que más val.
Creas me de çierto,
que más val vn beso de infanzón° — knight
que çinco de abadón,° — fat abbot
commo el tu 'baruj rapado° — beardless one
que sienpre anda en su capa ençerrado,° — wrapped
que la cabeça y la barua y el pescueço° — neck
non semeja senon escueso.° — frog
Mas el cuydado mayor
que ha aquel tu sennor
de su salterio rrezar,
e sus molaziellos° ensenar; — altar boys
la batalla faz con sus manos
quando bautiza sus afijados;° — children
comer e gastar
e dormir e folgar,
fijas de omnes bonos ennartar,° — deceive
casadas e por casar.
Non val 'nenguna rren° — nothing
quien non sabe de mal e de bien:
que el mío sabe dello e dello
e val más por ello».
María respuso tan yrada,
esa vegada:
«Elena, calla,
¿por qué dizes tal palabra?
Ca el tu amigo
'a pos° el mío non val vn mal figo. — next to

Quando él es en palaçio
non es en tal espaçio,° situation
oras° tien algo, oras tien nada, sometimes
que ayna falla 'ela solda.° his salary
Quando non tien qué despender
tórnase luego a jogar;
e joga dos vezes o tres,
que nunca gana vna vez;
quando torna a perder,
ayna sal el su auer:
joga el cauallo e el roçín
e elas armas otro sy,
el mantón, el tabardo
e el bestido e el calçado;
finca en auol° guisa, any
en panicos° e en camisa. underwear
Quando non tien que jogar
nin al a qué tornar,
vay e la siella empenar° pawn
alos francos° dela cal; French moneylenders
el freno° e el albardón° bit, packsaddle
dalo al su rapagón° stableboy
quelo vaya vender
e enpenar pora comer;
sé que ay oras° times
que allá van las espueras° spurs
a pie viene muchas vegadas,
desnudo e sin calças,
e 'se quier° a su amiga not even
nin conseja° nin la abriga; advise
ca omne con rancura
fría es la posada,
que asy faz do non ha vino
nin trigo nin farina nin toçino,
e averedes por lo a enpenar
el mantón e el brial.

Otro día asy se mucho dura
cada día sacará° sobrel vestido, — will gamble
fasta que sea comido.
Quando comido fuere,
¿qué será del sennor?
querrá yr a furtar;
mas se lo ouieron atomar,° — arrest
colgarlo han de vn palero,° — gallows
en somo de vn otero.° — hill
Ca el mío amigo, bien te lo digo,
a mucho trigo e muncho vino;
tien buenos çelleros° — coffers
de plata e de dineros;
viste° lo que quier, — wears
se quier° mantón, se quier piel; — either
non ha fanbre nin frío,
nin mengua de vestido.
Enla manana por la ylada° — cold
vieste su capa ençerrada
e 'enpenada en corderinos° — lined with wool
e vase a sus matines;
diz matines e misa
e sierue bien su eglisa,
e gana diezmos° e primençias° — tithes, first fruits
sin pecado e sin enganno;
e quando quier comer e beuer
e ha vida de rico omne.
E yo que esto digo,
a Dios grado e al mío amigo,
non ha fanbre nin frío,
nin mengua de vestido,
nin esto° deseosa — **=estoy**
de ninguna cosa».
Elena, do sedía,
cató contra María;
diz: «ve, astrosa,

e ¿non has ora vergüença?
¿Por qué dizes tal maldad° — evil
abuelta con torpedat?° — stupidity
querrieste alabar
se te yo quesiese otorgar
Ca tú non comes con sazón
esperando la obraçión;° — offering
lo que tú has a gastar,
ante la eglisa onrrada lo ha aganar;
beuides commo mesquinos,
de alimosna° de vuestros vezinos. — alms
Quando el abbad misa dezía,
a su moger maldezía;
enla primera oraçión
luego le echa la maldeçión.
Si tú fueres misa escuchar,
tras todos te has a estar;
ca yo estaré en la delantrera° — front row
e ofreçeré enla primera;
amí leuarán por el manto,
e tú yrás tras todas arrastrando;
amj leuarán commo condesa,
ati dirán commo monaguesa».
Quando María oyó esta razón,
pesól de coraçón;
respondió muy bien:
«todo esto non 'te prista ren;° — profit you at all
anos ¿qué nos val
por anbas nos denostar?
Ca yo bien sé asaz
el tu amigo lo que faz:
se él va 'en fonsado,° — army
non es de su grado;
se va conbater,
non es de su querer;
non puede refuyr

q*u*ando lo va otro ferir;
lazerar lo ha y,
senon tornar sobre sy.
Se bien lidia de sus mannos
es vna vez en treinta annos;
se vna vez vien descuidado
e vien aparejado,
s . . . . . uedes v . . . . .
endurades más de tres.
Muchas vegadas queredes comer
quenon podedes auer.
Ca bien telo juro por la mi camisa,
que siempre esto de buena guisa;
se bien janto e mejor çeno
que nunca lazdro nin peno,
ca ora he grand viçio
e biuo en grand deliçio;
ca bien ha mío sennor
que de la eglisa que de su lauor,
que siempre tien riqueza e bondat e honor.
Quando él misa dize,
bien sé que a mí non maldize;
ca quien vos amar en su coraçón
non vos maldizerá en nulla saçón.
Ca sy por uero lo sopiesen
e en escripto lo liesen,° read
que asy se perdía la moguer° quel clérigo touiese, **=mujer**
non faría otro abbad
senon el que touiese castidat;
ca non deue clérigo ser
el que alma ajena faz perder.
Mas otra onrra mejor
ha el mío sennor:
se fueren reys o condes
o otros ricos omnes
o duenas de linage

o caualleros de parage,° — noble
luego le van obedesçer
e vanle ofreçer;
bien se tiene por villano
quien le non besa la mano.
Villanía fablar
es asy me denostar;
se a mj dicen monaguesa,
ati diran cotayfesa.° — girlfriend of a lowly soldier
Mas se tú oujeses buen sen
bien te deujas conosçer;
ca do ha seso de prior,
conosçese enlo mejor.
Mas tú non as amor por mj
njn yo otrosí por ti;
vayamos anbas ala corte de vn rrey
que yo de mejor non sey;
este rey e enperador
nunca julga° senon de amor. — judges
Aquel es el rey Oriol,
sennor de buen valor,
non ha en todo el mundo corte
más alegre nin de mejor conorte;° — comfort
corte es de muy grand alegría
e de plazer e de jogrería;° — entertainment
omne non faz otro lauor
senon cantar sienpre de amor;
cantar e deportar° — entertaining
e viesos° nueuos contrubar;° — verses, composing
tanto ha entre ellos conorte
quenon han pauor de muerte.
El ruysennor,° que es buen jogral,° — nightingale, =**juglar**
aquella corte fue morar;
don açor e don gauilán° — sparrowhawk
en aquella corte están
don çerrenícolo° don falcón — kestrel

don . . . . .imo e don pauón,
el gayo° e la gaya,° crow, magpie
que son jograles 'de alfaya,° valued
el tordo° e el lengulado° starling, wryneck (
e don 'palonbo torcado° white-necked do
e el estornino° e la calandre,° starling, lark
que sienpre cantan de amor,
el pelisco° e la sirguera,° partridge, goldfinc
que de todos los buenos eran
s . . . . . tas . . . . .»
. . . . . . . . . . .
e mesura
que fuerça con locura.
Tórnate mj vasalla,
luego sin toda falla,
e besa me la mano
tres vezes enel anno ».
Elena dixo: «yo me quiero
tener mi razón
Mas selo el julgar,
e por derecho lo fallar,
que más val el tu barbirrapado
quel mío cauallero onrado,
tener me hey por cayda,
seré tu vasalla conosçida.
Mas selo el julgar mejor,
commo rey e commo sennor,
tú serás mi vasalla,
oy plaz me sin falla».
Anbas se auenieron,° agreed
al camino se metieron,
la . . . . . . . . . . . . . .
«Salvet el Criador
e vos dé el su amor.
Duenas somos de otras tierras
que venimos a estas sierras,

auos, sennor, demandar
por vn juyzio estremar;° — decide
sennor, por aquel queuos fizo,
departid° este juyzio!» — render
Esa ora dixo el rey:
«Yo vos lo departirey ».
Elena de primero
touo la voz del cauallero:
«Sennor, cudado° sy fuer de muerte, — **=cuidado**
ally ha el grand conorte;
luego lo va vegitar,° — dress
con su calze° comulgar. — chalice
Faz la casa delibrar,° — empty
mándalo manefestar,° — to confess
e valo consejar
quele de su auer pora misas cantar.
Ca diz que non ha tan buen ofiçio
commo de sacrifiçio
de salterios rezar
e de misas cantar.
Non manda dar a las puertas
nin a ospitales delos pobres;
tal cosa nunca vi,
todo lo quier para sy.
Mas se lo ve quexar
pora del siegro° pasar, — world
veredes yr pora la casa
cruz e agua sagrada,
e los molazinos° rezando, — altar boys
'requien eternan° cantando, — mass for the dead
los otros por las canpanas tirando,
los vnos a repicar
e los otros a encordar.° — ring the bells
Mas estas bondades
han todos los abades:
len° bien sus glosas — **=leen**

e cantan quirios° e prosas, — Lord have mercy
crismar° e bautizar — anoint
e omnes muertos soterrar.
Mas esto han los mesquinos,
sienpre sospiran por muerte de sus vezinos;
mucho les plaz
quando hay muchas viudas o viudos
por leuaren muchas obradas e muchos bodigos.
Bien cura su panza
quelo non fierga° la lança. — wound
Ca el mío sennor
cauallero es de grand ualor,
non vi nunca otro mejor
que más faga por mi amor.
Por amí fazer plazer,
de veluntad se va conbater;
non quier su escudo vedar
a ningund omne, se quier con él justar.
Ha castiellos do jaz
e muchas çibdades otro tal;
gana muchos aueres por su barraganía° — bravery
e por su cauallería,
gana mulas e cauallos
e otros aueres tantos,
oro e plata e escarlata
de que soy preçiada.
. . . . . . . . . . . . . . .

## *Hagiographic poetry*

*Santa María Egipciaca*, a long narrative saint's life, recounts the life of María, a courtesan of Alexandria, before she was converted, as well as after, when she did penance in the wilderness. Modeled upon a French original, the Castilian version shows some traces of originality. There is a mixture of eight and nine syllable lines.

The *Libre dels tres reys d'Orient* is a poem of 250 lines that relates the arrival of the Magi, the slaughter of the innocents, the flight into Egypt, and the story of the two thieves, Gestas and Dimas. Eight syllable lines predominate, but there are some of nine.

## *La vida de Santa María Egipciaca*

This is a hagiographic poem from the first half of the 13th century written in the minstrel style but with elements of *mester de clerecía.* It is written in couplets of irregular rhyme and narrates the life of Mary the Egyptian, a prostitute who later became a saint. We see her as a beautiful young woman with a corrupt spirit and later in the desert as an old hag but with a purified soul. She meets a monk by the name of Gozimas who serves as her spiritual mentor, hears her story and writes it down after her death. The Spanish version is based on a French poem of the same title and was a very popular theme of the Middle Ages.

*Açí comença la vida de Madona*
*Santa María Egipciaqua*

Oyt° varones huna razón — **=oíd**
en que non ha ssi verdat non;[1]
Escuchat de coraçón
sí ayades de Dios perdón.
Toda es fecha de uerdat:
'non ay ren° de falssedat. — there is nothing
Todos aquellos que a Dios amarán
estas palabras escucharán,
E los que de Dios non 'an cura° — are not concerned
esta palabra mucho les es dura.
Bien sé que de uoluntat la oyrán
aquellos que a Dios amarán;
Essos que a Dios amarán
grant gualardón ende reçibrán.
Si escucháredes esta palabra
más vos ualdrá que huna fabla.° — ficticious story

[1] **Non ha ssi...** *which is nothing but the truth*

De huna duenya que auedes oyda
quiero vos conptar° toda su uida: **=contar**
De santa María Egipçiaqua,
que fue huna duenya muy loçana,° beautiful
Et de su cuerpo muy loçana
quando era mançeba et ninya.
Beltad le dio Nuestro Sennyor
porque fue fermosa pecador.
Mas la merçet del Criador
después le fizo grant amor.
Esto sepa todo pecador
que 'fuere culpado del° Criador, have sinned against
Que non es pecado
tan grande ni tan orrible,
Que (non le faga) Dios non le faga perdón.
Por penitençia ho por conffessión,
quien 'se repinte° de coraçón, **=se arrepiente**
luego le faze Dios perdón.
Los que prenden° penitença receive
bien sen guarden de descreença,° disbelief
qua° el que descreye del Criador because
non puede auer la su amor.

Esta de qui quiero fablar
María la hoí nombrar;
El su nombre es en escripto
por que nasçió en Egipto.
De pequenya fue bautizada,
mala mientre fue ensenyada.
Mientre que fue 'en mancebía° a young girl
dexó bondat e 'priso follía.° took up folly
Tanto fue plena de lujuria° lust
que 'non entendié otra curia.° had no other interest
Por que era bella e genta° kind
mucho fiaua en su juuenta.° **=juventud**
Tanto amaua fer° sus plaçeres doing

que non ha cura dotros aueres,° — things
Mas despender e desbaldir° — wasted
que nol 'membraua de° morir. — think about
A sus parientes se daua,
a todos 'se baldonaua.° — she was generous
Bien creyo que daquel tiempo
non fue fembra° 'de tal enxemplo.° — woman, like her

Ninguna que fuesse María
non fue plena de tan gran luxiria.
Sus parientes, quando la veyen,
'por poco° que se non murien. — almost
Non preçiaua[2] su castigamiento° — counsel
más que si fuesse hun viento.° — empty air
«Fija cara, dixo su madre,
¿por qué non creyes al tu padre?
Si tú mantouieres el monesterio
nos ende auremos grant façerio.
Por ti ruego, fija María,
que tornes a buena vía.° — path
Quando desto te aurás partido
nos te daremos buen marido.
Non es derecho que seyas perdida
'por mengua dauer° en nuestra vida. — lack of wealth
Fija, tú eres de grant natura,
por que estás en mala uentura.
Que deues auer honor
como otras de linatge° peyor. — lineage
Tu padre te ha ayrado,
non será en su vida pagada;
Maldize essa hora en que tú nasçiste,
por que su consseio non prisiste».
La madre assí la castigaua
e de sus oios lloraua.
María poco lo preçiaua,

[2] **Non preciava...** *she did not value*

que mançebía la gouernaua.
Pues que xij anyos houo de edat,
con todos faze su uoluntat.
A ninguno non se queríe vedar,° refuse
'sol que° aya algo quel dar. as long as
E después 'le vino acordar° she decided
que dexasse su linatge° family.
Por más fer su voluntat
hirsse queríe de la çibdat.
María se ua en otro regno° kingdom
por 'acabar más de preçio.° to earn more
Sus parientes todos dexó,
assí que más nunqua los vio.
Sola salló° como ladrón **=salió**
que non demandó° companyón. look for
En su camino entró María
que non demandaua companya.
Vna aueziella° teníe en mano: little bird
assí canta yuierno° como verano; **=invierno**
María la teníe a grant honor
por que cada dia canta damor.
En Alexandría fue María:
aquí demanda aluerguía.° lodging
Allá va prender ostal° lodging
con las malas en la cal.
Las meretriçes,° quando la vieron, prostitutes
de buena miente la recibieron;
A gran honor la reçibieron
por la beltat que en ella vieron.
Los fijos de los burzeses° mandó llamar townspeople
que la viniessen mirar.
Ellos de ella auien grant sabor,
que tal era como la flor.
Todos la van cortejar° court
por el su cuerpo acabar.° enjoy
Ella los recibíe de uolonter

por que fiziessen su plazer,
E por fer todo su viçio
los mantenie a grant deliçio.
En beuer e en comer e follía
cuydaua noche e día.
Quando se lleua de yantar
con ellos va deportar.° sported
Tanto quiere iugar e reyr
que nol miembra que ha de morir.
Los mancebos de la çibdat
tanto les plaze de la beltat,
Que cada día la uan ha veyer
que non se pueden della toller[3]
Tantas hiuan de copanyas
que los iuegos tornan a sanyas.° quarrels
Ante las puertas en las entradas
dáuanse grandes espadadas.° sword blows
La sangre que dellos sallía
por medio de la cal corría.
La catina,° quando lo vedíe, wicked one
nulla piedat no le prendíe.
El que era más faldrido° valiant
aquell era su amigo.
El que vençíe dentro lo cogíe,° took
el que muríe pocol dolíe.
Sil muríen dos amigos,
ella auíe cinquenta biuos,
E por alma del ques muríe
ella más de vn riso non daríe.
Los que por ella eran plagados° wounded
non eran della visitados.
Más ama con los sanos iugar
que los enfermos visitar.
En Alexandría era María:
así sse mantenie noche e día.

[3] **Della toller** *tear themselves away from her*

En Alesandría es venida:
ahí mantenie aquesta vida.
En tal hora hi fue entrada
que toda la villa fue mesclada° — in turmoil
e tanta sangre fue derramada
que toda la villa fue menguada,
e las villas 'de en derredor° — around
todas eran en grant error.
De la beltat e de su figura,
como dize la escriptura,
ante que diga adelante,
diréuos de su semblante:
de aquell tiempo que fue ella,
depués no nasció tan bella;
nin reyna nin condessa
non viestes tal como ésta.
Redondas auíe las oreias,
blanquas como leche doueias;° — of sheep
oios negros e sobreçeias,° — eyebrows
alua° fruente fasta las çerneias.° — white, hairline
La faz tenie colorada° — rosy
como la rosa quando es granada;° — flowered
boqua chiqua e 'por mesura° — proportioned
muy fermosa la catadura.° — looks
Su cuello e su petrina° — bosom
tal como la flor dell espina.° — thorn bush
De sus tetiellas° bien es sana: — breasts
tales son como maçana.° — apple
Braços e cuerpo e todo lo ál
blanco es como cristal.
En buena forma fue taiada:° — shaped
nin era gorda nin muy delgada,
nin era luenga° nin corta, — tall
mas de mesura bona.
De so beltat dexemos estar
que non uos lo podría contar.

Contar uos e de los sus vestimentes
e de los sus guarnimentes.° accesories
El peyor día de la semana
non vistíe panyo de lana.
Assaz prende oro e argento° silver
bien sse viste a su talento.
Brial de xamit° se vistíe, silk cloth
manto erminyo cobríe
Nunqua calçaua° otras çapatas wore
sino de cordouán° 'entre talladas,° Cordovan leather, with designs
pintadas con oro e con plata,
cuerdas de sseda con que las ata.

En el mes de mayo hun día
leuantósse essa María.
Sallió al muro de la çibdat
por demostrar su beltad.
Cató ayuso a los puertos
on° solía fer sus depuertos° where, games
vio vna galeya° arribar galley
que estaua dentro en la mar.
Lena° era de pelegrinos° full, pilgrims
non auía hi omnes mesquinos.
Plena era de romeros,° pilgrims
de ricos omnes e caualleros.
Todos hiuan en romeatge° pilgrimage
a Iherusalem 'de buen oratge.° favorable wind
Mucho se quexauan de andar
que ellos hi cuydauan estar
a huna fiesta que es anyal° yearly
grande e general,
el día de la Açensión,
quando auría hi grant processión.
Allí posaron en est logar,
que allí queríen fer su yantar.
Queríen vn poco folgar

e depués que penssasen de andar.
Mançebos auía hi liuyanos° — happy
que se tomaron de las manos;
metieron se a andar:
por las riberas van solazar.
Corriendo uan por la ribera,
iugando por la eglera.° — open space
Quando se aperçibió María
non pudo estar que non se hiría.
Cerqua sí vio vn omne estar;
començól a demandar:
«Por Dios me digas tú, sennyor,
sí de Dios ayas amor,
aquelos que sallen del drumón° — ship
'a qual parte° van ho qué omnes son. — where
Si me podría con ellos hir,
grant talante daquí sallir.
Hir me querría daqueste logar:
non he talante daquí estar».
Allí respuso aquell varón
de lo que demanda díxol razón:
«Esto sé yo bien de plan
que aquellos en Iherusalem van.
Si tú ouiesses que les dar,
ellos te podrían levar».
Allí respuso essa:
«yo dieze° he buen cuerpo; — she says
este les daré 'a gran baldón,° — free
que non les daré otro don.
Non les daré otro logro,° — payment
que non tengo más dun dobro».° — small coin
Si en la naue me quisiéredes meter,
seruir uos e volonter.
Conbusco me hiré a vltra mar
si me quisiéredes leuar.
Por levar huna mesquina

non saldredes más tarde a riba.° shore
Si vos esta limosna° fer podedes, charity
más ayna arribaredes.
Por Dios vos ruego e por caridat
que conbusco me leuat».
Quando le hoyeron esta razón
no y houo° qui dixies de non. **=hubo**
Luego a las manos la prisieron
e dentro en la barqua la metieron.
La barqua van rimar° to row
e luego se meten a la mar.
Luego alçaron° las velas;° they raised, sails
toda la noche andan a las estrellas.
Mas de dormir non ay nada,
que María es aparellada.° available
Tanto la auía el diablo comprisa,° possessed
que toda la noche andó en camisa.
Tolló la toqua° de los cabellos head covering
nunqua vio omne más bellos.
Primerament los va tentando,° tempting
después los va abraçando.
E luego se ua con ellos echando
a grant sabor los besando.
Non auía hi tan enssenyado° experienced
siquier° vieiio° siquier cano,° neither, **=viejo**, gray haired
non hi fue tan casto
que con ella non fiziesse pecado.
Ninguno non se pudo tener,
tanto fue cortesa° de su mester. generous
Quando ella veye las grandes ondas
tan pavorosas° e tan fondas, frightening
E las lluuias con los vientos grandes
que trayen las tempestades,
Non le prende null pauor
nin llama al criador,
Antes° los comiença a confortar rather

e conbídalos a iugar.
Ellos tanto la queríen
que toda ssu voluntat conplíen.
Grant marauilla puede omne auer
que huna fembra tanto puede fer.
Mas non era aquella noche
que el diablo con ella non fuesse.
Bien la cuydaua enganyar
quella pereçiesse en la mar.
Mas non le fizo nengún tuerto,
que Dios la sacó a puerto.
Quando ffue arribada
dolienta fue e deserrada.° confused
Lorando sseye en la marina:
non ssabe qués faga la mesquina.
Non connoscíe homne nin fembra:
aquella tierra nada nol sembla.° recognize
Non sabe 'por qual manya° how
pueda beuir en aquella tierra.
'A la postremería° dixo: finally
«yo hiré a Iherusalem la çibdat.
A mi menester me tornaré,
que bien me gouernaré».
E llorosa e desconsseiada° helpless
en Iherusalem entraua.
Mas non dexó hi de pecar,
ante començó de peorar.° be worse
Agora oyt quál perdiçión
antes de la Açenssión.
Ella fue tan peyorada
meior le fuera 'non fues nada.° she were nothing
Los jóuenes homnes de la çibdat
tanto son presos de su beltat,
Que todos ffazíen con ella ssu voluntat.
El día vino de la Ascenssión,
allí fue grant proçessión

De los pelegrinos de 'vltra mar° — across the sea
que van a Dios rogar.
Los buenos omnes e los romeros
al templo van a rogar a Deos.
Non sse perçibió María:
metiósse entrellos en companya.
Metiósse entrellos en proçessión,
mas non por buena entençión.
Los pelegrinos, quando la veyen,
ssu coraçón non ge lo sabíen.
Que si ellos ssopiessen quien era María,
non auríen con ella companyía.
A las puertas viníen a los grados° — steps
e al templo son entrados.
Dentro entró la companiya,
mas non y entró María.
En la grant priessa se metíe,
mas nulla re nol valíe;
Que assí 'le era assemeiant° — it seemed to her
que veye huna gente muy grant
En ssemeiança de caualleros,
mas ssemeiauan le muy fieros.
Cada vno teníe ssu espada:
Menazauan° la a la entrada. — they threatened
Quando queríe a dentro entrar,
'a riedro° la fazíen tornar. — back
Quando vio que non podíe auer la entrada,
atrás faze la tornada.
Alli está muy desmayada:
a vn requexo° es assentada. — corner
Aquí comiença a pensar
e de coraçón a llorar.
Damas° manos tira a ssus cabellos, — both
grandes feridas dio a sus pechos.
Viol como [Dios] le era sanyudo
nol osó pedir conseio ninguno.

Ella asaz diziendo: «en mal hora
fuy tan pecadora;
Tan mal conseio houe prendudo° — taken
quando Dios me es assí sanyudo.
Tan sso plena de malueztat,° — wickedness
de luxuria e de maldat,
Que non puedo al templo entrar
ni a Dios me reclamar.° — invoke
¿Qué faré agora, catiua?
tanto me pesa porque sso biua».
Del cuerpo le sallió vn sospiro tan fuerte;
dixo: «Dios, dame la muerte».
Tornó la cara on sedía:° — was seated
vio huna ymagen de Santa María,
La ymagen bien figurada,
en su mesura taiada.° — carved
María, quando la vio,
leuantósse en pie, antella se paró
Los 'ynogos antella fincó;° — knelt before her
tan con uerguença la cató,
Atan piadosament la reclamó
e dixo: «Ay duenya dulçe madre,
que en el tu vientre touiste al tu padre,
Sant Gabriel te aduxo° el mandado° — brought, message
e túl respondiste con grant recabdo.° — prudence
Tan bueno fue aquell día
que él dixo: Aue María.
En ti puso Dios ssu amanca,° — love
llena fuste de la su graçia.
En ti puso humanidat
el fi° del Rey de la magestat. — son
Lo que él dixo tú lo otorgueste
e por su ançilla° te llameste. — handmaiden
Por esso eres del çiello reyna;
tú seyas oy de mí melezina.° — medicine
A las mis llagas, que son mortales,

non quiero otros melezinables.
En tu fijo metré° mi creyença: I will put
tornar me quiero a penitençia.
Tornar me quiero al mío senyor;
a tu metré por fiador;° guarantor
En toda mi vida lo seruiré:
iamás dél non me partiré.
Entiéndeme, duenya, esto que yo te fablo,
que me parto del diablo
E de sus companyías,
que no lo sierua en los míos días.
E dexaré aquesta vida
que mucho la e mantenida,
E ssienpre auré repinteçia,
más faré graue penitencia.
Creyo bien en mi creyençia,
que Dios fue en tu nascençia:° birth
En ti priso humanidat,
tú non perdiste virginidat.
Grant marauilla fue del padre,
que su fija fizo madre.
E fue marauillosa cosa
que de la espina sallió la rosa.
Et de la rosa ssallió friçio° fruit
porque todo el mundo saluó.
Virgo Reyna creyo por ti,
que si al tu fiio rogares por mí,
Si tú pides aqueste don,
bien ssé que hauré perdón.

Vna boz oyó veramente
que le dixo paladinamiente:° clearly
«Ve a la ribera de ssant Iordán° Jordan River
al monesterio de sant Iohan:° John
Vna melezina prenderás,
de todos tus pecados sanarás.

Corpus Christi° te darán, — Eucharist
e fuente° iordán te passarán, — river
Depué° entrarás en hun yermo° — =**después**, desert
e morarás hi vn grant tiempo.
En el yermo estarás
fasta que biuas hi 'te despendrás». ° — paid for your sins
Quando ella oyó esta ssanta boz,
en su fruente° fizo cruz. — forehead

Manyana sse levantó María:
contra oriente prende la vía.
Tanto anda noches e días,
e tanto ffalló ásperas° vías. — difficult
Atanto entró en la montanya,
Montesa° sse fizo e muy estranya, — like a mountain goat
Mas non oluidó noche e día
de rogar a Santa María.
Toda hora le miembra° lo quel dixiera — reminds
e lo que conella pusiera.° — she agreed
Como la metiera por fiador
ante la ymagen del ssu senyor.
Toda sse mudó dotra ffigura
qua non ha panyos nin vestidura.
Perdió las carnes° e la color, — flesh
que eran blancas como la flor;
E los sus cabellos, que eran ruuios,° — blond
tornaron blancos e suzios.
Las sus orejas, que eran aluas,
mucho eran negras e pegadas.° — like pitch
Entenebrados° auíe los oios, — without sparkle
perdidos auíe los mencoios.° — eyelashes
La boca era enpeleçida,° — hairy
derredor la carne muy denegrida.° — blackened
La faz, muy negra e arrugada,
de frío viento e elada.
La barbiella e el ssu grinyón° — facial hair

ssemeia 'cabo de tizón.° — black as soot
Tan negra era ssu petrina° — chest
como la pez e la resina.° — resin
En ssus pechos non auía tetas:° — breasts
como yo cuydo eran secas.
Braços luengos e ssecos dedos:
quando los tiende ssemeian espetos.
Las vnyas eran conuinentes,
que las taiaua° con los dientes. — cut
El vientre auíe sseco mucho,
que non comíe nengún conducho.
Los piedes eran quebraçados:° — cracked
en muchos logares eran plagados.° — wounded
E por nada non se desuiaua
delas espinas° on las ffallaua. — thorns
Semeiaua cortés,
mas non le ffallía hi res.
Quando huna espina la firía,
vno de sus pecados perdía.
E mucho era ella gozosa° — joyous
porque suffríe tan dura cosa.
Non es marauilla ssi es denegrida° — blackened
fembra que mantien tal vida.
Nin es marauilla ssi color muda
qui xl. annyos anda desnuda.

Quando María en esse logar posó,
huna oración acabó.
«Dios, dixo, si me quieres oyr,
daquí adelante non querría yr».
Ella sen tornó contra oriente,
acomendósse a Dios omnipotente.
Començó su oraçión
muy piadosa de coraçón.
Quando acabó su oraçión
vio huna buena visión:

«Buenos mandaderos° veyo yo aquí, — emissaries
mi cuerpo e mi alma acomiéndolo a ti».
Quando ella se estendió en tierra,
luego con ella era.
Quando en tierra fue echada
a Dios sse acomendaua.
Premió° los oios 'bien conuinientes,° — closed, appropriate
çerró su boca, cubrió sus dientes.
Enboluiós° en sus cabellos. — was wrapped
echó° sus braços sobre sus pechos. — put
El alma es de ella sallida,
los ángeles la an recebida.
Los ángeles la van leuando,
tan dulçe son que van cantando.
Mas bien podedes esto iurar
que el diablo noy° pudo llegar. — not there
Esta duenya da enxemplo
a todo omne que es en este sieglo.
Don Gozimás priso la vía:
tornóse a ssu abadía.
Mas de huna cosa es mucho yrado
porque su nombre no le a demandado.
A don Gozimás mucho le pesaua,
por la quaresma que tanto tardaua;
Mas quando vino essa sazón
el abat les dio su bendición.
Quando Gozimás ffue partido,
al fflumen° Iordán ayna° vino. — river, quickly
Alliende passó a la ribera
pora María prende carrera.
«Dios, dixo, muestra me aquell cuerpo,
por çierto cuydo que es muerto».
Bien quiso Dios a Gozimás,
non quiso que más penás.
Tornó los oios a diestra parte:
houo a oio huna claridat.

A aquella lumbre sse allegó,
vio el cuerpo, mucho se pagó,
Que iazíe contra oriente,
ssus oios floxos° fermosamientre. — closed
Sus crines° teníe 'por lençuelo.° — hair, as a shroud
a Gozimás prisso grant duelo.
Vno de ssus pañillos° desnudó, — clothing
llegós al cuerpo, con él lo cubrió.
Cató ayuso° contra° la tiesta, — up, toward
e vio hunas letras escritas en tierra.
Mucho eran claras e bien taiadas,
que en çielo fueron formadas.
Don Gozimás las leyó festino,° — quickly
como si ffuessen en pargamino:° — parchment
«Prent, Gozimás, el cuerpo de María,
ssotierral° oy en este día. — bury it
Quando lo aurás soterrado,
ruega por éll, que así te es acomendado».° — ordered
Quando Gozimás el nombre ffalló,
a Dios mucho lo agradesçió.
Después le ffizo el ministerio° — service for the dead
e dixo los salmos del salterio.
Mas de huna cosa es mucho marrido,° — sad
que non aduxo nada consigo
Conque pudiesse la tierra obrir° — **= abrir**
para el cuerpo ssobollir.° — bury
Mas por amor desta María
grant ayuda Dios le enbía:
Vn leyón salló desa montanya
a Gozimás faze conpanya.
Maguer que era bestia fiera,
Manso° va do el cuerpo era; — tamely
'Semblant fizo° del cuerpo seruir — he seemed
quel quiere ayudar a ssobollir.
Quando esto vio el buen varón,
muchol plaze de corazón.

Estonçe le dixo: «vos, amigo,
aquí estaredes comigo».
El leyón caua la tierra dura:
él le muestra la mesura.° size
La fuessa° fue ayna cauada° grave, dug
e de la tierra bien mondada.° cleaned
Amos la ponen en la fuesa
e vanse dende en fuera.
Don Gozimás faze la comendaçión° committal prayer
sin ayuda daquell leyón.
Mas quando le vio la tierra echar,
non quiso en balde estar.
Toda la tierra acarreyó:° brought
sobre el cuerpo la echó.
Echóse en tierra por se espedir;° say good-bye
senyas fizo ques quería yr,
«Compannyero, id uos en paz:
bien sé que Dios por María faz ».
Luego el leyón sen partió,
por la montanya sen metió.
«Agora creyo en mi creyençia
que santa cosa es penitençia,
E penitençia prendré,
piedat de mi cuerpo non auré ».
Tornós a su abadía
Gozimás e su companya.
Allí fablauan a grant razón,
non era hi entençión.° contention
Gozimás comiença de fablar,
non se quiso más çelar.° hide
De la egipçiana que non se le oluida
bien les conta toda su vida.
Contóles como la fallara
en la montanya do entrara,
E como la fallara
después al terçero annyo finada.

Contóles del leyón
como lo houiera por companyón.
El santo abat ploró muy fuerte,
quandol oyó contar su muerte.
E los monges que eran hi
todos plorauan otro sí.
Mucho emendaron° de su vida — corrected
por enxemplo desta María.
E nos mismos nos emendemos
que mucho mester° lo auemos. — need
E roguemos a esta María
cada noche e cada día.
Que ella ruegue al Criador
con quien ella ouo grant amor.
Quel podamos fer tal se*r*uiçio
que al día del Iuycio° — judgment
non nos falle en mal viçio.
Él nos dé grant partida° — share
en la perdurable vida.
Todo omne que ouiere seny° — good sense
responda e diga amén.
AMÉN

## *Libre dels tres reys d'Orient or Libro de la infancia y muerte de Jesús*

These are the names by which a poem from the first half of the 13th century is known. It is related to the scholar's poetry (mester de clerecía), written in 242 couplets in Castillian with traces of Aragonese. The poem narrates the legend of the Magi, the slaughter of the innocents, the flight into Egypt and the encounter of the Holy Family with the two thieves: the good one Dimas and the evil one Gestas.

Açí comença 'lo libre° dels tres reys dOrient =el libro

Pues muchas vezes oyestes contar
De los tres Reyes que vinieron buscar
A Jesucristo, que era nado, vna estrella los guiando;
Et de la grant maravilla
Que les auino° en la villa happened
Do Erodes° era el traydor, Herod
Enemigo del Criador.
Entraron los Reyes por Betlem la çibdat
Por saber Herodes si sabía verdat,
En qual logar podrían fallar
Aquell Senyor que hiuan° buscar; =iban
Que ellos nada non sabíen,
Erodes si lo queríe mal ho° bien. =o
E quando conell estudieron° =estuvieron
E el estrella nunqua la vieron.
Quando Erodes oyó el mandado
Mucho fue alegre e pagado.
E 'ffizo senblante° quel plazía, pretended
Mas nunqua vio tan negro° día. bad
Dixo que 'de que° fuera nado since
Nunqua oyera tan negro mandado,

Hitlo° buscar 'fe que deuedes,° =idlo, by your faith
Venit aquí mostrármelo edes;
En qual logar lo podredes fallar
Yo lo yré adorar.
Los Reyes sallen de çibdat,
E catan a toda part,
E vieron la su estrella
Tan luciente e tan bella,
Que nunqua de dellos se partió
Ffasta que dentro los metió.
Do° la Gloriosa° era where,Virgin Mary
El Rey del çielo e de la tierra.

Entraron los Reys mucho omildosos
E fincaron los ynoios;
E 'houieron gozo por mira,° — rejoiced looking at him
Offreçieron oro e ençiensso e mirra.
Baltasar offreçió horo
Porque era Rey poderoso.
Melchor mirra por dulçora,° — sweetness
Por condir° la mortal corona. — annoint
E Gaspar le dio ençiensso
Que assí era derecho.
Estos Reyes cumplieron sus mandados
E sson se tornados
Por otras carreras a sus regnados.
Quando Erodes ssopo
Que por hi° non le an venido, — there
Mucho 'sen touo por escarnido.° — felt scorned
E dixo todo 'me miro° — I am amazed
E quando vio esta maravilla,
Fuerte fue sanyoso por mira;° — amazement
E con grant hira que en sí auia
Dixo a sus vassallos, ¡Vía!
Quantos ninyos fallar podredes
Todos los descabeçedes;° — behead
¡Mezquinos° que sin dolor° — wretched ones, compunction
Obedeçieron mandado de su sennyor
Quantos ninyos fallauan
Todos los descabeçauan.
Por las manos los tomauan.
'Por poco° que los tirauan.° — almost, tore them apart
Sacauan 'a las vegadas° — at times
Los braços con las espaldas.
Mesquinas que cuytas° vieron — cruelties
Las madres que los parieron!
Toda madre puede entender
Qual duelo podríe seyer.° — **=ser**
Que en el çielo fue oydo

El planto° de Rachel. lament
Dexemos° los moçuelos let us leave
E non ayamos dellos duelos.
Por quien fueron martiriados
Suso° al çielo son leuados. up
Cantarán siempre delante Él
En huno con Sant Miguel,
La 'gloriosa tamanya° great glory
Será que nunqua más fin non haurá.
Destos ninyos que siempre ffiesta façedes
Si por enogo° non lo ouiéredes, **=enojo**
Dezir uos e huna cosa
De Christo e de la Gloriossa.
Josep jazía adormido,
El ángel fue a él venido.
Dixo lieua varón e vé tu vía,
Fuye con el ninyo e con María
Vete pora Egipto
Que así lo manda el escripto.
Leuantósse Josep mucho espantado,
Pensó de cumplir el mandado.
Prende el ninyo e la madre
E él guiólos como a padre.
Non leuó con ellos res° anything
Sino huna bestia e ellos tres.
Madrugaron grant manyana,
Solos pasan por la montanya.
Encontraron dos peyones° highwaymen
Grandes e fuertes ladrones,
Que robauan los caminos
E degollauan° los pelegrinos.° slit the throat, **=pe**
El que alguna cosa traxiesse **nos**
Non ha auer que le valiesse.
Presos fueron muy festino,° quickly
Sacáuanlos del camino.
De que fuera° los touieron off the road

Entre sí razón ouieron.
Dixo el ladrón más fellón,° — cruel
Así seya la partiçión.° — dividing of the spoils
Tú que mayor e meior eres
Descoig° dellos quál más quisieres — choose
Desi° partamos el más chiquiello — afterwards
Con el cuchiello.° — knife
El otro ladrón touo° que dizíe 'fuerte cosa° — thought, something foolish
Et fablar por miedo non osa.
Por miedo que 'sse hiraría° — would get angry
E que faría lo que dizía.
Antes dixo que dizía sseso° — prudently
E quel partiesen bien° por pesso.° — rather, weight
Et oyas me amigo por caridat
E por amor de piadat.
Penssemos de andar
Que hora es de aluergar.
En mi cassa aluergaremos
E cras como quisieres partiremos.
E ssi 'se fueren° por ninguna arte° — escape, trick
Yo te pecharé° tu parte. — make up
Dios, qué bien reçebidos son
De la muger daquell ladrón.
A los mayores daua plomaças° — bedding
E al ninyo toma en braços;
E fazíales tanto de plaçer
Quanto más les podíe fer.
Mas ell otro traydor quisiera luego
Que ante ques posasen° al fuego — sit
Manos e piedes les atar,
E en la cárçel los echar.
El otro ladrón començó de fablar
Como oyredes conptar.° — tell
Oyas me amigos por caridat
E por amor de piedad
Buena cosa e fuerte tenemos

Cras como quisieres partiremos.
E ssi se fueren por ninguna arte
Yo te pecharé tu parte.
La huéspeda° nin come nin posa — hostess
Siruendo a la Gloriosa.
E ruegal por amor de piedat
Que non le caya en pesar,
E que su fijo lo dé ha banyar.
La Gloriosa diz banyatle
E fet lo que quisiéredes,
Que en vuestro poder nos tenedes.
Va la huéspeda correntera° — hurriedly
E puso del agua en la caldera.° — pot
De que el agua houo asaz caliente
El ninyo en braços prende.
Mientre lo banya al non faz
Sino cayer lágrimas por su faz.
La Gloriosa la cataua
Demandól porque lloraua;
Huéspeda por que llorades,
Non me lo çeledes° si bien ayades.° — hide, if you please
Ella dixo, non lo çelaré amiga
Mas queredes que uos diga.
Yo obtengo tamanya cueyta
Que querría seyer muerta.
Vn fijuelo que hauía
Que parí el otro día,
Afelo allí don jaz gafo° — leper
Por mi pecado despugado.° — condemned
La Gloriosa diz: dármelo varona
Yo lo banyaré que no so ascorosa.° — bothered
E podedes dezir que en este annyo
Non puede auer meior vannyo.
Ffue la madre e prísolo en los braços,
A la Gloriosa lo puso en las manos.
La Gloriosa lo metió en el agua

Do banyado era el Rey del çielo e de la tierra.
La virtut fue fecha 'man a mano,° immediately
Metiól gaffo e sacó sano.
En el agua fincó todo el mal,° disease
Tal lo sacó com vn crispal.° glass
Quando la madre vio el fijo guarido
Grant alegría a consigo.
Huéspeda en buen día a mi casa viniestes
Que a mi fijo me diestes.
Et aquell ninyo que allí jaz
Que tales miraglos faz,
A tal es mi esperança
Que Dios es sines dubdança.
Corre la madre muy gozosa,
Al padre dize la cosa.
Contól todo comol auino,
Mostról el fijo guarido.
Quando el padre lo vio sano
Non vio cosa mas fues pagado;
E por pauor del otro despertar
Pensó quedo° des leuantar; quietly
E con pauor de non tardar
Priso carne, vino e pan.
Pero que media noche era
'Metiese con° ellos a la carrera. led
Escurriólos° fasta en Egipto, accompanied
Así lo dize el escripto.
E quando de ellos sse houo a partir
Merçet° les començó de pedir. favor
Que el fiio que ell ha sanado
Suyo 'seya acomendado.° be under his protection
A tanto ge lo acomendó° de suerte° commended, so that
Que suyo fues a la muerte.
La Gloriosa ge lo ha otorgado,
El ladrón es ya tornado.
Al otro aleuoso° ladrón treacherous

Naçiól vn fijo varón.
Los ninyos fueron creçiendo,
Las manyas° de los padres aprendiendo. practices
Sallíen robar caminos
E degollauan los pelegrinos.
E ffaçían mal a tanto
Fasta on los priso° Pilato. captured
A Iherusalem los aduz,° leads
Mándalos poner en cruz;
En aquell día senyalado
Que Christus fue cruçificado.
El que en su agua fue banyado
Fue puesto al su diestro lado,
Luego quel vio en él creyó,
E merçet le demandó.
Nuestro Senyor dixo
Oy serás conmigo
En el santo parayso.
El fi° de traydor quando fablaua son
Todo lo despreçiaua.
Diz, varón, como eres loco,
Que Christus non te valdrá tan poco.
A ssí non puede prestar,° help
¡como puede a ti huuiar!° help
Este fue en infierno miso° placed
E el otro en paraysso.
Dimas fu saluo
E Gestas fe° condapnado. **fe=fue**
Dimas e Gestas
Medio° 'diuina potestas.° in the middle, Christ
*FFINITO LIBRO SIT LAUS GLORIA CHRISTI.*[4]

---

[4] ***Ffinito libro sit*** *This book is finished, praise and glory to Christ.*

## *Galician-Portuguese Narrative Poetry*

The *Cantigas de Santa Maria* were written partly by, and partly for, king Alfonso X, the Learned, who ruled Castile and Leon from 1252 to 1284 and who was the most prolific poet in Galician-Portuguese. The *Cantigas* contain more than 400 poems that sing of the miracles and praise of the Holy Virgin. The sources are the great Latin collections of miracle stories known all over Europe as well as from the Spanish tradition and folklore. The manuscripts of the *Cantigas* are important also as early Spanish art , for the poems/songs are illustrated with beautiful miniatures. These illustrations offer a vivid picture of daily life in Alfonso's reign.

Prologue to the Cantigas de Santa Maria

*[Este é o prólogo das cantigas de Santa Maria,*
*ementando as cousas que á mester eno trobar]*

*Porque trobar é cousa en que jaz*
*entendimento, poren queno faz*
*á-o d'aver e de razon assaz,*
*per que entenda e sábia dizer*
*o que entend' e de dizer lle praz,*
*ca ben trobar assi s'á de ffazer.*

*E macar eu estas duas non ey*
*com'eu querria, pero provarei*
*a mostrar ende un pouco que sei,*
*confiand' en Deus, ond' o saber ven;*
*ca per ele tenno que poderei*
*mostrar do que quero algũa ren.*

*E o que quero é dizer loor*
*da Virgen, Madre de Nostro Sennor,*
*Santa Maria, que ést' a mellor*
*cousa que el fez; e por aquest' eu*
*quero seer oy mais seu trobador,*
*e rogo-lle que me queira por seu*

*Trobador e que queira meu trobar*
*reçeber, ca per el quer' eu mostrar*
*dos miragres que ela fez; e ar*
*querrei-me leixar de trobar des i*
*por outra dona, e cuid' a cobrar*
*per esta quant' enas outras perdi.*

*Ca o amor desta Sen[n]or é tal,*
*que queno á sempre per i mais val;*
*e pol-lo gaannad' á, no lle fal,*
*senon se é per sa grand' ocajon,*
*querendo leixar ben e fazer mal,*

Éste es el prólogo de las cantigas de Santa María,
recordando lo que es menester en el trovar.° — to write poetry

Porque trovar es cosa en que yace° — lies
entendimiento, por eso, quien lo hace
ha de tenerlo, y razón bastante,
para que entienda y sepa decir
lo que entiende y le place expresar
porque el bien trovar así ha de ser hecho.

Y aunque yo estas dos cualidades no tengo
tal como tener quisiera, sin embargo, probaré
de mostrar 'en adelante° lo poco que sé, — from this point on
confiando en Dios, de donde el saber viene,
pues por Él supongo que podré
mostrar algo de lo que mostrar quiero.

Y lo que quiero es 'decir loor° — tell the praises
de la Virgen, Madre de Nuestro Señor,
Santa María, que es lo mejor
que Él hizo, y, por esto, yo
quiero ser desde hoy trovador suyo,
y le ruego que me quiera por su

Trovador, y que quiera recibir mi trovar,
porque por él quiero mostrar
los milagros que Ella hizo; y además
quiero dejarme de trovar, desde ahora,
por otra dama, y pienso recobrar,
por ésta, cuanto por las otras perdí.

Porque el amor de esta Señora es tal
que, quien lo tiene, siempre por ello vale más,
y lo que haya ganado ya no lo pierde,
si no es que, por su gran desgracia,
quiera dejar bien y hacer mal,

*ca per esto o perd' e per al non.*

*Poren dela non me quer' eu partir,*
*ca sei de pran que, se a ben servir,*
*que non poderei en seu ben falir*
*de o aver, ca nunca y faliu*
*quen llo soube con merçee pedir,*
*ca tal rogo sempr' ela ben oyu.*

*Onde lle rogo, se ela quiser,*
*que lle praza do que dela disser*
*en meus cantares e, se ll'aprouguer,*
*que me dé gualardon com' ela dá*
*aos que ama; e queno souber,*
*por ela mais de grado trobará.*

*Cantiga 7*
*Esta é como Santa Maria livrou a abadessa prenne,*
*que adormecera ant' o seu altar chorando.*

Santa Maria amar
devemos muit' e rogar
que a ssa graça ponna
sobre nos, por que errar
non nos faça, nen peccar,
o demo sen vergonna.

*Porende vos contarey*
*un miragre que achei*
*que por hũa badessa*
*fez a Madre do gran Rei,*
*ca, per com' eu apres' ei,*
*era –xe sua essa.*
*Mas o demo enartar*
*a foi, por que emprennar*
*s'ouve dun de Bolonna,*

ya que por esto lo pierde, y no por otro motivo.

Por tanto, ya no quiero separarme de Ella,
porque sé cabalmente° que, si bien la sirviere, perfectly
no podré perder su bien,
porque nunca faltó
a quien supo, con piedad, pedirle,
porque tales ruegos siempre fueron bien oídos por Ella.

Por ello, le ruego, si Ella quisiere,
que le plazca lo que de Ella yo dijere
en mis cantares, y si a Ella le agradara,
que me dé un galardón° tal como el que Ella da reward
a los que ama, y quien lo supiere,
con mayor agrado° trovará por Ella. pleasure

Cantiga 7
Esta es cómo Santa María libró a la abadesa° preñada° abbess, pregnant
que 'se adormeció° llorando ante su altar. fell asleep

*Mucho debemos amar*
*y rogar a Santa María,*
*para que ponga su gracia*
*sobre nos para que*
*no nos haga ni pecar,*
*el desvergonzante ° demonio.* shameless

Por eso, os contaré
un milagro que he encontrado,
que, a favor de una abadesa,
hizo la Madre del Gran Rey,
pues, como he sabido, la tenía 'por suya,° as hers
pero el demonio fue a enredarla° trap her
para que quedase preñada
de un hombre de Bolonia,° **=Bologna**

*ome que de recadar*
*avia e de guardar*
*seu feit' e sa besonna.*
Santa Maria amar…

*As monjas, pois entender*
*foron esto e saber,*
*ouveron gran lediça;*
*ca, porque lles non sofrer*
*queria de mal fazer,*
*avian-lle mayça.*
*E fórona acusar*
*ao Bispo do logar,*
*e el ben de Colonna*
*chegou y; e pois chamar*
*a fez, vẽo sen vagar,*
*leda e mui risonna.*
Santa Maria amar…

*O Bispo lle diss' assi;*
*"Dona, per quant' aprendi,*
*mui mal vossa fazenda*
*fezestes; e vin aquí*
*por esto, que ante mi*
*façades end' emenda."*
*Mas a dona sen tardar*
*a Madre de Deus rogar*
*foi; e, come quen sonna,*
*Santa Maria tirar*
*lle fez o fill' e criar*
*lo mandou en Sanssonna.*
Santa Maria amar…

*Pois s' a dona espertou*
*e se guarida achou,*

que se gobernaba muy bien,
tanto en sus hechos° deeds
como en sus negocios.
*Mucho debemos amar…*

Las monjas, cuando tal oyeron
y supieron esto,
se regocijaron° mucho, were overjoyed
porque no les toleraba
cosa mal hecha
y le tenían ojeriza.° grudge
Y fueron en seguida a acusarla
al obispo del lugar,
que llegó luego desde Colonna, **=Cologne**
y cuando la mandó llamar,
ella vino en seguida
muy alegre y risueña.° smiling
*Mucho debemos amar…*

El obispo le dijo así:
"Dueña, por cuanto he sabido,
muy mal negocio
habéis hecho, y he venido aquí
por esto, para que ante mí
hagáis enmienda."° amends
Pero la dueña, sin tardanza,
rogó a la Madre de Dios;
y como quien sueña,° is sleeping
Santa María hizo
sacarle el hijo y mandarlo a criar° reared
a Soissons.° city in France
*Mucho debemos amar…*

Cuando la dueña se despertó
y se encontró librada,° unencumbered

*log' ant' o Bispo vẽo;*
*e el muito a catou*
*e desnua-la mandou;*
*e pois lle vyu o sẽo,*
*começou Deus a loar*
*e as donas a brasmar,*
*que eran d'ordin d'Onna,*
*dizendo: "Se Deus m'anpar,*
*por salva poss' esta dar,*
*que non sei que ll'aponna."*
Santa Maria amar…

Cantiga 10
*Esta é de loor de Santa Maria,*
*com'é fremosa e bõa e á gran poder.*

Rosa das rosas e Fror das frores,
Dona das donas, Señor das sennores.

*Rosa de beldad' e de parecer*
*e Fror d'alegria e de prazer.*
*Dona en mui piadosa seer,*
*Sennor en toller coitas e doores.*
Rosa das rosas e Fror das frores…

*Atal Sennor dev'ome muit' amar,*
*que de todo mal o pode guardar;*
*e pode-ll' os peccados perdõar,*
*que faz no mundo per maos sabores.*
Rosa das rosas e Fror das frores…

*Devemo-la muit' amar e servir,*
*ca punna de nos guardar de falir;*
*des i dos erros nos faz repentir,*
*que nos fazemos come pecadores.*
Rosa das rosas e Fror das frores…

vino ante el obispo
que la miró mucho
y la mandó desnudar,° to take off her
y cuando le vio el seno,° clothes; breasts
comenzó a loar a Dios
y a criticar a las dueñas,
que eran de la 'Orden de Oña° order of nuns
diciendo: "Así Dios me ampare,° help
por salva° puedo darla, innocent
que no sé de qué puedo acusarla."
*Mucho debemos amar...*

Cantiga 10
Esta es de loor de Santa María,
como es hermosa, y buena, y de gran poder.

*Rosa de las rosas, flor de las flores,*
*Dueña de las dueñas, Señora de las señoras.*

Rosa de beldad* y de belleza, beauty
y flor de alegría y de placer;
Dueña, en muy 'piadosa ser;° being merciful
Señora, en quitar cuitas° y dolores. worries
*Rosa de las rosas, flor de las flores...*

Tal Señora debe el hombre amar,
porque de todo mal puede guardarlo,
y puede perdonarle los pecados
que hace en el mundo por apetitos° malos. desires
*Rosa de las rosas, flor de las flores...*

Debemos amarla mucho y servirla,
porque 'pugna por° guardarnos de errar strives
y de los yerros nos hace arrepentir
que como pecadores cometemos.
*Rosa de las rosas, flor de las flores...*

*Esta dona que tenno por Señor*
*e de que Quero seer trobador,*
*se eu per ren poss' aver seu amor,*
*dou aos demo os outros amores.*
Rosa das rosas e Fror das frores…

Cantiga 18
*Esta é como Santa Maria fez fazer aos babous que crian a seda duas toucas, porque a dona que os guardava lle prometera hũa e non lla dera.*

*Por nos de dulta tirar,*
*praz a Santa Maria*
*de seus miragres mostrar*
*fremosos cada dia.*

*E por nos fazer veer*
*sa apostura,*
*gran miragre foi fazer*
*en Extremadura,*
*en Segovia, u morar*
*hũa dona soya,*
*que muito sirgo criar*
*en ssa casa fazia.*
Por nos de dulta tirar…

*Porque os babous perdeu*
*e ouve pouca*
*seda, poren prometeu*
*dar hũa touca*
*per' a omagen onrrar*
*que no altar siia*
*da Virgen que non á par,*
*en que muito criya.*
Por nos de dulta tirar…

De esta dama que tengo por señora
y de la que quiero ser trovador,
si no logro por nada su amor,
doy al diablo los demás amores.
*Rosa de las rosas, flor de las flores…*

Cantiga 18
Esta es como Santa María hizo hacer dos tocas
a los 'gusanos que crían la seda,° porque la dueña que los guardaba le prometió una y no se la había dado. — silkworms

Para sacarnos de dudas,
place a Santa María
mostrarnos, cada día,
hermosos milagros suyos.

Y por hacernos ver
su belleza
gran milagro hizo
en Extremadura,
en Segovia, donde solía morar° — dwell
una dama
que criaba en casa
mucha seda.
*Para sacarnos de dudas…*

Porque había perdido los gusanos
y tuvo poca
seda, prometió
dar una toca,
para honrar la imagen
que estaba en el altar
de la Virgen, 'sin par,° — peerless
en la que mucho creía.
*Para sacarnos de dudas…*

*Pois que a promessa fez,*
*senpre creceron*
*os babous ben dessa vez*
*e non morreron;*
*mas a dona con vagar*
*grande que y prendia,*
*d' a touca da seda dar*
*senpre ll' escaecia.*
Por nos de dulta tirar…

*Onde ll' avẽo assi*
*ena gran festa*
*d'Agosto, que vẽo y*
*con mui gran sesta*
*ant' a omagen orar;*
*e ali u jazia*
*a prezes, foi-lle nenbrar*
*a touca que devia.*
Por nos de dulta tirar…

*Chorando de coraçon*
*foi-sse correndo*
*a casa, e viu enton*
*estar fazendo*
*os bischocos e obrar*
*na touca a perfia,*
*e começou a chorar*
*con mui grand' alegria.*
Por nos de dulta tirar…

*E pois que assi chorou,*
*meteu ben mentes*
*na touca; des i chamou*
*muitas das gentes*

Después que hizo la promesa
siempre crecieron
los gusanos,
y no murieron
pero a la señora, tras la demora° — delay
que se fue tomando,
siempre se le olvidaba
dar la toca de seda.
*Para sacarnos de dudas…*

Cuando le sucedió,
en la gran fiesta
de agosto,[5] que yendo a la hora
de gran calor,
a orar ante la imagen, → Faithful to the Virgin Mary
y estando allí
rezando, se recordó
de la toca que debía.
*Para sacarnos de dudas…*

Llorando de corazón
se fue corriendo
a casa, y vio entonces
cómo estaban trabajando
'a porfía° los bichitos — dilligently
Por tejer° la toca, — weave
y comenzó a llorar
con alegría muy grande.
*Para sacarnos de dudas…*

Y después que así lloró,
'paró mientes° — noticed
en la toca, y en seguida llamó
a mucha gente

[5] **Fiesta de agosto** August 15, Feast of the Assumption

*y, que vẽessen parar*
*mentes como sabia*
*a Madre de Deus lavrar*
*per santa maestria.*
Por nos de dulta tirar…

*As gentes, con gran sabor,*
*quand' est'oyron*
*dando aa Madre loor*
*de Deus, sayron*
*aas ruas braadar,*
*dizendo: "Via, via*
*o gran miragre catar*
*que fez a que nos guia."*
Por nos de dulta tirar…

*Un e un, e dous e dous*
*log' y vẽeron ;*
*ontre tanto os babous*
*outra fezeron*
*touca, per que fossen par,*
*que se alguen queria*
*a hũa delas levar,*
*a outra leixaria.*
Por nos de dulta tirar…

*Poren don Affons' el Rei*
*na ssa capela*
*trage, per quant' apres' ei,*
*end' a mais bela,*
*que faz nas festas sacar*
*por toller eregia*
*dos que na Virgen dultar*
*van per sa gran folia.*
Por nos de dulta tirar…

para que vinieran a fijarse
cómo sabía
la Madre de Dios labrar° (weave)
por santa maestría.° (mastery)
*Para sacarnos de dudas…*

Las gentes con gran placer,
cuando esto vieron,
salieron dando loor a la Madre
de Dios,
por las calles, cantando:
paso,° paso, (quickly)
mirad el gran milagro
que hizo la que nos guía."
*Para sacarnos de dudas…*

Uno a uno y de dos en dos,
luego fueron
viniendo; entretanto los gusanos
tejieron otra
toca, para que fuesen pareja,
y si alguien quería
llevar una de ellas,
otra se quedaría.
*Para sacarnos de dudas…*

Por esto, el rey don Alfonso
trajo una a su capilla.
por cuanto he sabido
es la más bella,
y la hace sacar en las fiestas
para desechar° la herejía (fight against)
de los que por su gran locura
van a dudar de la Virgen.
*Para sacarnos de dudas…*

Cantiga 47
*Esta é como Santa Maria guardou o monge,*
*que o demo quis espantar por lo fazer perder.*

Virgen Santa Maria,
guarda-nos, se te praz,
da gran sabedoria
que eno demo jaz.

*Ca ele noit' e dia | punna de nos meter*
*per que façamos erro, | porque a Deus perder*
*ajamo-, lo teu Fillo, | que quis por nos sofrer*
*na cruz paxon e morte, | que ouvessemos paz.*
Virgen Santa Maria…

*E desto, meus amigos, | vos quer' ora contar*
*un miragre fremoso, | de que fix meu cantar,*
*como Santa Maria | foi un monge guardar*
*da tentaçon do demo, | a que do ben despraz.*
Virgen Santa Maria…

*Este mong' ordÿado | era, segund' oý,*
*muit', e mui ben sa orden | tĩia, com' aprendi;*
*mas o demo arteiro | o contorvou assy*
*que o fez na adega | bever do vÿ 'assaz.*
*Virgen Santa Maria…*

*Pero beved' estava | muit, o monge quis s' ir*
*dereit' aa eigreja; | mas o dem' a sair*
*en.figura de touro | o foi, polo ferir*
*con seus cornos merjudos, | ben como touro faz.*
Virgen Santa Maria…

*Quand' esto viu o monge, | feramen s' espantou*
*e a Santa Maria | mui de rrijo chamou,*
*que ll' appareceu log' e | o tour' amẽaçou,*
*dizendo: "Vai ta via, | muit' es de mal solaz."*
Virgen Santa Maria…

Cantiga 47
Esta es cómo Santa María guardó al monje
que el demonio quiso asustar, para hacerlo perder.

*Virgen Santa María,*
*librarnos, si te place,*
*de la gran sabiduría*
*que hay en el demonio.*

Porque él, noche y día, lucha por hacernos
caer en yerros, para que perdamos a Dios,
tu Hijo, que quiso sufrir,
en la cruz, pasión y muerte, para que tuviésemos paz.
*Virgen Santa María...*

Y de esto, amigos míos, quiero referiros
un hermoso milagro, del que hice mi cantar,
cómo Santa María fue a guardar a un monje
de la tentación del demonio, al que el bien desagrada.
*Virgen Santa María...*

Este monje estaba ordenado y, según oí,
observaba muy bien las sus reglas, como he aprendido,
pero el demonio artero° lo turbó de manera — artful
que, en la bodega,° bebiera demasiado vino. — wine cellar
*Virgen Santa María...*

Cuando estaba bebido, el monje quiso irse
'en derechura° a la iglesia, pero el demonio le salió — straight
al encuentro, en figura de toro, y fue a herirlo
con sus cuernos, bajos, tal como lo hace el toro.
*Virgen Santa María...*

Cuando esto vio el monje, se llenó de espanto
y a Santa María llamó, muy recio;° — insistently
Ella se apareció en seguida y amenazó al toro,
diciendo: "Sigue tu camino, que malos juegos tienes."
*Virgen Santa María...*

*Pois en figura d' ome | pareceu-ll' outra vez,*
*longu' e magr' e veloso | e negro come pez;*
*mas acorreu-lle logo | e Virgen de bon prez,*
*dizendo: "Fuge, mao | mui peor que rapz."*
Virgen Santa Maria…

*Pois entrou na eigreja, | ar pareceu-ll' enton*
*o demo en figura | de mui bravo leon;*
*mas a Virgen mui santa | deu-lle con un baston,*
*dizendo: "Tol-t', astroso, | e logo te desfaz."*
Virgen Santa Maria…

*Pois que Santa Maria | o seu mong' acorreu,*
*como vos ei ja dito, | e ll'o medo tolleu*
*do demo e do vinno, | con que era sandeu,*
*disse-ll': "Oy mais te guarda | e non sejas malvaz."*
Virgen Santa Maria…

| | |
|---|---|
| Después, en hechura° de hombre, se le apareció otra vez, | guise |
| alto, de negro y velludo,° negro como la pez;° | hairy, pitch |
| pero le acudió luego la Virgen de buena prez,° | reputation |
| diciendo: "Huye,° malo, que eres peor que un chiquillo." | scat |
| *Virgen Santa María…* | |
| | |
| Después cuando entró en la iglesia, todavía volvió a aparecérsele | |
| el demonio, en figura de un bravo° león, | fierce |
| pero la Virgen muy Santa le dio con un báculo,° | stick |
| diciendo: "Quítate, astroso,° y desaparece." | vile one |
| *Virgen Santa María…* | |
| | |
| Después de que Santa María hubo socorrido al monje, | |
| como os he dicho, y le quitó el miedo | |
| del demonio y el vino, con el que estaba enloquecido,° | crazed |
| le dijo: "Guárdate, desde hoy, y no seas malvado."° | bad |
| *Virgen Santa María…* | |

## Scholar's Poetry: *mester de clerecía*

In the 13th century and in the 14th the *mester de clerecía* flourished. It was characterized by monorhymed quatrains rather than assonance, regular lines of fourteen syllables with a caesura or pause in the middle of each. This poetry is also known as *cuaderna vía* (the four-fold way).

The *Poema de Fernán González* is the only poem that has survived using epic material and written in *cuaderna vía*. Fernán González (d. 970) was the founder of Castilian independence. The poem was written about 1250 and relates the wonderful, yet realistic events connected with this count's conquests for Castile.

The *Libro de Apolonio*, which was written during the first half of the 13th century, is the first appearance of a Byzantine tale to emerge in Spanish. Based probably upon a lost Greek novel, it is more romantic and less heroic than *Fernán González*.

The *Libro de Alexandre* of the mid-13th century contains 10,500 lines and was written by a poet of considerable culture and education. This book portrays Alexander the Great as the perfect medieval knight and shows that Spanish literature of the period was of a universal scope rather than confined to themes of the Iberian Peninsula.

## *POEMA DE FERNÁN GONZÁLEZ* [6]

This is an epic poem in *mester de clerecía* about the life of Fernán González, count of Castile, who struggled to obtain the independence of Castile from Leon. The count died in 970 but the poem was written by a monk of the monastery of San Pedro de Arlanza between 1250 and 1266 and is conserved in only one 15th century manuscript. It tells the story of the count's campaigns against the Moors, his wars against the Kingdom of

[6] Preliminary note. Digital edition based on that of Ramón Menéndez Pidal's in *Reliquias de la poesía épica española*, Madrid: M. Rivadeneyra, 1951, pp. 34-153, and compared with the critical editions by Alonso Zamora Vicente, Madrid: Clásicos Castellanos, 1944; reedited 1953 and 1978, and Juan Victorio, Madrid: Cátedra, 1998, 4th ed.

Navarre, his debates with the King of Leon, and his protection of San Pedro de Arlanza, where he was eventually laid to rest. Although the poem is based on an historic character and historic events, folklore and imagination often shape the narrative.

Justificación

1 En el nonbre del Padre que fizo toda cosa,
del que quiso nasçer la Virgen preciosa
e del Spíritu Santo, que igual dellos posa,° — is
del conde de Castiella quiero fer una prosa.

2 El Señor que crió la tierra e la mar,
—e las cosas passadas que yo pueda contar—
El, que es buen maestro, me deve demostrar
commo cobró s' la tierra toda de mar a mar.

3 Contar vos he primero de commo la perdieron
nuestros antecessores, en qual coita visquieron;° — lived
commo omnes deserdados° fuidos andodieron;° — defenseless, went
¡essa rabia llevaron que ende non morieron!

4 Muchas coitas passaron nuestros anteçessores,
muchos malos espantos, muchos malos sabores,° — troubles
sufríen frío e fanbre e muchos amargores:° — bitterness
estos viçios° d'agora estonz eran dolores. — delights

5 En tanto, desde tienpo ir vos he yo contando
commo fueron la tierra perdiendo e cobrando,
. . . . . . . . . . . . . . . . . . . . . . . . . . . . . . . . . . . .
fasta que todas fueron al conde don Fernando.

6 Commo es mucho luenga desde el tienpo antigo
commo se dio la tierra al buen rey don Rodrigo,— last King of visigodos
commo la ovo a ganar el mortal enemigo:
de grand honor que era tornó l' pobre mendigo.

7 Esto fizo Mafomat,° de la mala creençia, — Mohammed
. . . . . . . . . . . . . . . . . . . . . . . . . . . . . . . . . . . . . .
. . . . . . . . . . . . . . . . . . . . . . . . . . . . . . . . . . . . . .
predicó por su boca mucha mala sentençia.

8 Desque ovo Mafomat a todos predicados,
avien los coraçones las gentes demudados,° — changed
. . . . . . . . . . . . . . . . . . . . . . . . . . . . . . . . . . . . . .
e la muerte de Cristus avían la olvidado.

9 Desque los españones° a Cristus conosçieron, — **=españoles**
desque en la su ley° bautismo resçibieron, — religion
nunca en otra ley tornar se non quisieron,
mas por guarda d'aquesto muchos males sufrieron.

85 Fueron, commo oyestes, de los moros rancados:° — conquered
muchos eran los muertos, muchos los cativados;
fuíen los que fincaron maldiziendo sus fados;
fueron por todo el mundo luego estos mandados.

86 Pero, con todo esto, buen consejo prendieron:
tomaron las reliquias quantas tomar podieron,
alçaron se en Castiella, assí se defendieron,
los de las otras tierras por espadas murieron.

87 Era Castiella Vieja un puerto bien çerrado,
non avíe más entrada de un sólo forado,° — entrance
tovieron castellanos el puerto bien guardado,
por end' de toda España esse ovo fincado.

88 Fincaron las Asturias, un pequeño lugar
con valles e montañas que son çerca la mar;
non podieron los moros por los puertos° passar — passes
e ovieron, por tanto, las Asturias fincar.

89 España la gentil fue luego destruida,
eran señores d'ella la gente descreída;
los cristianos mesquinos avíen muy mala vida,

nunca fue en cristianos tan grand cuita venida.

90 Dentro en las iglesias fazían establías,° stables
fazien en los altares muchas fieras follías,
rovavan los tesoros de las sacristanías,
lloravan los cristianos las noches e los días.

91 Quiero vos dezir cosa que fizo retraer:
prendíen a los cristianos, mandavan los cozer,° cook
fazían semejante que los ivan comer
por tal que les podiessen mayor miedo meter.

92 Tenían otros presos, dexavan los foír
por que veíen las penas a los otros sofrir,
avían por do ivan las nuevas a dezir
. . . . . . . . . . . . . . . . . . . . . . . . . . . . . . . . . . . . . .

93 Dezían e afirmavan que los vieran cozer,
cozían e asavan omnes pora comer;
quantos que lo oían ivan se a perder,
non sabíen, con grand miedo, adonde se asconder.

94 Assí ivan foyendo de las gentes estrañas
. . . . . . . . . . . . . . . . . . . . . . . . . . . . . . . . . . . . . .
murían de grand fanbre todos por las montañas,
non diez, veinte nin treinta, mas muchas de conpañas.

95 Perdieron muchos d'ellos con miedo los sentidos,
matavan a las madres, en braços a sus fijos,
no s' podíen dar consejo mugeres nin maridos,
avían, con grand miedo, muchos enloqueçidos.

96 E los omnes mesquinos que estavan alçados
del grand bien que ovieron estavan muy menguados:
querían más ser muertos o yacer soterrados
que non vesquir tal vida, fanbrientos e lazrados.

97 Los omnes d'otro tienpo que fueran segurados,

veían se de nuevo en la tierra tornados:
comíen el paneziello de sus fijos amados,
los pobres eran ricos e los ricos menguados.

98 Dezíen los malfadados: «En mal ora nasçimos;
diera nos Dios España, guardar la non sopimos;
si en grand coita somos, nos bien lo meresçimos,
por nuestro mal sentido en grand yerro caímos.

99 Si nos atales fuéssemos commo nuestros parientes,
non avrían poder aquestas malas gentes;
ellos fueron muy buenos, e nos menos valientes,
traen nos commo lobos a corderos rezientes.° new born

100 Nos a Dios falesçiendo,° ha nos él falesçido, failing
lo que otros ganaron, hemos lo nos perdido;
partiendo nos de Dios, ha se de nos partido,
todo el bien de los godos por end es confondido.»

101 Diera Dios essas oras grand poder al pecado,
fasta allende del puerto todo fuera astragado;° laid waste
semeja fiera cosa, más diz lo el ditado,
a San Martín de Torres[7] ovieron allegado.

102 Visquieron castellanos grand tienpo mala vida
en tierra muy angosta, de viandas° muy fallida, meat
lazrados muy grand tienpo a la mayor medida;
vien se en muy grand miedo con la gent' descreída.

103 En todas estas coitas, pero que mal andantes,
en la merçet de Cristus eran enfiuzantes,° trusting
que les avríe merçed contra non bautizantes:
«Val nos, Señor,—dixeron— ond' seamos cobrantes.»° conquerors

104 Avían en todo esto a Almançor[8] a dar

[7] **San Martín de Torres** is the French city Saint Martin de Tours.

[8] **Almançor** was the ruler of Al-Andalus in the late 10th to early 11th centuries.

çien donzellas fermosas que fuessen por casar;
avíen las por Castiella cada una a buscar,
avíen lo de cunplir, pero con grand pesar.

Batalla de Roncesvalles

127 Hemos esta razón por fuerça d'alongar,
quiero en el rey Carlos este cuento tornar;
ovo al rey Alfonso mandado de enbiar
que venie en España pora gela ganar.

128 Enbió el rey Alfonso al rey Carlos mandado
que en ser atributado° non era acordado, — one who pays tribute
por dar parias° por él non quería el reignado, — tribute payments
seríe llamado torpe en fer atal mercado.° — business

129 Dixo que más quería commo estava estar,
que el reigno d'España a Francia sojuzgar,
que non se podríen d'esso franceses alabar,
¡que más la queríen ellos, en çinco años ganar!

130 Carlos ovo consejo sobre este mandado;
commo menester fuera non fue bien consejado;
dieron le por consejo el su pueblo famado
que veníessen a España con todo su fonsado.° — army

131 Ayuntó sus poderes, grandes e sin mesura,
movió pora Castiella, ¡tengo que fue locura!;
al que lo consejó nuncal' marre° rencura,° — lack, affliction
ca fue essa venida plaga de su ventura.

132 Sopo Bernald del Carpio que françeses passavan,
que a Fuente Rabia[9] todos y arribavan
por conquerir a España, segunt que ellos cuidavan
que ge la conquerrían, mas non lo bien asmavan.

[9] **Fuente Rabia** is the area of Roncesvalles.

133 Ovo grandes poderes Bernaldo d'ayuntar,
e dessí enbió los al puerto de la mar,
ovo l' todas sus gentes el rey casto a dar,
non dexó a esse puerto al rey Carlos passar.

134 Mató y de françeses reyes e potestades,
com' diz' la escriptura, siete fueron, sepades;
muchos morieron y, esto bien lo creades,
que nunca más tornaron a las sus vezindades.

135 Tovo se por 'mal trecho° Carlos essa vegada; ill-treated
'quando vio que por y le tollió la entrada,
movió s' con assaz gentes e toda su mesnada,
al puerto de Marsilla[10] fizo luego tornada.

136 Quando fueron al puerto los françeses llegados,
rendieron a Dios graçias que los avíe guiados;
folgaron e dormieron, que eran muy cansados,
¡si essora se tornaran, fueran bien venturados!

137 Ovieron su acuerdo de passar a España,
onde non les fincasse nin torre nin cabaña.
. . . . . . . . . . . . . . . . . . . . . . . . . . . . . . . . . . .
. . . . . . . . . . . . . . . . . . . . . . . . . . . . . . . . . . .

138 Fueron y los poderes con toda su mesnada,
al puerto de Gitarea[11] fizieron la tornada.
. . . . . . . . . . . . . . . . . . . . . . . . . . . . . . . . . . .
. . . . . . . . . . . . . . . . . . . . . . . . . . . . . . . . . . .

139 Los poderes de Francia, todos muy bien guarnidos,
por los puertos de Aspa[12] fueron luego troçidos;° passed through
¡fueran de buen acuerdo si non fueran venidos,
que nunca más tornaron a do fueron nasçidos!

[10] **Marsilla** is Marseille, France.
[11] **Gitarea** mountain pass in area of Roncesvalles.
[12] **Aspa** mountain pass in present-day Huesca, Spain.

140 Dexemos los françeses en España tornados,
por conquerir la tierra todos muy bien guisados;
tornemos en Bernaldo de los fechos granados,
que avíe d' espannones los poderes juntados.

141 Movió Bernald del Carpio con toda su mesnada,
si sobre moros fuesse, era buena tornada;
movieron pora un agua muy fuerte e muy irada,° swift
Ebro l' dixeron sienpre, assí es oy llamada.

142 Fueron a Çaragoça° a los pueblos paganos, **=Zaragoza**
besó Bernald del Carpio al rey Marsil[13] las manos
que dies' la delantera° a pueblos castellanos front lines
contra los Doze Pares, essos pueblos loçanos.

143 Otorgó gela luego e dio gela de grado,
nunca oyó Marsil otro nin tal mandado:
movió Bernald del Carpio con su pueblo dudado,° feared
de gentes castellanas, era bien aguardado.

144 Tovo la delantera Bernaldo essa vez
con gentes espannones, ¡gentes de muy grand prez!;
vençieron essas oras a françeses refez,° vile
bien fue essa más negra que la primera vez.

IV
Elogio de España Temperate Land

145 Por esso vos lo digo que bien lo entendades:
mejor es que otras tierras en la que vos morades,
de todo es bien conplida° en la que vos estades, filled
dezir vos e agora quantas ha de bondades.

146 Tierra es muy tenprada, sin grandes calenturas,
non fazen en ivierno destenpradas friuras;° cold
non es tierra en el mundo que aya tales pasturas,

---

[13] **Marsil** was the Moorish king of Zaragoza

árboles pora fruta siquier de mil naturas.

147 Sobre todas las tierras mejor es la montaña,
de vacas e de ovejas non ha tierra tamaña,
tantos ha y de puercos que es fiera fazaña,
sirven se muchas tierras de las cosas d'España.

148 Es de lino° e de lana° tierra mucho abastada, linen, wool
de çera° sobre todas buena tierra provada, wax
non sería d'azeite en mundo tal fallada,
Inglatierra nin Francia d'esto es abondada.

149 Buena tierra de caça° e buena de venados,° hunting, deer
de río e de mar muchos buenos pescados,
quien los quiere rezientes,° quien los quiere salados, fresh
son d'estas cosas tales pueblos muy abastados.

150 De panes e de vinos tierra muy comunal,
non fallaríen en mundo otra mejor nin tal,
muchas de buenas fuentes, mucho río cabdal,° large
otras muchas mineras de que fazen la sal.

151 Ha y venas de oro, son de mejor barata,° value
muchas de buenas venas de fierro e de plata;
ha en sierras e valles mucha de buena mata,° trees
todas llenas de grana° pora fer escarlata. seed (for dyeing)

152 Por lo que ella más val aun non lo dixemos:
es mucho mejor tierra de las que nunca viemos,
de los buenos caveros° aun mençión non fiziemos, horses
nunca tales caveros en el mundo non viemos.

153 Dexar vos quiero d'esto, assaz vos he contado,
non quiero más dezir, que podríe ser errado,
pero non olvidemos al apóstol honrado,
fijo del Zebedeo, Santiago llamado.

154 Fuerte mient quiso Dios a España honrar,

quando al santo apóstol quiso y enbiar;
d'Inglatierra e Françia quiso la mejorar,
sabet, non yaz apóstol en todo aquel logar.

155 Onró le otra guisa el preçioso Señor,
fueron y muchos santos muertos por el su amor,
de morir a cochillo° non ovieron temor, knife
muchas vírgenes santas, mucho buen confessor.

156 Commo ella es mejor de las sus vezindades,
assí sodes mejores los que España morades,
omnes sodes sesudos, mesura heredades,
d'esto por todo el mundo muy grand preçio ganades.

V
Castilla y su protohistoria

Elogio de Castilla
157 Pero de toda España Castiella es mejor,
por que fue de los otros el comienço mayor,
guardando e temiendo sienpre a su señor,
quiso acreçentar la assí el Criador.

Fernan Gonzalez
heroe de Castilla

158 Aun Castiella Vieja, al mi entendimiento,
mejor es que lo al, por que fue el çimiento,
ca conquirieron mucho maguer poco convento:° population
bien lo podedes ver en el acabamiento.° outcome

159 Pues quiero me con tanto d'esta razón dexar,
temo, si más dixesse que podría herrar;° **=errar**
otrossí non vos quiero la razón alongar,
quiero en don Alfonso, el Casto rey, tornar.

Desamparo° del condado — abandonment

160 Rey fue de grand sentido e de muy grand valor,
siervo fue e amigo mucho del Criador;
fue se d'aqueste mundo para el otro mayor,
fincó toda la tierra essora sin señor.

161 Eran en muy grand coita españones caídos,
duraron muy grand tienpo todos desavenidos.° — disconcerted
commo omnes sin señor, tristes e doloridos:
«Mucho nos valdríe más que nunca ser nasçidos.»

162 Quand vieron castellanos la cosa assí ir
e que pora alçar rey no s' podíen avenir,
vieron que sin pastor non podíen bien vevir,
posieron quien podiesse los canes referir.° — keep away

Elección de los alcaldes

163 Todos los castellanos en uno se acordaron:
dos omnes de grand guisa° por alcaldes alçaron; — quality
los pueblos castellanos por ellos se guiaron;
que non posieron rey muy grand tienpo duraron.

164 Diré de los alcaldes quales nonbres ovieron,
e dende en adelante los que d'ellos venieron;
muchas buenas batallas con los moros ovieron,
con su fiero esfuerço grand tierra conquirieron.

165 Don Nuño fue el uno, omne de grand valor,
vino de su linaje el buen batallador;
el otro don Laíno, el buen guerreador,
vino de su linaje el buen Çid Canpeador,

166 Fi de Nuño Rasura, omne bien entendido,
Gonçalo ovo nonbre, omne muy atrevido;
anparó bien la tierra, fizo quanto a podido,

este fue referiendo al pueblo descreído.

167 Ovo Gonçalo Núñez tres fijuelos varones,
todos tres de grand guisa, de grandes coraçones;
estos partieron tierra e dieron la a infançones,° nobles
por donde ellos partieron y están los mojones.° borders

168 Don Diego Gonçález, el ermano mayor;
Rodrigo, el mediano; Fernando, el menor;
todos tres fueron buenos, mas Fernando el mejor,
ca quitó muy grand tierra al moro Almançor.

169 Finó Diego Gonçález, cavero muy loçano,
quedó toda la tierra en el otro ermano,
don Rodrigo por nonbre, que era el mediano,
señor fue muy grand tienpo del pueblo castellano.

170 Quando vino la ora puesta del Criador,
fue se don Ruy Gonçález, pora el mundo mejor;
fincó toda la tierra al ermano menor,
don Fernando por nonbre, cuerpo de grand valor.

171 Estonçe era Castiella un pequeño rincón,
era de castellanos Montes d'Oca° mojón,° boundary, east of
e de la otra parte Fitero el fondón,° Burgos, below
moros teníen Caraço en aquesta sazón.

172 Era toda Castiella sólo una alcaldía;° jurisdiction
maguer que era pobre e de poca valía,
nunca de buenos omnes fue Castiella vazía,
de quales ellos fueron paresçe aun oy día.

173 Varones castellanos, este fue su cuidado:
de llegar su señor al más alto estado;
d'un alcaldía pobre fizieron la condado,
tornaron la después cabeça de reinado.

VI
Castilla, condado

174 Ovo nonbre Fernando esse conde primero,
nunca fue en el mundo otro tal cavallero;
este fue de los moros un mortal omiçero,° murderer
dizíen le por sus lides el 'vueitre carniçero.° meat-eating vultur

175 Fizo grandes batallas con la gent descreída,
e les fizo lazrar a la mayor medida,
ensanchó° en Castiella una muy grand medida, increased
ovo en el su tienpo mucha sangre vertida.

176 El conde don Fernando, con muy poca conpaña
—en contar lo que fizo semejaríe fazaña—
mantovo sienpre guerra con los reys d'España
non dava más por ellos que por una castaña.° chestnut

San Pedro de Arlanza

226 El conde don Fernando, cuerpo de buenas mañas,
cavalgó en su cavallo, partió s' de sus conpañas,
por ir buscar el puerco, metió s' por las montañas,
falló lo en un arroyo çerca de Vasquebañas.

227 'Acojió se° el puerco a un fiero° lugar, took refuge, wild
do tenía su cueva e solía albergar;
non se osó el puerco en cueva asegurar,° trust his safety
fuxó a una ermita, metió s' tras el altar.

228 Era essa ermita d'una yedra° techada,° ivy, disguised
por que de toda ella non parescía nada;
tres monjes y vevían vida fuerte lazrada,
San Pedro avía nonbre essa casa sagrada.

229 Non pudo por la peña el conde aguijar;
sorrendo° el cavallo, ovo se d'apear; taking the reins

por do s' metió el puerco, metió s' por es' lugar,
entró por la ermita, llegó fasta el altar.

230 Quando vio don Fernando tan onrado logar,
Desanparó° el puerco, no l' quiso y matar: spared
«Señor—dixo—a quien temen los vientos e la mar,
si yo erré en esto, deves me perdonar.

231 A ti me manifiesto, Virgen Santa María,
que d'esta santidat, Señora, non sabía:
por y fazer enojo yo aquí non entraría,
si non por dar ofrenda o por fer romería.° pilgrimage

232 Señor, tú me perdona, e me vale e me ayuda
contra la gent pagana que tanto me es erguda;° pursue
anpara a Castiella de la gent descreúda;
si tú non la anparas, tengo la por perduda.»

233 Quando ovo el conde la oraçión acabada,
vino a él un monje de la pobre posada,
Pelayo avía nonbre, vivie vida lazrada,
preguntó le quién era e quál era su andada.

234 Dixo que tras el puerco ay era venido,
era de su mesnada arredrado° e partido; separated
si por pecados fuesse de Almançor sabido,
non fincaría tierra donde escapasse vivo.

235 Recudió el monje e dixo: «Ruego t' por Dios, amigo,
si fuesse tu mesura° que ospedasses conmigo, pleasure
dar te he yo pan d'ordio,° ca non tengo de trigo, barley
sabrás commo has de fer contra el tu enemigo.»

236 El conde don Fernando, de todo bien conplido,
contra el monje Pelayo resçibió su convido,° invitation
del ermitaño santo tovo s' por bien servido:
mejor non albergara después que fuera vivo.

Promesa de ayuda divina

237 Dixo don fray Pelayo escontra su señor:
«Fago te, el buen conde, de tanto sabidor,
que quiere tu fazienda° guiar el Criador: deeds
vençerás el poder del moro Almançor.

238 Farás grandes batallas en la gent descreída,
muchas serán las gentes a quien toldrás° la vida, take
cobrarás de la tierra una buena partida,
la sangre de los reyes por ti será vertida.

239 Non quiero más dezir te de toda tu andança,
será por todo el mundo temida la tu lança;
quanto que te yo digo, ten lo por segurança,
dos vezes serás preso, creí me sin dudança,

240 Antes de terçer día serás en grand cuidado,
ca verás el tu pueblo todo muy espantado:
verán un fuerte signo qual nunca vio omne nado,
el más loçano d'ellos será muy desmayado.

241 Tú confortar los has quanto mejor podieres,
dezir les has a todos que semejan mugieres,
departir has° el signo quanto mejor sopieres, will explain
perderán todo el miedo quand' gelo departieres.

242 Espídete° agora con lo que has oído, leave
aqueste lugar pobre non lo eches en olvido;
fallarás el tu pueblo triste e dolorido,
faziendo lloro e llanto e 'metiendo apellido.° complaining

243 Por lloro nin por llanto non fazen ningún tuerto,
ca piensan que eres preso o que moros te han muerto,
que quedan sin señor e sin ningún confuerto,
coidavan con los moros por ti salir a puerto.

244 Mas ruego te, amigo, e pido lo de grado

que quando ovieres tú el canpo arrancado,
venga se te en mientes d'est convento lazrado,
e non se te olvide el pobre ospedado.

245 Señor, tres monjes somos, assaz pobre convento,
la nuestra pobre vida non ha nin par nin cuento;
si Dios non nos envia algún consolamiento,
daremos a las sierpes° el nuestro avitamiento.»° snakes, house

246 El conde dio l' respuesta commo omne enseñado.
Dixo: «Don fray Pelayo, non ayades cuidado,
quanto que demandastes ser vos ha otorgado,
conosçeré a donde me diestes ospedado.

247 Si Dios aquesta lid me dexa arrancar,
quiero todo el mío quinto° a este lugar dar; fifth part of the booty
demás, quando muriere, aquí me soterrar,
que mejore por mí sienpre este lugar.

248 Faré otra iglesia de más fuerte çimiento,° foundation
faré dentro en ella el mi soterramiento,
daré y donde vivan de monjes más de çiento,
sirvan todos a Dios, fagan su mandamiento.»

249 Despidió se del monje alegre e muy pagado,
vino se pora Lara el conde aventurado;
quando allá llegó e le vio su fonsado,
el lloro e el llanto en gozo fue tornado.

250 Contó a sus varones commo le avie contido,° happened
del monje que fallara que yazía ascondido,
commo fuera su uésped, tomara su convido,
mejor non albergara después que fue nasçido.

Batalla de Lara
Inferioridad de fuerzas. Miedo en el campo cristiano

251 Otro día mañana mandó mover sus gentes;
pora cada cristiano avíe mill descreyentes;
los del conde eran pocos, mas buenos conbatientes,
todos eran iguales, d'un coraçón ardientes.

252 Bien se veíen por ojo los moros e cristianos;
non es omne en el mundo que asmasse los paganos,
todos veníen cobiertos, los oteros e llanos:
a cristianos cuidavan prender se los a manos.

253 Fazíen grand alegría los pueblos descreídos,
veníen tañendo tronpas° e dando alaridos, horns
davan los malfadados atamaños roídos,
que los montes e valles semejavan movidos.

254 El conde don Fernando estava muy quexado,
queríe morir por ver se con moros en el canpo;
bien cuidava esse día reignar y el pecado,
que metió grand espanto en el pueblo cruzado.

255 Uno de los del conde, de la Puente Ytero,
cavalgava un cavallo fermoso e ligero;
puso l' de las espuelas por çima d'un otero,
partió s' con él la tierra e 'somió se° el cavero. died

256 Fueron los castellanos todos muy espantados:
«Esto que nos conteçe es por nuestros pecados;
bien semeja que Dios nos ha desamparados,
mejor seso fiziéramos si fuéramos tornados.

La arenga

257 Bien vemos nos que a moros quiere Dios ayudar;
¿cómmo podremos nos contra ellos lidiar.»
Dixo estonçes el conde: «Querades me escuchar:
non querades en poco 'mal prez° sienpre ganar. dishonor

258 Lo que muestra este signo quiero vos departir,
amigos e vassallos, si queredes me oír:
si tierra dura e fuerte vos fazedes somir,
pues ¿cuáles cosas otras vos podrían sofrir?

259 Los vuestros coraçones los veo enflaquesçer
contra gentes que son de muy menos valer.
Non devedes, varones, ningún miedo aver,
ca yo en este día me cobdiciava ver.

260 Amigos, d'una cosa so yo bien sabidor:
ellos serán vençidos, yo seré vençedor;
en gran afruenta° en canpo seré con Almançor: contest, battle
veré de castellanos com' guardan su señor.»

La batalla

261 Pues que ovo acabada el conde su razón,
e esforçadas sus gentes commo omne de sazón,
mandó a sus conpañas desbolver° su pendón: to wave
firieron en los moros todos d'un coraçón.

262 Ferió luego el conde en los pueblos paganos,
quien con él se encontravan non se ivan d'él sanos;
dizie « Yo so el conde; esforçad, castellanos,
ferid los bien de rezio, amigos e hermanos.»

263 Otrossi un rico omne que dezíen don Velasco
. . . . . . . . . . . . . . . . . . . . . . . . . . . . . . . . . . . . . . . .
. . . . . . . . . . . . . . . . . . . . . . . . . . . . . . . . . . . . . . . .
. . . . . . . . . . . . . . . . . . . . . . . . . . . . . . . . . . . . . . . .

264 Metíen toda su fuerça en guardar su señor,
non avíen de su muerte nin pesar nin dolor,
tollié les el grand depdo de la muerte el pavor,
non avíe pora buenos d'este mundo mejor.

265 Commo todos fizieron refez° es d'entender, — easy
tanto non fizo omne con tan poco poder;
semeja poca cosa pesada de creer
con trezientos caveros tan grand pueblo vençer.

266 Caveros e peones firme miente lidiavan,
todos quanto podían a su señor guardavan,
quando dezíe «Castiella» con él se esforzavan;
los moros, en todo esto, las espaldas tornavan.

267 Fue les de una lid el conde acuitando,° — pursuing
iva s' contra la tienda d'Almançor acostando.
. . . . . . . . . . . . . . . . . . . . . . . . . . . . . . . . . . . . .
. . . . . . . . . . . . . . . . . . . . . . . . . . . . . . . . . . . . .

268 Llegaron a Almançor estos malos roídos
sabiendo commo eran sus poderes vençidos;
eran muchos los muertos e muchos los feridos,
avía de sus reyes los mejores perdidos.

Fuga del enemigo
269 Demandó su cavallo por lidiar con sus manos,
fueran y venturados caveros castellanos:
muerto fuera o preso de los pueblos cristianos,
mas non lo consejaron los sus pueblos cristianos.

270 Por non vos detener en otras ledanías,° — stories
fue Almançor vençido con sus cavallerías:
allí fue demostrado el poder del Mexías,
el conde fue David e Almançor Gollías.

271 Foía Almançor a guisa d'algarivo° — grieved
«Todo el mi grand poder es muerto o cativo;
pues ellos muertos son, ¿por qué finco yo vivo»
. . . . . . . . . . . . . . . . . . . . . . . . . . . . . . . . . . . . .

272 Dizíe: «Ay, Mafomat, en mal ora en ti fío
non vale tres arvejas° todo el tu poderío.» — beans

Fincaron en el canpo muertos muchos gentíos,
de los que sanos eran estonz fueron vazíos.

Persecución y botín. Riqueza de éste
273 Quando fueron vençidos essos pueblos paganos,
fueron los vençedores los pueblos castellanos;
el conde don Fernando con todos los cristianos
fueron en su alcançe° por cuestas e por llanos. pursuit

274 Rendieron a Dios graçias e a Santa María
por que dexó les ver tamaña maravilla:
duró les el alcançe quanto que medio día,
enriqueçió s' por sienpre la pobre alcaldía.

275 Quando fue Almançor grand tierra alexado,
fincó de sus averes el canpo bien poblado;
cojieron sus averes que Dios les avíe dado;
tan grand aver fallaron que non seríe contado.

276 Fallaron en las tiendas sobejano tesoro,
muchas copas e vasos que eran d'un fino oro:
nunca vio atal riqueza nin cristiano nin moro,
seríen ende abondados Alexander e Poro.[14]

277 Fallaron y maletas e muchos de çurrones° leather sacks
llenos d'oro e de plata, que non de pepiones,° worthless things
muchas tiendas de seda e muchos tendejones,° tents
'espadas e lorigas e muchas guarniçiones.

Donación a San Pedro de Arlanza
278 Fallaron de marfil° arquetas° muy preçiadas, ivory, chests
con tantas de noblezas° que non seríen contadas; riches
fueron pora San Pedro las más d'aquellas dadas,
están todas oy día en su altar asentadas.

---

[14] **Alexander e Porro** Alexander the Great defeated King Porus of India at the Battle of the Hydaspes River in 326 B.C.

279 Tomaron d'esto todo lo que sabor ovieron,
mas fincó de dos partes que levar non podieron;
las armas que fallaron dexar non las quisieron,
con toda su ganançia a San Pedro venieron.

280 Quand' fueron y llegados a Dios graçias rendieron,
todos, chicos e grandes, su oraçión fizieron,
todos por una boca «Deo gratias» dixeron,
cada uno sus joyas al altar ofreçieron.

281 De toda su ganançia que Dios les avíe dado,
mandó tomar el quinto el conde aventurado,
qualquier cosa que l' copo,° ovo lo bien conprado, corresponded
mandó lo dar al monje que le diera ospedado.

282 El conde e sus gentes e todos los cruzados
a la çibdat de Burgos fueron todos llegados;
folgaron e dormieron, que eran muy cansados,
demandaron maestros° por sanar los llagados. doctors

Aparición en sueños de San Pelayo y San Millán
405 Teniendo su vegilia, con Dios se razonando,
un sueño muy sabroso al conde fue tomando:
con sus armas guarnido assí se fue acostando,
'la carne adormida, assí yaze soñando.

406 Non podría el conde aun ser adormido,
el monje San Pelayo de suso l' fue venido,
de paños commo el sol todo veníe vestido,
nunca más bella cosa veyera omne nasçido,

407 Llamó le por su nonbre al conde don Fernando,
dixo l': «¿Duermes o cómmo estás assí callando?
Despierta e ve tu vía, ca te creçe oy grand bando,
ve te pora el tu pueblo, que te está esperando.

408 El Criador te otorga quanto pedido le has,
en los pueblos paganos grand mortandat° farás, killing

de tus buenas conpañas muchas y perderás,
pero, con todo el daño, tú el canpo vençerás.

409 Aun te dize más el alto Criador:
que tú eres su vassallo e él es tu Señor,
con los pueblos paganos lidiarás por su amor,
manda te que te vayas lidiar con Almançor.

410 Yo seré y contigo, que me lo ha otorgado,
y será el apóstol Santiago llamado,
enbiar nos ha Cristo valer a su criado,
será con tal ayuda Almançor enbargado.° overwhelmed

411 Otros vernán y muchos commo en una visión
en blancas armaduras, ángeles de Dios son;
traerá cada uno la cruz en su pendón:
moros, quando nos vieren, perdrán° el coraçón. **=perderán**

412 Amigo, dicho te he lo que a mí mandaron,
vo me pora aquellos que me acá enviaron.»
Los ángeles fermosos de tierra lo alçaron,
grand alegría faziendo al çielo lo levaron.

413 Despertó don Fernando commo con grand pavor:
«¡Qué puede ser aquesto! ¡Vala me el Criador!
Pecado es que me quiere echar en un error;
Cristo, yo tuyo so, guarda me tú, Señor.»

414 Estando en el sueño que soñara pensando,
oyó una grand voz que le estava llamando.
«'Lieva dend,° ve tu vía, el conde don Fernando, get up from here
espera te Almançor con el su fuerte bando.

415 Non tardes, ve tu vía; si non, tuerto me azes,
porque tanto me tardas en grand culpa me yazes,
no l' des ninguna tregua nin fagas con él pazes,
a todo el tu pueblo fazer lo has tres azes.

416 Tú entra con los menos de partes de oriente,
entrante de la lid ver me has 'vesible miente;° =visiblemente
manda entrar la otra az de partes d'oçidente,
y será Santiago, esto sin fallimiente.

417 Entre la otra terçera de partes d'aquilón,° north
vençremos los poderes d'este bravo león;
farás tú, si esto fazes, a guisa de Sansón° Sampson
quando con las sus manos lidió con el bestión.

418 Non quiero más dezir: lieva dend', ve tu vía.
¿Quieres saber quien trae esta mensajería?
Millán so yo por nonbre, Jesucristo me enbía,
durará la batalla fasta terçero día.»

Los castellanos, molestos con su señor

419 Quando ovo don Fernando todo esto oído,
el varón don Millán a los çielos fue ido:
fue luego de la ermita el conde espedido,
tornó se a Piedrafita d'onde fuera salido.

420 Quando el conde llegó a su buena conpaña,
falló a sus vassallos todos con fuerte saña,
maltraían° le tanto que eran grand fazaña, mistreated
non davan más por él que por una castaña.° chesnut

421 Commo eran malincónicos° todos con grand despecho, angry
de chicos e de grandes, de todos fue maltrecho.
«Fazes—dixeron—conde, sin guisa grand malfecho,
si algún yerro tomamos, será muy grand derecho.

422 Assí commo ladrón que anda a furtar,° to steal
assí solo señero te amas apartar;
quando nos te buscamos no t' podemos fallar,
abremos por aquesto algún yerro tomar.

423 Por que tanto t' sofrimos    por end somos peores,
pedimos te merçed,    non nos fagas traidores,
ca non lo fueron nunca    nuestros anteçessores,
mas non ovo en el mundo    leales nin mejores.»

Fernán González les arenga

424 Quando a toda su guisa    lo ovieron maltraído,
dixo les don Fernando:    «Por Dios, sea oído:
de quanto que yo fize    non so arrepentido,
no m' devedes tener    assí por tan fallido.°    false

425 Fui yo a la ermita    por mi amigo ver,
por él e yo en uno    amos aver plazer;
quando y fui llegado,    demandé d'él saber,
por nuevas me dixeron    que era en otro poder.

426 Sope yo como era    mi amigo finado,
mostraron me el logar    do yazíe soterrado;
rogué a Jesucristo    que, si él fizo pecado,
por la su grand mesura    le sea perdonado.

427 Entrante de la puerta    y fize mi oraçión,
tal qual me dio Dios seso    e m' metió en coraçón;
vino a mí este monje    commo en una visión:
"Despierta—dixo—amigo,    que ora es e sazón."

428 Dixo me lo en sueños,    non lo quise creer,
desperté e non pude    ninguna cosa ver;
oí una grand voz    de çielo desçender,
voz era de los santos    según mi entender.

429 Esta es la razón    que la voz me dezía:
"Conde Fernán González,    lieva dend', ve tu vía,
todo el poder de África    e del Andaluzía
vençer lo has en el canpo    d'este terçero día."

430 Dixo m' que mal fazía    por tanto que tardava
a aquel Rey de los Reyes    por cuya amor lidiava,
que fuesse e non tardasse    contra la gent pagana,
que por qué avíe miedo,    pues que él me ayudava.

431 Otras cosas me dixo    que me quiero callar,
seríe grand alongança    de todo lo contar,
mas vos aver lo hedes    aína de provar,
fasta que lo provedes,    aver me he de callar.

432 En aquella ermita    fui yo bien consejado
del monje San Pelayo,    siervo de Dios amado,
que por el su consejo    Almançor fue arrancado;
fui lo a buscar agora    e fallé l' soterrado.

433 Fasta que lo sepades    com' lo fui yo a saber
por end non me devedes    por fallido tener;
aguardar vos querría    a todo mi poder
de por mengua de mí    en yerro non caer.

Disposición del ejército cristiano

450 Mandó que fuessen prestos    otro día mañana,
fuessen puestas las azes    en medio de la plana,
todos fuessen armados    a primera canpana,
darían lid canpal    a aquella gent pagana.

451 A don Gustio Gonçález    el que de Salas era,
a él e a sus fijos    dio les la delantera,
con ellos don Velasco    —también de Salas era—
que por miedo de muerte    non dexaríe carrera.

452 Entró Gonçalo Díaz,    en esta misma faz,
era en los consejos    bueno de toda paz,
era por en faziendas    crudo° commo agraz,°    harsh, sour grape
quienquier que l' demandasse    fallar lo ie de faz.

453 Dos sobrinos del conde, valientes e ligeros,
—fiziera los el conde estonçes cavalleros—
devieran ser contados en los golpes primeros,
fueron estos llamados los lobos carniçeros.

454 Los que Gustio Gonçález avíe d'acabdillar,° lead
—dozientos fueron estos caveros de prestar—
el conde los mandó por una parte entrar;
de quales ellos fueron no s' podríen mejorar.

455 Dio les seis mill peones pora la delantera,
omnes de la Montaña, gente fuerte e ligera:
si bien guisados fuessen, commo mester les era,
por tres tantos de moros non dexaríen carrera.

456 Dexemos esta az toda muy bien parada,
non podría el cabdiello° mejorar se por nada, leader
seríe por nulla fuerça a duro quebrantada;
ya era en todo esto la otra az guisada.

457 Fue dado por cabdiello don Lope el vizcaíno,
bien rico de mançanas, pobre de pan e vino;
en la faz° se contaron fijos de don Laíno, battle line
e otro de la Montaña que dizíen don Martino.

458 Avíe de buroveses,° otrossi treviñanos,° from La Bureva, from Treviño
caveros bien ligeros, de coraçón loçanos,
de Castiella la Vieja muy buenos castellanos,
que muchos buenos fechos fizieron por sus manos.

459 Venían y de Castro unas buenas conpañas,
e venían con ellos otros de las montañas;
fueron y estorianos,° gentes muy bien guisadas, from Asturias
muy buenos eran d'armas, bien conplidos de mañas.

460 Veníen estos caveros en essa az mediana,
estos eran dozientos de la flor castellana;
todos fueron en canpo otro día mañana,

essa fue pora moros     una negra semana.

X
Castilla y León
El rey de León convoca cortes

570 Enbió Sancho Ordóñez     al buen conde mandado
que queríe fazer cortes     e que fuesse priado,° ready
e que eran ayuntados     todos los del reinado;
por él solo tardava,     que non era uviado.° arrived

571 Ovo ir a las cortes,     pero con grand pesar,
era muy fiera cosa     la mano le besar:
«Señor Dios de los çielos,     quieras me ayudar
que yo pueda a Castiella     d'esta premia sacar.»

572 El rey e sus varones     muy bien lo reçebieron,
todos con el buen conde     muy grand gozo ovieron,
fasta en su posada     todos con él venieron,
entrante de la puerta     todos se despedieron.

573 A chicos e a grandes     de toda la çibdad
la venida del conde     plazíe de voluntad;
a la reina sola     pesava por verdad,
que avía con él     muy grande enemistad.

574 Avíe en estas cortes     muy gran pueblo sobejo,
después que el conde vino     duró les poquellejo,° very few
ca dio les el buen conde     mucho de buen consejo,
d'ellos en poridad,     d'ellos por buen conçejo.

Venta del caballo y el azor

575 Llevara don Fernando     un mudado açor,
non avía en Castiella     otro tal nin mejor,
otrossí un cavallo     que fuera d'Almançor:

avíe de todo ello el rey muy grand sabor.

576 El rey, de grand sabor de a ellos llevar,
luego dixo al conde que los queríe conprar.
«Non los vendríe, señor, mas mandes los tomar;
vender non vos los quiero, mas quiero vos los dar.»

577 El rey dixo al conde que non los tomaría,
mas açor e cavallo que gelos conpraría,
que d'aquella moneda mill marcos le daría
por açor e cavallo si dar gelos quería.

578 'Avenieron se° amos, fizieron su mercado, agreed
puso quando lo diesse a día señalado;
si el aver non fuesse aquel día pagado
sienpre fues' cada día 'al gallarín° doblado. doubling geometrically

579 Cartas por ABC° partidas y fizieron, copies of same document; oaths
todos los paramentos° allí los escrivieron,
en cabo de la carta los testigos pusieron
quantos a esta merca° delante estovieron. matter

580 Assaz avía el rey buen cavallo conprado,
mas salió le a tres años muy caro el mercado:
con el aver de Françia nunca seríe pagado,
por y perdió el rey Castiella su condado.

668 Fizieron su imagen commo antes dicho era,
a figura del conde, d'essa misma manera;
pusieron le en un carro de muy fuerte madera;
sobido en el carro, entraron en carrera.

669 Todos, chicos e grandes, a la piedra juraron,
commo a su señor assí la aguardaron;
pora ir a Navarra el camino tomaron,
en el primero día a Arlançón llegaron.

670 Desende otro día, essa buena conpaña,

su señor mucho onrado, su seña mucho estraña,° special
passaron Montes d'Oca, una fiera montaña,
solíe ser de los buenos e los grandes d'España.

671 Caveros castellanos, conpaña muy lazrada,
fueron a Bilforado fazer otra albergada;
qual a Dios demandaron ovieron tal posada,
movieron se otro día quando al alborada.° dawn

Encuentro de los castellanos y los fugitivos
672 Enantes que oviessen una legua andado,
salida fue la noche e el día aclarado;
el conde con su dueña veníe mucho lazrado:
quando vio aquella seña, muy mal fue desmayado.

673 La dueña la vio antes e ovo gran pavor;
dixo luego la dueña: «¿Qué faremos, señor?
Veo una grand seña, non sé de qué color,
o es de mi hermano, o es de Almançor.»

674 Fueron en fuerte quexa, non sabíen qué fiziessen,
non veían montaña do meter se pudiessen,
non sabíen con la quexa qué consejo prendiessen,
ca non veíen logar do guarida oviessen.

675 Eran en fuerte quexa, nunca fuera tamaña,
quisieran, si podieran, alçar se a la montaña,
que se asconderían siquiera en cabaña;
fue catando la seña, otrossí la conpaña.

676 Conosçió en las armas commo eran cristianos,
non eran de Navarra nin eran de paganos;
conosçió commo eran de pueblos castellanos,
que ivan a su señor sacar d'agenas° manos. other

677 «Dueña—dixo el conde-, non dedes por end' nada,
será la vuestra mano d'ellos todos besada:
la seña e la gente que vos vedes armada,

aquella es mi seña, e ellos mi mesnada.

678 Oy vos faré señora de pueblos castellanos,
serán todos convusco alegres e pagados,
todos, chicos e grandes, besar vos han las manos,
dar vos he yo en Castiella fortalezas e llanos.»

679 La dueña, que estava triste e desmayada,
fue con aquestas nuevas alegre e pagada;
quando ella vio que era a Castiella llegada,
rendió graçias a Dios, que la avíe bien guiada.

680 Enantes que el su pueblo al conde fues' llegado,
fue delante un cavero e sopo este mandado:
como venía el conde, bien alegre e pagado,
traía a la infante e veníe muy cansado.

681 Las gentes castellanas, quando aquesto oyeron
que veníe su señor e por çierto lo ovieron,
nunca tamaño gozo castellanos ovieron,
todos con alegría a Dios graçias rendieron.

682 Tanto avíen de grand gozo que creer no l' quisieron,
dieron se a correr quant' de rezio pudieron;
enantes que llegassen, al conde conosçieron,
allegaron se a él, en braços le cojieron.

683 Fueron besar las manos todos a su señora,
diziendo, «Somos ricos castellanos agora.
Infante doña Sancha, nasçiestes en buen hora,
por end' vos resçebimos nos todos por señora.

684 Fiziestes nos merçed, nunca otra tal ovíemos,
quanto bien nos fiziestes, contar non lo sabríemos;
. . . . . . . . . . . . . . . . . . . . . . . . . . . . . . . . . . . . . .
si non fuera por vos, cobrar non lo podríemos.

685 Sacastes a Castiella de grand cautividat,

fiziestes grand merçed a toda cristiandat,
mucho pesar a moros, esto es la verdat,
todo esto vos gradesca el Rey de Magestat.»

686 Todos, ella con ellos, con grand gozo lloravan,
tenían que eran muertos e que resuçitavan;
aquel Rey de los çielos bendezíen e laudavan,
el llanto que fazían en grand gozo tornavan.

687 Llegaron de venida todos a Bilforado,
—aquesta villa era en cabo del condado-;
un ferrero° muy bueno demandaron priado:° blacksmith, quickl
el conde don Fernando de fierros fue sacado.

Bodas en Burgos

688 Fueron se pora Burgos quanto ir se podieron,
luego que allí llegaron, grandes bodas fezieron:
non alongaron plazo, bendiçiones prendieron,
todos, grandes e chicos, muy grand gozo ovieron.

689 Alançavan tablados[15] todos los cavalleros,
a tablas° e escaques° jugan los escuderos, backgammon, che
d'otra parte matavan los toros los monteros,° huntsmen
avíe y muchas çítulas° e muchos de violeros.° stringed instrume lute players

690 Fazían muy grand gozo que mayor non podían,
dos bodas, que non una, castellanos fazían:
una, por su señor, que cobrado avían,
otra, por que entramos 'bendiçiones prendían.° they were b

*Libro de Apolonio*
The poem tells the story of Apollonius, King of Tyre, in 2624

[15] **Alançavan tablados**...game that knights play throwing objects to knock down a wooden castle.

lines, in mester de clerecía. He finds his lost daughter Tarsiana after shipwrecks, separations, and strange adventures all characteristics of the Byzantine novel. The exact source of the Spanish version is not known, but its author might have drawn from the Latin or French redactions which were available to him. The book had great influence in Europe and appeared in most of the vernacular literatures in the Middle Ages. Like so many books in 13th century Spain, the *Libro de Apolonio* drew from oriental tales and had a moral message that good always conquers evil.

| | |
|---|---|
| 426 Luego el otro día, de buena madurguada,° | **=madrugada** |
| levantóse la dueña ricamiente adobada;° | dressed |
| priso una viola° buena y bien temprada,° | lute, tuned |
| e sallió al mercado violar° por soldada. | play the lute |
| | |
| 427 Comenzó unos viesos° y unos sones° tales, | songs, tones |
| que trayén grant dulzor y eran naturales;° | excellent |
| finchiénse° de homes apriesa los portales, | filled |
| non les cabién en las plazas, subiénse a los poyales.° | high benches |
| | |
| 428 Cuando con su viola hobo bien solazado, | |
| a sabor de los pueblos hobo asaz cantado, | |
| tornóles a rezar un romance bien rimado,[1] | |
| de la su razón° misma, por ò° había pasado. | story, which |
| | |
| 429 Fizo bien a los pueblos su razón entender, | |
| más valié de cien marcos ese día el loguer;° | earnings |
| fuese el traidor pagando del menester,° | work |
| ganaba por ello soberano° grant haber. | very |
| | |
| 430 Cogieron con la dueña todos muy grant amor, | |
| todos de su facienda° habían grant sabor; | story |
| demás, como sabían que había mal señor, | |
| ayudábanla todos de voluntat mejor. | |
| | |
| 431 El príncipe Antinágora mejor la querié, | |

[1] **Tornóles a rezar ...** She began to tell them a rhymed story

que si su fija fuese más non la amarié;
el día que su voz o su canto non oyé,
conducho° que comiese 'mala pro° le tenié. meal, no benefit

432 Tan bien sopo la dueña su cosa aguisar,
que sabía a su amo la ganancia tornar.
Reyendo y gabando° con el su buen catar, joking
sópose, maguer niña, de follía° quitar. sadness

433 Visco en esta vida un tiempo porlongado,
fasta que a Dios plogo, bien quita de pecado.
Mas dejemos a ella su menester usando,
tornemos en el padre que andaba lazdrado.° suffering

434 A cabo de diez años que la hobo lejada,° left
Recudió° Apolonio con su barba trenzada,° came back, braided
cuidó fallar la fija dueña grant y criada,
mas era la facienda 'otramiente trastornada.° reversed

435 Estrángilo, el de Tarso, cuando lo vio entrar,
perdió toda la sangre con cuita° y con pesar; cares
tornó en su encubierta° a la mujer a rebtar, deceit
mas cuidábase ella con mentiras salvar.

436 Salvó° el rey sus huéspedes y fuelos abrazar, greeted
fue dellos recebido como debía estar.
Cataba por su fija que les dio a criar,
non se podié sin ella reír ni alegrar.

437 «Huéspedes, dijo el rey, ¿qué puede esto seer?
Pésame de mi fija, que non me viene veyer;
querría desta cosa la verdat entender,
que veyo a vos tristes, mala color tener».

438 Recudiól' Dionisa, díjol' grant falsedat:
«Rey, de tu fija, ésta es la verdat:
al corazón le priso mortal enfermedat,
pasada es del sieglo, ésta es la verdat».

439 Por poco Apolonio qu'el seso non perdió,
pasó bien un gran rato qu'él no les recudió,
que tan mala colpada° él nunca recibió. — blow
Paróse endurido,° la cabeza primió.° — afflicted, lowered

440 Después, bien a la tarde, recudió el varón,
demandó a beber agua, que vino non,
tornó contra la huéspeda y díjol' una razón,
que debié a la falsa quebrar el corazón.

441 «Huéspeda, diz, querría más la muerte que la vida,
cuando por míos pecados, la fija he perdida;
la cuita de la madre, que me era venida,
con ésta lo cuidaba aducir a medida.[2]

442 Cuando cuidé agora que podría sanar,
que cuidaba la llagua guarir y encerrar,
he preso otro colpe en ese mismo logar,
non he melezina que me pueda sanar.

443 Pero las sus abtezas° y los sus ricos vestidos, — jewels
poco ha que es muerta, aún non son mollidos;° — moldy
tenérvoslo he a grado que me sean vendidos,
de que fagamos fatilas° los que somos feridos. — bandages

444 Demás quiero ir luego veyer la sepultura,
abrazaré la piedra, maguer frida° y dura; — cold
sobre mi fija Tarsiana plañeré mi rencura,
sabré de su facienda algo por aventura».

445 Cosa endiablada, la burcesa° Dionisa, — citizen
ministra del pecado, fizo grant astrosía:° — evil
fizo un monumento, rico a muy gran guisa,
de un mármol tan blanco como una camisa.

446 Fizo sobre la piedra las letras escrebir:

---

[2] **Aducir a medida** mitigate the suffering in some way

«Aquí fizo Estrángilo a Tarsiana sobollir,° bury
fija de Apolonio, el buen rey de Tir,
que a los XII años avés° pudo sobir». hardly

447 Recibió Apolonio lo que pudo cobrar,
mandólo a las naves a los homnes levar;
fue él al monumento su ventura plorar,
por algunas reliquias del sepulcro tomar.

448 Cuando en el sepulcro cayó el buen varón,
quiso facer su duelo como habié razón;
abajósele el duelo y el mal del corazón,
non pudo echar lágrima por nenguna misión.° reason

449 Tornó contra sí mismo, comenzó de asmar:° consider
«¡Ay, Dios! ¿qué puede esta cosa estar?
Si mi fija Tarsiana yoguiese° en este logar, were lying
non debién los mis ojos 'tan en caro se parar.° refrain from crying

450 Asmo que todo aquesto es mentira probada,
non creyo que mi fija aquí es soterrada;
mas, o me la han vendida o en mal logar echada.
Seya, muerta o viva, a Dios acomendada».

451 Non quiso Apolonio en Tarso más estar,
ca habié recebido en ella gran pesar;
tornóse a sus naves, cansado de llorar,
su cabeza cubierta, no les quiso fablar.

452 Mandóles que moviesen y que pensasen de andar,
la carrera de Tiro pensasen de tomar,
que sus días eran pocos y querrié allá finar,
que entre sus parientes se querrié soterrar.

453 Fueron luego las áncoras a las naves tiradas,
los rimos° aguisados,° las velas enfestadas;° oars, raised, unfurled
tenién viento bueno, las ondas bien pagadas,
fueron de la ribera aína° alongadas. quickly

454 Bien la media carrera o más habién andada,
habían sabrosos vientos, la mar yacié pagada,
fue en poco de rato toda la cosa camiada,° =cambiada
tollióles la carrera que tenién comenzada.

455 De guisa fue revuelta y irada la mar,
que non habién nengún consejo de guiar;
el poder del gobernó° hubiéronlo a desemparar,° rudder, abandon
non cuidaron ningunos de la muerte escapar.

456 Prísolos la tempesta y el mal temporal,
sacólos de caminos el oratge° mortal, storm
echólos su ventura y el Rey Espirital
en la vila que Tarsiana pasaba mucho mal.

457 Fueron en Mitalena los romeros arribados,
habían mucho mal pasado y andaban lazdrados.
'Prisieron luego lengua,° los vientos ya quedados: received news
rendían a Dios gracias porque eran escapados.

458 Ancoraron las naves en ribera del puerto,
encendieron su fuego, que se les era muerto,
enjugaron sus paños, lasos° y del mal puerto; tired
el rey en todo esto no tenié nuyl conhuerto.° encouragement

459 El rey Apolonio, lazdrado caballero,
naciera en tal día y era disantero;° feast day
mandóles que comprasen conducho muy llenero,° abundant
e ficiesen rica fiesta y 'octavario plenero.° a whole week

460 En cabo de la nave, en un rencón destajado,° apart
echóse en un lecho el rey tan deserrado;° depressed
juró que quien le fablase serié mal soldado,° paid
del uno de los pies serié estemado.° cut off

461 Non quisieron los homes sallir de su mandado,
compraron gran conducho de cuanto que fue fallado.

Fue ante de mediodía el comer aguisado,
cualquiere que vinié non era repoyado.° rejected

462 Non osaban ningunos al señor decir nada,
ca habié dura ley puesta y confirmada;
cabdellaron° su cosa, como cuerda° mesnada, carried out, obedi
pensaron de comer la compaña lazdrada.

463 En esto Antinágora, por la fiesta pasar,
salló contra el puerto, queríase deportar.° have a good time
Vio en esta nave tal compaña estar,
entendió que andaban como homnes 'de prestar.° honorable

464 Ellos, cuando lo vieron de tal guisa venir,
levantáronse todos, fuéronlo recebir;
gradescíólo él mucho, non los quiso fallir,° be discourteous
asentóse con ellos por non los desdecir.° scorn

465 Estando a la tabla, en solaz natural,
demandóles cuál era el señor 'del reyal.° encampment
«Yaze, dijieron todos, enfermo muy mal,
e por derecho duelo es perdido non por ál.

466 Menazados nos ha que aquel que li fablare,
de comer nin de beber nada le ementare,° mention
perderá el un pie de los dos que levare,
por aventura amos, si mucho lo porfiare».

467 Demandó quel' dijiesen por cuál ocasión
cayó en tal tristicia y en tal ocasión.
Contáronle la estoria y toda la razón,
quel' dicién Apolonio de 'la primera sazón.° beginning

468 Díjoles él: «Como yo creyo, si non soy trastornado,
tal nombre suele Tarsiana haber mucho usado.
A lo que me saliere, ferme quiero osado;
decirle he que me semeja 'villano descoraznado».° unfeeling peasant

469 Mostráronle los homnes el logar on yazía,
que com el homne bueno a todos mucho placié;
violo con fiera barba que los pechos le cobrié,
tóvolo por fazaña porque atal facié.

470 Díjol': «Dios te salve, Apolonio amigo,
oí fablar de tu facienda, vengo fablar contigo.
Si tú me conoscieses, habriés placer comigo,
ca non ando pidiendo nin soy homne mendigo».

471 Volvióse Apolonio un poco en el escaño,
si de los suyos fuese recibría mal daño;
mas, cuando de tal guisa vio homne extraño,
no le recudió nada, enfogó° el sosaño.° — he repressed, anger

472 Afincólo el otro, non le quiso dejar,
homne era de precio, queríalo esforzar.
Dijo: «Apolonio, mal te sabes guardar,
debiéste de otra guisa contra mí mesurar.° — behave

473 Señor soy desta villa, mía es para mandar,
dícenme Antinágora, si me oíste nombrar;
cabalgué de la villa y sallíme a deportar,
las naves que yacién por el puerto a mirar.

474 Cuando toda la hobe la ribera andada,
paguéme desta tu nave, vila bien adobada;° — outfitted
salliéronme a recebir toda la tu mesnada,
recebí su convido, yanté en su posada.° — camp

475 Vi homnes enseñados, compaña mesurada,
la cocina bien rica, la mesa bien abondada;
demandé que cuál era el señor de la albergada,
dijéronme tu nombre y tu vida lazdrada.

476 Mas si tú a mí quisieres escuchar y creyer,
saldriés desta tiniebra,° la mi cibdat veyer, — darkness
veriés por ella cosas que habriés gran placer,

por que podriés del duelo gran partida perder.

477 Debiés en otra cosa poner tu voluntat,
que te puede Dios facer aún gran piedat;
que cobrarás tu pérdida, cuido que será verdat,
perderás esta tristicia y esta crueldat».

478 Recudió Apolonio y tornó ha él la faz,
díjol': «Quienquier que seyas, amigo, ve en patz.° =paz
Gradézcotelo mucho, fecísteme buen solaz,
entiendo que me dices buen consejo asaz.

479 Mas soy por mis pecados de tal guisa llagado
que el corazón me siento todo atravesado;° pierced through
desque vevir non puedo y soy de todo desfriado,° bored
de cielo nin de tierra veyer non he cuidado».

480 Partióse Antinágora d'él mal deserrado,° afflicted
veyé por 'mal achaque° homne bueno dañado; sad reason
tornó a la mesnada fieramiente conturbado,
díjoles que el homne bueno fuert era deserrado.

481 Non pudo comedir° nin asmar tal manera reflect
por cual guisa pudiés' meterlo en la carrera:
«Só en sobejana cuita, más que yer° non era; yesterday
nunca en tal fui, por la creenza vera.

516 Tres demandas° tengo que son asaz rafeces.° riddles, easy
Por tan poca de cosa, por Dios, non empereces,° be lazy
si demandar quisieres, yo te daré las veces».° chances

517 «Nunca, ditz el rey, vi cosa tan porfiosa,° persistent person
si Dios me benediga, que eres mucho enojosa.
Si más de tres dijeres, tenert'é por mintrosa,
non te esperaría más por ninguna cosa».

518 «De dentro soy vellosa° y de fuera raída,° hairy, smooth
siempre trayo en seno mi crin° bien escondida; mane

ando de mano en mano, tráenme escarnida,
cuando van a yantar negún non me convida».

519 «Cuando en Pentápolin entré desbaratado,° — impoverished
si non fuese por ésa andaría lazdrado;
fui del rey Architrastres por ella honrado,
si no, non me hobiera a yantar convidado».

520 «Nin soy negro nin blanco, nin he color certero,
nin lengua con que fable un proverbio señero,
mas sé rendar° a todos, siempre soy refertero,° — give, quarrelsome
valo en el mercado apenas un dinero».

521 «Dalo por poco precio el bufón° el espejo; — peddlar
nin es rubio nin negro, nin blanco nin bermejo;
el que en él se cata veye su mismo cejo,
a altos y a bajos riéndelos° 'en parejo».° — makes them, alike

522 «Cuatro hermanas somos, so un techo moramos,
corremos en parejo, siempre nos segudamos,
andamos 'cada 'l día,° nunca nos alcanzamos,° — every day, reach
yacemos abrazadas, nunca nos ayuntamos».° — meet

523 «Rafez es de contar aquesta tu cuestión,
que las cuatro hermanas las cuatro ruedas son;
dos a dos enlazadas, tíralas un timón,° — rudder
andan y non se ayuntan en ninguna sazón».

524 Quísol' aún otra pregunta demandar,
asaz lo quiso ella 'de cuenta° engañar; — in the story
mas sopo cuántos eran Apolonio contar,
díjol' que se dejase y que estoviés' en paz.

525 «Amiga, dijo, debes de mí seyer pagada,
de cuanto tú pidiste bien te he abondada,° — granted
et te quiero aún añader en soldada;
vete luego tu vía, mas non me digas nada.

526 Mas por ninguna cosa non te lo sofriría,
querriésme, bien lo veyo, tornar en alegría,
terniélo a escarnio toda mi compañía;
demás, de mi palabra, por ren no me toldría».

527 Nunca tanto le pudo decir nin predicar,
que en otra leticia° le pudiese tornar. — joy
Con grant cuita que hobo non sopo qué asmar,
fuele amos los brazos al cuello a echar.

528 Hóbose ya con esto el rey a ensañar,
hobo con fellonía° el brazo a tornar, — anger
hóbole una ferida en el rostro a dar,
tanto que las narices le hobo ensangrentar.

529 La dueña fue irada, comenzó de llorar,
comenzó sus rencuras todas ha ementar.
Bien querrié Antinágora grant haber a dar,
que non fuese entrado en aquella yantar.

530 Dicía: «¡Ay, mezquina, en mal hora fui nada!
Siempre fue mi ventura de andar ahontada;° — shamed
por las tierras ajenas ando mal sorostrada,° — insulted
por bien y por servicio, prendo mala soldada.

531 ¡Ay, madre Luciana, si mal fado hubiste,
a tu fija Tarsiana mejor non lo diste;
peligraste° sobre mar y de parto moriste, — ventured
ante quen parieses afogarme° debiste! — drowned

532 Mi padre Apolonio non te pudo prestar,° — help
a fonsario° sagrado non te pudo levar; — burial place
en ataúd muy rico echóte en la mar,
non sabemos del cuerpo dó pudo arribar.

533 A mí tobo° a vida por tanto pesar tomar, — =tuvo
diome a Dionisa de Tarso a criar;
por derecha envidia quísome fer matar.

Si entonces fuese muerta non me debiera pesar.

534 Hobe por mis pecados la muerte a excusar,° escape
los que me acorrieron no me quisieron dejar,
vendiéronme a homne que non es de prestar,
que me quiso el alma y el cuerpo dañar.

535 Por la gracia del cielo, que me quiso valer,
non me pudo ninguno fasta aquí vencer;
diéronme homnes buenos tanto de su haber,
por que pague mi amo de todo mío loguer.° earnings

536 Entre las otras cuitas ésta m'es la peyor:
a homne que buscaba servicio y amor,
hame ahontada a tan gran deshonor.
¡Debría tan gran soberbia pesar al Criador!

537 ¡Ay, rey Apolonio, de ventura pesada,
si sopieses de tu fija tan mal es ahontada,
pesar habriés y duelo, y sería bien vengada,
mas cuido que non vives, onde non soy yo buscada!

538 De padre nin de madre, por míos graves pecados,
non sabré el ciminterio do fueron soterrados;
tráyenme como a bestia siempre por los mercados,
de peyores de mí faciendo sus mandados».

539 Revisco° Apolonio, plógol' de corazón, revived
entendió las palabras que vinién por razón.
Tornóse contra ella, demandol' si mintié o non,
preguntól' por paraula° de grado el varón: **=palabra**

540 «Dueña, si Dios te deje al tu padre veyer,
perdóname el fecho, dart'é de mío haber;
erré con felonía, puédeslo bien creyer,
ca nunca fiz tal yerro nin lo cuidé facer.

541 Demás, si me dijiese, ca puédete membrar,

e nombre del ama que te solié criar,
podríemosnos por ventura amos alegerar,
yo podría la fija, tú el padre cobrar."

542 Perdonólo la dueña, perdió el mal taliento,
dio a la demanda leyal recudimiento:
"La ama, dice, de que siempre menguada me siento,
dijiéronlo Licórides, sepades que no vos miento."

543 Vio bien Apolonio que andaba carrera,
entendió bien senes° falla° que la su fija era; without, doubt
salló fuera del lecho luego de la primera
diciendo: "¡Valme Dios, que eres vertut vera!"

544 Prísola en sus brazos con muy grant alegría,
diciendo: "Ay, mi fija, que yo por vos muría,
agora he perdido la cuita que había.
Fija, non amanesció para mí tan buen día.

545 Nunca este día no lo cuidé veyer,
nunca en los míos brazos yo vos cuidé tener.
Hobe por vos tristicia, agora he placer;
Siempre habré por ello a Dios que gradecer."

## *Libro de Alexandre*

The *Libro de Alexandre*, written in *mester de clerecía*, from the first half of the 13th century narrates the life of Alexander the Great. It is composed of 2675 strophes and 10,500 lines. It draws heavily upon the knowledge surviving from the ancient world, and includes so much information that it is a veritable encyclopedia of medieval knowledge. Geography, history, astronomy, human customs, and animal behavior are all to be found in this work. The author, not content to deal with the life of Alexander, relates apologues and fables, includes letters supposedly exchanged between famous personages (for example Aristotle and Alexander), inserts long didactic passages, and presents allegorical treatments of many subjects. The book represents the urge of the 13th century to teach and to offer all that was available in the way of knowledge.

*Libro de Alexandre*

1 Señores, se° quisierdes 'mío serviçio prender,° — **=si,** accept my work
Querríavos de grado servir de mío mester;° — work
deve de lo que sabe ome largo seer,
si non, podrié en culpa e en riebto caer[3]

2 Mester° trago hermoso, 'non es de joglaría,° — verse, different from that of minstrels; perfect
mester es 'sen pecado,° ca es de clerecía:[4]
fablar° cunado° por la cuaderna vía,[5] — to compose, poem
a síllavas cuntadas, ca es grant maestría.° — skill

3 Qui° oír lo quisier', a todo mío creer,[6] — **=quien**
avrá de mí solaz,° 'en cabo° grant plazer, — entertainment, in the end

---

[3] **Deve de...** *a man must be generous with what he knows, if not he could be blamed and commit a crime.*

[4] **Que es....** *because it is a work of someone learned*

[5] **Cuaderna vía...**Cuaderna vía or the four-fold way is a verse form of full-rhyme consonant quatrains with fourteen syllable lines and a cæsura, or pause, in the middle of each line.

[6] **A todo...** *as I believe completely*

aprendrá bonas gestas° que sepa retraer,° — stories of deeds, tell
averlo an por ello muchos a conocer.

4 Non vos quiero grant prólogo nen
grandes novas° fazer, — news
luego° a la materia me vos quiero coger;[7] — immediately
el Crïador nos lexe° bien apresos° seer, — **=deje**, informed
si en algo pecarmos,° 'Él nos deñe valer.° — err, may He help us

5 Quiero leer un livro de un rey noble, pagano ← Alexander
que fue de gran esforçio,° 'de coraçón loçano,° — courage, valiant
conquistó tod' el mundo, 'metiól' so su mano;° — put it under his power
Terné se lo comptiere, que soe bon escrivano.[8]

Canto de mayo

1950 El mes era de mayo, el tienpo glorïoso,
cuando fazen las aves un solaz deleitoso;
son cubiertos los prados° de vestido hermoso: — meadows
da suspiros la dueña la que non ha esposo.

1951 Tienpo dulçe e sabroso pora bastir° casamientos, — arrange
porque lo tenpran° las flores e los sabrosos vientos: — moderate
cantan las donçelletas° suyos mayos° 'a conventos,° — maidens, May songs, in groups; tidings
fazen unas a otras buenos pronunçiamientos.°

1952 Caen en el sereno° las buenas ruçiadas,° — evening, dew
entran en la flor las mieses, ca son ya espigadas,[9]
fazen las dueñas triscas,° en camisas delgadas: — dances
estonçes casan algunos que después 'se mesan las barvas.° — regret it

1953 Andan moças e viejas 'bueltas en amores,° — around in love
van a coger° por la siesta a los prados las flores, — to gather

[7] **A la...** *I want to bring the story to you.*
[8] **Terné se...** *If I achieve this, I will be a good writer.*
[9] **Entran en...** *the crops have gone to seed because the fields have been gleaned*

dicen unas a otras buenos pronunçiadores° — secrets
e aquellos 'más tiernos° tiénense por mejores. — younger

1954 Los días son bien grandes,° los canpos reverdidos,° — long, very green
son los paxarillos° de mal pello sallidos,° — =**pajarillos**, moulted
los távanos° que muerden° non son aún venidos, — horseflies, bite
luchan° los moçüelos° en bragas,° sin vestidos. — wrestle, =**mozuelos**, underwear

1955 El rey Alixandre, 'un cuerpo tan acabado,° — a man so perfect
'a la sabor del tienpo, que era tan tenprado,° — because of the fine weather; held court,
'fizo corte° general con coraçón pagado:° — happy man, =**Persia**, gathered
non fue varón° en Presia° que no fuese allí juntado.°

1956 A menos que supiésedes sobre 'qué fue la cosa,° — what was happening
bien podríedes tener la razón por mintrosa,[10]
mas quiérovos dexar° toda la otra cosa, — to tell
descobrirvos he el testo, enpeçarvos la glosa.[11]

1957 Quiérovos brevement dezir el brevïario,° — story
non vos quiero 'de un poco° fer° 'luengo sermonario:° — short, =**hacer,** long sermon
quiero casar el rëy con la filla de Dario,
con Risane[12] la genta,° 'fenbra de grant contrario.° — beautiful, a lady, ill-tempered woman

1958 Las bodas fueron fechas ricas e abondadas,° — abundant
andavan las carreras° 'de conducho poblados:° — streets, full of food
sedién° noches e días las mesas aguisadas,° — were, set
de tovajas° cubiertas e conducho cargadas.° — napkins, heavy

1959 Avié grant abondança de carnes e de pescados,
de toros e de vacas, de caças°e de venados:° — game, deer
aduzién° los conduchos todos bien adobados,° — brought, prepared
a cada uno con sus salsas° le eran presentados. — sauces

---

[10] **Bien podríedes...** *you could have been mistaken*

[11] **Descobrirvos he...** *I will tell you the story and begin to gloss (explain) it.*

[12] **Dario con...** Persian king Darius III who was defeated for the second time by Alexander in 331 B.C., Roxasana or Roxena, in literature the daughter of Darius III.

1960 Eran grandes e muchas 'las mudas e los dones,° gift exchanges
non querien los juglares çendales nin çiclatones:[13]
d'éstos avié allí muchos que fazién diversos sones,° songs
otros que meneavan° ximios 'e çaratones.° led, men with masks

1961 Duraron estas bodas 'quinze días conplidos,° a full two weeks
eran todos los días los tablados feridos,[14]
tenién que de la guerra non eran mal sallidos,
teniénse los varones de Persia por guaridos.[15]

2305 Una façaña suelen las gentes retraer,
non yaze en escripto, es grave° de creer; hard
si es verdat o non yo 'non he í que fer,° I'm not to say
Moguer° non la quiero 'en olvido poner.° but, forgotten

2306 Dizen que por saber qué fazen los pescados,
cómo biven los chicos entre los más granados,° big
fizo arca° de vidrio con muzos° bien cerrados; chest, seams
metió se él de dentro con dos de sus criados.

2307 Éstos fueron captados °de todos los mejores, selected
por tal que non oviessen° dono° de traidores; receive, taint
ca que el o que ellos avrién aguardadores,° escorts
non farién a su guisa los malos reboltores.° conspirators

2308 Fue de buena betume° la casa aguisada,° tar, caulked
fue con buenas cadenas bien presa° e calcada;° held, provided
fue con pliegos° bien firmes a las naves plegada,° ropes, bound
que fundir° non se podiesse e 'soviesse colgada °. sink, be suspended

2309 Mandó que lo dexassen quinze días folgar,° rest

---

[13] Normally minstrels asked for food and clothing as remuneration for their performance but the food and gifts were so abundant that they did not even ask for fine silk garments.
[14] **Tablados feridos...** these are wooden scaffolds against which knights hurled their lances as a form of sport.
[15] **Tenién que...** *they felt that they had come out well in the battle, the men from Persia considered themselves well protected.*

las naves con tod esto pensassen de andar;
assaz podrié 'en esto° saber e mesurar — in this time
e meter en escripto los secretos del mar.

2310 La cuba° 'fue echada° en que el rey yazié, — chest, thrown over board
a los unos pesava, a los otros plazié;
bien cuidavan° algunos que nunca end °saldrié, — thought, from it
mas destajado° era que en mar non morrié. — destined

2311 Andava el buen rey en su casa cerrada,
sedié grant corazón° en angosta° posada;° — valor, narrow, place
vedié toda la mar de pescados poblada,
non es bestia en sieglo que no fues *í* trobada.° — found

2312 Non bive en el mundo ninguna criatura
que non cría° el mar su semejant figura;° — rear, form
'traen enemiztades° entre sí por natura, — there are enemies
los fuertes a los flacos 'dan les mala ventura.° — they attack them

2313 Estonz vió el rey en aquellas andadas° — travels
cómo 'echan los unos a los otros celadas;° — lie in wait for each other; lured
dizen que ende fueron presas i sossacadas,°
fueron desent° acá en el sieglo usadas. — later

2314 Tanto se acogién' al rey los pescados — came
como si los oviesse por armas subyugados;
vinién fasta la cuba todos cabez colgados,° — hanging down
tremién° todos ant él como moços mojados.° — trembled, wet

2315 Jurava Alixandre por el su diestro lado
que nunca fue de omnes mejor aconpañado;
de los pueblos del mar 'tovo se° por pagado, — considered himself
contava que avié grant emperio ganado. (...)

2329 Pesó al Criador que crió la Natura;
ovo de Alixandre saña° e grant rencura;° — anger, resentment
dixo, "Este lunático° que non 'cata mesura° — madman, practice

yo-l tornaré° el gozo todo en amargura. moderation; turn

2330 "Él sopo° la soberbia de los peces judgar, **=supo**
la que en sí tenié non la sopo asmar;° judge
omne que tan bien sabe judicios de librar° give
por qual judizio dio por tal deve pasar."[16]

2331 Cuand vío la Natura que al Señor pesava,
ovo grant alegría, maguer triste andava;
movió se de las nuves, de dó siempre morava;
por mostrar su rencura '¡cuál quebranto tomaba!° how afflicted she was

2332 Bien veyé° que por omne nunca serié vengada, saw
ca moros e judíos temién la su espada;
asmó° que le echassen una mala celada: plotted
buscar como le diessen 'collación enconada.° poisoned meal

2333 Pospuso sus labores, las que solié° usar, **=solía**
por nuevas creaturas las almas guerrear;
descendió al infierno 'su pleito recabdar,° state her case
por al rey Alixandre mala carrera° dar. journey

---

[16] **Por cual...** *because of giving this judgment, he must be judged*

## Gonzalo de Berceo

Gonzalo de Berceo was born toward the end of the 12th century in the region known as La Rioja in the hamlet of Berceo, which exists today. He was still alive in the early years of the 1250's. He is the first Castilian writer whose name we know, proclaiming his identity at a time when authors preferred to remain anonymous. Part of his education was received in the Benedictine monastery in San Millán de la Cogolla, which is still active and thriving. Berceo was not a monk but rather a secular priest. His work was for the most part administrative and legalistic. It is likely that he served the abbot as his notary.

Berceo's works can be classified according to form and content into four groups: 1) poems concerned with the Virgin Mary—*Los milagros de Nuestra Señora*, the *Loores de Nuestra Señora*, and the *Duelo que fizo la Virgen*; 2) the lives of local saints—*Vida de San Millán*, *Vida de Santo Domingo de Silos*, *Vida de Santa Oria*, and the unfinished *Martyrio de San Laurencio*; 3) two doctrinal poems and 4) three hymns.

Berceo's poems are the first in Castilian written in a metrical form known as the *mester de clercía*, a learned form of poetry of fourteen syllable monorhymed quatrains with a caesura after the seventh syllable.

*Los milagros de Nuestra Señora* is a collection of twenty-five miracle stories of the Virgin Mary preceded by an allegorical introduction. Each story tells the plight of a devotee of the Virgin and his or her way out of this circumstance with Her help. The end of many of these stories encourages the audience's devotion to the Virgin who is the help and key to salvation. Berceo uses the we form of the verb in these stanzas, thereby including himself in his own advice.

### *Los milagros de Nuestra Señora*

MILAGRO XX
El monje beodo° — drunk

461. De un otro miraclo° vos querría contar — **=milagro**

Que cuntió° en un monge° de 'ábito reglar:° — happened, =**monje**,
Quísolo el diablo durament° espantar, — religious order; really
Mas la Madre gloriosa sópogelo° vedar.° — =**se lo supo**, prevent

462. 'De que° fo° enna° orden, 'bien de que° fo noviçio — since, =**fue**, =**en la**, e
Amó a la Gloriosa° siempre façer serviçio: — since; Virgin Mary
Quitándose° de follía° de fablar en forniçio.° — avoided, folly, fornica-
Pero ovo° 'en cabo° de caer en un viçio. — **tion**; =**tuvo**, in the
463. Entró enna bodega° un día por ventura,° — wine cellar, chance
Bebió mucho del vino, esto fo sin mesura,° — moderation
Embebdóse° el locco, 'issió de° su cordura,° — he got drunk, lost, san
Iogó° hasta las viésperas° sobre la tierra dura. — -ity; he lay, vespers

464. Bien a ora de vísperas el sol bien enflaquido,° — weak
Recordó° malamientre andaba estordido:° — awoke, dazed
Issió contra la claustra hascas° sin nul sentido: — almost
Entendíengelo todos que bien avíe° bebido. — =**había**

465. Peroque° en sus piedes non se podíe tener,° — although, stand
Iba a la eglesia° commo solía façer , — =**iglesia**
Quísoli el diablo 'zancajada poner,° — trip
Ca bien se lo cuidaba° rehezmientre° vençer. — intended, easily

466. En figura de toro que es escalentado,° — raging
Cavando° con los piedes, el çeio° demudado,° — pawing, face, angry
Con fiera cornadura° sannoso° e yrado° — horns, angry, irate
Paróseli delante el traydor probado.

467. Façíeli gestos malos la cosa diablada,° — devilish
Que li metríe los cuernos por media la corada° — entrails
Priso° el omne° bueno muy mala espantada,° — took, =**hombre**, fright
Mas valiól° la Gloriosa reyna coronada. — helped him

468. Vino Sancta María con 'ábito onrrado,° — noble dress
Tal que de omne vivo non seríe apreçiado,
Methíeselis° in medio a él e al peccado,° — She put herself, devil
El toro tan superbio fue luego amansado.° — tamed

| | |
|---|---|
| 469. Menazóli° la duenna con la falda del manto,° | threatened him, cape |
| Esto fo pora elli° un muy mal quebranto,° | **=él**, punishment |
| Fusó° e desterrósse° façiendo muy grant planto,° | fled, left, complaint |
| Fincó° en paz el monge, graçias al Padre sancto. | remained |
| | |
| 470. Luego a poco rato, a pocas depassadas° | steps |
| Ante que empezasse a sobir ennas gradas,° | stairs |
| Cometiólo° 'de cabo° con 'figuras pesadas,° | attacked, again, threatening |
| En manera de can° 'firiendo colmelladas.° | faces; dog, striking with fangs |
| | |
| 471. Viníe de mala guisa,° los dientes regannados,° | way, bared |
| En çeio muy turbio,° los oios remellados° | angry, wide open |
| Por ferlo° todo piezas, espaldas e costados:° | **=hacerlo**, tear him, sides; wretched one |
| Mesiello,° diçíe elli, graves son mis pecados. | |
| | |
| 472. Vien° se cuidó el monge seer despedazado,° | **=bien**, torn to pieces |
| Sedíe en 'fiera cueta,° era mal dessarrado,° | great trouble, disturbed |
| Mas valiól la Gloriosa, es cuerpo adonado,° | gifted |
| Commo fizo el toro, fo el can segudado.° | driven away |
| | |
| 473. Entrante de la eglesia enna somera° grada | highest |
| Cometiólo de cabo la terçera vegada° | time |
| En forma de león, una bestia dubdada,° | fearsome |
| Que traíe tal fereza° que non seríe asmada.° | ferocity, imagined |
| | |
| 474. Allí cuidó el monge que era devorado, | |
| Ca vidíe por verdat un fiero encontrado:° | encounter |
| Peor li era esto que todo lo passado, | |
| Entre su voluntad° maldiçíe° al peccado. | mind, cursed |
| | |
| 475. Diçíe: valme Gloriosa madre Sancta María, | |
| Válame la tu graçia oi° en esti día, | **=hoy** |
| Ca só en grant afruento,° en maior non podría: | danger |
| Madre, non 'pares mientes° a la mi grant follía | look at |
| | |
| 476. Abes° podió el monge la palabra cumplir | scarcely |
| veno Sancta María commo solíe venir | |
| Con un palo en mano pora león ferir:° | strike |

Methióselis delante, empezó a deçir:

477. Don falso alevoso,° 'non vos escarmentades° — traitor, you do not lea[rn] a lesson
Mas io vos daré oi lo que vos demandades:
Ante lo compraredes° que daquend° vos vayades, — you will pay, from he[re]
Con quien volvistes° guerra quiero que lo sepades. — waged

478.Empezóli a dar de grandes palancadas,° — blows with a stick
Non podíen las menudas escuchar las grannadas,[17]
Lazraba° el león 'a buenas dinaradas,° — suffered, a lot
Non ovo en sus días las cuestas tan sovadas.° — beaten

479. Diçíel la buena duena: don falso traydor
Que siempre en mal andas, eres de mal sennor:
Si más aquí te prendo° en esti derredor,° — catch, place
De lo que oi prendes aun prendrás peor.

480. Desfizo° la figura, empezó a foír, — vanished
Nunqua más fo osado al monge escarnir,° — mock
Ante passó grant tiempo que podiesse guarir,° — be cured
Plógoli° al diablo quando lo mandó ir. — pleased

481. El monge que por todo esto avía pasado,
De la carga° del vino non era bien folgado,° — weight, recovered
Que vino e que miedo avíenlo tan sovado,
Que tornar non podió a su lecho usado.

482. La Reyna preçiosa e de preçioso fecho° — deed
Prísolo por la mano, levólo por al lecho,
Cubriólo con la manta e con el sobrelecho,° — bedspread
Púsol so° la cabeza el cabezal° derecho. — under, pillow

483. Demás° quando lo ovo en su lecho echado° — also, lying down
Sanctiguól° con su diestra e fo bien sanctiguado: — she made the sign of
Amigo, díssol, fuelga,° ca eres muy lazrado, — cross over him; rest
Con un pocco que duermas luego serás folgado.

[17] **Non podíen las...** *The big blows drowned out the small ones.*

484. Pero esto te mando, afirmes te lo digo,
Cras° mannana demanda a fulán° mi amigo, — tomorrow, so and so
Conffiéssate con elli e serás bien comigo,
Ca es muy buen omne, e 'dart ha° buen castigo.° — **=te dará**, penance

485. Quiero io que mi vía° salvar algún cuitado,° — see, suffering soul
Esto es mi deliçio,° mi offiçio° usado:° — delight, work, usual
Tú finca bendicho° a Dios acomendado;° — blessed, commended
Mas non se te oblide° lo que te e° mandado. — forget, **=he**

486. Dísol el omne bueno: duenna, 'fe que debedes,° — by your word
Vos que en mí fiçiestes atán grandes merçedes,
Quiero saber quí sodes,° o qué nomne avedes,° — **=sois**, **=tenéis**
Ca° io gano en ello, vos nada non perdedes. — because

487. Disso la buena duenna: seas bien sabidor,° — informed
Io so la que parí° al vero° Salvador, — gave birth to, true
Que por salvar el mundo sufrió muert e dolor,
Al que façen los ángeles serviçio e onor.

488. Disso el omne bono: esto es de creer:
De ti podríe, sennora, esta cosa naçer:
Dessáteme,° sennora, los tus piedes tanner° — let me, touch
Nunqua en esti sieglo° veré tan grant plaçer. — world

489. Contendié° el bon omne, queríesse levantar, — insisted
Por 'fincar los inoios,° los piedes li besar; — kneel
Mas la Virgo Gloriosa non lo quiso esperar,
Tollióseli° de oios,° ovo él grant pesar. — withdrew, **=ojos**

490. Non la podíe a ella por do iba veer,
Mas vedíe grandes lumnes° redor ella arder:° — lights, shine
Non la podíe por nada de los oios toller,° — take
Façíe° muy 'grant derecho,° ca fízol grant plaçer.° — acted, rightly, favor

491. Otro día mannana venida la luz clara
Buscó al omne bono que ella li mandara:
Fizo su confessión con umildosa° cara, — humble

Non li çeló° un punto de quanto que pasara. — hide

492. El maestro al monge fecha la confessión,<br>
Dioli conseio bueno, dioli absoluçión,<br>
Methió Sancta María en él tal bendiçión,<br>
Que valió más por elli toda essa congregaçión.

493. Si ante fora bono, fo desende° meior: — from then on<br>
A la sancta reyna Madre del Criador<br>
Amóla siempre mucho, fízol siempre onor:<br>
Feliz fo el que ella cogió en su amor.

494. El otro omne bono non lo sabríe nomnar,<br>
Al que Sancta María lo mandó maestrar:° — confess<br>
Cogió amor tan firme de tanto la amar<br>
Que dessarsíe° por ella la cabeza cortar. — would allow

495. Todas las otras gentes legos° e coronados,° — lay, tonsured<br>
Clérigos e canonges° e los escapulados,° — canons, monks<br>
Fueron de la Gloriosa todos enamorados<br>
Que sabe acorrer° tan bien a los cuitados. — help

496. Todos la bendiçíen e todos la laudaban,<br>
Las manos e los oios a ella los alzaban,<br>
Retraíen° los sos fechos, las sos laudes cantaban, — recounted<br>
Los días e las noches en esso las passaban.

497. Sennores e amigos, muévanos esta cosa,<br>
Amemos e laudemos todos a la Gloriosa,<br>
Non echaremos° mano en cosa tan preçiosa — lay<br>
Que también nos acorra en ora periglosa.° — **=peligrosa**

498. Si nos bien la sirviéremos, 'quequiere quel° pidamos — whatever of her<br>
Todo lo ganaremos, bien seguro seamos:<br>
Aquí lo entendremos bien ante que muramos,<br>
Lo que allí methiéremos que bien lo empleamos.

499. Ella nos dé su graçia e su bendiçión

Guárdenos de peccado e de tribulaçión,
De nuestras liviandades° ganemos remissión, — follies
Que no vaian las almas nuestras en perdiçión.° — damnation

MILAGRO XXI
La abadesa encinta

500. Sennores e amigos companna 'de prestar° — noble
De que Dios se vos quiso traer a est logar,
Aun si me quissiéssedes un poco esperar,
En un otro miraclo vos querría fablar.

501. De un otro miraclo vos querría contar
Que fizo la Gloriosa estrella de la mar:
Si oírme quisiéredes, bien podedes iurar
Que de meior boccado° non podríedes tastar. — morsel

502. Ennos tiempos derechos° que corría° la verdat, — righteous, was wide-spread
Que non diçíen por nada los omnes falsedat,
Estonz vivíen 'a buenas,° viníen a vegedat,° — happily, old age
Vedíen a sus trasnietos° en séptima edat.° — great grandchildren, generation

503. Façíe Dios por los omnes miraclos cutiano,° — daily
Ca non queríe ninguno mentir a su xpiano,° — Christian neighbor
Avíen 'tiempos derechos° ivierno e verano, — fair weather
Semeiaba el sieglo° que todo era plano.° — world, simple

504. Si pecaban los omnes, façíen bien penitençia,
Perdonábalis luego Dios toda la malquerençia,° — ill will
'Avíen con° Jesu Xpo° toda su atenençia:° — put in, Christ, friendship;
Quiérovos dar a esto una buena sentençia.° — example

505. De una abbatissa° vos quiero fer conseia,° — **=abadesa**, story
Que peccó 'en buen punto° commo a mí semeia, — at a propitious time
Quissiéronli sus duennas 'revolver mala çeia,° — to frown on her
Mas nol empedeçieron° 'valient una erveia.° — harm, a bean's worth

506. En esta abbadesa iaçíe mucha bondat,
Era de grant recabdo° e de grant caridat, — judgment
Guiaba su conviento de toda voluntat,
Vivient segunt regla en toda onestat.° — chastity

507. Pero la abbadesa cadió° una vegada, — fell
Fizo una locura que es mucho vedada,° — prohibited
Pisó° 'por su ventura° yerba fuert enconada,° — stepped, by chance,
Quando 'bien se catido,° falló se embargada.° — poisonous; looked ca fully; pregnant

508. Fol creçiendo el vientre 'en contra° las terniellas,° — to, breasts
Fuéronseli façiendo peccas° ennas masiellas,° — freckles, cheeks
Las unas eran grandes, las otras más poquiellas,
Ca ennas primerizas° caen° estas cosiellas. — first pregnancies, hap pen

509. Fo de las companneras la cosa entendida,
Non se podíe çelar° la flama ençendida, — hide
Pesaba a las unas que era mal caída,
Mas plaçíelis sobrio° a la otra partida. — very much

510. Apremiábalas mucho, teníelas ençerradas,° — was strict, cloistered
E non les consintíe fer las cosas vedadas° — forbidden:
Querríen veerla muerta las locas malfadadas,° — unhappy
Cunte° a los prelados° esto a las vegadas. — happens, superiors

511. Vidieron que non era cosa de encobrir,° — to be covered up
Si non, podríe de todas el diablo reír:
Embiaron al bispo por su carta deçir
Que non las visitaba, e debíelo padir.° — to do it

512.Entendió el bispo enna mesagería,° — letter
O que avíen contienda,° o fiçieron follía: — problem
Vino fer° su offiçio,° visitar la mongía,° — carry out, duty, conve
Ovo a entender toda la pletesía.° — business

513.Deiemos al obispo folgar° en su posada,° — rest, house
Finque en paz e duerma elli con su mesnada:° — household
Digamos nos que fizo la duenna embargada,

Ca sabía que otro día sería porfazada.° — harshly accused

514.Çerca de la su cámara° do solía albergar,° — room, lodge
Tenía un apartado,° un apuesto° logar: — retreat, convenient
Era su oratorio, en que solía orar,° — to pray
De la Gloriosa era vocación° el altar. — dedicated

515.Y tenía la imagen de la Sancta Reigna,
La que fue para el mundo salut e mediçina:
Teníala afeytada° de codrada° cortina,° — adorned, red, veil
Ca por todos 'en cabo° essa fue su madrina. — after all

516.Sabía que otro día sería mal porfazada,
Non avía alguna escusa a la cosa probada,
Tomó un buen conseio la bienaventurada,
Esto fue maravilla commo fue acordada.° — prudent

517.Debatióse° en tierra delante el altar, — prostrated
Cató a la imagen, empezó a llorar:
Valme, dixo, Gloriosa, estrella de la mar:
Ca non e° nul conseio queme pueda prestar. — =he

518.Madre, bien lo leemos, díçelo la escriptura,
Que eres de tal gratia° e de tan grant mesura — =gracia
Que qui de voluntat te diçe su rencura,° — fear
Tú luego li acorres en toda su ardura.° — anxiety

519.Entró al oratorio ella sola sennera,
Non demandó consigo ninguna compannera,
Paróse desarrada° luego de la primera;° — helpless, in her first
Mas Dios e su ventura abriéronli carrera. — prayer

520. Tú acorriste,° sennora, a Theóphilo[18] que
era desesperado — helped

---

[18] **Theóphilo**according to legend sold his soul to the Devil and repents. He asked Holy Mary to retrieve the letter he had signed from Hell. This story is recounted in Miracle 25.

Que de su sangre fizo carta con el peccado:° — the devil
Por el tu buen conseio fue reconçiliado,
Onde todos los omnes 'te lo tienen a grado.° — give you thanks
521. Tú acorriste, sennora, a la Egiptiana,[19]
Que fue peccador mucho, ca fue muger liviana:° — loose
Sennora benedicta, de qui todo bien mana,° — flows
Dame algún conseio ante de la mannana.

522. Sennora benedicta, non te podí servir;
Pero améte siempre laudar e bendeçir:
Sennora, verdat digo e non cuydo° mentir, — intend
Querría seer muerta sy podiesse morir.

523. Madre del Rey de gloria de los çielos Reigna,
Mane de la tu graçia alguna mediçina,
Libra de mal porfazo una muger mezquina:
Esto si tú quisieres, puede ser ayna.° — quickly

524. Madre, por el amor del fijo querido,
Fijo tan 'sin embargo,° tan dulçe e tan cumplido, — unblemished
Non finque repoiada,° esta merçet te pido, — refused
Ca veo que me segudan° 'sobre grant apellido°. — persuing, loudly

525. Si non prendes, sennora, de mí algun conseio,
Veo mal aguisada° de salir a conseio:° — prepared, council
Aquí quiero morir en esti logareio,° — little place
Ca sy allá salliero, 'fernle an mal trebeio.° — they will surely mock me

526. Reyna coronada, templo de castidat,
Fuente de misericordia, torre de salvedat,
Fes° en aquesta cuyta alguna piadat, — take
En mí non se agote° la tu grant piadat. — used up

527. Quiero contra tu Fijo dar a ti por fianza,° — pledge

---

[19] **Egiptiana** this is a reference to St. Mary of Egypt (354?-431?), famous as a penitent prostitute.

Que nunca más non torne° en aquesta erranza:° — repeat, error
Madre, si fallesçiero, fes en mí tal venganza,
Que todo el mundo fable de la mi malandanza.° — disgrace

528. Tan afincadamente° fizo su oratión, — earnestly
Que la oió la Madre llena de bendiçión:
Commo qui amodorrida° vio grant visión, — asleep
Tal que debía en omne 'façer ediffiçaçión.° — be edifying
529. Traspúsose° la duena con la grant cansedat,° — remaind asleep, weariness
Dios lo obraba todo por la su piadat,
Apareçió la Madre del Rey de magestat,
Dos ángeles con ella de muy grant claridat.

530. Ovo pavor la duenna e fo mal espantada,
Ca de tal vissión nunqua era usada,
De la grant claridat fo mucho embargada,° — disturbed
Pero de la su cuita fo mucho alleviada.

531. Díssoli la Gloriosa: aforzat,° abbadesa, — take courage
Bien estades comigo, non 'vos pongades quessa,° — do not complain
Sepades que vos traio muy buena promessa,
Meior que non querríe la vuestra prioressa.

532. Non aiades nul miedo de caer en porfazo,
Bien vos a Dios guardada de caer en es° lazo, — **=ese**
Bien lis hid° 'a osadas° a tenerlis el plazo, — **=id**, boldly
Non lazrará por esso el vuestro espinazo.° — back

533. 'Al sabor del solat° de la Virgo gloriosa — protected
Non sintiendo la madre del dolor nulla cosa,
Naçió la creatura, cosiella muy fermosa,
Mandóla a los ángeles prender la Gloriosa.

534. Díssolis a los ángeles: a vos ambos castigo,° — I charge
Levad esti ninnuelo a fulán mi amigo,
Deçid quem lo críe, io assín° gelo digo, — thus
Ca bien vos creerá, luego seed conmigo. — return

535. Moviéronse los ángeles 'a muy grant ligereza,° — very speedily
Recabdaron° la cosa sin ninguna pereza,° — executed, delay
Plógol al ermitanno más que con grant riqueza,
Ca de verdad bien era una rica nobleza.° — honor

536. Recudió° la parida,° fízose santiguada, — came to, new mot
Diçié: val me Gloriosa, reyna coronada,
Si es esto verdat o si so engannada,
Sennora beneíta, val a esta errada.° — wayward person

537. Palpóse° con sus manos quando fo recordada, — touched herself
Por ventre, por costados, e por cada ijada:° — below her ribs
Trobó° so vientre llaçio,° la çinta° muy delgada, — found, flat, waist
Commo muger que es de tal cosa librada.

538. Non lo podié creer por ninguna manera,
Cuidaba que fo suenno, non cosa verdadera,
Palpóse e catóse la vegada terçera,
'Tiróse de° la dubda en cabo bien çertera. — cast away

539. Quando se sintió libre la prennada mesquina,
Fo el saco vaçío de la mala farina,° — **=harina**
Empezó con grant gozo cantar Salve Regina,[20]
Que es de los cuitados solaz e mediçina.

540. Ploraba de los oios de muy grant alegría,
Diçié laudes preçiosas a la Virgo María,
Non se temié del bispo nin de su cofradría,° — companions
Ca terminada era de la fuert malatía.° — malady

541. Ploraba de los oios e façie oraçiones,
Diçie a la Gloriosa laudes e bendiçiones,
Diçie: laudada seas, Madre, 'todas sazones,° — at all times
Laudarte deben siempre mugieres e varones.

---

[20] **Salve Regina...** a Latin hymn in praise of the Virgin Mary.

542. Era en fiera° cuyta e en fiera pavura,° — great, fear
Cay a los tos piedes, díssite mi ardura,° — concern
Acorrióme,° sennora, la tu buena mesura:° — helped me, remedy
Debes laudada seer de toda creatura.

543. Madre, io sobre todos te debo bendeçir,
Laudar, magnificar, adorar e servir,
Que de tan grant infamia me dennesti° guarir , — deigned
Que podrie tod el mundo siempre de mí reír.

544. Si esta mi nemiga° issiesse° a conçeio, — evil deed, had come
De todas las mugieres serie 'riso sobeio.° — laughing stock
Quand° grant es e quam° bono, Madre, el to conseio, — how, how
Non lo asmarie° omne° nin grant nin poquielleio. — imagine, no one

545. La merçed e la graçia que me denesti fer,
Non lo sabría, Madre, io a ti gradeçer,
Nin lo podrie, sennora, io nunqua mereçer:° — deserve
Mas non çessaré° nunqua graçias a ti render. — stop

546. Bien fincarie la duenna en su contemplaçión,
Laudando la Gloriosa, façiendo oraçión;
Mas vínoli mandado de la congregaçión
Que fuesse a cabillo° 'façer responsión.° — meeting, to respond

547. Commo en el porfazo non se temie caer,
Fo luego a los piedes del obispo seer:
Quísol besar las manos, ca lo debie fer;
Mas él non gelas quiso a ella ofreçer.

548. Empezóla el bispo luego a increpar,° — rebuke
Que avíe fecha cosa por que debie lazrar,
E non debíe por nada abbadessa estar,
Nin entre otras monias non debíe abitar.

549. Toda monia que façe tan grant desonestat,
Que non guarda so cuerpo nin tiene castidat,
Debíe seer echada de la soçiedat:° — order

Allá por do quisiere faga tal suçiedat.

550. Sennor, díssoli ella, ¿por qué me maltraedes?° — mistreat
Non so 'por aventura° tal commo vos tenedes:° — fortunately, think
Duenna, disso el bispo, porque vos lo neguedes,
Non seredes creída, ca a probar seredes.

551. Duenna, disso el bispo, essit vos al ostal,° — common room
Nos abremos conseio, depues faremos al:
Sennor, disso la duenna, non deçides nul° mal: — nothing
Io a Dios me acomiendo, al que puede e val.

552. Issió la abbadessa fuera del consistorio,° — assembly
Commo mandó el bispo, fo poral diversorio,° — common room
Fiçieron su cabillo la ira o el odio,
Amasaron su massa de farina de ordio.° — barley flour

553. Díssolis el obispo: amigos non podemos
Condepnar° esta duenna 'menos que° la probemos. — **=condenar**, unless
Díssoli el conviento: de lo que bien sabemos,
Sennor, en otra prueba nos ¿por qué entraremos?

554. Díssolis el obispo: quando fuere vençida,° — convicted
Vos seredes más salvos, ella más confondida:° — ashamed
Si non nuestra sentençia serie mal retraída:° — criticized
Non li puede en cabo prestar nula guarida.° — remedy

555. Envió de sus clérigos en qui él más fiaba,
Que probassen la cosa de qual guisa estaba:
Tolliéronli la saia° maguer que li pesaba, — skirt
Falláronla tan secca que tabla° semeiaba. — plank of wood

556.Non trovaron en ella signo de prennedat,° — pregnancy
Nin leche nin batuda° de nulla malveztat:° — trace, evil deed
Dissieron: non es esto fuera grant vanidat,° — illusion
Nunqua fo levantada,° tan fiera falsedat.° — made, false charge

557.Tornaron al obispo, dissiéronli: sennor,

Sabet que es culpada 'de valde° la seror: — without cause
Quiquiere que ál vos diga, salva° vuestra onor, — except
Dizvos tan grant mentira, que non podríe maior.

558. Cuidóse el obispo que eran deçebidos,° — deceived
Que lis avie la duenna dineros prometidos:
Dixo: domnos° maliellos, non seredes creíos, — men
Ca otra quilma° tiene 'de iusso° los vestidos. — sack, under

559. Disso: non vos lo quiero tan aína creer,
O sodes vergonzosos, o prisiestes aver:° — money
Io quiero esta cosa por mis ojos veer;
Si non, qui lo apuso° lo debe padeçer. — accused

560. Levantóse el bispo onde estaba assentado,
Fo pora la abbadessa sannoso e irado,
Fízoli despuiar° la cogulla° 'sin grado,° — take off, habit, unwillingly
Probó quel aponíen crimen falsso probado.

561. Tornóse al conviento bravo e muy fellón:° — violent
Duennas, disso, fiçiestes una grant traiçión,
Pussiestes la sennora en tan mala razón[21]
Que es muy despreçiada° vuestra religión.° — dishonored, order

562. Esta cosa non puede sin iustiçia passar,
La culpa que quissiestes vos a ella echar,
El decreto lo manda, en vos debe tornar,
Que debedes seer echadas desti logar.

563. Vio la abbadessa las duennas mal iudgadas,
Que avíen a seer de la casa echadas,
Sacó a part al bispo bien a quinçe passadas:
Sennor, disso, las duennas non son mucho culpadas.

564. Díssoli su façienda,° porque era pasada, — business
Por sus graves peccados commo fo engannada,

---

[21] **Pussiestes la...** *You accused the lady falsely.*

Commo la acorrió la Virgo coronada:
Si por ella non fuesse, fuera mal porfazada:° censured

565. E commo mandó ella el ninnuelo levar,
Commo al ermitanno gelo mandó criar;
Sennor, si vos quisiéredes podédeslo probar:
Por caridat non pierdan las duennas el logar.

566. Mas quiero io sennera seer embergonzada° shamed
Que tanta buena duenna sea desamparada:
Sennor, merçet vos pido, parçid° esta vegada: pardon
Por todas a mí sea la penitençia dada.

567. Espantóse el bispo, 'fo todo demudado,° his expresión was completely changed
Disso: duenna, si esto puede seer probado,
Veré don Iesu Xpo que es vuestro pagado:
Io mientre° fuero vivo, faré vuestro mandado.° while, command

568. Envió dos calonges luego al ermitanno
Probar esti si era o verdat o enganno,
Trovaron al bon omne con ábito estranno
Teniendo el ninnuelo envuelto en un panno.° cloth

569. Mostrólis el infant reçien nado° del día, born
Disso que lo mandara criar Sancta María:
Quien esto dubdase, faria bavequía,° foolishness
Ca era verdat pura, ca non vallitanía.° a lie

570. Tornaron al obispo luego con el mandado,
Dissiéronli por nuevas lo que avíen probado:
Sennor, dissieron, desto sei çertificado:
Si non, farás grant ierro, ganarás grant peccado.

571. Tóvos el obispo enna duenna por errado,
Cadióli a los piedes en el suelo postrado,
Duenna, disso, merçet, ca mucho so errado:
Ruégovos que me sea el ierro perdonado.

572. Sennor, disso la duenna, por Dios e la Gloriosa
Catat vuestra mesura,° non fagades tal cosa: — position
Vos sodes omne sancto, io peccadriz doliosa,° — grievious
'Si en al non tornades,° seré de vos sannosa. — if you don't get up

573. La duenna con el bispo avíe esta entençia,° — discussion
Mas finaronlo todo en buena avenençia,° — agreememt
Iamas° ovieron ambos amor e bienquerençia,° — evermore, good will
Ençerraron su vida en buena paciençia.

574. 'Methió paz° el obispo enna congregaçión, — established peace
Amató° lo contienda,° e la dissensión, — ended, disagreement
Quando quiso despedirse, diolis su bendiçión,
Fo bona pora todos essa visitaçión.

575. Envió sus saludes° al sancto ermitanno, — greeting
Commo a buen amigo, a 'cuempadre fontano,° — baptismal godfather
Que criase el ninno hastal seteno° anno: — seventh
Desende° él pensaríe de ferlo buen christiano. — then

576. Quando vino el término,° los siet annos passados, — time
Envió de sos clérigos dos de los más onrrados
Que trasquiessen el ninno del mont a los poblados:
Recabdáronlo° ellos commo bien castigados. — did it

577. Adussieron el ninno en el yermo° criado,° — wilderness, reared
'De los días que era,° era bien ensennado: — for his age
Plógol al obispo, fo ende muy pagado:
Mandól 'poner a letras° con maestro letrado. — to study

578. Issió° muy bon omne en todo mesurado:° — turned out, temperate
Pareçíe bien que fuera de bon amo criado:
Era el pueblo todo delli mucho pagado:
Quando murió el bispo diéronli el bispado.

579. Guiólo la Gloriosa que lo dio a criar,
Sabíe su obispado con Dios bien gobernar,

Guiaba bien las almas commo debie guiar,
Sabíe en todas cosas mesura bien catar.

580. Amábanlo los pueblos e las sus clereçías,° clergy
Amábanlo calonges e todas las mongías,
Todos 'por ond° estaban rogaban por sos días, wherever
Fuera° algunos foles que amaban follías. except

581. Quando vino el término que ovo de finar,
Non lo dessó su ama° luengamiente lazrar: Virgin Mary
Levólo a la gloria, a seguro logar,
Do ladrón nin merino° nunqua puede entrar. judge

582. A la Virgo gloriosa todos graçias rendamos,
De qui tantos miraclos leemos e probamos;
Ella nos dé su gratia que servirla podamos,
E nos guíe fer cosas por ond salvos seamos. AMÉN.

## *La Vida de Santa Oria*

This is a saint's life in *mester de clerecía* written by Gonzalo de Berceo in his old age. It is a versification of a Latin account of Oria's life, narrated by her confessor a certain Munno or Munnio shortly after her death in 1069.

Most saint's lives follow a similar tripartite division of childhood and adolescence, followed by miracles while the saint was alive and those accomplished after his or her death and entry into heaven. However, here Berceo constructs the life from three visions that Oria experienced and ends with the last that she had just before she died, having confessed these visions to Munno. The first vision occurs when Oria is 18 years old and visits heaven where she sees the blessed and a throne designated for her. The second vision is set in her cell with the appearance of the Virgin Mary who foretells Oria's future entry into heaven. In the third vision Oria is transported to a spiritual garden setting, the Mount of Olives.

| | |
|---|---|
| 1. En el nombre de el Padre que nos quiso criar,° | =crear |
| E de don Ihesu Christo que nos vino salvar, | |
| E del Spiritu Sancto lumbre° de confortar , | light |
| De una Sancta Virgen quiero versificar.° | tell in verse |
| | |
| 2. Quiero en mi vegez,° maguer so ya cansado, | =vejez |
| De esta sancta Virgen romanzar su dictado,[1] | |
| Que Dios por el 'su ruego° sea de mi pagado,° | her prayer, pleased |
| E non quiera venganza tomar del° mi pecado. | because of |
| 3. Luego° en el comienzo e 'en la primería° | here, at the start |
| A ella merçet pido, ella sea mi guía, | |
| Ruegue° a la Gloriosa Madre Sancta María, | that she ask |
| Que sea nuestra guarda° de noche e de día. | guardian |
| | |
| 4. Essa Virgen preçiosa de quien fablar solemos, | |
| Fue de Villa Velayo, segunt lo que leemos: | |
| Amunna fue su madre, escrito lo tenemos, | |
| Graçía fue el padre, en letra lo avemos. | |
| | |
| 5. Munno era su nombre, omne fue bien letrado,° | learned |
| Sopo bien su façienda:° el fizo° el dictado, | deeds, wrote |
| Havíagelo la madre todo, bien razonado,[2] | |
| Que non quería mentir por° un rico condado.° | even for, county |
| | |
| 6. De suso° la nombramos, acordarvos podedes, | above |
| Emparedada° era, yaçía entre paredes, | recluse |
| Havía vida lazrada° qual entender podedes, | harsh |
| Si su vida leyerdes, así lo probaredes. | |
| | |
| 7. Sanctos° fueron sin dubda e iustos° los parientes, | =santos, justos |
| Que fueron de tal fixa° engendrar meresçientes:° | =fija, deserving |
| De ninnes° façía ella fechos muy convenientes,° | =niñez, good |
| Estaban maravilladas ende° todas las gentes. | from this |
| | |
| 8. Commo diçe del apóstol Sant Paulo la lectión° | reading |

[1] **Romanzar su...** *tell her story in Spanish*

[2] **Havíagelo la...** *her mother had told it to him completely and very well*

Fue esta sancta Virgen vaso° de oraçión, — vessel
Ca puso Dios en ella cumplida bendiçión,° — blessing
E vido° en los çielos mucha grant visión.° — saw, vision

9. Bien es que bos digamos luego en la entrada
Qual nombre li° pusieron quando fue bautizada — to her
Commo era preçiosa° más que piedra preçiada° — precious, valuable
Nombre había de oro, Oria era llamada.

10. Havemos en el prólogo mucho detardado,° — tarried
Sigamos la estoria, esto es aguisado,° — proper
Los días son non grandes, anocheçerá° privado° — it will be dark, soon
Escribir en tiniebla° es un mester° pesado. — darkness, task

11. Fue de Villa Velayo Amunna natural,° — native
El su marido sancto, García 'otro tal,° — also
Siempre en bien punaron,° partiéronse° de mal, — strove, avoided
Cobdiçiaban° la graçia de el Rey çelestial. — longed for

12. Omnes eran católicos, vivían vida derecha,° — righteous
Daban a los sennores° a cada uno su pecha,° — lords, tribute
Non fallaba en ellos el diablo retrecha,° — fault
El que 'todas sazones° a los buenos açecha.° — always, stalks

13. Nunca querían 'sus carnes mantener° a grant viçio,° — indulge, pleasure
Ponían toda femençia° en fer a Dios serviçio, — effort
Esso avían por pascua° e por muy grant deliçio, — great feast
A Dios ponían delante° en todo su offiçio.° — first, undertakings

14. Rogaban a Dios siempre de firme corazón
Que lis quissiese dar alguna criazón,° — child
Que para el su serviçio fuese, que para 'al non,° — to no other
E siempre meiorase° esta devoçión. — might improve

15. Si lis dio otros fixos non lo diçe la leyenda:° — story
Más diolis una fixa de spiritual façienda,° — deeds
Que hovo con su carne baraia° e contienda,° — struggle, battle
Por consentir° al cuerpo nunca soltó la rienda.° — indulge, the reins

16.Apriso° las costumbres de los buenos parientes, — she learned
Quanto li castigaban ponía en ello mientes,[3]
Con ambos sus labriellos° apretaba° sus dientes, — little lips, pressed
Que non saliessen dende° palabras desconvenientes.° — from them, improper

17.Quiso seer la madre de más áspera vida,
Entró emparedada de çeliçio° vestida, — hairshirt
Martiriaba sus carnes a la mayor medida,[4]
Que non fuese la alma del diablo vençida.

18. Si ante fuera buena, fue después muy meyor,° — **=mejor**
Plaçía su serviçio a Dios nuestro sennor,
Los pueblos de la tierra façíanli grant honor,
Salía a luengas° tierras la su buena loor.° — distant, praise

19 Dexemos de la madre, en la fixa tornemos,
Essas laudes tengamos cuyas bodas comemos:[5]
Si nos cantar sopiéremos,° grant materia tenemos, — are to sing
Menester° nos será todo el seso° que avemos. — necessary, mind

20 .Desque mudó° los dientes, luego a pocos annos — lost
'Pagábase muy poco° de los seglares pannos[6]: — did not like
Vistió otros vestidos de los monges calannos,° — just like
Podrían valer pocos dineros los sus peannos.° — garments

21. Desamparó° el mundo Oria toca° negrada, — abandoned, habit
En un rencón° angosto entró emparedada, — cell
Sofría grant astinençia,° vivía vida lazrada,° — abstinence, harsh
Por onde° ganó en cabo de Dios rica soldada.° — which, reward

22. Era esta reclusa vaso de caridat,
Templo de paçiençia e de humildat,

---

[3] **Quanto li...** *all that they taught her, she kept in mind*
[4] **Martiriaba sus..** *she martyred her flesh to the utmost*
[5] **Essas laudes...** *let us praise the one whose feast we celebrate*
[6] **Los seglares...** her worldly clothes

Non amaba oír palabras de vanidat,
Luz era e confuerto° de la su veçindat. consolation

23. Porque angosta era la emparedaçión,° cell
Teníala por muy larga° el su buen corazón: wide
Siempre rezaba psalmos e façía oraçión,
Foradaba° los çielos la su devoçión. pierced

24.Tanto fue Dios pagado de las sus oraçiones
Que li mostró en çielo tan grandes visiones
Que debían a los omnes cambiar los corazones:
Non las podrían contar palabras nin sermones.

25.Terçera noche era después de Navidat,
De Sancta Eugenia[7] era festividat,
Vido de visiones una infinidat,
Onde pareçe que era plena de sanctidat.

26. Después de las matinas° leída la lecçión matins
Escuchóla bien Oria con grant devoçión:
Quiso dormir un poco, tomar consolaçión,
Vido 'en poca hora° un grant visión. in a short time

27. Vido tres sanctas vírgines de grant auctoridat,
Todas tres fueron mártires en poquiella° edat, very young
Agatha en Catania[8] essa rica çiudat,
Olalia en Mérida[9] ninna de grant beldat.

28. Çeçilia[10] fue terçera, una martir preçiosa
Que de don Ihesu Christo quiso seer esposa:
Non quiso otra suegra sinon° la Gloriosa except
Que fue más bella que 'nin lilio nin rosa.° a lily or a rose

---

[7] Eugenia was a Roman virgin martyred in the 3rd century under the emperor Valerian.
[8] St. Agatha was martyred in Catania (Sicily) in the 3rd century.
[9] St. Eulalia was martyred at the beginning of the 4th century in Mérida, Spain.
[10] St. Cecilia was martyred in Rome in the 2nd or 3rd century.

29. Todas estas tres vírgines que avedes oídas,
Todas eran iguales de un color vestidas:
Semejaba° que eran en un día naçidas, — it seemed
Luçían commo estrellas, tanto eran de bellidas.° — beautiful

30. Estas tres sanctas vírgines en çielo coronadas
Tenían sendas palombas° en sus manos alzadas,° — **=palomas**, raised
Más blancas que las nieves que 'non son coçeadas:° — untrodden
Paresçía que non fueran en palombar° criadas. — dovecote

31. La ninna que yaçía en paredes çerrada
Con esta visión fue mucho embargada;° — frightened
Pero del Spíritu Sancto fue luego conortada:
Demandólis quí eran, e fue bien aforzada.° — heartened

32. Fabláronli las vírgines de fermosa manera,
Agatha e Eolalia, Çeçilia la terçera:
Oria, por ti tomamos esta tan grant carrera:° — trip
Sepas bien que te tengas por nuestra compannera.

33. Combidarte° venimos, nuestra hermana, — to invite
Embíanos don Christo, de quien todo bien mana,° — flows
Que° subas a los çielos, e que veas qué gana — **=para que**
El serviçio que façes e la saya de lana. — habit

34. Tu mucho te deleitas en las nuestras passiones,
'De amor e de grado° leyes nuestras razones, — lovingly and gladly
Queremos que entiendas entre las visiones
Quál gloria reçibíemos, e quáles galardones.° — rewards
35. Respondió la reclusa que avía nombre Oria:
Yo non sería digna de veer tan grant gloria;
Mas si me reçibiésedes° vos en vuestra memoria, — hold
Allá sería complida toda la mi estoria.

36. Fixa, dixo Ollallia, tú tal cosa non digas,
Ca as sobre los çielos amigos e amigas:
Así mandas° tus carnes, e assí las aguissas° — discipline, chastise

Que por subir a los çielos tu digna te predigas.[11]

37. Resçibe este conseio, la mi fixa querida,
Guarda° esta palomba, 'todo lo al° olvida: — look at, all else
Tú vé do ella fuere,° non seas deçebida,° — went, deceived
Guíate por nos, fixa, ca Christus te combida.

38.Oyendo este conseio que Olalia li daba,
Alzó Oria los oios, arriba onde estaba,
Vido una columna, a los çielos pujaba,° — piercing
Tanto era de enfiesta° que avés° la cataba°. — tall, scarcely, see

39.Avía en la coluna 'escalones e gradas:° — stairs and steps
Veer solemos tales en las torres obradas:° — worked into
Yo sobí° por algunas, esto muchas vegadas° — **=subí,** times
Por tal suben las almas que son aventuradas.° — fortunate

40.Movióse la palomba, comenzó de volar,
Suso contra los çielos comenzó de pujar:° — rose
Catábala don Oria dónde iría a posar,° — land
Non la podía por nada de voluntat sacar.° — get it out of her m

41.Empezaron las vírgines lazradas° a sobir , — martyred
Empezólas la duenna reclusa a seguir:
Quando don Oria cató Dios lo quiso complir,° — permit
Fue puia° ensomo° por verdat vos deçir. — raised, on high

42.Quando dormía Iacob[12] çerca de la carrera,
Vido sobir los ángeles por una escalera:
A esta reluçía° ca obra de Dios era, — shone
Entonçe perdió la pierna en essa 'liz veçera.° — arduous battle
43.Ya eran, Deo graçias, las vírgines ribadas,° — arrived
Eran de la columpna ensomo aplanadas,° — even
Vieron un buen árbol, 'çimas bien compasadas,° — well-formed top

---

[11] **Tú digna...***you declare yourself worthy*

[12] **Iacob;** this is a reference to Jacob and his dream of the ladder in Genesis 28:10-22 and the angel touching his thigh which withers in Genesis 32:24-32.

Que de diversas flores estaban bien pobladas.

44.Verde era el ramo de foyas° bien cargado,° — = **hojas** ***leaves***, laden
Façía sombra sabrosa° e logar muy temprado,° — delightful, temperate
Tenía redor el tronco maravilloso prado, — = **alrededor**
Más valía esso solo que un rico regnado.° — kingdom

45.Estas quatro donçellas ligeras más° que viento — lighter
Ovieron con este árbol plaçer e pagamento:° — contentment
Subieron en él todas, todas 'de buen taliento,° — eagerly
Ça avían en él forgura° en él grant cumplimiento.° — rest, fulfillment

46.Estando en el árbol estas duennas contadas,
Sus palomas en manos alegres e pagadas,
Vieron en el çielo finiestras° foradadas,° — windows, opened
Lumbres° salían por ellas, 'de duro° serían contadas. — lights, difficult

47. Salieron tres personas por essas aberturas,° — openings
Cosas eran angélicas con blancas vestiduras,
Sendas vergas° en manos de preçiosas pinturas,° — staffs, colors
Vinieron contra° ellas en humanas figuras.° — towards, form

48. Tomaron estas vírgines estos sanctos varones
Commo a sendas pennolas° en aquellos bordones:°[13] — feathers, staffs
Pusiéronlas más altas en otras regiones,
Allá vidieron muchas honradas proçessiones.

49. Don Oria la reclusa de Dios mucho amada,
Commo la ovo ante Olalia castigada,
Catando la palomba commo bien acordada° — prudent
Subió en pos° las otras a essa grant posada.° — after, dwelling

50. Puyaba a los çielos sin ayuda ninguna,
Non li façía embargo,° nin el sol, nin la luna, — obstacle
A Dios havía pagado por manera alguna,

---

[13] **Tomaron estas...**Read: Estos sanctos varones tomaron estas vírgenes, en aquellos bordones como (si fueran) sendas pennolas.

Si non, non subría tanto la fixa de Amunna.

51. Entraron por el çielo que abierto estaba,
Alegróse con ellas la corte que y moraba;° — dwelt
Plógolis con la quarta que las tres aguardaba,° — accompanied
Por essa serraniella° menos non 'se preçiaba.° — peasant, consider

52. Apareçiólis luego una muy grant companna,
En vestiduras albas fermosas 'por fazanna:° — as a fact
Semeioli° a Oria una cosa estranna, — it seemed to (her)
Ca nunca vido cosa 'de aquesta su calanna.° — like this

53. Preguntó a las otras la de Villa Velayo:
Deçitme, qué es esto por Dios e Sant Pelayo?[14]
En el mi corazón una grant dubda trayo:
Meior paresçen estos que las flores de mayo.

54. Dixéronli las otras: oye, fixa querida,
Colonges° fueron estos, omnes de sancta vida; — canons
Tuvieron en el mundo la carne apremida,° — disciplined
Agora son en gloria en leticia° complida. — happiness

55. Conosçió la fixa buenos quatro varones,
Los que nunca vidiera en ningunas sazones:
Bartolomeo ducho° de escribir passiones, — skilled
Don Gomes de Masiella, que daba bien raçiones° — alms

56. Don Xemeno terçero un veçino leal,
De el barrio de Velayo fue esti natural:
Galindo su criado, qual° él, bien otro tal, — like
Que sopo de bien mucho e sabía poco mal.

57. Fueron más adelante en esa romería,° — pilgrimage
Los mártires delante, la freira° en su guía, — anchoress (Oria)
Aparesçiolis otra asaz grant compannía,

[14] **Sant Pelayo…** Saint Pelagius, a Spanish martyr, born in Zaragoza (c. 912-925).

De la de los colonges avía 'grant meioría.° — even greater

58. Todos vestían casullas° de preçiosas colores, — chasubles
Blagos° en las siniestras commo predicadores, — staffs
Cálices° en las diestras de oro muy meiores, — chalices
Semeiaba ministros de preçiosos° sennores. — important

59. Demandó la serrana, ¿qué eran esta cosa?
¿Qué proçesión es esta tan grant e tan preçiosa?
Dixéronli las mártires respuestas muy sabrosa:
Obispos fueron estos siervos de la Gloriosa.° — Holy Mary

60. Porque daban al pueblo beber de buen castigo,° — teaching
Por ende tienen los cáliçes cada uno consigo:
Refirían con los quentos al mortal enemigo
Que engannó a Eva con un astroso° figo. — vile

61.Conoçió la reclusa en essa proçessión
Al obispo don Sancho, un preçioso varón:
Con él a don García su leal compannón
Que sirvió a don Christo de firme corazón.

62. Dixéronli las mártires a Oria la serrana:
El obispo don Gómez non es aquí, hermana:
Peroque° trayo mitra fue cosa muy llana,° — although, unworthy
Tal fue commo el árbol que floreçe non grana.° — doesn't bear fruit

63. Visto este convento,° esta sancta mesnada,° — assembly. company
Fue a otra comarca° esta freyra levada: — area
El coro de las vírgines proçesión tan honrrada
Salieron resçibirla de voluntat pagada.

64. Salieron reçibirla con 'responsos doblados,° — two part responses
Fueron abrazarla con los brazos alzados:
Tenían con esta novia los corazones bien pagados,
Non 'fiçieran tal gozo° 'annos havía passados.° — celebrated, for years

65. Embargada° fue Oria con el reçibimiento, — bewildered

Ca tenía que non era de tal mereçimiento:
Estaba aturdida° en grant desarramiento;° — flustered, confusion
Pero nunca de cosas ovo tal pagamiento.

66: Si del Rey de la gloria li fuese otorgado,
Finearía° con las vírgines de amor e de grado: — would stay
Mas aún esi tiempo non era allegado
Para reçibir soldada° de el lazerio passado. — reward

67. El coro de las vírgines una fermosa az° — line
Diéronli a la freyra todas por orden paz:° — kiss of peace
Dixéronli: contigo mucho nos plaz:
Para en esta companna digna eres assaz.

68. Esto por nuestro mérito nos non lo ganaríemos,
Esto en que somos, nos non lo mereçíemos;
Mas el nuestro Esposo a quien voto fiçíemos
Fízonos esta graçia porque bien lo quisíemos.

69. Oria, que ante estaba mucho embergonzada,° — embarassed
Con estos dichos buenos fízose más osada:
Preguntó a las vírgines esa sancta mesnada
Por una su maestra que la ovo criada.

70. Una maestra ovo de muy sancta vida,
Urraca li dixeron muger buena complida,
Emparedada visco° una buena partida, — =vivió
Era de la maestra Oria muy querida.

71. Preguntólis por ella la freyra que oydes:
Deçitme, mis sennoras, por Dios, ¿a qui servides
Urraca es en estas las que aquí venides?
Grant graçia me faredes, si esto me deçides.

72. Mi ama fue al mundo esta por quien demando,
Lazrró conmigo mucho, e a mí castigando,
Querría yo que fuesse en esti vuestro vando,° — company
Por su deudor me tengo durmiendo, e velando.

73. Dixéronli las vírgines nuevas 'de grant sabor:° — happy
Esa que tú demandas, Urraca la seror,° — sister
Compannera es nuestra e 'nuestra morador:° — dwells with us
Con Iusta su disçípula sierva del Criador.

74. Ruégovos, dixo Oria, por Dios que la llamedes:
Si me la demostrardes, grant merçet me faredes:
Io por la su doctrina entré entre paredes,
Io ganaré y mucho, vos nada non paredes.

75. Clamáronla por nombre las otras companneras,
Respondiolis Urraca a las voçes° primeras: — calls
Conoçió la voz Oria, entendió 'las senneras;° — characteristics
Mas ver non la podió por ningunas maneras.

76. La az era muy luenga, eso la embargaba,° — impeded
Que non podía verla, ca en cabo° estaba: — end
Levóla a delante la voz que la guiaba,
Pero a la maestra nunca la olvidaba.

77. En cabo de las vírgines, toda la az pasada
Falló muy rica siella° de oro bien labrada: — throne
De piedras muy preçiosas toda engastonada,° — encrusted
Mas estaba vaçía e muy bien seellada.° — sealed

78.Vedía sobre la siella muy rica açitara,° — tapestry
Non podría en este mundo cosa ser tan clara:° — bright
Dios solo faz tal cosa que sus siervos empara,° — protects
Que non podría comprarla toda alfoz de Lara.[15]

79. Una duenna hermosa de edat mançebiella° — young
Voxmea havía nombre, guardaba esta siella:
Daría por tal su reyno el rey de Castiella,
E sería tal mercado° que sería 'por fabliella.° — trade, fabled

---

[15] **Alfoz de...** district of Lara, one of the most important and richest districts of Castile in the Middle Ages.

80.Alzó Oria los oios escontra° aquilón,° — toward, north
Vido grandes compannas, fermosa criazón° — group
Semeiaban vestidos todos de vermeión,° — red
Preguntó a las otras: estos, ¿qué cosas son?

81.Dixéronli las vírgines que eran sus guionas,° — guides
Todos estos son mártires, unas nobles personas,
Dexáronse matar a golpes de azconas,° — darts
Ihesu Christo por ende diolis ricas coronas.

82. Allí es Sant Estevan[16] el que fue apedreado,° — stoned
Sant Lorente[17] el que Çesar ovo después asado,° — roasted
Sant Viçente[18] el caboso° de Valerio criado: — virtuous
Mucho otro buen lego,° mucho buen ordenado° — laymen, clergy.

83. Vido más adelante en un apartamiento° — place apart
De sanctos hermitannos un preçioso conviento,
Que sufrieron por Christo mucho amargo viento° — adversity
Por ganar a las almas vida e guarimiento.° — salvation

84.Conosçió entre todos un monge ordenado:
Monio li dixeron, commo diz el dictado:° — book
A otro su disçípulo, Munno era llamado,
Que de Valvanera fue abat consagrado.

85. Y vido a Galindo en esa compannía,
Ladrones lo mataron en la hermitannía:
y vido a su padre que llamaban Garçía,
Aquelli que non quiso seguir nulla folía.° — folly

86. Vido a los apóstolos más en alto logar,
Cada uno en su trono en que debía jusgar:
A los evangelistas y los vido estar,
La su claridad° omne non la podríe contar. — brightness

[16] **Sant Estevan** first Christian martyr who died ca. 35 A.D.
[17] **Sant Lorente** was martyred in 238 A.D.
[18] **Sant Viçente** was martyred in Valencia in 304 A.D.

87. Estos son los nuestros padres cabdiellos° generales, — leaders
Prínçipes de los pueblos, son omnes prinçipales,
Ihesu Christo fue papa, estos los cardenales,
Que sacaron de el mundo las serpientes mortales.

88. Commo asmaba° Oria a su entendimiento, — was thinking
Oió fablar a Christo en esse buen conviento;
Mas non podió veerlo 'a todo su taliento,° — to her satisfaction
Ca 'bien lieve° non era de tal mereçimiento. — apparently

89. Dexemos lo al todo, a la siella tornemos,° — return
La materia° es alta,° temo que pecaremos; — subject, lofty
Mas en esto culpados nos seer non debemos,
Ca al non escribimos, 'si non° lo que leemos. — except

90. De suso lo dixiemos, la materia lo daba,
Voxmea avia nombre la que la siella guardaba
Commo rayos de el sol, assi relampagaba.° — it was shining
Bien fue felix la alma para quien estaba.

91. Vistía esta mançeba preçiosa vestidura,
Más preçiosa que oro, más que la seda pura;
Era sobresennada° de buena escritura, — inscribed
Non cubrió omne vivo tan rica cobertura.

92. Avíe en ella nombres de omnes de grant vida,
Que sirvieron a Christo con voluntat complida;
Pero de los reclusos° fue la mayor partida — recluses
Que domaron° sus carnes a la mayor medida. — tamed

93. Las letras de los iustos de mayor sanctidat
Pareçían más leybles de mayor claridat: — legible
Los otros más sorienda° de menor claridat — lower
Eran más tenebrosas° de grant obscuridat. — darkness

94. Non se podía la freyra de la siella toller:° — take away
Díxole a Voxmea que lo querría saber:

Este tan 'grant adobo° ¿cuyo podría ser? — beautiful garment
Ca non sería por nada comprado por haver .° — money

95. Respondióli Voxmea, díxoli buen mandado,° — news
Amiga, bien has fecho e bien has demandado;
Todo esto que vees a ti es otorgado,
Ca es del tu serviçio el Criador pagado.

96. Todo esti adobo a ti es comendado,
El solar° e la siella, Dios sea ende laudado, — place
Si non te lo quitare conseio del pecado° — devil
El que hizo a Eva comer el mal bocado° — bite.

97. Si commo tú me diçes, díxoli Sancta Oria.
A mí es prometida esta tamaña° gloria, — great
Luego en esti tálamo° querría ser novia; — wedding bed
Non querría de el oro tornar a la escoria.° — slag

98. Respondióli la otra commo bien razonada:
Non puede seer esto, Oria, esta vegada,
'De tornar as° a el cuerpo, yaçer emparedada, — **=has de tornar**
Fasta que sea toda tu vida acabada.

99. Las tres mártires sanctas que con ella vinieron
En ninguna sazón° de ella non se partieron; — time
Siempre fueron con ella, con ella andidieron° — **=anduvieron**
Fasta que a su casa misma la tragieron.

100. Rogó a estas sanctas de toda voluntat
Que rogassen por ella al Rey de maiestat,
Que gelo condonase° por la su piedat — grant
De fincar con Voxmea en essa heredat.° — promised place

101. Rogaron a Dios ellas quanto meior supieron,
Más lo que pedía ella ganar non lo podieron:
Fablóles Dios de el çielo, la voz bien la oieron,
La su majestat grant; pero non la vieron.

102. Díxolis: piense Oria de ir a su logar,
Non vino tiempo aún de aquí habitar:
Aún ave un poco el cuerpo a lazrar,
Después verná° el tiempo de la siella cobrar.° — **=vendrá**, claim

103. Sennor, dixo, e padre, peroque non te veo,
De ganar la tu graçia siempre ovi° desseo: — **=tuve**
Si una vez salliero del solar en que seo,
Non tornaré y nunca según lo que yo creo.

104. Los çielos son mucho altos, yo pecadriz° mezquina, — sinner
Si una vez tornaro en la mi calabrina,° — mortal condition
Non fallaré en el mundo sennora nin madrina,° — godmother
Por qui yo esto cobre nin tarde nin ayna.° — sooner

105. Díxoli 'aún de cabo° la voz del Criador — furthermore
Oria, del poco mérito non ayas temor:
Con lo que has lazrado ganesti el mi amor,
Quitar non te lo puede ningún escantador.° — **=encantador**

106. Lo que tú tanto temes e estás desmedrida,° — frightened
Que los çielos son altos, enfiesta° la subida, — steep
Io te los faré llanos,° la mi fixa querida, — flat
Que non havrás embargo en toda tu venida.

107. De lo que tú temes non serás embargada,
Non abrás nul embargo, non te temas por nada:
Mi fixa, benedicta° vaias° e sanctiguada, — blessed, **=vayas**
Torna a tu casiella, reza tu matinada.° — morning prayer

108. Tomáronla las mártires que ante la guiaron
Por essa escalera por la que la levaron.
En muy poquiello rato al cuerpo la tornaron,
Espertó° ella luego que ellas la dexaron. — **=despertó**

109. Abrió ella los oios, cató enderredor,
Non vido a las mártires, ovo muy mal sabor:
Vídose alongada de muy grant dulzor,

Havía muy grande cuyta e sobeio° dolor. extreme
110. Non cuidaba veer la hora nin el día
Que podiese tornar a essa confradía:
Dolíase de la siella que estaba vaçía,
Siella que Dios fiçiera a tan grant maestría.° skill

111. Por estas visiones la reclusa don Oria
Non dio en sí entrada a nulla vanagloria:
Por amor de la alma non perder la victoria
Non façía a sus carnes nulla misericordia.

112 .Martiriaba las carnes dándolis grant laçerio,
Complía días e noches todo su ministerio:° duties
Ieiunios° e vigilias e rezar el psalterio, fastings
Quería a todas guisas° seguir el Evangelio. ways

113 .El Rey de los reyes, sennor de los sennores,
En cuya mano iaçen justos e pecadores,
Quiso sacar a Oria de estos baticores,° sufferings
E ferla compannera de compannas meiores.

114. Once meses, sennores, podrí haber pasados
Desque vido los pleitos° que avemos contados: things
De sanctos e de sanctas conventos mucho onrrados,
Mas non los havía Oria encara° olvidados. still

115. En esi mes onçeno vido grant vissión,
Tan grande commo las otras las que escritas son:
Non se partía Dios de ella en ninguna sazón,
Ca siempre tenía ella en el su corazón.

116. Terçera noche ante de el mártir Saturnino[19]
Que cae en noviembre de Sant Andrés[20] veçino,
Vínoli una graçia, meior nunca le vino,

---

[19] **Saturnino** martyred missionary in the Pamplona region and first bishop of Toulouse. His feast day is November 29.
[20] **Sant Andrés,** one of the twelve apostles whose feast day is November 30.

Más dulçe e más sabrosa era que pan nin vino.

117. Sería la meatat° de la noche pasada, =**mitad**
Avía mucho velado, Oria era cansada,
Acostóse un poco flaca e muy lazrada,
Non era la camenna° de molsa° ablentada.° bed, down, soft
118. Vido venir tres vírgines, todas de una guisa,
Todas venían vestidas de una blanca frisa° cloth
Nunca tan blanca vido nin toca° nin camisa, wimple
Nunca tal cosa ovo nin Genua° nin Pisa. Genoa

119. Ende a poco rato vino Sancta María,
Vínolis a las vírgines gozo e alegría,
Commo con tal sennora todas havían buen día,
Allí fue adonada° toda la confradría. blessed

120. Dixéronli a Oria: tú que yaçes sonnosa,° in sleep
Levántate y reçibe a la Virgen gloriosa,
Que es Madre de Christo e fixa e esposa:
Serás 'mal acordada° si faces otra cosa. foolish

121. Respondiólis la freira con grant humildat:
Si a ella ploguiesse pora la su piadat
Que yo llegar podiesse a la su maiestat,
Cadría° a sus pies desde buena voluntat. =**caería**

122. Aves° avía don Oria el vierbo acabado scarcely
Plegó° la Gloriosa: ¡Dios tan buen encontrado!° =**llegó**, encounter
Relumbró la confita° de relumbor° doblado: cell, light
Qui oviese tal huéspeda° sería bien venturado. guest

123. La Madre benedicta de los çielos sennora
Más fermosa de mucho 'que non° es la aurora, than
'Non lo puso por plazo nin sola una hora,° did not hesitate
Fue luego abrazarla a Oria la serora.

124. Ovo en el falago° Oria grant alegría: compliment
Preguntóla si era ella Sancta María:

Non ayas nulla dubda, díxol, fijuela mía:
Yo so la que tú ruegas de noche e de día.

125. Yo so Sancta María la que tú mucho quieres,
Que saqué de porfazo° a todas las mugieres: disgrace
Fixa, Dios es contigo: si tú firme estovieres,
Irás a grant riqueza, fixa, quando morieres.° **=mueras**

126. Todas eran iguales de una calidat,
De una captenençia° e de una edat: behavior
Ninguna a las otras non vençía de bondat,
Trahían° en todas cosas todas tres igualdat. **=traían**

127. Trahían estas tres vírgines una noble lechiga,° bed
Con adobos° reales non pobres nin mendiga: bed linen
Fabláronli a Oria de Dios buena amiga:
Fixa, oy° un poco, si Dios te bendiga. listen

128. Liévate de la tierra que es fría e dura,
Subi en este lecho, yazrás más en mollura:° softness
E aquí la reyna, de esto sei° segura, be
Si te falla en tierra avrá de ti rencura.

129. Duennas, díxolis Oria, non es eso derecho,
Para vieio e flaco conviene este lecho:
Yo valiente so e ninna por sofrir 'todo fecho:° anything
Si yo y me echase, Dios avría ende despecho.

130. Lecho quiero yo áspero de 'sedas aguijosas.° prickly cloth
Non mereçen mis carnes iaçer tan viçiosas:° at ease
Por Dios que non seades en esto porfidiosas,° stubborn
Para muy grandes omnes son cosas tan preçiosas.

131. Tomáronla las vírgines dándol grandes sosannos.° reproaches
Echáronla a Oria en esos ricos pannos:
Oria con grant cochura° daba gemidos estrannos, displeasure
Ca non era vezada de entrar en tales bannos.

132. Luego que fue la freira en el lecho echada
Fue de bien grandes lumbres la çiella alumbrada,
Fue de vírgines muchas en un rato poblada,
Todas venían honrrarla a la emparedada.

133. Madre, díxoli Oria, si tú eres María,
De la que fabló tanto el varón Isaía,
Por seer bien çertera algún signo quería
Porque segura fuese que salvarme podría.

134. Díxol la Gloriosa: Oria, la mi lazrada,
Que de tan luengos tiempos eres emparedada,
Io te daré un signo, sennal buena probada:
Si la sennal vidieres, estonçe serás pagada
. . . . . .
NOTA: *Aquí faltaba una hoja en los códices del monasterio de San Millán.*

135. Esto ten tú por signo por çertera sennal:
Ante de pocos días enfermarás muy mal,
Serás fuerte embargada de enfermedat mortal,
Qual nunca la oviste, 'terrasla bien por tal.° — this will be the sign

136. Veraste° en grant quexa, de° muerte serás cortada, — **=te verás**, by
Serás a pocos días desti mundo passada,
Irás do tú cobdiçias° a la silla honrrada, — desire
La que tiene Voxmea para ti bien guardada.

137. En cuita° yaçía Oria dentro en su casiella,° — distress, cell
Estaba un grant conviento° de fuera de la çiella, — gathering
Rezando su psalterio cada uno en su siella,
E non tenía ninguno enjuta° la maxiella.° — dry, cheek

138. Iaçiendo la enferma en tal tribulaçión,
Maguera° 'entre dientes° façía su oraçión: — nevertheless, mumbling
Quería batir sus pechos, mas non había sazón,° — time
Pero quería la mano alzar en esi son.

139. Traspósose° un poco, ca era quebrantada,° slept, exhausted
Fue a 'monte Olivote° en visión levada, Mount of Olives
Vido y tales cosas de que fue saborgada,° pleased
Si non la despertasen, cuidó seer folgada.° at peace

140. La madre en la rabia° non se podía folgar,° distress, rest
Ca todos se cuidaban que se quería pasar:
Metióse° en la casa por la cosa probar, entered
Comenzó de traerla°, ovo de despertar. shake her

141. Vido redor el monte una bella anchura,° wide plain
En ella de olivos una grant espesura,° thickness
Cargados de olivas mucho sobre mesura,
Podría vevir so° ellos omne a grant folgura. under

142. Vido por esa sombra muchas gentes venir,
Todas venían gradosas° a Oria resçebir, joyfully
Todas 'bien aguisadas° de calzar e de vestir, elegantly
Querían si fuese tiempo, al çielo la sobir.

143. Eran estas compannas de preçiosos varones,
Todos vestidos eran de blancos çiclatones,
Semeiaban de ángeles todas sus guarniçiones:° adornments
Otras tales vidieran en algunas sazones.

144. Vido entre los otros un omne ançiano,
Don Sancho li dixeron, varón fue masellano,° from Mansilla
Nunca lo ovo visto nil tanso° de la mano; touched
Pero la sierraniella° conoçió al serrano. mountain girl

145. Con esto la enferma ovo muy grant pesar,
En aquella sazón non querría espertar,
Ca estaba en grant gloria en sabroso logar,
E cuydaba que nunca allá podría tornar.

146. Avíales poco grado a los despertadores,
Siquiera a la madre, siquiera a los serores.
ca estaba en grant gloria entre buenos sennores,

Que non sentía un punto de todos los dolores.

147. Diçía entre los dientes con una voz cansada:
Monte Olivete, monte Olivete, ca non diçía al nada:
Non gelo entendía nadi de la su posada,
Ca non era la voz 'de tal guisa formada.° garbled

148. Otras buenas mugieres qui çerca li sedíen,
Vidían que murmuraba, mas non la entendíen:
Por una maravilla esta cosa havíen,
Estaban en grant dubda si era mal o bien.

149. La madre de la duenna fizo a mi clamar,
Fízome en la casa de la fija entrar.
Io que 'la afincasse° si podiesse fablar , urge her
Ca queríe deçir algo, non la podían entrar.° understand

150. Dixéronli a ella quando yo fui entrado:
Oria, abre los oios, e oirás buen mandado:° news
Reçibe a don Munno el tu amo honrrado
Que viene despedirse del tu buen gasaiado.° company

151. Luego que oió este mandado Oria,
Abrió ambos los oios, entró en su memoria,
E dixo: ¡ay mesquina! estaba en grant gloria,
Porque me despertaron so en grant querimonia.° distress
152. Si sólo un poquiello me oviesen dexada,
Grant amor me fiçieran, sería terminada,° dead
Ca entre tales omnes era yo arribada
Que contra° los sus bienes el mundo non es nada. compared to

153. Ovo de estas palabras don Munno mucho plaçer:
Amiga, dixo, esto fáznoslo entender:
Bien non lo entendemos, querríamoslo saber,
Esto que te rogamos tú débeslo façer.

154. Amigo, dijo ella, non te mintré° en nada, **=mentiré**
Por façer el tu ruego mucho so adebdada,° obligated

A monte Oliveti fui en vissión levada,
Vidi y tales cosas por qui so muy pagada.

155. Vidi y logar bueno sobra buen arbolado,° grove
El fruto de los árboles non sería preçiado,° valued
De campos grant anchura, de flores grant mercado,° abundance
Guarría° la su olor a omne entecado.° would cure, sick

156. Vidi y grandes gentes de personas honrradas,
Que eran bien vestidas todas, e bien calzadas,
Todas me reçibieron con laudes bien cantadas,
Todas eran en una voluntat acordadas.

157. Tal era la companna, tal era el logar;
Omne que y morase° nunca vería pesar:° dwell, grief
Si oviesse más un poco y estar,
Podría muchos bienes ende acarrear.° bring

158. Díixol Munno a Oria: ¿cobdiçias allá ir?
Díxol a Munno Oria: yo sí, más que vivir:
E tú non perdrías° nada de conmigo venir: **=perderías**
Díixol Munno: quisiésselo eso Dios consentir.

159. Con sabor de la cosa quísose levantar,
Commo omne que quiere en carrera entrar:
Díxoli Munno: Oria fuelga en tu logar,
Non es agora tiempo por 'en naves entrar.° embark

160. En esta pleitesía non quiero detardar;
Si por bien lo tovierdes, quiérovos destaiar,° cut it short
A la fin de la duenna me quiero acostar,° come
Levarla a la siella, después ir a folgar.

161. El mes era de marzo la segunda semana
Fiesta de Sant Gregorio de Leandre cormana[21]

---

[21] **Fiesta de Sant...** St. Gregory's feast day is March 12 and St. Leander's is March 13; we can say they are "cousin" feast days.

Hora quando los omnes façen meridiana,° — siesta
Fue quexada° la duenna que siempre vistía lana.° — sick, hairshirt

162. La madre de la duenna, cosa de Dios amada,
Del duelo de la fixa estaba muy lazrada:
Non dormiera la noche, estaba apesgada,° — very grieved
Lo que ella comía non era fascas° nada. — almost

163. Yo Munno e don Gómez çellerer° del logar — majordomo
Oviemos a Amunna de firmes a rogar
Que fuese a su lecho un poquiello a folgar,
Ca nos la guardaríamos,° si quisiesse passar.° — attend, were to die

164. Quanto fue acostada fue luego adormida,
Un visión vido que fue luego complida:° — ended
Vido a su marido omne de sancta vida,
Padre de la reclusa que yaçía mal tanida.° — ill

165. Vido a don Garçía que fuera su marido,
Padre era de Oria, 'bien ante° fue transido:° — long ago, died
Entendió bien que era por la fixa venido,
E que era sin dubda el su curso° complido. — life

166. Preguntóli Amunna, decitme, don Garçía,
¿Quál es vuestra venida? yo saberlo querría:
Si vos vala don Christo, Madre Sancta María,
Deçitme de la fixa si verá cras° el día. — tomorrow

167. Sepas, dixo Garçía, fágote bien çertera,
çerca anda del cabo Oria de la carrera:
Cuenta que es finada, ca la hora espera,
Es de las sus iornadas esta la postremera.° — last

168. Vido con don Garçía, tres personas seer
Tan blancas que nul omne non lo podría creer:
Todas de edat una e de un paresçer,
Mas non fablaban nada nin querían signas fer.

169. Despierta fue Amunna, la vissión pasada,
Si ante fue en cuita, después fue más coitada,
Ca sabía que la fixa sería luego pasada,
E que fincaria ella triste e dessarrada.° forlorn

170. Non echó esti suenno la duenna en olvido
Nin lo que li dixiera Garçía su marido:
Recontógelo todo a Munno su querido:
El decorólo° todo commo bien entendido. memorized it

171. Bien lo decoró eso commo todo lo al,
Bien gelo contó ella, non lo aprendió él mal,
Por ende de la su vida fizo libro caudal:° important
Yo ende lo saqué esto de esi su misal.[22]

172. Conjuróla° Amunna a su fixuela Oria: begged her
Fixa, sí Dios vos lieve a la su sancta gloria,
Si visión vidiestes o alguna historia,
Deçítmelo demientre avedes la memoria.

173. Madre, dixo la fixa, ¿qué me afincades° tanto? do you insist
Dexatme, si vos vala Dios el buen padre sancto:
Asaz tengo en mi laçerio e quebranto:
Más me pesa la lengua que un pesado canto.° stone

174. Queredes que vos fable, yo non puedo fablar:
Veedes que non puedo la palabra formar:
Madre, si me quisierdes tan mucho afincar,
Ante de la mi hora me puedo enfogar.° choke

175. Madre, si Dios quisiesse que pudiese vevir ,
Aún asaz tenía cosas que vos deçir;
Mas quando non lo quiere el Criador sofrir,
Lo que a él ploguiere es todo de sofrir.

---

[22] **Yo ende lo...** *I took it (the story) from Munno's missal* who apparently wrote it on blank pages in the missal.

176. Fuel' viniendo a Oria la hora postremera:
Fuese más aquejando, 'a boca de noche era;° — it was getting dark
Alzó la mano diestra de fermosa manera:
Fizo cruz en su fruente, sanctiguó su mollera.° — head

177. Alzó ambas las manos, juntólas en igual,
Commo qui riende graçias al buen Rey espiritual:
Çerró oios e boca la reclusa leal:
Rindió a Dios la alma, nunca más sintió mal.

178. Avía buenas companna en essi pasamiento,° — passing (death)
El buen abat don Pedro persona 'de buen tiento,° — prudent
Monges e hermitannos, un general conviento,
Estos façían obsequio e todo complimiento.° — respect

179. Fue esti sancto cuerpo ricamente guardado,
En sus pannos de orden ricamente aguisado:
Fue muchas de vegadas el psalterio rezado:
Non se partieron de elli fasta fue soterrado.° — buried

180. Si entender queredes toda çertanidat,
Do yaçe esta duenna de grant sanctidat,
En Sant Millán de Suso, esta es la verdat:
Fáganos Dios por ella merçet e caridat.

181. Çerca de la iglesia es la su sepultura,
A pocas de pasadas en una angostura,° — narrow place
Dentro en una cueba° so una piedra dura, — **=cueva**
Commo mereçía ella, non de tal apostura.° — quality

182. La fija e la madre ambas de sancta vida,
Commo ovieron siempre grant amor e complida,
En la muerte y todo non an cosa partida,
Çerca yaçe de Oria Amunna sepelida.° — buried

183. Cuerpos son derecheros° que sean adorados, — honored
Ca sufrieron por Christo laçerios muy granados:
Ellas fagan a Dios ruegos multiplicados

Que nos salve las almas, perdone los pecados.

184. Gonzalo li dixeron al versificador,° — poet
Que en su portaleyo° fizo esta labor: — door
Ponga en él su graçia Dios el nuestro sennor,
Que vea la su gloria en el reyno mayor.

185. Aún non me quería, sennores, espedir,° — say good-bye
Aún fincan cosiellas que vos e de deçir:
La obra comenzada bien la quiero complir,
Que non aya ninguno porque me escarnir.° — criticize

186. Desque murió la fixa sancta emparedada,
Andaba la su madre por ella fetillada:° — grieving
Solo que la podiesse sonnar una vegada,
Teníase por guarida° e por muy confortada. — cured

187.Sopo Dios entender bien el su corazón,
Demostróli a Amunna una grant vissión,
Que sopo de la fixa que era o que non:
Aún esso nos finca de todo el sermón.[23]

188. Cayó una grant fiesta un día sennalado,
Día de çincuesma° que es mayo mediado, — Pentecost
Ensonnó esta duenna un suenno desseado,
Por qual muchas vegadas ovo a Dios rogado.

189. Cantadas las matinas, la 'liçençia soltada,° — permission granted
Que fuesse qui's quissiese folgar a su posada,
Acostósse un poco Amunna bien lazrada,
E luego ensonnó la su fixa amada.

190. Abrazáronse ambas commo façían en vida:
Fixa, dixo la madre, avédesme guarida:
Quiero que me digades quál es vuestra venida,
O si sodes en pena° o sodes ende salida. — purgatory

---

[23] **Aún esso non…** *the end of the story is yet to be told*

191. Madre, dixo la fixa, fiesta es general,
Commo es Resurectión, o commo la Natal:° — Christmas
Oy prenden los christianos el çebo° espiritual, — food
El cuerpo de don Christo mi sennor natural.

192. Pasqua es en que deben christianos comulgar,
Reçibir 'corpus domini° sagrado en el altar. — Eucharist
Io essi quiero, madre, resçibir e tomar,
E tener mi carrera, allá me quiero andar.

193. Madre, si bien me quieres, e pro° me quieres buscar, — something good
Manda llamar los clérigos, vénganme comulgar,
Que luego me querría de mi grado tornar,
E nin poco nin mucho non querría tardar.

194. Fixa, dixo la madre, ¿dó vos queredes ir?
Madre, dixo la fixa, a los çielos sobir,
Sin razón me façes, fixa, quiero vos lo deçir,
Que tan luego queredes de mí vos despartir.° — distance

195. Mas fixa, una cosa vos quiero demandar:
¿Si en el passamiento reçibiestes pesar?
¿O si vos dieron luego en el çielo logar?
¿O vos fiçieron ante a la puerta musar?° — wait

196. Madre, dixo la fixa, en la noche primera
Non entré al palaçio, non sé por quál manera.
Otro día mannana abrióme la portera,
Reçibiéronme, madre, todos por compannera.

197. Fixa, en esa noche que entrar non podiestes,
¿Quién vos fizo companna mientre fuera estoviestes?
Madre, las sanctas vírgines que de suso oiestes:
Estovi en tal deliçio en qual nunca oyestes.

198. La Virgo gloriosa lo que me prometió,
Ella sea laudada, bien me lo guardó:

En el mi passamiento de mí non se partió
De la su sancta graçia en mí mucha metió.

199. Otra cosa vos quiero, mi fixa, preguntar,
¿En quál compannía sodes,? façétmelo entrar.
Madre, dixo la fixa, estó en buen logar,
Qual nunca por mi mérito non podría ganar.

200. Entre los inocentes so, madre, heredada,
Los que puso Erodes° por Christo a espada, — Herod
Yo non lo merezría° de seer tan honrrada; — **=merecería**
Mas plogo a don Christo la su virtut sagrada.

201. Estas palabras dichas e muchas otras tales,
Oria la benedicta de fechos espiritales
Fuyóli a la madre de los oios corales,° — of her heart
Despertó luego ella, moyó° los lagremales. — wept

202. Vido sin estas otras muy grandes visiones,
De que formaría omne asaz buenas razones;
Mas tengo otras priesas de fer mis cabazones:[24]
Quiero 'alzarme desto° fasta otras sazones. — leave this

203. Qui en esto dubdare que nos versificamos,
Que non es esta cosa tal commo nos contamos,
Pecará duramientre en Dios que adoramos:
Ca todo quanto deçimos, escrito lo fallamos.

204. El que lo escribió non dirá falsedat,
Que omne bueno era de muy grant sanctidat.
Bien conosçió a Oria, sopo su poridat:° — secrets
En todo quanto dixo, dixo toda verdat.

205. De ello sopo de Oria, de la madre 'lo al,° — the rest
De ambas era elli maestro muy leal,
Dios nos dé la graçia el buen Rey Spirital

---

[24] **Tengo otras priesas…** *I am in a hurry to end this*

Que allá nin aquí nunca veamos mal. Amén.

...................
Hic liber est scriptus, qui scripsit sit benedictus.[25]

Sánchez, al fin de la Vida de Santa Oria, publica estos
versos, que dice están en la lápida° tombstone
del sepulcro de santa Auria, virgen:
*Hunc quem cernis lapidem scultum sacra tegit membra*
*Beata. Simul Auria Virgo cum matre Amunnia quiesunt*
*Femina. Et quia pro Xpo arctam duxerunt vitam,*
*Simul cum eo meruerunt coronari in gloria.*
So esta piedra que vedes yace el cuerpo de santa Oria,
E el de su madre Amunna fembra de buena memoria:
Fueron de grant abstinencia en esta vida transitoria,
Por que son con los angeles las sus almas en gloria.

[25] **Hic liber est...** *This book is written, may the writer be blessed.*

# *XIV Century*

## Historical Background

This was a period of war and civil war, of political upheaval, and a continuation of the Reconquest. The study of the arts and sciences, so avidly pursued by the scholars of Alfonso X, waned. The Black Death struck Spain, just as it struck the rest of Europe. The kings of Spain were not outstanding patrons of literature. In spite of all of this, literature was written, and at least two writers have earned a place among the immortals. One, a prince, don Juan Manuel, nephew of Alfonso X, wrote a collection of prose tales; the other, a priest, Juan Ruiz, Archpriest of Hita, wrote the perennially famous *Libro de buen amor*. The ruling house of Trastamara had its beginning in the 14th century and was to produce a number of kings, and in the 15th century, the famous Isabella of Castile.

## Lyric Poetry

Poetry written in the Galician-Portuguese language continued to be in vogue among erudite poets, although Castilian was coming into its own. The lyric in Galician still modeled itself after the Provençal school, although folk or native Spanish themes and ideas were included. A number of poets who preferred Galician lived in the 14th century, but are considered 15th century poets because their writings appear in the fifteenth-century *Cancionero de Baena.*

## Narrative Poetry

### *Minstrel Poetry: Juglaría*

Interest in the epic did not die in the 14th century, although there was a considerable change in tone and a pulling away from the old epic formula of the *Poema de Mio Cid* (12th century) and *Poema de Fernán González* (13th century) which survived only in *clerecía.* The interest in the human aspects of the lives and characters of epic heroes brought about redactions of old themes and created new roles for these heroes.

The *Siete infantes de Lara* or Salas, which is the account of a feud, the murder of seven brothers, and the vengeance taken by a half-brother named Mudarra historically occurred in the $10^{th}$ century but the only version we have is from the $14^{th}$ century. The *Cantar de Rodrigo*, or *Mocedades del Cid*, was written in the poetry of the minstrels (juglares), possibly as late as the early $15^{th}$ century, but in tone it belongs to the $14^{th}$, if not even to earlier times. Its date of composition is usually given as 1400.

The *Poema de Alfonso XI* is a long (10,000 lines) historical poem dealing with the life and Moorish wars of King Alfonso XI (d. 1350) of Castile. It is realistic and filled with a great deal of daily life and customs of the time.

## *Los Siete infantes de Lara*

This is a fragment of an epic poem in the minstrel style. The legend starts with the wedding of Doña Lambra (the aunt of the seven *infantes*) and Ruy Velázquez (the brother of the *infantes'* mother, Doña Sancha). The wedding is in Burgos and is hosted by Garci Fernández, the Count of Castile. It is a five-week celebration and there are many festivities. One of them is a kind of javelin throwing contest. Muño Salido is the tutor of the seven nobles.

Primero lançó° su vara° el conde Garci Fernández — hurled, javelin
e después lançó otrosí el bueno de Ruy Velázquez,
e después Muño Salido, el que bien cató° las aves, — observed
e desí adelant lançaron otros muchos de otras partes.

*In one of the events, Doña Lambra's cousin, Álvar Sánchez, excels, and she declares him to be worth all the rest. At this, the youngest of the seven infantes, Gonzalo, takes offense, and does even better than Álvar Sánchez. A dispute erupts, and Gonzalo kills Álvar Sánchez. This is an enormous offense to Doña Lambra—not only killing her cousin, but at her wedding as well—and she asks her husband, Ruy Velázquez, to retaliate:*

"Ruégovos, don Rodrigo, que vos pese° de mi male° — grieve, offense
pésevos de mi dolor, de vuestra desonra grande
que vuestros sobrinos nos han fecho tan male."

"Non curedes,° doña Lambra, non tomedes más pesare — worry
que si yo vivo e no muero, yo vos entiendo vengare
e darvos he tal derecho de que todo el mundo fable."

*So Ruy Velázquez devises a plan. He will send Gonzalo Gustioz, the infantes' father to Cordova to get promised funds, so he says, from Almanzor, the caliph, to help pay for his extravagant wedding, and meanwhile he'll have the seven infantes killed. Velázquez gives Gonzalo Gustioz a letter of introduction to the caliph. But the lettter really asks Almanzor to detain and behead him.*

*Ruy Velázquez then asks the seven infantes to accompany him on a sortie, which is really going to be an ambush to capture and kill the infantes. Along the way, Muño Salido sees bad omens— the first one is an eagle that kills itself— and says they should go back.*

un águila cabdal° ferrera[26] que estava encima de un pino. — large
Muchol pesó de coraçón a ese Nuño Salido:
"Estas aves nos lo muestran: tornemos° nos, míos fijos."... — let's return
e dexóse caer en tierra muerta a pié del pino.

*His prediction was right, and the ambush is now obvious, as 10,000 Moors appear. The seven infantes and Muño Salido are attacked and all are beheaded. The heads are placed in a chest to take back to Almanzor. From the Moorish army, king Alicante has lost a lot of his soldiers owing to the fierce battle that the infantes and their men waged before their deaths. Ruy Velázquez had promised Alicante, for his help, safe conduct in Castile for him and his soldiers (for plundering sorties).*

Ya son muertos los infantes ¡Dios les aya las almas!
Alicante a Ruy Velázquez en el ombro° le besava, — **=hombro**
Ruy Velázquez a Alicante de coraçón le abraçava:
"Daquí adelant nuestra facienda° avémosla librada,° — business, completed
non ha de qui° nos temer en Castiella nin en Lara." — whom
"Don Rodrigo, esta batalla cuesta a nos muy cara."

*Alicante goes back to Cordova and speaks with Almanzor:*

---

**Ferrera** the color of iron which indicates a bad omen.

Alicante pasó el puerto,° comensó de más andar, mountain pass
por sus 'jornadas contadas° a Cordova fue a llegar. number of days
"Ganamos ocho cabeças de omnes de alta° sangre, noble
mas tales ganancias caras nos cuestan asaz;° very
tres reys e quinze mill de otros perdiémoslos allá."

*Now that Almanzor has the chest, he is curious to learn whom the heads belonged to, so he asks the imprisoned Gonzalo Gustioz if he can recognize any of them.*

e díxol: "Gonçalo Gustios, bien te quiero preguntar:
lidiaron° los míos poderes° en el canpo de Almenar, fought, armies
ganaron ocho cabeças, todas son de gran linaje;
e dizen míos adalides° que de Lara son naturales, scouts
si Dios te salve, que me digas la verdad."
Respondió Gonçalo Gustios: "Presto os la entiendo declarar:
si ellas son de Castiella conocer he de qué logar,
otrosí si de alfoz° de Lara, ca serán de mi linaje." region
Violas Gonçalo Gustioz bueltas° en polvo° e en sangre; covered, dust
con la manta° en que estavan començólas de alinpiar, cloth
tan bien las afemenció,° conosciólas 'por su mal.° looked intently, sadly
Llorando de los sus ojos dixo entonces a Almançor:
"Bien conosco estas cabeças por mis pecados, señor;
conosco las siete, ca de los míos fijos son,
la otra es de Muño Salido, su amo° que los crió. tutor
¡Non las quiso muy grant bien quien aquí las ayuntó!° gathered
Captivo desconortado° para siempre so." disconsolate
Alinpiólas muy bien del polvo e de la sangre
cada una como nasció púsolas en aze° order
estavan lo oteando° Almançor e Alicante. watching
Tomó primero en sus bracos la cabeça de Muño Salido
e razonóse° con ella como si fuese bivo: spoke
"Sálvevos Dios, Muño Salido, mi conpadre e mi amigo,
dadme cuenta de los míos fijos
que en vuestras manos ove metido,
por do° en Castiella e en León érades vos muy temido. everywhere
Cataríades° los agüeros como amo e padrino, read

non vos querría creer Gonçalo Gonçález mi fijo,
ca se dolería° de mí que yazía en cativo. grieved
E perdonatme, conpadre e mi buen amigo."

La cabeça de Muño Salido tornóla en su lugar
e la de Diego Gonçález su fijo el mayor fue a tornar,
mesando° sus cabellos e las barbas de su faz. pulling out
"¡Viejo so mesquino° para estas bodas bofordare!° wretched, jousting
Fijo Diego Gonçález, a vos quería yo máse° **=más**
fazíalo con derecho ca vos naciérades ante.° first
Grant bien vos quería el conde ca érades su mayor alcaide"° first lieutenant
Besó la cabeça llorando e tornóla a su lugar.
Cada uno como nasçió así las va tomare.

La cabeça de Martín Gonçález en braços la tomava.
"O fijo Martín Gonçález, persona mucho onrada,
¿quién podría asurar que en vos avía tan buena maña?° skill
Tal jugador de tablas° non avía en toda España; jouster
muy mesurada miente vos fablávades en plaça,
bien plazía ende a todos los que vos escuchavan.
Pues vos sodes muertos, por mí non daría nada,
que viva o que muera de mí ya no me incala,° matters
mas he muy fiero° duelo de vuestra madre doña Sancha: strong
sin fijos e sin marido fincará tan desconortada."
Besó la cabeça llorando e a su lugar la tornava
e la de Suer Gonçález en bracos la tomava.
"Fijo Suero Gonçález, cuerpo tan leale,
de las vuestras buenas mañas un rey se devía pagare,
de muy buen caçador no avíe en el mundo vuestro par
en caçar muy bien con aves e a su tiempo las mudar.° molt
¡Malas bodas vos guisó° el hermano de vuestra madre, prepared
metió a mí en cativo e a vos fizo descabeçar!
los nasçidos e por nasçer traidor por ende le dirán."
Besó la cabeça llorando e en su lugar la dexóve,
la de Fernant Gonçález en braços la tomóve.
"Fijo, cuerpo honrado, e nombre de buen señore,
del conde Fernant Gonçález, ca él vos bateó.
De las vuestras mañas, fijo, pagar se devía un enperador;

matador de oso e de puerco e de cavalleros señore,
quier° de cavallo quier de pie que ningún otro mejor. — whether
Nunca rafezes° compañas, fijo, amastes vos, — vile
e muy bien vos aveníades° con las más altas e mejores. — get along
¡Vuestro tío don Rodrigo malas bodas vos guisó:
a vos fizo matar e a mí metió en prisión!
¡traidor le llamarán quantos por nascer son!"

Besó la cabeça llorando e en su lugar la miso;° — **=metió**
la de Ruy Gonçález en braços la priso.
"Fijo Ruy Gonçález, 'cuerpo muy entendido,° — very intelligent pe[rson]
de las vuestras buenas mañas un rey sería conplido,
muy leal a señor e verdadero amigo,
mejor cavallero de armas que nunca omne vido.
¡Malas bodas vos guisó vuestro tío don Rodrigo:
a vos fizo descabeçar e a mí metió en cativo!
Hevos° finados deste mundo mesquino, — here you are
él por sienpre avía perdido el paraíso."

Besó la cabeça llorando e en su lugar la dexava;
la de Gustios Gonçález en braços la tomava,
del polvo e de la sangre muy bien la alinpiava,
faziendo fiero duelo por los ojos la besava.
"Fijo Gustios Goncález, avíades buena maña:
non dixérades una mentira por quant maña° es España. — great
Cavallero de buena guisa, buen feridor d'espada:
ninguno feristes con ella que no perdiese el alma.
¡Malas nuevas irán, fijo, de vos al alfoz° de Lara!" — territory
Besó la cabeça con lágrimas e púsola en su lugar,
e la de Gonçalo Gonçález su fijo el menor fue tomar,
mesando sus cabellos, faziendo duelo grande.
"Fijo Gonçalo Gonçález, a vos amava más vuestra madre.
Las vuestras buenas mañas ¿qui las podría contare?
buen amigo para amigos e para señor leale;
conosçedor de derecho, amávades lo judgar;° — doing justice
en armas esforçado, a los vuestros franquear,° — generous
alançador° de tablado nunca omne lo vido tale; — lance thrower
con dueñas e donzellas sabíades muy bien fablar

e dávades las vuestras donas muy de voluntad
donde erades más amado que otro cavallero de prestar
menester avía agudeza quien con vos razonase,
Los que me temían por vos, enemigos me serán,
aunque yo torne a Lara, nunca valdré un pan;
non he pariente ni amigo que me pueda vengar:
¡más me valdría la muerte que esta vida tal!"
E en esto comediendo,° amortesçido se ha, — considering
la cabeça de las manos sobre las otras se le cae,
quando cayó en tierra de sí no sabía parte.° — where he was

Almançor mandó llamar una infante, su hermana...
e muy bien e muy apuestamiente° fablava: — courteously
"Hermana, si me vos amades, entrad en esa casa
do yaz ese christiano que es ome de sangre alta...
vos, mi hermana, conortatlo con muy buenas palabras..."

*Almanzor's sister goes to comfort Gonzalo Gustioz.*

"¡Conortatvos, christiano, mucho vos veo cobarde!
los moros e los christianos quando avedes lid canpal
passades los bivos sobre los muertos con
grant coyta° de lidiar. — haste
E pues vos esto non podedes librar,
lo que yo, muger, sofrí,° cuedo° sofreríades mal: — endured, think
yo avía pocos años quando murió mi madre
e yo nunca ove marido nin 'amigo en poridat° — seceret lover
e mi hermano Almançor a Sevilla me fue a casar
con un rey muy poderoso e de muy grant rictat...° — wealth
Mi hermano envió° por nos una fiesta de Sant Johan: — ordered
en el axaraf° de Sevilla christianos fuimos topar,° — plain, met
mataron a mío marido, mis siete fijos otro tal;
yo escapé a vida, metíme en un axarafe,
lazré noches e días e non me quis por end matar.
Veovos los cabellos blancos, mas el rostro fresco° asaz: — young
por ventura aún faredes fijos que a los otros vengarán."
Ella dezía mentira por lo haber de conortar,
ca nunca fuera casada, nin fijos fuera engendrar,

mas era donzella e fermosa asaz."

Don Gonçalo 'paró en ella mientes° e della fue trabar.° — set his eyes on her, gra[b]
"Dueña, vos 'açomastes el sueño,° Dios lo quiera soltar,[27] — you proposed the idea
ca conbusco faré el fijo que a los otros vengará..."

*The princess gets pregnant from this encounter. When Gonzalo Gustioz leaves Cordova, he gives her half of a ring with which their offspring can identify himself.*

*Mudarra, now fully grown, goes to his mother and threatens her to force her to tell him about his father.*

"Denuéstanme° en vuestra casa, e dízenme que non he padre, — scorn me
e yo si vuestra merçed fuere, quiérolo ir buscar:
si él fuere bueno e onrado para vos he de tornarme,
si fuese fijo de villano nunca me veredes más."

*In the* Chronica de 1344 *version, she says: " 'Fijo, padre avedes muy onrrado qual saben en toda España e ha nonbre Gonzalo Gustioz, e es natural de Salas' e aquí lo tovo vuestro tío en cárçel, y me empreñé de vos, en yaziendo preso. Aquí le troxeron siete cabeças de sus fijos, quel mataron en una lid... e yo fablando con él, díxele que aún podría aver otros fijos que le vengarían la muerte de aquéllos." She gives him the half ring, and he goes off to find his father.*

*Meanwhile Doña Sancha, Gonzalo's wife, has a dream
and tells him about it:*

"...descuentra° Córdova veía venir volando un açor... — toward
tan grande que la su sombra cubría a mí e a vos...
ívase posar en el onbro de Ruy Velázquez, el traidor."

*In her dream, the hawk pecks at Ruy Velázquez's shoulder until it bleeds, and Doña Sancha drinks his blood.*

Mudarra's squire goes to Salas first and talks with Sancha

[27] **Dios lo quiera...** *may God carry it out*

"Tomad, señora, estos paños 'en nombre de° — as
estrena° honrada; — gift
buen huésped vos viene, e seed bien conortada,
ca vos viene por huésped el infante don Mudarra,
sobrino del rey Almançor, fijo de la infante su hermana."
Con fondo sospiro allí dixo doña Sancha:
"¡Dios quiera que sea el açor que yo esta noche soñava!"

*Mudarra goes to church in Salas where the eight heads are on display.*

e yendo por el camino una eglesia falló
e entró en ella a fazer su oración...

"A Dios digo verdat que del mundo es señor,
poca seríe la mi vida si estas cabeças non vengo yo."

Saliéronse de la eglesia, fuéronse para don Gonçalo,
e todos los de Salas le vinieron besar las manos;
dixeron que lo servirían e farían su mandado.
Don Mudarra Gonçález diçió° a la puerta del palacio — =dijo

"Yo so sobrino de Almançor, fijo de la su hermana,
vos me avedes engendrado, vuestro fijo so sin dubdança."
Dixo Gonçalo Gustioz: "Desque casé con doña Sancha,
nunca ove fazimiento° con mora nin con christiana; — friendship
vos servido seredes en quanto fuerdes en Salas;
e desto que vos digo non podedes saber más nada."

Respondió sañudamiente ese Mudarra Gonçález:
"Si me non queredes por fijo, nin yo a vos por padre,
ca donde yo menos valgo así es de vuestra parte.
Mas déxeme Dios vengar míos hermanos los infantes
e recebir cristiandat por mi ánima salvar,
que por vuestro heredamiento non doy quanto un figo vale."
Allí dixo doña Sancha: "¡Si vos viésedes como ante!
Si viésedes agora su rostro e su faz,
diríades que este era vuestro fijo Gonçalo Gonçález.

E vos con miedo de mí non neguedes lo que errastes,
ca quien yaze en captivo non puede ley guardare,
ca conviene pecar con lazeria, sed o fanbre.
E por vergüença de mí non neguedes vuestra sangre:
pecariedes mortal miente e yo avría enojo grande.
¡Tales pecados como este oviésedes siete o más!
vos tomaríedes penitencia e yo tomaría la meetad."° =mitad

Estonce dixo don Gonçalo toda la verdat:
"Si él es fijo de la infante, él me dará señal…"

*Mudarra gives him the half-ring, which Gonzalo compares with his half, and everybody is joyful that Mudarra will avenge his brothers and their tutor.*

E fueron aquestas nuevas a Ruy Velázquez onde estava
con dozientos cavalleros en el castiello de Amaya.
Pesól de coraçón, pero que dixo fuertes palabras:
"Por todo aquesto non do quanto una paja;
ante que salga este año ayuntar me he con él en batalla,
e onde fize traer de los siete sus cabeças a Salas,
si me Dios non es contrallo,° eso faré a don Mudarra" against it

*After an enormous chase, Mudarra finally corners Ruy Velázquez.*

Dixo Ruy Velázquez a Mudarra González:
"¿Qui sodes vos, cavallero, e qué venides buscare?"
Respondióle don Mudarra: "Yo so vuestro enemigo mortal,
vengo vengar la muerte de mis hermanos los infantes
que vos como traidor levastes a descabeçar."
"Vos sodes el traidor," dixo Ruy Velázquez,
"ca desque que a Lara entrastes me fiziestes mucho mal:
matastes me mis vasallos e las mis villas quemastes;
agora me lo pagaredes que en tal tiempo estades."
Dixo don Mudarra: "Mientes, don falso traidor desleal;
de quantas traiciones pensaste oy derecho tú darás.
de quantos males uvedes fecho oi derecho me dorás
Castiguemos la cavallería estén quedas nuestras azes,

lidiemos nos uno por otro si esto a vos plaze,
que las nuestras gentes, ¿por qué se an de matare?
Entregar vos he mi cuerpo o vengaré los infantes."
Dixo Ruy Velázquez: "Todo esso a mí plaze."
Respondióle don Mudarra: "pues los vuestros castigad,
castigaré yo los míos que ninguno non derranche,° — leave the field
traidor sea como Judás quien i fiziere al."
Amos se desafiaron, uno de otro muy cerca están:
e sus gentes castigadas, dixo Mudarra Gonçález:
"Este es el día que yo deseava más!
Señor, tú cuida al que andava con verdad."
Allí le dixo Gonçalo Gustioz su padre:
"Fijo, por amor de mí non lidiedes con él aparte;
fuerte cavallero es el traidor, non ha en España su pare;
yo que lo conozco con él me dexad lidiare,
vengaré mis fijos e lo que me fizo cativare."
Dixo don Mudarra: "Señor, non me mandades
tale omenaje° le tengo fecho, no lo puedo quebrantare; — sworn promise
no falsaría mi palabra por quanto el mundo vale.
Veámonos con salud, si al nuestro Señor plaze."
Espoloneó el cavallo e deçendió por el valle.
Muy agradoso° el traidor a reçebirlo sale. — pleased
Alli espolonean los cavallos, a acometerse van;
abaxadas las lanças fieros golpes se dan,
quebrantaron los escudos que ninguna pro° les han, — benefit
'desmallávanse las lorigas° como si fueran çendal. — mail coat became undone
El poder de Jesucristo siempre amó verdad:
el golpe que el traidor dio a Mudarra Gonçález
non quiso Dios quel prendiese en la carne
pero non dexó la lança de salir de la otra parte.
La lançada que don Mudarra dio al traidor de
Ruy Velázquez
firiól por meytad de los pechos, la loriga le fue a falsar;° — break
más de la media lança salió de la otra parte,
sacóle de la silla° en tierra lo fue derribar: — saddle
nunca otro cavallero diérale golpe tal.
Don Mudarra tiró de la lança por otra ferida le dar,
desde encima del cavallo queríale golpear;

díxol don Rodrigo: "Amigo, ¿qué ganas en me matar?
ca el golpe que me diste me abonda asaz; sufficient
más por la fe que a Dios deves tanto te quiero rogar:
mis vasallos non han culpa, non les quieras fazer mal."
Desque Gonçalo Gustioz vio al traidor en tierra estar,
aguijó el cavallo, quanto pudo fuese para allá:
"Fijo, ese traidor non mates, liévalo a doña Sancha
tu madre que soltara el su sueño que soñava beber de su sangre."
"Por Dios, señor," dixo Mudarra, "en Salas non entrará,
en Vilvestre, su casa, allí lo justiciarán."
Cárganlo en una azémila,° comiénçanlo de levar; pack mule,
tamaño gozo han los de Lara, comiençan a bofordar.° joust

Los vasallos de Ruy Velázquez vanse para don Mudarra:
"Señor, non nos culpedes, ca servimos nuestras soldadas;
si vos ploguiere, seremos en vuestra conpaña."
Entonce les dixo ese infante don Mudarra:
"Amigos, id vos en buen ora, vuestro servicio no me incala.° doesn't matter
Más dadme agora recabdo como me dedes Castro e Amaya,
finquen al conde las heredades que dél avedes tomadas,
e vos id catar señor que bien vos faga,
que en vida del conde ni en la mía non ganaredes nada."

Dallí enbían los mandados a Salas, a doña Sancha,
que viniese a las bodas de don Mudarra.
E ella desque lo sopo, vino muy loçana.
Doña Sancha entró en Vilvestre, todos a reçebirla salen,
°coberturas villutadas,° bofordando van; plush clothes
Mudarra a doña Sancha las manos le fue besare,
diziendo 'a altas bozes:° "¡Justicia el cielo faze! shouting
Señor, deste traidor tú me quieras vengar."
Deçienden todos de las bestias, al palacio van entrar.
Entonce dixo don Mudarra a doña Sancha su madre:
"Vedes aquí el traidor, agora lo mandat justiciar."
El traidor cerró los ojos e la non quiso mirar;
catávalo doña Sancha en el suelo donde yaz,
echado en unas colchas vio correr d'él mucha sangre:
"¡Grado e gracias a ti, Señor rey celestial,

que veo el sueño que soñé que bevía de la su sangre!"
E fincó los inojos para beber, d'él a par;
mas desque así la vio esse Mudarra Gonçález,
rebatóla° en los braços, ayudóla a levantar: — took her
"Non lo fagades, señora, non quiera Dios que tal pase,
que sangre de omne traidor entre en cuerpo atan leal;
afelo en vuestras manos, mandatlo justiciar."
en vuestras manos lo tenedes mandaldo justiciar
Los unos dezían: "Señora, cada día un mienbro le tajad";
los otros dezían: "Señora, mandaldo desollar"; ° — flay
otros le dezían: "Por Dios, vámoslo a quemar";
los otros le dezían: "Señora, vámoslo a apedrear."° — stone
Allí fabló doña Sancha, oiredes que dirá:
"A todos lo agradezco que vos sentides de mi mal,
mas quiero esta justicia fazer a toda mi voluntad;
plaziendo a Dios e a don Mudarra yo quiero
ser desto alcalde:° — judge
en Burgos fueron las bodas, al tablado alançare,
sobresto se levantó esta traición atan grande,
por cativar mi marido, mis fijos descabeçare;
alçaldo° agora en dos vigas,° pies e manos le atade,° — raise him, posts, tie
de los que finaron en la batalla vénguese agora su linaje:
escuderos e cavalleros, e los que pudieren alcançare,
con lanças e con bofordos todos vengan alançar,
con dardos e con asconas° o con varas de lançar — throwing weapons
que las carnes del traidor hayan a despedaçar,
e desque cayere en tierra apedreallo han."
Como doña Sancha mandó, así a fazerlo van.
Veriedes las carnes del traidor todas a tierra caen,
ca la compaña era mucha, aína° lo van despedaçar; — quickly
ayuntaron los pedaços, piedras sobre él van lançar,
cubierto fue dellas, diez carradas° sobre él yazen. — cartloads
Agora quantos por i pasan de Paternóster° en lugar, — Our Father
con sendas piedras al luziello° van dare, — grave
e dizen: " 'Mal sieglo aya° la su alma. AMÉN." — cursed be her soul
Non levarán mil azémilas la piedra que y yaze
Por esta guisa es maldito aquel que traición faze;
non fallaredes en España qui su pariente se llame.

Hoy non se quiere ninguno llamar de su linaje.
La mala de doña Lambra para el conde ha adelinado° headed
en sus vestidos grandes duelos, los rabos° tails
de las bestias tajados;
llegado ha a Burgos, entrado ha en el palacio,
echóse a los pies del conde e besóle las manos:

"¡Merçed, conde señor, fija so de vuestra prima!
Lo que don Rodrigo fizo yo culpa non avría,
e non me desanparedes ca pocos serán los mis días."
El conde dixo: "¡Mentidos, doña alevosa° sabida!° treacherous, crafty
ca todas estas traiciones vos avedes bastecidas;° prepared
vos de las mis fortaleças érades señora e reina.
Non vos 'atreguo el cuerpo° de oy en este día; guarantee your safety
mandaré a don Mudarra que vos faga quemar viva
e que canes° espedaçen esas carnes malditas, dogs
e, por lo que fezistes, el alma avredes perdida."
Así fincó doña Lambra pobre e muy mezquina.

Desque esta cuitada de dueña del conde fue desamparada,
fuyendo por la tierra do sabía que era Mudarra,
con una manceba sola andava apeonada,° on foot
e non avía que comer sinon lo que por Dios les davan.
Murió en la sierra de Neila, e en Neila yaze soterrada
e hoy en día quantos por i pasan
nunca dizen Paternoster, dízenle: "¡Mal sieglo haya!"
AMÉN.

## *Mocedades del Cid (Cantar de Rodrigo)*

This poem (1360) is an important redaction of epic material in the *juglaría* style which gives a character to the Cid different from that presented in the *Cantar de Mio Cid* and shows him as a young man filled with vim, vigor, and even humor. After killing his father's enemy, Count Gómez, father of doña Jimena, King Ferdinand orders Rodrigo to marry her. Our hero postpones the marriage until he has won five battles and is therefore deserving of such a bride. Added to the material taken from historical sources is a great deal of folklore, legend, and tradition, and possibly even from the imagination of the redactor. It was this version and one in prose found in the *Crónica de 1344* as well as certain ballads of the next century that served as the source of the *Mocedades del Cid* of Guillén de Castro and *Le Cid* of Corneille, important developments of Spanish and French drama of the Early Modern period. It should be noted that the *Cantar de Rodrigo* forms a part (lines 280-1125) of a longer work, *la Crónica rimada de las cosas de España.* The importance of these redactions of the Cid's life is great, because of their influence on subsequent literature.

425 Allegó don Diego Laínez° al rey bessarle la mano; — Cid's father
cuando esto vio Rodrigo non le quisso bessar la mano
.....
Rodrigo fincó los inojos por le bessar la mano,
el espada traía luenga, el rey fue mal espantado.
A grandes bozes dixo: "Tiratme allá esse pecado."° — devil

430 Dixo estonçe don Rodrigo: "Querría más un clavo° — nail
que vos seades mi señor nin yo vuestro vassallo:
porque vos la bessó mi padre soy yo mal amanzellado."° — dishonored
'Essas oras° dixo el rey al conde don Ossorio su amo:[28] — then
"Dadme vos acá essa doncella: despossaremos° — we will marry
este lozano."° — haughty one

435 Aún no lo creyó don Diego, tanto estava espantado.
Salió la doncella et tráela el conde por la mano
ella tendió° los ojos et a Rodrigo comenzó de catarlo. — opened
Dixo: "Señor, muchas mercedes,
ca este es el conde que yo demando."
Allí despossavan a doña Ximena Gómez
con Rodrigo el Castellano.

---

[28] **Don Osorio su..** Doña Jimena's guardian.

440 Rodrigo respondió muy sañudo° contra el rey castellano. — angry
"Señor, vos me despossastes, más a mi pessar° que de grado: — grief
mas prométolo a Christus que vos non besse la mano,
nin me vea con ella en yermo° nin en poblado, — unpopulated place
fasta que venza çinco lides° en buena lid en canpo." — battles

445 Cuando esto oyó el rey fízose maravillado.
Dixo: "Non es este omne, mas figura a de pecado."

581 A los caminos entró Rodrigo, con treçientos fijosdalgo.
Al vado° de Cascajar, a do Duero fue apartado — ford
—fuerte día fazía de frío—, 'a la posiesta° en llegando, — late
a la horilla° del vado, estava un pecador de malato,° — **=orilla**, leper

585 A todos pediendo piedad, que le passasen el vado.
los cavalleros todos escopían,° et 'ívanse d'él arredrando.° — spit, left him
Rodrigo ovo dél duelo, et tomólo por la mano;
so una capa verde aguadera° passólo por el vado, — raincoat
en un mulo andador que su padre le avía dado,

590 e fuesse para Grejalva, do es Cerrato llamado;
so unas piedras cavadas, que era el poblado,
so la capa verde aguadera, alvergó° el Castellano e el malato. — protected
E en siendo dormiendo, a la oreja le fabló el gafo:° — leper
"¿Dormides Rodrigo de Bivar? Tiempo has de ser acordado:° — wake up

595 mensagero só de Christus, que non soy malato;
Sant Lázaro só, a ti me ovo Dios enviado,
que 'te dé un resollo en las espaldas,° que en calentura° sea tornado; — blow on your back; fever
que cuando esta calentura ovieres, que te sea menbrado,
cuantas cosas comenzares 'arrematarl'as° con tu mano." — finish them

600 Diol' un resollo en las espaldas que a los pechos le ha passado.
Rodrigo despertó, e fue muy mal espantado;

cató en derredor de sí, et non pudo fallar el gafo.
Menbróle d'aquel sueño, et cavalgó muy privado;° — fast
fuesse para Calahorra, de día et de noche andando.

750 En esta querella llegó otro mandado;° — message
cartas del rey de Françia e del emperador alemano,
cartas del patriarca e del papa romano,
que diesse tributo España desde Aspa fasta en Santiago:
el rey que en España visquiese° siempre se llamasse tributario, — live

755 'diese fuero° e tributo cada año; — issued laws
cinco son los reinados de España, así 'viníe afirmado;° — was declared
que diessen quinze donçellas vírgines en cada año,
...e fuesen fijasdalgo,
e diez cavallos, los mejores del reinado,

760 et treinta marcos de plata, que despensasen° los fijosdalgo, — pay
et azores mudados, et tres falcones, los mejores de los reinados;
este tributo que diesse cada año
en cuanto fuessen bivos cristianos.
Cuando esto oyó el buen rey don Fernando

765 batiendo va amas las palmas, las azes° quebrantando;° — face, scratching
"¡Pecador sin ventura, a qué tiempo só llegado!° — come
Cuantos en España visquieron nunca se llamaron tributarios;
a mí véenme niño e 'in sesso,° et vanme soverviando:° — immature, humiliating
¡Más me valdría la muerte que la vida que yo fago!

770 Agora enbiaré por mis vassallos, que me semeja guissado,° — opportune
et consejarme he con ellos si seré tributario."
Allí embió por Rodrigo et por todos los fijosdalgo;
enbiara atreguar° los condes, que non temiessen de daño. — arrange a truce

Allí fabló Ruy Diaz, ante que el rey don Fernando

1110 "¡Dévos Dios malas graçias, ay papa romano!
que por lo por ganar venimos, que non por lo ganado;
ca los çinco reinos de España sin vos le besan la mano;
viene por conquerir el emperio de Alemania,
que de derecho ha de heredarlo;
assentósse en la silla, por ende sea Dios loado:

1115 veré que le dan avantaja de la cual será ossado° — emboldened
conde alemano que l' dé la corona et el blago!."° — staff of religious authority
En tanto se levantó el buen rey don Fernando;
"A treguas venimos, que non por fazer daño.
Vos adeliñat,° mi señor Ruy Diaz el Castellano." — go on

1120 Estonçe apriessa se fue levantado:
"Oítme—dixo—rey de Françia e enperador alemano,
oítme patriarca e papa romano:
.......
enbiástesme pedir tributario:
traérvoslo ha el buen rey don Fernando,

1125 cras° vos entregará en buena lid en el campo — tomorrow
los marcos que l'pedistes.......
Vos, rey de Françia, de mí seredes buscado:
veré si vos acorrerrán° los Doçe Pares o algún francés loçano." — help
'Emplaçados fincan° para otro día en el campo. — set the date

## *Poema de Alfonso XI*[29]

Rodrigo Yáñez

This is a poem which relates the life of Alfonso XI from his rise to the throne to the conquest of Algeciras in 1344 and his battles against the Moors, in particular the Benimerines. The victory of the Christians over the Moors is described in a prophecy

[29] *Alfonso XI reigned from 1312-1350.*

by the Arthurian wizard Merlin. The authorship has been attributed to Ruy Yáñez, but some scholars believe that he was only a copyist. The work praises the king and his mistress Leonor de Guzmán. The verse form is important, for it is regarded as a link between the epic meter of minstrel poetry and the ballad. Some regard it as verse of 16 syllables broken by a caesura with rhyme ABAB at the end of each hemistich; others prefer to think of it as two separate quatrains set side by side, each rhyming ABAB.

*Virtudes y cualidades de Alfonso XI*

| | |
|---|---|
| 274 Espejo° fué de la ley, | observant |
| del Gran Criador vasallo: | |
| éste fué el mejor rey | |
| que estido° en cavallo. | was |
| Rey noble, entendido,° | intelligent |
| muy 'fiel de coraçón,° | loyal |
| con Dios Padre muy te*n*ido,° | close |
| bien devoto en oraçión. | |
| Conpañero graçioso, | |
| real, ssin mala codiçia,° | greed |
| cavallero muy fermoso,° | handsome |
| 'peso igual° de justiçia. | even handed |
| Caçador, real montero,° | flushes out the game |
| muy fiel batallador, | |
| en lidiar fuerte braçero,° | arm |
| de espada 'bien feridor.° | good wielder |

*Cortes en Madrid. Alfonso XI como legislador*

| | |
|---|---|
| Salió de Valladolid | |
| con todos ssus naturales,° | men |
| en la villa de Madrit | |
| fizo cortes muy reales. | |
| Commo lo ussan° los reys | do |
| por más 'cumunal provecho,° | common good |

publicó muy bien ssus leys
otorgadas° en derecho.° based, justice

330 Ffizo una ley cumunal
que fué una real cossa,
por todos en general
ffizo ley provechosa.

[La Batalla del Río de Salado, 1340: victoria sobre los moros. Profecía de Merlín]
Dios ayudó la su ley
e África quebrantó,° defeated
por honra del noble rey
España adelantó
en nobleza e en señorío,° dominion
en valor e en altura,° merit
en fama e en poderío,
al buen rey dio la ventura.° fortune
Mal desonrado salió
de Tarifa el moro marín:° Benamarines tribe
en aquel día Dios conplió
una profecía de Merlín.[30]
1811 Merlín fabló d' España
e dixo esta profeçía
estando en la Bretaña
a un maestro que í avía.
1812 Don Antón era llamado
este maestro que vos digo,
sabidor° y letrado,° wise, learned
de don Merlín mucho amigo.
1813 Este maestro sabidor
así le fué preguntar:
"Don Merlín, por el mi amor
'sepádesme declarer° tell me
la profeçía de España,

[30] ***Merlín*** *a magician with powers to predict the future in the time of King Arthur of Celtic lore.*

que yo querría saber
por vos alguna fazaña° — event
de lo que 'se ha de fazer."° — is to happen

*Profecía de Merlín*

1815 Merlín, sabidor sotil,
dixo luego esta razón:
"acabados los años mill
e los trezientos de la encarnaçión
cincuenta e nueve conplirán
los años desta fazaña
la mar fonda pasarán° — cross
de bestias muy grand conpaña.
1817 Muchas cosas aconteçerán,
maestro, creeldo çiertamiente,
fuertes° batallas serán — fierce
en las tierras del Poniente.° — west
1818 Reynará un león coronado
en la provençia de España,
será fuerte e apoderado,
señor de muy grand conpaña.
1819 Sabidor e de coraçón,
bivirá sienpre en guerra,
muy bravo del coraçón
e muy señor de la su tierra.
1820 Escontra° el sol poniente — toward
en el tienpo deste león
reyna un león dormiente,° — **=durmiente**
muy manso del coraçón.
1821 E el león coronado
que en este tienpo regnar
él será desafiado° — challenged
del puerco° de allén° la mar. — Moor, beyond
1822 Salirse ha el 'puerco espín,° — porcupine
señor de la grand espada;
de tierras de Benamarín

ayuntará° grand albergada.° gather, army
1823 Con bestias bravas e perros marinos° sailors
las aguas fondas pasará,
cobrirá montes e caminos,
en la España aportará.° arrive
1824 Pasarán por ponte seca
grand poder a maravilla
del falso pueblo de Meca
e çercarán una villa
1825 que es puerto de la mar
en tierras de la frontera,
e este fecho ha de llegar
*a*l dragón de la grand f*r*omera."° den
1835 Estas palabras apuestas° fine
de los leones e puerco espín
así commo son conpuestas
profetizólas Merlín.
1836 Non las quiso más declarar
Merlín, el de gran saber;
yo las quiero apaladinar° explain
cómmo las pueden entender:
1837 El león coronado
sobre que fundó° razón based
fué este rey bien aventurado
1838 de Castiella e de León.
E el otro león dormiente
aquel rey fué su natural,° liege
que regnó en el poniente
que llaman de Portogal.
1839 E el bravo puerco espín,
señor de la grand espada,
fué el rey de Benamarín
que a Tarifa tovo çercada,° under siege
1840 Rey de Granada fuel el dragón,
Granada la grand f*r*omera;
este rey de grand coraçón
cuydó° ganar la frontera. intended
1841 Las bestias bravas e perros marinos

que aportavan en la España
moros fueron viejos e niños
que í perderán grand conpaña
1842 que el buen rey fué matar
el día de la batalla;
la ponte seca del mar
las galeas° fueron sin falla. galleys (ships)
1843 La espada que dixo Merlín
que el puerco í perdería
la honra fué del rey de Benamarín
que se í perdió aquel día.
1844 La profeçía conté
e torné en dezer llano
yo, Rodrigo Yáñez la noté
en linguaje castellano.

## *Scholar's Poetry: Clerecía*

The greatest poet of the 14th century was Juan Ruiz, Archpriest of Hita. He regarded his *Libro de buen amor* as a kind of *ars poetica* and used a wide variety of verse forms, some of which like his own *serranillas*, appear to be forerunners of the *serranillas* of the following century. He writes both lyric and narrative verse in the *clerecía* meter and offers poems in the traditional *cuaderna vía* as well as poems of 5, 6, 7 and 8 syllable lines.

## Juan Ruiz, Arcipreste de Hita

He was a cleric who was elevated to the rank of Archpriest and was imprisoned for his writings by Gil de Albornoz, Archbishop of Toledo.

His masterpiece, *El libro de buen amor*, is more than 7000 lines long and written largely in *cuaderna vía*. It contains tales, moral satires, burlesques, fables and lyric poetry. The predominant theme is love which conquers all. The work appears in two versions, 1330 and 1343, the second of which is an expansion of the first and believed to have been written while he was in prison. The work is a manual of spiritual and carnal love as well as one of poetic composition.

*Aquí dize de cómo el Açipreste rogó a Dios que le diese graçia que podiese fazer este libro*

11. Dios Padre, Dios Fijo, Dios Spíritu Santo,
el que nasçió de la Virgen esfuérçenos° de tanto, strengthen us
que sienpre lo loemos en prosa e en canto,
sea de nuestras almas cobertura° e manto.° protection, shield

12. El que fizo el çielo, la tierra e el mar,
Él me done° su graçia e me quiera alunbrar,° give, enlighten
que pueda de cantares un librete rimar,
que los que lo oyeren puedan solaz tomar.

13. Tú Señor Dios mío que 'l omne crieste,° created
informa° e ayuda a mí el tu açipreste, teach
que pueda fazer un libro de buen amor aqueste,
que los cuerpos alegre e a las almas preste.° minister

14. Si queredes, señores, oír un buen solaz,
escuchad el rromanze° sosegadvos° en paz; in vernacular, be
non vos diré mentira en cuanto en él yaz,
Ca por todo el mundo se usa e se faz.

15. E por que mejor de todos sea escuchado,
fablarvos he 'por trovas° e cuento rrimado; in verse
es un dezir fermoso e saber sin pecado,
rrazón más plazentera, fablar más apostado.° delicate

16. Non tengades que es libro neçio 'de devaneo,° frivolous
nin creades que es chufa° algo que en él leo,° joke, teach
ca segund buen dinero yaze en vil correo,° leather pouch
ansí en feo libro está saber non feo.

17. El axenuz° de fuera más negro es que caldera,° fennel seed, kettle
es de dentro muy blanco más que la peñavera:° ermine
blanca farina está so negra cobertera;

açúcar negro e blanco está en vil cañavera.° sugar cane

18. Sobre la espina está la noble rosa flor;
en fea letra está saber de grand dotor:
como so mala capa yaze buen bevedor,° drinker
ansí so el mal tabardo° está buen amor. cloak

19. E porque de todo bien es comienço e raíz
la Virgen Santa Maria, por ende yo Juan Rroíz
açipreste de Fita, della primero fiz
cantar de los sus gozos siete, que ansí diz.

*Gozos de Santa María*

20. ¡O Santa María
luz del día
tú me guía
toda vía!

21. Gáname graçia e bendiçión,
e de Jhesú consolación,
que pueda con devoçión
cantar de tu alegría.

22. El primero gozo que's lea:
en çibdad de Galilea,
Nazaret creo que sea,
oviste mensajería

23. del ángel que a ti vino,
Grabiel santo e digno;
tróxote mensaz° divino, message
díxote: «Ave María.»

24. Tú, desque el mandado oíste,
omilmente rresçebiste;
luego virgen conçebiste

al fijo que Dios en ti enbía.

25. En Belém acaesçió
el Segundo, cuando nasçió
e sin dolor aparesçió
de ti, Virgen, el Mexía.

26. El terçero cuentan las leyes
cuando venieron los Reyes
E adoraron al que veys
En tu braço do yazía.

27. Ofreçió'l mira Gaspar,
Melchior fue ençienso dar,
oro ofreció Baltasar
al que Dios e omne seía.° was

28. Alegría cuarta e buena
fue cuando la Madalena
te dixo goço sin pena,
qu'el tu fijo vevía.

29. El quinto plazer oviste
cuando al tu fijo viste
sobir al çielo e diste
graçias a Dios ó subía.

30. Madre el tu gozo sesto,
cuando en los discípulos presto
fue Spíritu Santo puesto
en tu santa conpañía.

31. Del septeno, Madre Santa
la iglesia toda canta;
sobiste con gloria tanta
al çielo e cuanto y avía.

32. Reynas con tu fijo quisto,° beloved

nuestro Señor Jhesu Xpisto;
por ti sea de nós visto
en la gloria sin fallía.

*Aquí dize de cómo segund natura los omes e las otras animalias quieren haver conpañía con las fenbras*

71. Commo dize Aristótiles, cosa es verdadera,
el mundo por dos cosas trabaja: por la primera,
por haver mantenençia:° la otra cosa era — sustenance
por haver juntamiento con fenbra° plazentera. — woman

72. Si lo dixiese de mío, sería de culpar;
dízelo grand filósofo, non só yo de rebtar:° — challenge
de lo que dize el sabio non devemos dubdar,
que por obra se prueva el sabio e su fablar.

73. Que diz verdat el sabio claramente se prueva;
omnes, aves, animalias, toda bestia de cueva
quieren segund natura conpañía sienpre nueva,
e cuánto más el omne que a toda cosa se mueva.

74. Digo muy más del omne que de toda creatura;
todos a tienpo çierto se juntan con natura;
el omne 'de mal seso,° todo tienpo sin mesura, — without thinking
cada que puede e quiere fazer esta locura.

75. El fuego sienpre quiere estar en la çeniza,
commoquier que más arde cuanto más se atiza:° — stirring
el omne cuando peca bien vee que desliza,° — is slipping
mas non se parte ende ca natura 'lo enriza.° — urges him on

76. E yo como soy omne commo otro, pecador,
ove de las mugeres a las vezes grand amor;
provar omne las cosas non es por ende peor,
e saber bien e mal, e usar lo mejor.

*Aquí fabla de la constelación e de la planeta en que los omnes nasçen e del juizio que los çinco sabios naturales dieron en el nasçemiento del fijo del Rey Alcaraz*

123. Los antiguos astrólogos dizen en la çiençia
de la astrología, una buena sabiençia,° — wise saying
qu'el omne, cuando nasçe, luego en su naçençia,° — birth
el signo en que nasçe le juzgan por sentençia.° — destiny

124. Esto diz Tholomeo° e dízelo Platón, — Ptolemy
otros muchos maestros en este acuerdo son;
cuál es el ascendente° e la costellaçión — rising star
del que naçe, tal es su fado° e su don. — fate

125. Muchos hay que trabajan sienpre por clerezía,° — learning
deprenden° grandes tienpos, espienden° grant cuantía: — spend, spend
'en cabo° saben poco, que su fado les guía, — in the end
non pueden desmentir° a la astrología. — belie

126. Otros entran en orden° por salvar las sus almas, — religious order
otros toman esfuerço en querer usar armas,
otros sirven señores con las manos anbas;
pero muchos de aquestos 'dan en tierra de palmas.° — fall on their faces

127. Non acaban en orden nin son más cavalleros,
nin han merçed de señores nin han de sus dineros;
porque puede ser esto, creo ser verdaderos,
segund natural curso, los dichos estrelleros. — astrologers

128. Por que creas el curso destos signos atales,
dezirte he un juizio de çinco naturales
que judgaron un niño por sus çiertas señales,
dieron juizios fuertes de acabados° males. — great

129. Era un rey de moros, Alcaraz nonbre avía;
nasçióle un fijo bello, más de aquél non tenía;
enbió por sus sabios, dellos saber querría
el signo e la planeta del fijo que'l nasçía.

130. Entre los estrelleros que·l vinieron a ver,
vinieron çinco dellos de más conplido saber;
desque vieron el punto en que ovo de nasçer,
dixo el un maestro: «Apedreado° ha de ser». stoned

131. Judgó el otro: «Este ha de ser quemado»;
el terçero dize: «El niño ha de ser despeñado»;° hurled from a cliff
el cuarto dixo: «El infante ha de ser colgado»;° hanged
dixo el quinto maestro: «Morrá° en agua afogado».° **morirá**, drowned

132. Quando oyó el rey juizios desacordados,
mandó que los maestros fuesen muy bien guardados;
fízolos tener presos en logares apartados,
dio todos sus juizios por mintrosos° provados. lies

133. Desque fue el infante a buena hedat° llegado, **edad**
pidió al rrey su padre que le fuese otorgado
de ir a correr monte, caçar algún venado;° deer
respondióle el rey que le plazía de grado.

134. Cataron° día claro para ir a caçar; waited
desque fueron en el monte, óvose a levantar
un rebatado° nublo,° començó de agranizar,° dark, cloud, hail
e a poca de ora començó de apedrear.

135. Acordóse su ayo° de cómmo lo judgaron tutor
los sabios naturales que su signo cataron;
diz: «Vayámosnos, señor, que los que a vos fadaron° predicted your fate
non sean verdaderos en lo que adevinaron».° predicted

136. Pensaron mucho aína todos de se acojer:
mas commo es verdat e non puede fallesçer
en lo que Dios ordena en cómmo ha de ser,
segund natural curso, non se puede estorçer.° deviate

137. Façiendo la grand piedra, el infante aguijó,° spurred on
pasando por la puente, un grand rayo° le dio, bolt of lightning
foradóse° la puente, por allí se despeñó, made an opening

en un árbol del río de sus faldas se colgó.

138. Estando ansí colgado adó todos lo vieron,
afogóse en el agua, acorrer non lo podieron;
los çinco fados dichos todos bien se conplieron,
los sabios naturales verdaderos salieron.

139. Desque vido el rey conplido su pesar,
mandó los estrelleros de la presión soltar;
fízoles mucho bien e mandóles usar
de su astrología, en que non avíe que dubdar.

140. Yo creo los estrólogos verdad naturalmente;
pero Dios que crió natura e açidente,
puédelos demudar° e fazer otramente; change
segund la fe cathólica yo desto só creyente.

141. En creer lo de natura non es 'mal estança,° bad condition
e creer muy más en Dios con firme esperança;
por que creas mis dichos e non tomes dubdança,
pruévotelo brevemente con esta semejança.° example

142. Cierto es que el rey en su regno ha poder
de dar fueros° e leyes e derechos fazer; customary privile
desto manda fazer libros e cuadernos conponer,
para quien faze el yerro, qué pena deve haver.

143. Acaesçe que alguno faze grand traiçión,
ansí que por el fuero deve morir con raçón;
pero por los privados que en su ayuda son,
si piden merçed al Rey, dale conplido° perdón. full

144. O si por aventura, aqueste que lo erró,
al rey en algund tienpo atanto le servió,
que piedat e serviçio mucho al rey movió,
por que del yerro fecho conplido perdón le dio.

145. E ansí commo por fuero avía de morir,

el fazedor del fuero non lo quiere consentir;
dyspensa contra el fuero e déxalo bevir,
quien puede fazer leyes puede contra ellas yr.

146. Otrosí puede el papa sus decretales far,
en que a sus súbditos manda çierta pena° dar; punishment
pero puede muy bien contra ellas dispensar,
por graçia o por serviçio toda la pena soltar.

147. Veemos cada día pasar esto de fecho,
pero por todo eso las leyes y el derecho
e el fuero escripto non es por ende desfecho,
ante es çierta çiençia e de mucho provecho.

148. Bien ansí nuestro señor Dios, cuando el çielo crió,
puso en él sus signos e planetas ordenó;
sus poderíos çiertos e juizios otorgó,
pero mayor poder retuvo en sí que les non dio.

149. Ansí que por ayuno° e limosna° e oración fasting, alms
e por servir a Dios con mucha contriçión
non ha poder mal signo nin su costellaçión;
el poderío de Dios tuelle° la tribulaçión. takes away

150. Non son por todo aquesto los estrelleros mintrosos,
que judgan segund natura por sus cuentos fermosos;
ellos e la çiençia son çiertos e non dubdosos,
mas non pueden contra Dios ir, nin son poderosos.

151. Non sé astrología nin só ende maestro,
nin sé astralabio más que 'buey de cabestro;° lead ox
mas porque cada día veo pasar esto,
por aqueso lo digo; otrosí veo aquesto;

152. Muchos nasçen en Venus, que lo más de su vida
es amar las mugeres, nunca se les olvida;
trabajan e afanan° mucho, sin medida, toil
e los más non recabdan° la cosa más querida. get

153. En este signo atal creo que yo nasçí,
sienpre puné° en servir dueñas que conosçí; — strove
el bien que me feçieron non lo desagradesçí,° — I was not ungrateful
a muchas serví mucho que nada non acabesçí.° — I never got anything

154. Commoquier que he provado mi signo ser atal,
en servir a las dueñas punar, e non en ál,
pero aunque omne non goste° la pera del peral, — taste
en estar a la sonbra es plazer comunal.

155. Muchas noblezas ha en el que a las dueñas sirve,
loçano fablador en ser franco° se abive:° — generous, strives
en servir a las dueñas el bueno non se esquive,
que si mucho trabaja en mucho plazer byve.

156. El amor faz sotil al omne que es rudo;
fázele fabrar° fermoso al que antes es mudo; — **fablar**
al omne que es cobarde fázelo muy atrevudo:° — daring
al perezoso faze ser presto° e agudo.° — quick, sharp

157. Al mançebo° mantiene mucho en mançebez° — young man, youth
e al viejo faz perder mucho la vejez;
faze blanco e fermoso del negro como pez,° — pitch
lo que non vale una nuez,° amor le da grand prez.° — farthing, value

158. El que es enamorado, por muy feo que sea,
otrosí su amiga, maguer que sea muy fea,
el uno e el otro non ha cosa que vea
que tan bien le paresca nin que tanto desea.

159. El bavieca,° el torpe,° el neçio, el pobre, — stupid, slow person
a su amiga bueno paresçe e rico onbre,
más noble que los otros por ende todo onbre,
como un amor pierde, luego otro cobre.

160. Ca puesto que su signo sea de tal natura
commo es este mío, dize una escriptura

que «buen esfuerço vençe a la mala ventura»,
e a toda pera dura grand tienpo la madura.

161. Una tacha° le fallo al amor poderoso, defect
la cual a vos, dueñas, yo descobrir non oso:
mas por que non me tengades por dezidor medroso,° fearful
es ésta: que el amor sienpre fabla mentiroso.

162. Ca segund vos he dicho en la otra conseja,
lo que en sí es torpe con amor bien semeja,
tiene por noble cosa lo que non vale una arveja,° bean
lo que semeja non es; oya bien tu oreja.

163. Si las mançanas sienpre oviesen tal sabor
de dentro, cual de fuera dan vista e color,
non avríe de las plantas fructa de tal valor;
mas ante pudren° que otra, pero dan buen olor. rot

164. Bien atal es el amor, que da palabra llena,
toda cosa que dize paresçe mucho buena;
non es todo cantar cuanto ruido suena;
por vos descobrir esto, dueña, non haya pena.

165. Diz: «Por las verdades se pierden los amigos,
e por las non dezir se fazen desamigos»;
ansí entendet sano los proverbios antiguos,
e nunca vos creades loores de enemigos.

*De cómo el Amor vino al Arçipreste e de la pelea que con él ovo el dicho Arçipreste*

181. Dirévos una pelea que una noche me vino,
pensando en mi ventura, sañudo e non con vino:
un omne grande, fermoso, mesurado, a mí vino;
yo le pregunté quién era; dixo: «Amor, tu vezino.»

182. Con saña que tenía, fuilo a denostar:

dixe˙l: «Si amor eres non puedes aquí estar;
eres mentiroso, falso en muchos enartar:
salvar non puedes uno, puedes çient mill matar.

183. «Con engaños e lisonjas e sotiles mentiras
enpoçonas las lenguas, enervolas° tus viras: poison
al que mejor te sirve, a él fieres cuando tiras;
párteslo del amiga al omne que aíras.° anger

184. «Traes enloqueçidos a muchos con tu saber,
fázeslos perder el sueño, el comer y el bever,
fazes a muchos omes tanto se atrever
en ti, fasta que el cuerpo e el alma van perder.

185. «Non tienes regla çierta nin tienes en ti tiento,
a las vegadas prendes con grand arrevatamiento,° attack
a vezes poco a poco con maestrías çiento;
de cuanto yo te digo tú sabes que non miento.

186. «Desque los omnes prendes, non das por ellos nada,
tráeslos de hoy en cras en vida muy penada;
fazes al que te crea lazar ° en tu mesnada entangle
e por plazer poquillo andar luenga jornada.

187. «Eres tan enconado° que, do fieres de golpe, poisonous
non lo sana mengía,° enplasto nin xarope; medicine
non sé fuerte nin rrecio que se contigo tope
que no˙l debatas° luego, por mucho que se enforçe. defeat

188. «De cómmo enflaquezes las gentes e las dapñas,° harm
muchos libros hay desto, de cómmo las engañas
con tus muchos doñeos° e con tus malas mañas; flatteries
sienpre tiras° la fuerza, dízenlo en fazañas. take away

*Enxienplo de la propiedat qu'el dinero ha*

490. «Mucho faz el dinero e mucho es de amar,

al torpe° faze bueno e omne 'de prestar,° — awkward, worthy
faze correr al coxo° e al mudo fablar; — lame
el que non tiene manos, dineros quiere tomar.

491. «Sea un ome nesçio e rudo° labrador, — coarse
los dineros le fazen fidalgo e sabidor:
cuanto más algo tiene, tanto es más de valor;
el que non ha dineros non es de sí señor.

492. «Si tovieres dineros, avrás consolaçión,
plazer e alegría, del Papa ración;[1]
conprarás paraíso, ganarás salvaçión;
do son muchos dineros, está mucha bendiçión.

493. «Yo vi en corte de Roma, do es la santidad,
que todos al dinero fazen grand homildat;° — homage
grand onrra le fazían con grand solepnidat,° — **=solemnidad**
todos a él se omillan,° commo a la magestat. — kneel

494. «Fazíe muchos priores, obispos e abbades
arçobispos, doctores, patriarcas, potestades;° — potentates
a muchos clérigos nesçios dábales dinidades:° — high honors
fazíe de verdat mentiras e de mintiras verdades.

495. «Fazía muchos clérigos e muchos ordenados,
muchos monges e mongas, religiosos sagrados;
el dinero los daba por bien examinados,
a los pobres dezían que non eran letrados.° — educated

496. «Daba muchos juizios, mucha mala sentençia;
con muchos abogados era su mantenencia° — dealings
en tener pleitos malos e fazer abenençia:° — settlement
en cabo, por dineros avía penitençia.° — absolution

497. «El dinero quebranta las cadenas dañosas,

---

[1]**Ración** prebend, an allowance paid by a cathedral or collegiate church to a member of its clergy.

| | |
|---|---|
| tira çepos° e gruillos° e cadenas peligrosas, | stocks, shackles |
| el que non tiene dineros échanle las posas:° | handcuffs |
| por todo el mundo faze cosas maravillosas. | |
| | |
| 498. «Yo vi fer maravillas do él mucho usaba; | |
| muchos meresçían muerte, que la vida les daba, | |
| otros eran sin culpa, e luego los mataba, | |
| muchas almas perdían, e muchas salvaba. | |
| | |
| 499. «Fazer perder al pobre su casa e su viña, | |
| sus muebles e razes° todo lo desaliña:° | land, ruins |
| por todo el mundo anda su sarna° e su tiña:° | itch, mange |
| do el dinero juega, allí el ojo guiña.° | winks |
| | |
| 500. «Él faze cavalleros de neçios aldeanos, | |
| condes e Ricos omnes de algunos villanos; | |
| con el dinero andan todos los omnes loçanos: | |
| cuantos son en el mundo le besan hoy las manos. | |
| | |
| 501. «Vi tener al dinero las mejores moradas, | |
| altas e muy costosas, fermosas e pintadas, | |
| castillos, heredades e villas entorreadas° | turreted |
| todas al dinero sirven e suyas son conpladas.° | bought |
| | |
| 502. «Comía muchos manjares de diversas naturas, | |
| vistía los nobles paños, doradas vestiduras, | |
| traía joyas preçiosas en viçios e folguras,° | luxury |
| guarnimientos° estraños, nobles cabalgaduras. | trappings |
| | |
| 503. «Yo vi a muchos monges en sus predicaciones | |
| denostar al dinero e a sus tenptaçiones, | |
| en cabo, por dinero otorgan los perdones, | |
| asuelven el ayuno, ansí fazen oraçiones. | |
| | |
| 504. «Pero que le denuestan los monges por las plaças, | |
| guardándolo en convento en vasos e en taças, | |
| con el dinero cunplen sus menguas e sus raças,° | tatters |
| más condesiguos° tienen que tordos° nin picaças.° | hiding places, thr |

magpies

505. «Commoquier que los frailes e clérigos dizen
que aman a Dios servir,
si barruntan° que el rrico está ya para morir, — suspect
cuando oyen sus dineros que comiençan a retenir,° — jingle
cuál dellos los levarán comiençan luego a reñir.

506. «Monges, frailes, clérigos non toman los dineros,
bien les 'dan de la çeja° do son sus parçioneros,° — frown, inheritors
luego los toman prestos sus 'omes despenseros;° — stewards
pues que se dizen pobles, ¿qué quieren thesoreros?

507. «Allí están esperando cuál havrá más rico tuero:° — share
non es muerto ya dizen "Pater Noster"° a mal agüero, — Our Father
commo los cuervos al asno cuando le desuellan° el cuero: — strip off
"Cras, cras nós lo avremos, que nuestro es ya por fuero.° — custom

508. «Toda muger del mundo e dueña de alteza
págase del dinero e de mucha riqueza;
yo nunca vi fermosa que quisiese pobleza;
do son muchos dineros, y es mucha nobleza.

509. «El dinero es alcalde e juez mucho loado,
este es consejero e sotil abogado,
alguaçil e merino, bien ardit,° esforçado; — bold
de todos los ofiçios es muy apoderado.

510. «En suma te lo digo, tómalo tu mejor,
el dinero del mundo es grand rrevolvedor:° — disrupter
señor faze del siervo, de señor servidor:
toda cosa del sigro° se faze por su amor. — world

511. «Por dineros se muda el mundo e su manera;
toda muger cobdiçiosa de algo es falaguera,° — flatterer
por joyas e dineros salirá de carrera;
el dar quebranta peñas,° fiende° dura madera. — rocks, splits

512. «Derrueca° fuerte muro e derriba grant torre; — knocks down

a coita° e a grand priesa° el mucho dar acorre;° — stress, straits, relieve
non ha siervo cabtivo que el dinero non le aforre:° — free
el que non tiene qué dar, su caballo non corre.

513. «Las cosas que son graves fázelas de ligero,
por ende a tu vieja sé 'franco e llenero,° — liberal and generous
que poco o que mucho, non vaya sin logrero:° — money lender
non me pago de joguetes do non anda el dinero.

514. «Si algo non le dieres, cosa mucha o poca,
sey franco de palabla, non le digas razón loca;
quien non tiene miel en la orça,° téngala en la boca, — honey jar
mercador que esto faze bien vende e bien troca.

515. «Si sabes estromentos bien tañer o tenplar,
si sabes o avienes° en fermoso cantar, — can
a las vegadas poco, en onesto lugar
do la muger te oya, non dexes probar.° — attempt it

516. «Si una cosa sola a la muger non muda,
muchas cosas juntadas facerte han ayuda:
desque lo oye la dueña, mucho en ello coida,° — thinks
non puede ser que a tienpo a bien non te rrecabda.° — responds

517. «Con una flaca cuerda non alçarás grand trança° — beam
nin por un solo "¡farre!"° non anda bestia manca, — "giddyup"
a la peña pesada non la mueve una palanca,° — lever
con cuños° e almádanas° poco a poco se arranca. — wedges, sledgehamm

518. «Prueba fazer ligerezas° e fazer valentía, — skillful acts
'quier lo vea o non, saberlo ha algund día;
non será tan esquiva° que non ayas mejoría, — elusive
non canses de seguirla, vençerás su porfía.° — stubbornness

519. «El que la mucho sigue, e que la mucho usa,
en el coraçón lo tiene, maguer se le escusa;
pero que todo el mundo por esto le acusa,
en éste coida sienpre, por éste 'faz la musa.° — muses

520. «Cuanto es más sosañada,° cuanto es más corrida,° — mocked, shamed
cuanto por omne es magada° e ferida, — beaten
tanto más por él anda loca, muerta e perdida;
non coida ver la ora que con él seya ida.

521. «Coida su madre cara que por la sosañar,
por corrella e ferilla e por la denostar,
que por ende será casta e la fará estar;
estos son aguijones° que la fazen saltar. — spurs

522. «Debía pensar su madre de cuando era donzella,
que su madre non 'quedaba de° ferirla e correlia, — cease
que más la ençendie:° pues debía por ella — stirred up
judgar todas las otras e a su fija bella.

523. «Toda muger nasçida es fecha de tal masa,° — stuff
lo que más le defienden, aquello ante pasa,
aquello la ençiende, e aquello la traspasa:° — torments
do non es tan seguida, anda más 'floxa laxa.° — listless and weak

524. «A toda cosa brava grand uso la amansa,
la çierva montesina mucho corrida cansa,
caçador que la sigue tómala cuando descansa;
la dueña mucho brava usando° se faz mansa. — pursued

525. «Por una vez al día que omne gelo pida,
çient vegadas de noche, de amor es rrequerida,
doña Venus gelo pide por él toda su vida,
en lo que'l mucho piden anda muy ençendida.

526. «Muy blanda es el agua, más dando en piedra dura,
muchas vegadas dando, faze grand cavadura:° — crevice
por grand uso el rrudo sabe grand letura:
muger mucho seguida olvida la cordura.

527. «Guárdate non te avuelvas° a la casamentera:° — get involved with, matchmaker
doñear non la quieras; ca es una manera

por que te faría perder a la entendera,° — lady love
ca una congrueca° de otra sienpre 'tiene dentera.° — mistress, resentful

*De cómmo Doña Endrina fue a casa de la vieja*
*e el Arçipreste acabó lo que quiso*

871. Después fue de Santiago, otro día seguiente,
a ora de mediodía, cuando yanta la gente,
vino Doña Endrina con la mi vieja sabiente,
entró con ella en su tienda bien sosegadamente.

872. Commo la mi vejezuela me avía aperçebido,
non me detove mucho, para allá fui luego ido;
fallé la puerta çerrada, mas la vieja bien me vido:
«¡Yuy!», diz, «qué es aquello, qué faz aquel rroído?

873. «¿Es omne o es viento? Creo que es omne, non miento;
¡vedes, vedes cómo otea° el pecado carboniento!° — black, looking aroun
¿Es aquél? ¿Non es aquél? Él me semeja, yo lo siento,
¡A la fe, aquel es Don Melón! Yo lo conosco, yo lo viento.° — smell

874. «Aquella es la su cara e su ojo de bezerro;° — calf
¡catat, catat cómmo asecha!° Barrúntanos commo perro; — stalking
allí rraviaría° agora, que non puede 'tirar el fierro,° — going crazy, open th
mas quebrantaría las puertas, menéalas commo çencerro.° — door; cow bell

875. «Cierto aquí quiere entrar; mas ¿por qué yo non le fablo?
¡Don Melón, tiradvos° dende! ¿Tróxovos el diablo? — go away
¡Non queblantedes mis puertas! que del abbad de Sant Pablo
las ove ganado; non posistes aí un clavo.

876. «Yo vos abriré la puerta, ¡esperat, non la quebredes!
E con bien e con sosiego dezid si algo queredes;
luego vos id de mi puerta, non nos alhaonedes:° — bother
entrad mucho en buen ora; yo veré lo que faredes».

877. «¡Señora Doña Endrina! ¡Vos la mi enamorada!

¡Vieja! ¿por esto teníades a mí la puerta çerrada?
¡Tan buen día es hoy éste que fallé atal çelada!° — ambush
Dios e mi buena ventura me la tovieron guardada».

[.........]

878. «Cuando yo salí de casa, pues que veyades las rredes,
¿por qué fincávades con él sola entre estas paredes?
a mí non Retebdes, fija, que vos lo meresçedes;
El mejor cobro° que tenedes, vuestro mal que lo calledes. — remedy

879. «Menos de mal será que esto poco çeledes,
que non que vos descobrades e ansí vos pregonedes;° — make it known
casamiento que vos venga, por esto non lo perderedes;
mejor me paresçe esto que non que vos enfamedes.° — defame

880. «E pues que vos dezides que es el daño fecho,
defiéndavos e ayúdevos 'a tuerto e a derecho;° — right or wrong
fija, a daño fecho 'aved rruego e pecho,° — show courage
¡callad! guardat la fama, non salga de so techo.

881. «Si non parlase la picaça más que la codorniz,° — quail
non la colgarían en la plaça, nin reirían de lo que diz;
castigadvos, amiga, de otra tal contraíz,° — unhappy experience
que todos los omnes fazen commo Don Melón Ortiz».

882. Doña Endrina le dixo: «¡Ay viejas tan perdidas!
a las mugeres trahedes engañadas, vendidas;
ayer mill cobros me dabas, mill artes, mill salidas,
hoy, que só escarnida, todas me son fallidas.

883. «Si las aves lo podiesen bien saber e entender
cuántos laços les paran, non las podrían prender;
cuando el lazo veen, ya las lievan a vender,
mueren por el poco çebo,° non se pueden defender. — bait

884. «Sí° los peçes de las aguas, cuando veen el anzuelo,° — thus, hook
ya el pescador los tiene e los trahe por el suelo;

la muger vee su daño cuando ya finca con duelo,
non la quieren los parientes, padre, madre nin abuelo.

885. «El que la ha desonrrada déxala, non la mantiene,
vase perder por el mundo, pues otro cobro non tiene,
pierde el cuerpo e el alma, a muchos esto aviene:
pues otro cobro yo non he, así fazer me conviene».

886. Está en los antiguos seso e sabiençia,
es en el mucho tienpo el saber e la çiençia;
la mi vieja maestra ovo ya conçiençia
E dio en este pleito una buena sentençia.

887. «El cuerdo gravemente non se debe quexar,
cuando el quexamiento non le puede pro° tornar; advantage
lo que nunca se puede reparar nin emendar,
débelo cuerdamente sofrir e endurar.

888. «A las grandes dolençias, a las desaventuras,
a los acaesçimientos, a los yerros de locuras,
debe buscar consejo, melezinas e curas;
el sabidor se prueba en coytas e en presuras.

889. «La ira, la discordia a los amigos mal faz,
pone sospechas malas en cuerpo do yaz;
haved entre vos anbos concordia e paz,
el pesar e la saña tornadlo en buen solaz.

890. «Pues que por mí dezides que el daño es venido,
por mi quiero que sea el vuestro bien avido;° come
vós sed muger suya e él vuestro marido,
todo vuestro deseo es bien por mí conplido».

891. Doña Endrina e Don Melón en uno casados son,
alégranse las conpañas en las bodas con rrazón;
si villanía he dicho, haya de vos perdón,

que lo feo de la estoria diz Pánfilo e Nasón.[2]

*De lo que contesçió al Arçipreste con la serrana e de las figuras della*

1006. Sienpre ha la mala manera la sierra e la altura,
si nieua o si yela, nunca da calentura;
bien ençima del puerto, fazía oruela° dura, — wind
viento con grand elada, rozio con grand friura.

1007. Commo omne non siente tanto frío si corre,
corrí la cuesta ayuso, ca diz: «Quien da a la torre,
antes dize la piedra que sale el alhorre»;[3]
yo dixe: «Só perdido, si Dios non me acorre».

1008. Nunca desque nasçí pasé tan grand peligro
de frío: al pie del puerto falléme con vestiglo,° — monster
la más grande fantasma que vy en este siglo,
yeguariza,° trifuda,° talla de mal çeñiglo.° — mare herder, large, white goosefoot bush

1009. Con la coyta del frío e de aquella grand elada,
rrogué·l que me quisiese ese día dar posada;
díxome que·l plazía si·l fuese bien pagada,
tóvelo a Dios en merçed e levóme a la Tablada.

1010. Sus mienbros e su talla non son para callar,
ca bien creed que era una grand yegua cavallar;
quien con ella luchase non se podría bien fallar;
si ella non quisiese, non la podría aballar.° — pin her down

1011. En l' Apocalipsi Sant Johan Evangelista
no vydo tal figura nin de tan mala vista;

---

[2] **Pánfilo e Nasón...** Reference to the Archpriest's sources, *Pamphilus de amore* and Ovid. In this work the lady was raped by her suitor. The thrity-two stanzas which recount this event are missing from all manuscripts of the *Libro de buen amor*.

[3] **Quien da a...** when you throw a stone at a tower it hits you before the falcon comes out.

a grand hato° daría lucha e grand conquista; herd
non sé de cuál diablo es tal fantasma quista.

1012. Havía la cabeça mucho grand 'sin gujsa,° out of proportion
cabellos muy negros, más que corneja lysa,° sleek
ojos fondos,° bermejos, poco e mal deuisa,° sunken, saw
mayor es que de yegua la patada° do pisa. footprint

1013. Las orejas mayores que de añal° burrico, yearling
el su pescueço negro, ancho, velloso, chico,
las narizes muy gordas, luengas, de çarapico;° sea bird
beuería en pocos días cabdal° de buhón° rico. wealth, peddler

1014. Su boca de alana,° e los rrostros° muy gordos, mastiff, lips
dyentes anchos e luengos, asnudos° e moxmordos,° donkey-like, protrudi
las sobreçejas anchas e más negras que tordos;° thrushes
¡los que quieren casarse, aquí non sean sordos!

1015. Mayores que las mías tiene sus prietas baruas;° whiskers
yo non vy en ella ál, mas si tú en ella escaruas,° dig
creo que fallarás de las chufetas° daruas; jokes
valdríasete más trillar en las tus paruas.° heap of grain

1016. Mas, en verdat, sí, bien vy fasta la rrodilla,
los huesos mucho grandes, la çanca° non chiquilla, thigh
de las cabras 'de fuego° una grand manadilla,° singe marks, number
sus touillos° mayores que de una añal novilla.° ankles, cow

1017. Más ancha que mi mano tiene la su muñeca,° wrist
vellosa, pelos grandes, pero non mucho seca;
boz gorda° e gangosa,° a todo omne enteca,° thick, nasal, bothers
tardía,° como ronca, desdonada° e hueca. slow, unpleasant

1018. El su dedo chiquillo mayor es que mi pulgar,° thumb
piensa de los mayores si te podrías pagar;
si ella algund día te quisiese espulgar,° delice
bien sentiría tu cabeça que son viga de lagar.° winepress

1019. Por el su garnacho° tenía tetas colgadas,
dáuanle a la çinta° pues que estavan dobladas,°
ca estando senzillas° 'darlen° so las yjadas:°
a todo son de çítola° andarían° sin ser mostradas.°

blouse
waist, folded
unfolded, would reach
thighs; stringed instrument, dance,
taught; ribs, filthy

1020. Costillas° mucho grandes en su negro° costado,
unas tres vezes contélas estando arredrado;°
dígote que non vy más nin te será más contado,
ca moço mesturero° non es bueno para mandado.°

at a distance
gossipy, message

1021. De cuanto que me dixo e de su mala talla,
fize bien tres cantigas, mas non pud' bien pintalla;
las dos son chançonetas la otra 'de trotalla;°
de la que te non pagares, veyla e ríe e calla.

for dancing

*De las figuras del Arçipreste*

1485. «Señora», diz la vieja, «yo˙l veo a menudo,
el cuerpo ha bien largo, mienbros grandes e trifudo,°
la cabeça non chica, velloso, pescoçudo,°
el cuello non muy luengo, cabezprieto,° orejudo:°

muscular
thick-necked
black-haired, big eared

1486. «las çejas apartadas,° prietas como carbón,
el su andar enfiesto,° bien como de pauón,°
su paso sosegado e de buena razón;
la su nariz es luenga, esto le desconpón:°

wide-set
erect, peacock
spoils (his looks)

1487. «las ençiuas° bermejas e la fabla° tunbal,°
la boca non pequeña, labros al comunal,
más gordos que delgados, bermejos como coral;
las espaldas bien grandes, las muñecas atal.

gums, speech, hollow

1488. «Los ojos ha pequeños, es un poquillo baço;°
los pechos delanteros, bien trifudo el braço,
bien conplidas las piernas, del pie chico pedaço;
Señora, dél non vy más, por su amor vos abraço.

dark-skinned

1489. «Es ligero, valiente, bien mançebo 'de días,°

young

sabe los instrumentos e todas juglerías,
doñeador° alegre, ¡para las çapatas mías! suitor
tal omne como éste non es 'en todas erías».° everywhere

*De las propiedades que las dueñas chicas han*

1606. Quiérovos abreuiar° la predicaçión,° shorten, preaching
que sienpre me pagué de pequeño sermón
e de dueña pequeña e de breue razón,
ca poco e bien dicho afincase° el coraçón. stays

1607. Del que mucho fabla ríen, quien mucho rríe es loco;
es en la dueña chica amor e non poco;
dueñas hay muy grandes, que por chicas non troco,° exchange
mas las chicas e las grandes non 'se rrepienden° del troco. regret

1608. De las chicas que bien diga el Amor me fizo ruego,
que diga de sus noblezas; yo quiérolas dezir luego;
dezirvos he de dueñas chicas que lo havredes por juego,° pleasantry
son frías como la nieue e arden commo el fuego.

1609. Son frías de fuera, con el amor ardientes,
en la cama solaz, trebejo,° plazenteras, ryentes, sporting
en casa cuerdas, donosas, sosegadas, bienfazientes;° well behaved
mucho ál fallaredes, adó bien pararedes mientes.

1610. En pequeña girgonça° yaze grand rresplandor, gemstone
en açúcar muy poco yaze mucho dulçor,
en la dueña pequeña yaze muy grand amor;
pocas palabras cunplen° al buen entendedor. suffice

1611. Es pequeño el grano de la buena pemienta,
pero más que la nuez conorta e calienta; comforts
así dueña pequeña, si todo amor consienta,
non ha plazer del mundo que en ella non sienta.

1612. Commo en chica rrosa está mucha color,

en oro muy poco grand preçio e grand valor,
commo en poco blasmo° yaze grand buen olor, — balm
ansí en dueña chica yaze muy grand sabor.

1613. Como robí pequeño tiene mucha bondat,
color, virtud e preçio e noble claridad,
ansí dueña pequeña tiene mucha beldat,
fermosura, donayre,° amor e lealtad. — gracefulness

1614. Chica es la calandria° e chico el rruiseñor,° — lark, nightingale
pero más dulçe canta que otra ave mayor;
la muger que es chica por eso es mejor;
con doñeo es más dulçe que açúcar nin flor.

1615. Son aves pequeñas papagayo° e orior,° — parrot, oriole
pero cualquier dellas es dulçe gritador,° — warbler
adonada,° fermosa, preçiada cantador; — gifted
bien atal es la dueña pequeña con amor.

1616. De la muger pequeña non hay conparaçión,
terrenal paraíso es e grand consolaçión,
solaz e alegría, plazer e bendiçión;
mejor es en la prueua que en la salutaçión.

1617. Sienpre quis' muger chica más que grande nin mayor,
non es desaguisado° del grand mal 'ser foidor;° — unwise, flee
del mal tomar lo menos, dízelo el sabidor,
por ende de las mugeres la mejor es la menor.

## *Didactic poetry*

Didactic poetry flourished, and indeed many of the works, treated under minstrel poetry and *clerecía* poetry were didactic. Part of the *Libro de buen amor* is considered didactic. There are several poems, however, surviving from the 14th century, which are almost entirely didactic. The *Proverbios morales* of the Rabbi Sem Tob (also called Santob and Santo) are of this variety.

## *Proverbios morales*

SEM TOB (SANTOB) DE CARRIÓN

The *Proverbios morales* of Rabbi Sem Tob are didactic in nature. The author lived in the first half of the 14th century and dedicated this work to King Pedro el Cruel whose father Alfonso XI, owed a debt to the author. The metrical form was the quatrain of seven syllables, brought about by the division into two hemistichs of the Alexandrine line of the *clerecía* verse with rhyme, ABAB rather than the *clerecía* rhyme AAAA. His proverbs are the quintessence of concise wisdom. They point to a philosophical, sad, and pacific acceptance of life's trials. The rabbi recommends that action triumph over excessive prudence. He condemns greed and praises knowledge, appropriate silence and writing. The language is popular and many of the proverbs are from Spanish sources. This is Spain's first example of gnomic literature (the literature of maxims and aphorisms). The work is also called *Consejos e documentos al rey don Pedro*, and was written between 1355 and 1360.

1 Señor, rey, noble, alto:
oí sermón
que viene dezir Santo,
judío de Carrión;

2 comunalmente trobado,
de glosas moralmente
de filosofía sacado,
segunt aquí va siguiente

3 Quando el rey don Alfonso
finó, fincó la gente
commo quando el pulso
fallesçe al doliente;

4 que luego non cuidavan
que tan grant mejoría
a ellos fincava,
nin omne lo entendía.

5 Quando la rosa seca
e en su tienpo sale
el agua della finca,
rosada, que más vale.

6 Así vos fincastes dél
para mucho turar° — last
e fazer lo que él
cobdiçiava librar.° — realize

47 Pues trabajo me mengua
donde puede aver
pro, diré de mi lengua
algo de mi saber.

48 Si non es lo que quiero,
quiera yo lo que es;
si pesar he primero,
placer avré después.

49 Mas, pues aquella rueda,
del çielo una ora
jamás non está queda,
peora e mejora;

50 aún aqueste lasso° — tired
renovará el esprito,
es de' pandero manso,° — reference to author
aún el su retinto° — message

51 sonará; verná día,
avrá su libra tal,
presçio como solía
valer el su quintal.° — money

52 Yo prové lo pesado,
provaré lo liviano;
quiçá mudare fado

cuando mudare la mano.

53 Resçelé, si fablase,
que enojo faría;
pero si me callase,
por torpe° fincaría. dull

54 Que el que non se muda,
non falla lo que plaz';
dizen que ave muda,
agüero nunca faz'.

55 Porque pisan poquiella° little
sazón tierra, parlando,
omes que pisan ella
para siempre, callando,

56 entendí que en callar
avrí grant mejoría,
aborresçi fablar,
e fueme peoría.

57 Que non só para menos
que otros de mi ley,
que ovieron buenos
donadíos° del Rey. gifts

58 Mas vergüença afuera
me tiró y apró,° withdrew
si no, tanto no fincara
sin honra y sin pro.

59 Si mi razón es buena,
non sea despreçiada
porque la diz' presona
rafez°; que mucha espada vile

60 de fino azero sano

sabe de rota vaina° — sword sheath
salir, e del gusano
se faze la seda fina.

61 E astroso° garrote° — terrible, catapult
faze muy çiertos trechos,° — breaches
e algunt roto pellote° — cloak
descubre blancos pechos;

62 e muy sotil trotero° — messenger
aduze buenas nuevas,
e muy vil bozerro° — lawyer
presenta çiertas pruevas.

63 Por nasçer en el espino,
non val' la rosa çierto
menos, nin el buen vino
por salir del sarmiento.

64 Non val' el açor menos
por nasçer de mal nido,° — nest
nin los enxenplos buenos
por los dezir judío.

65 Non me desdeñen por corto:
que mucho judío largo° — generous
non entraría 'a coto° — without hesitation
a fazer lo que fago.

66 Bien sé que nunca tanto
cuatro tiros° de lança — throws
alcançaría cuanto
la saeta° alcança. — arrow

67 E razón muy granada
se diz' en pocos versos,
e çinta muy delgada
sufre costados gruesos.

68 E mucho omne entendido,
por seer vergonçoso,
es torpe tenido
e llamado astroso;° wretched

69 e si viese sazón,
mejor e más apuesta
diría su razón
aquel que lo denuesta.

70 Quiero dezir, del mundo
e de las sus maneras
e cómo d'él dubdo,
palabras muy çerteras.

71 Que non sé tomar tiento° moderation
nin fazer pleitesía;
de acuerdos más de ciento
me torno cada día.

300 De una gota suzia,
podrida e dañada:
e tienes te por lusia° shining
estrella, muy preçiada.

301 Pues dos vezes pasaste
camino muy biltado,° vile
locura es preçiarte:
daste por muy menguado.° humble

302 E más que un mosquito
el tu cuerpo non vale
desque° aquel esprito once
que lo meçe° dél sale. moves

313 Conoçe tu medida
e nunca errarás,
e en toda tu vida

soberuia non farás.

314 Cual quieres reçebir,
atal de tí reçiban:
conviénete servir,
si quieres que te sirvan;

315 conviénete que onres,
si quieres ser onrado;
faz pagados los omres,° men
e fazerte han pagado.

316 Nunca omre naçió
que cuanto le pluguiese,
segum lo cobdiçió,
que tal se le cunpliese.

317 Quien quiere fazer pesar,
conbiénele aperçebir:
que non se puede escusar
de atal reçebir.

318 Si quieres fazer mal,
pues fazlo atal pleito
de reçebir atal
cual tú fizieres. Çierto

319 non puedes escapar,
si una mala obra
fizieres, de topar° finding yourself
en resçebir tú otra.

320 Que sabe que non nasçiste
por bevir apartado;
al mundo non veniste
por ser aventajado.

321 En el rey mete mientes,

toma enxenplo d'él:
más lazra por las gentes
que las gentes por él.

322 Por sus mañas el omre
se pierde o se gana,
e por la su costunbre
adolesçe o sana.

421 El omre que es omre
senpre vive cueitado:
si rico o si pobre,
non le mengua cuidado.

422 El afán° el hidalgo
sufre en sus cuidados,
e el villano, largo
afán a en sus costados.

fatigue

423 Omre pobre preçiado
non es más que el muerto:
el rico guerreado°
es, non teniendo tuerto.

warred against

424 Del omre vivo dizen
las gentes sus maldades,
e desque muere fazen
cuenta de sus bondades.

425 Quando pro nol terná,
lóanlo bien la gente:
de lo que nol verná
bien, danle larga mente.

566 Mal es mucho fablar,
mas peor es ser mudo,
que non fue por callar

la lengua, segunt cuido.

567 Pero la mejoría
del callar non podemos
negar, mas todavía
convién' que la contemos.

568 Por que la mitad de
cuanto oyamos fablemos,
una lengua por ende
e dos orejas avemos.

569 Quien mucho quier' fablar
sin gran sabiduría,
çierto en se callar
mejor baratería.° — make a better bargain

570 El sabio que loar
el callar bien querría,
e el fablar afear,
esta razón dezía:

571 "Si fuese el fablar
de plata figurado,° — represented
sería el callar
de oro debuxado.° — represented

572 "De bienes del callar,
la paz, una de çiento;
de males del fablar,
el menor es el riebto."° — challenge

573 E dize más, abuelta° — with
de mucha mejoría,
que el callar, sin ésta,
sobr'el fablar avía:

574 "Sus orejas fazían

pro solamente a él,
de su lengua avían
pro los otros, non él.

575 Aconteçe al que escucha
a mí, cuando yo fablo,
del bien se aprovecha
e réutame° lo malo."    attribute to me

576 El sabio, por aquesta
razón callar querría:
porque su fabla presta°    benefits
sólo al que lo oía;

577 e querría castigarse°    learn
en otro, él callando,
mas que castigarse
otro en él, fablando.

578 Las bestias an afán
e mal por no fablar,
e los omres lo an
lo más por no callar.

579 El callar tienpo non pierde,
e piérdelo el fablar:
por ende omre non puede
perder por el callar.

580 El que calla razón
quel' cumpliera fablar,
non menguará sazón°    occasion
que perdió por callar.

581 Mas quien fabla razón
que debiera callar,
perdió ya la sazón
que perdió por fablar.

582 Lo que oy se callare,
puédese cras fablar;
mas lo que oy fablare,
no se puede callar.

583 Lo dicho, dicho es:
lo que dicho non as,
dezirlo as después,
si non oy, será cras.

607 Buenos nomres sabemos
en loor del fablar,
cuantos males podemos
afeando al callar:

608 el fablar es clareza,
el callar, escureza;
el fablar es franqueza
e el callar, escaseza;° lack

609 el fablar, ligereza,
e el callar, pereza;° laziness
el fablar es riqueza,
e el callar, pobreza;

610 el callar, torpedat,° dullness
e el fablar, saber;
el callar, çeguedat,
e el fablar, vista aver.

611 Cuerpo es el callar,
e el fablar, su saber;
omne es el fablar,
e el callar, su cama.

612 El callar es dormir,
el fablar, despertar;
el callar es primir,° go down

el fablar, levantar.

613 El callar es tardada,
e el fablar, aína;
el fablar es espada
e el callar su vaïna.

614 Talega° es el callar, — sack
e el algo que yase
en ella es el fablar,
e provecho no faze

615 en cuanto ençerrado
en ella estuviere:
non sera más honrado
por ello cuyo fuere.

616 El callar es ninguno,
que no meresçe nonbre,
e el fablar es alguno:
por él es omne honbre.

617 Figura el fablar
al callar, e así
non sabe el callar
de otro nin de sí.

710 Mantener avenidos° — in agreement
en onra e en paz:
sus fechos son conplidos
del rey que esto faz'.

711 Con el bueno trebeja° — takes pleasure
e al malo enpoxa;° — knocks down
defiende la oveja
e la cabrilla coxa° — limps

712 del lobo° e del zebro: — wolf

¿por qué alongaremos?
Al noble rey don Pedro
estas mañas veemos.

713 Toda la suma d'ellas
en él es muy entera.
Sus mañas son estrellas,
e él es la espera° — sphere

714 del çielo, que sostiene
a derecho la tierra.
A los buenos mantiene,
a los malos atierra.

715 Si él solo del mundo
fuese la mano diestra
de mil reys, bien cuido,
non faríe la siniestra.

716 Es meatad° muy fea — half
poder con desmesura:
¡nunca Dios quiera que sea
luenga tal vestidura!

717 Que si muy luenga fuese,
muchas acortaría,
e él que la vistiese,
muchas despojaría.° — ruin

718 El poder con mesura
es cosa muy apuesta,
como en rostro blancura
con bermejura° buelta: — red

719 mesura que levanta
simpleza° e cordura,° — humility, prudence
e poder que quebranta
sobervia e locura.

720 Dos son mantenimiento
mundanal: una, ley
que es ordenamiento,
e la ota es el rey,

721 que·l' puso Dios por guarda
que ninguno non vaya
contra lo que Dios manda,
si non en pena caya.

722 Por guardar que las gentes
fazer mal non se pongan,
e que los omnes fuertes
a los flacos non coman.

723 Dé Dios vida al Rey,
nuestro mantenedor,
que guarda d'esta grey° — flock
es e defendedor.

724 Las gentes de su tierra,
todas a su serviçio
traiga, e aparte guerra
d'ella e mal bolliçio.° — disturbance

725 E la merçed que el noble,
su padre prometió,
la terná, como cunple,
al Santob el Judío.

# *XV Century*

## HISTORICAL BACKGROUND

The 15th century brought many changes to Spanish life. The reigns of Juan II and Enrique IV had been politically a period of dissension and morally a time of decadence. With the ascension of Isabella and Ferdinand there was great change: the rebellious nobles were suppressed; the danger of Portuguese invasion was ended; the Kingdom of Granada, last stronghold of the Moors, surrendered in 1492; in this same year Columbus discovered the New World and set Spain on the road to conquest and colonization there; the Spanish Inquisition came into power; the Jews were expelled, an act that had many lasting and bad effects upon the country, and Antonio Nebrija published the first grammar of the Castilian language.

Printing came to Spain in the last years of the century, and as Spain turned from Moorish culture, she turned toward the revived classical culture of the Renaissance.

## Lyric Poetry

Lyric poetry continued to flourish and there were numerous collections of lyric verse. The works of troubadour poets from the 14th century were often included, and indeed, Galician-Portuguese poems were still being written, although the 15th century marks the beginnings of Italianate forms. The *cancioneros*, therefore, show poetry in transition from the troubadour verse (Galician-Portuguese) of the Middle Ages to the Italianate poetry of the Renaissance. Some collections of verse were *cancioneros* put together by known collectors. Two of the largest and most important are the *Cancionero de Baena* and the *Cancionero de Stúñiga.*

The *Cancionero de Baena* of Juan Alfonso de Baena, Royal Secretary of Juan II, contains some 576 poems by 54 poets whose names are known and 35 whose names are not. He dedicated the *cancionero* to King Juan II around 1445. All the poets included were erudite men, and even those who wrote in Galician-Portuguese must be considered polished, courtly poets who entirely disregarded the poetry of the people. Most of the *cancionero* poets are not great, and this fact has led many to say of the *Cancionero de Baena*, "*muchos poetas, poca poesía.*" To some the most valuable contribution of the *cancionero* is its description of the life of the times.

The *Cancionero de Stúñiga* was compiled at the court of Alfonso V, who had won Naples for Aragon, by Lope de Stúñiga, and thus the name of this *cancionero*. The poems in it are more lyric than those of Baena's collection, but there are also ballads and other popular poetry. This *Cancionero* gives something of a picture of Naples under Spanish domination. The largest number of poems by a single author are those of Carvajal or Carvajales

The *Cancionero general* was compiled by Hernando del Castillo in Valencia in 1511. This cancionero gathers the works of minor poets of the time of the Catholic monarchs, Isabella and Ferdinand, as well as those of some other famous troubadours. It includes some 1000 long compositions and almost 200 poets and is the most extensive and inclusive of the cancioneros.

## *Cancionero de Baena*

Juan Alfonso de Baena (c.1375- c. 1434) was a Castilian troubadour. Born at Baena, Cordoba, he served as *escribano escribiente* (notarial secretary) at the court of John II of Castile. He collected poems written during the reigns of several kings: John I of Castile, Henry III of Castile and John II of Castile. The cancionero was compiled between 1426-1430. The complete title of the work is *Cancionero de poetas antiguos que fizo é ordenó e compuso é acopiló el judino Johan Alfon de Baena.*

## Micer Francisco Imperial ¿1350-1409?

He was a Genoese and the son of a jewel merchant in Seville. He wrote very early in the 15th century and received words of praise from Santillana. He was an admirer of Dante whose influence is seen in some of his works. He wrote love poetry and didactic poetry that spoke about changeable Fortune.

Este desir fizo el dicho Micer Francisco Imperial por amor e loores de vna fermosa muger de Seuilla que llamó el estrella Diana, e físolo vn día que vid e la miró a ssu guysa, ella yendo por la puente de Sseuilla a la yglesia de Ssant' Ana fuera de la cibdat

Non fue por cierto mi carrera vana,° — in vain
Pasando la puente de Guadalquivir,
Atan buen encuentro que yo vi venir
Rribera del río, en medio Triana,° — section of Seville
(5) a la muy fermosa Estrella Diana,
Qual sale por mayo al alua del día,
Por los santos passos de la romería:
Muchos loores haya Santa Ana.

E por galardón demostrar me quiso
(10) la muy delicada flor de jasmín,
Rossa nouela de oliente jardín,
E de verde prado gentil flor de lysa,° — lily
El su gracioso e honesto rysso,° — smile
Ssenblante amorosso e viso ssuaue,
(15) propio me parece al que dixo: *Aue,*
quando enbiado fue del paraysso.

Callen poetas e callen abtores,
Omero, Oracio, Vergilio e Dante,
E con ellos calle Ovidio *D'amante*
(20) e quantos escripuieron loando señores,
Que tal es aqueste entre las mejores,
Commo el lucero entre las estrellas,
Llama muy clara a par de centellas,
E commo la rrosa entre las flores.

(25) Non se desdeñe la muy delicada
Eufregymio[1] griega, de las griegas flor,
Nin de las troyanas 'la noble señor,° — Helen of Troy

[1] Euphrosyne, one of the Graces

Por ser aquesta atanto loada;
Que en tierra llana e no muy labrada
(30) nasce a las veses muy oliente rrosa,
Assy es aquesta gentil e fermosa,
Que tan alto meresce de ser comprada.

## Macías ¿1340-1370?

This Galician poet came to be known as the epitome of the unlucky lover. He fell in love with a woman, doña Elvira, who later married another man. He continued to court her causing her husband to kill him while he was imprisoned. Twenty-one of the cantigas in this Cancionero are attributed to him and are characterized by a blend of traditional Galician poetry and courtly poetry.

Esta cantyga fizo Macías contra el amor; enpero algunos
trobadores disen que la fiso contra el rrey don Pedro° — King Pedro el Cruel

Amor cruel e bryoso,° — spirited
Mal aya la tu altesa
Pues non fases ygualesa
seyendo tal poderoso.
(5) Abaxóme mi ventura
Non por mi merecimiento
E por ende la ventura
Púsome en grant tormento.
Amor, por tu fallimiento° — failing
(10) e por la tu grant cruesa,° — cruelty
Mi coraçón con tristesa
Es puesto en pensamiento.

Rey eres sobre los rreyes
Coronado enperador,
(15) dó te plase van tus leyes,
Todos an de ty pauor;
E pues eres tal sseñor

Non 'fases comunalesa,° — practise moderation
Sy entiendes que es proesa
(20) non soy ende judgador.° — judge
So la tu cruel espada
Todo onne es 'en omildança° — humiliated
Toda dueña mesurada
En ty deue aver fiança;° — trust
(25) con la tu brillosa° lança — shiny
Ençalsas° toda vilesa, — praise
E abaxas° la noblesa — debase
De quien en ty ovo fiança.
Ves, amor, por que lo digo,
(30) sé que eres cruel e forte,
Aduersaryo o nemigo,
Desamador de tu corte;
Al vyl hechas° en tal sorte — put
Que por pres° le das [altesa]; — payment
(35) quien te sirue en gentylesa
Por galardón le das morte.

Alfonso Alvarez de Villasandino (¿1340-1428?) began writing about 1370 and died circa 1428. He has the most poems in the *Cancionero de Baena* (more than 100) and was a professional poet in the service of Enrique II and other noblemen who paid for his work. According to Alan Deyermond, he was a poet of great flexibility writing courtly love poetry, panegyrics (poems of praise), mocking poems and beggars' poems. His poetry is written first in Galician-Portuguese, as was the tradition of that time, and later in Castilian.

*Esta cantiga fizo Alfonso Alvarez de Villasandino por ruego del conde don Pedro Niño, por amor e loores de doña Beatriz, su mujer.*

La que siempre obedecí
E obedezco todavía,
¡mal pecado!° sólo un día — alas

Non se le membra° de mí. — remember
Perdí
Meu° tempo en servir — =mi
A la que me faz vevir
Cuidoso° desque° la vi. — suffering, since

Eu la vi por meu mal,
Pois 'me traje° conquistado — I am
E de mí non ha cuidado
Ningunt tiempo, nin me val.
Leal
Le fui siempre, e non sé
'Cal he° a razón porque — what is
Me da morte desigual.° — sad

E pois que non ha mansela° — compassion
De miña° cuitada morte, — my
Si osase, en toda corte
Diría miña querela:
Mais° della — = mas
He pavor, que ha poder
Tal, que no oso disir
Si es doña nin doncella.

*Esta cantiga fizo Alfonso Álvarez por ruego del adelantado Pero Manrique, cuando andaba enamorado de esta su mujer, fija que es del señor duque de Benavente*

Señora, flor de açuçena,° — lily
Claro° viso angelical, — bright

Vuestro amor me da grant pena.
Muchas en Estremadura
Vos han grant emvidia pura,
Porque quantas han fermusura;
Dubdo mucho sy fue tal
En su tienpo Polyçena.

Fyzo vos Dios delycada,
Honesta,° bien enseñada; — chaste
Vuestra color matyzada
Más que rosa del rosal,
Me tormenta e desordena.° — confuse
Donayre,° graçioso brío,° — grace, spirit
Es todo vuestro atauío;° — adornment
Lynda flor, deleyte mío,
Yo vos fuy sienpre leal,
Más que fue Parys a Elena.

Vuestra vysta deleytosa
Más que lirio nin que rosa,
Me conquista, pues non osa
Mi coraçón dezir quál
Es quien asy lo enagena.° — intoxicates

Cunplida de noble asseo,° — cleanliness
quando vuestra ymagen veo
Otro plazer non desseo
Synon sufryr bien o mal,
Andando en vuestra cadena.

Non me basta más mi seso,
Plazerme ser vuestro presso;
Señora: por ende beso
Vuestras manos de crystal,
Clara luna en mayo llena.

*Esta cantiga fizo el dicho Alfonso Álvares por alabanza e loores de la redundable[2] cibdat de Sevilla*

Fuente de grant maravilla,
Jardyn de dulçe olor,
Morada de enperador,

[2] **Redundable** remarkable, exhuberant

Ryca, fermosa vaxilla,° — vessel
Digan esto por Sevilla
Trobadores e poetas,
Pues que synos° e planetas — constellations
Lo sostienen syn manzilla.

En ella los elementos,
Agua, tierra, fuego e ayre,
Son ryquezas e donayres,° — pleasant
Viçios° e abondamientos; — pleasures
Loores, ensalzamientos° — exhaltations
Sean dados, yo lo mando,
Al sancto rey don Ferrando
Pues ganó tales çimientos.° — foundation

Morar deue en paraíso
Quien guerreando con moros
Ganó tan rycos tesoros
E tanta tierra 'en proviso;° — at one time
Esta çibdat que 'de vyso° — sight
Será en el mundo llamada
La muy bien aventurada
A quien Dios bien quiere e quisso.

Clarydat e dyscreçión,
Esfuerço e caualleryа,
Grant linpieza e loçanía
Mora en su poblaçión;
Pues fazer deue mençión
Todo el mundo en verdat
De tan perfecta çibdat
E de su costelaçión.

## *Cancionero de Stúñiga*

The name of this *Cancionero* derives from the fact that Lope de Stúñiga is the first poet in the collection. It is the poetic production of the court of Alfonso V of Aragon who, after conquering

Naples in 1443, created a court with Castilian, Aragonese, Alicante and Catalan poets, influenced by Italian poets of this period.
Lope de Stúñiga was the son of the Castilian Marshall Íñigo Ortiz. He was a member of the Order of Santiago and an enemy of don Álvaro de Luna, the Condestable of Juan II. On his return to Castile he was imprisoned due to this enmity.

In the following poem, six ladies request gifts from the poet and he has six poppies brought. He dyes them white, blue, black, red, green and yellow. He composed a poem in the form of a copla for each poppy and put them in his sleeve. Each lady took a poppy with its *copla* out of the sleeve and received it as a sign of her fate.

Primera: la blanca

Ve, dormidera cuytada,
Llena de gran amargura:
Amarte syn ser amada
Fue siempre la mi ventura.

La azul

Bien segura fue de estar
qualquiera que me tomare,
que nunca verá pesar
de cosa que bien amare.

La prieta

Dama de gran gentileza,
Guárdate Dios de mi suerte,
La qual fue siempre tristeza,
Muy más áspera que muerte.

La colorada

A mí me llaman plazer,
Que fago tal juramento
De nunca te fallecer
Por ningúnd mal nin tormento.

La verde

Esperança, los que esperan
Me suelen todos llamar;
Mas algunos desesperan
Por mucho tiempo esperar.

La amarilla

A mí llaman conplimiento° fulfillment
De verdaderos amores;
Mas las dubdas y temores
Me ponen mucho tormento.

## Carvajales

He wrote the largest number of poems in this cancionero and is the first known author of ballads, the first Spanish poet to write in Italian, and an imitator of Santillana. We do not know very much about him but he did write *serranillas,* some like those of the *Libro de buen amor* and others more refined like those of the Marqués de Santillana.

XXII

Si tan fermosa como uos
Fasta oy fuera nascida,
Non seríades tan querida.

Non seríades tanto amada
Nin io de tanto mal sufriente,
Non seríades uos espada
Para mí tan perseguiente;

Contemplad, quered por Dios,
En reparo° de mi uida — remedy
Qu'es en punto de perdida.

XXIII

¡O qué poca cortesía
Para ser tan lynda dama,
Desamar a quien uos ama!

Doleduos de mí, que peno,
La uida triste que biuo,
Non fagáys de mi ageno° — stranger
Que nascí uuestro catiuo;
Renegad° mala porfía,° — renounce, insistence
¿Non sentís que uos disfama
desamar a quien uos ama?

XXIV

Saliendo de un oliuar
Más fermosa que arreada° — elegant
Vi serrana que tornar° — turn away
Me fiso de mi iornada.° — journey

Tornéme en su compannía
Por faldas de una montanna,
Suplicando sil'° plasía — **=si le**
Demostrarme su cabanna;
Dixo: "Non podéys librar,° — judge
Sennor, aquesta uegada,
Que superfluo es demandar
[a] quien non suele dar nada".

Si lealtad non me acordara
De la más lynda figura,

Del todo me enamorara:
Tanta ui su hermosura.
Dixe: "¿Qué queréys mandar
sennora, pues soys casada
que uos non quiero enoiar
nin offender mi enamorada?"

Replicó: "Yd en buen hora,
Non cures de amar uillana,
Pues seruís a tal sennora,
Non troques seda por lana,
Njn queráys de mí burlar,
Pues sabéys que só enaienada.° distant from you
Vi serrana que tornar
Me fizo de mi iornada.

XXV

Más triste que non María,
Aflita° con mucha pena afflicted
Vi tristesa en sennoría,° worship
Que iniusto amor condena;
Mas bella que Madalena:
Cabellos, cara llorosa,
Mostrándose, más fermosa
La cara syempre serena.

## Juan de Tapia (¿-1462)

We know very little about him except that he was born in Spain in the early years of the XVth century. He was in the battle of Ponza (1435) and imprisoned in Genoa. He obtained his freedom perhaps by influence from Milan and spent time in Naples. His verses extol Alfonso of Aragon, known as the Magnanimous, as well as his court. Sixteen of his poems are found in the *Cancionero de Stuñiga* and most of his poetry reflects the influence of the Italian humanists.

Canción a madama Lucrecia
Dama de tan buen semblante,° — face
Que la vuestra gran beldat
Fase la guerra
A quien fa temblar la tierra
Desde poniente° a levante.° — west, east

Vos fuistes la más fermosa
Donsella que fue nascida,
Muy honesta et virtuosa,
De todos bienes conplida;
Señora, que a tal amante
Con tan poca piedat
Faséis la guerra,
A quien fa temblar la tierra
Desde poniente a levante.

Vos fuistes la combatida° — embattled one
Que venció al vencedor,
Vos fuistes quien por amor
Jamás nunca fue vencida;
Vos pasáis tan adelante
Et con tanta crueldat
Faséis la guerra,
A quien fa temblar la tierra
Desde poniente a levante.

*Cancionero general*

This cancionero includes poetry by Fernán Pérez de Guzmán, Gómez and Jorge Manrique, Pero Guillén de Segovia, Florencia Pinar, Pedro de Cartagena as well as Juan de Mena and Íñigo López de Mendoza.

The compiler is Hernando del Castillo who began to gather poems about 1490 with the first edition published in Valencia in 1511. In this collection we find nine sections containing works of devotion and morality, love, satire, romances, villancicos, canciones and others.

## Florencia Pinar

She is one of the few Castilian women poets of the XVth century whose name we know. Her poems are recognized for her passionate wit and novelty of theme which include *canciones* about objects. She often speaks of love which she depicts as causing both pleasure and pain. Obviously, she was a member of the upper class and well-educated.

*Canción de unas perdices °que le enviaron vivas...* — partridges

Destas aves su nación° — nature
Es cantar con alegría,
Y de vellas° en prisión — seeing them
Siento yo grave° pasión,° — deep, suffering
Sin sentir nadie la mía.
Ellas lloran que se vieron
Sin temor de ser cativas,° — captives
Y a quien eran más esquivas° — shy
Esos mismos las prendieron:° — took
Sus nombres mi vida son
Que va perdiendo alegría,
Y de vellas en prisión
Siento yo grave pasión,
Sin sentir nadie la mía.

*Canción*

¡Ay!, que hay quien más no vive
Porque no hay quien d'¡ay! se duele,
Y si hay ¡ay! que recele,° — distrust
Hay un ¡ay! con que s'esquive — escape
Quien sin ¡ay! vevir no suele.
¡Ay plazeres!, ¡ay pesares!,
¡ay glorias!, ¡ay mil dolores!,
¡Ay, donde hay penas d'amores

Muy gran bien si d'él gozares!,° enjoy
Aunque vida se cative,
Si hay quien tal ¡ay! consuele,
No hay razón porque se cele,
Aunque hay con que se esquive
Quien sin ¡ay! vevir no suele.

## Guevara

He is one of the best poets of the *Cancionero general.* We only know his last name and that he probably was the father or uncle of fray Antonio de Guevara.

CXXVI

El seso turbio pensando,
La vida muerte sintiendo,
Los ojos tristes llorando,
La voz cuitada plañendo,
Vivo yo, triste, sin vida,
Ya partido,
No partido de partida
Me despido.

Y voy a donde el morir
Buscaré'n tierras ajenas,
Que en tantos males y penas,
Ya no puedo más vevir:
A do yo triste, cativo,
No muriendo,
Seré muerto, siendo vivo,
No te viendo.

Y las aves dulces, ledas,° happy
Cantarán sus alboradas,° dawn songs
Y a vista de sus amadas
Harán los pavos las ruedas;° their showy fan tail
Pues a mí, triste, no queda
Sino suerte° fate

De, sin verte, ver la rueda
De mi muerte.

Y verás cómo se encienden° — are inflamed
Las mis coplas en tormentos,
Tan altas en pensamientos
Que muy pocos las entienden:
Y verás que siempre vivos
Dieron males,
Pero no males iguales
De los míos.

Allí verás mi querer
Que no te quiso por vicio,
Y verás más, mi servicio
Más triste que mi plazer:
Y verás cómo se parte,
Siendo viva,
Mi sola fe que sin arte
Fue cativa.

Y verás allí los años
Que serán tan sin mesura,
Y verás a mi tristura
Más triste que mis engaños:
Y verás cómo trocaste
Sin derecho
Mi querer, y desamaste
Tu provecho.

Y no llores mi tormento,
Mas assí tú vevirás,
Que jamás no hallarás
Quien tal afán te consienta:
Do serás importunada,
No querida,
Requerida, más burlada
Que servida.

Cabo
Y con esta fe llorosa° mournful
Sin c'a mi seso te escondas,
Bogaré° en las altas ondas I will row
De aquella mar peligrosa,
Do, si vivo, beviré
Con gran dolor,
Y si muero, moriré
Tu servidor.

Esparsa
Las aves andan volando,
Cantando canciones ledas,
Las verdes hojas temblando,
Las aguas dulces sonando,
Los pavos hazen las ruedas:
Yo, sin ventura amador,
Contemplando mi tristura
Deshago por mi dolor
La gentil rueda d'amor
Que hize por mi ventura.

## Quirós

He is known for his great variety of *canciones* and as an agile poet who adheres to the exact norms of the *Cancionero general.*

Canción

Dos enemigos hallaron
Las hadas, y a mí los dieron,
Mis ojos que me perdieron,
Los vuestros que me mataron.

Hiciendo yo mal tractado
Muestra amor esta crueldad,
Que pidiendo yo amistad,

Ni sólo soy escuchado:
Contra mí solo se armaron,
Assí que me destruyeron,
Mis ojos que me prendieron,
Los vuestros que me mataron.

Villancico

Pues la triste vida dize
Que es la muerte mejor d'ella,
¿Qué se perderá en perdella?

Razón es, alma, que creas
Que sin vida estás conmigo;
Vete y llévame contigo
A donde verte desseas.
De tal vida nunca seas
Temerosa de perdella,
Qu'es la muerte mejor d'ella.

Mejor es morir por cierto,
Pues que con la vida dexa
Este mal de tanta quexa
Que no sana sino el muerto:
Vida de tal desconcierto
Que es la muerte mejor d'ella,
¿qué se perderá en perdella?

## Other Lyric Poets

Marqués de Santillana, Don Íñigo López de Mendoza (1398-1458), was the greatest poet of the 15th century. He was a man of great culture and deep learning, and his delicate taste and fine discrimination made it possible for him to see excellence in troubadour poetry of the Galician-Portuguese school and even in folk poetry, as well as in the new Italian forms of verse. He produced some of the best lyrics of the entire period.

Juan de Mena (1411-1456) was a Cordovan who studied at

Salamanca and traveled to Rome. He was a supporter of the royal favorite, don Álvaro de Luna, and an official in the pay of Juan II. Little else is known of his life. He was the first Spaniard to translate the *Illiad* (about which he also wrote a commentary). After Santillana he ranks as the greatest poet of the century.

## Marqués de Santillana,
## Don Íñigo López de Mendoza (1398-1458)

This most famous poet of the 15th century wrote *villancicos, serranillas, canciones,* and *decires* which are unpretentious, and though modeled after popular poetry, are polished and erudite, maintaining a charming simplicity. He was also subject to Italian influence and was the first to write sonnets (42 of them) in Spanish. He wrote long allegorical poems in the style of Petrarch and Dante, and was the first to comment on the development of poetry in his *Prohemio y carta al Condestable de Portugal.* In the Italian style was his most famous single poem, *Comedieta de Ponza.* Such allegorical poems as the *Infierno de los enamorados, De funsión de don Enrique de Villena,* the dialogue, *Bías contra fortuna, Doctrinal de privados,* and the *Proverbios de gloriosos y fructuosa enseñanza* all have their merits, but are little read today.

### *Sonetos fechos al itálico modo*

En este primero soneto quiere mostrar el actor que quando los cuerpos superiores, que son las estrellas, se acuerdan con la natura, que son las cosas baxas, fasen la cosa muy más linpia e muy más neta (*pure*).

Quando yo veo la gentil° criatura — graceful
qu'el çielo, acorde° con naturaleza — in agreement
formaron, loo° mi buena ventura, — praise
el punto° e hora que tanta belleza — moment
me demostraron, e su fermosura,
ca sola de loor es la pureza;
mas luego torno con ygual tristura° — **=tristeza**

e plango° e quéxome de su crueza.° — weep, cruelty
Ca non fue tanta la del mal Thereo,[3]
nin fizo la de Achila e de Potino,
falsos ministros de ti, Ptolomeo.[4]
Assí que lloro mi serviçio indigno
e la mi loca fiebre, pues que veo
e me fallo cansado e peregrino.° — pilgrim

VIII

En este octavo soneto muestra el actor commo, non enbgargante (***a pesar* de)** su señora o amiga lo oviese ferido e cativado, que a él non pesava (*displease*) de la tal presyón (**prisión**).

¡O dulce esguarde,° vida e honor mía, — look
segunda Helena,° templo de beldad, — Helen of Troy
so cuya mano, mando° e señoría° — rule, power
es el arbitrio° mío e voluntad! — reason

Yo soy tu prisionero, e 'sin porfía° — without a struggle
fueste señora de mi libertad;
e non te pienses fuyga° tu valía,° — **huya**, power
nin me desplega° tal cautividad. — displeases

Verdad sea que Amor gasta° e dirruye° — wastes, destroys
las mis entrañas con fuego amoroso,
e la mi pena jamás diminuye;° — **disminuye**

nin punto fuelgo° nin soy en reposo, — relax
más bivo alegre con quien me destruye;
siento que muero e non soy quexoso.

---

[3] **Thereo** is a prince in Greek mythology (Tereus) who married Procne and then forced himself on Philomela, her sister. He then cut off Philomela's tongue and told Procne that she had died.

[4] **Achila, Potino** and **Ptolomeno**. Achillas and Potinus, the Eunuch, were ministers of the pharaoh Ptolemy XIII. By their disservice involving Cleopatra VII, Ptolemy's sister, they caused a civil war.

IX

*En este noveno soneto el actor muestra commo en un día de grand fiesta vio a la señora suya en cabello; dise ser los cabellos suyos muy ruvios (**=rubios**) e de la color de la tupaça (topaz), que es una piedra que ha la color commo de oro. Alý dó dise "filos de Arabia" muestra asymismo que eran tales commo filos (**=hilos**) de oro, por quanto ° (since) en Arabia nasçe el oro. Dise asymismo que los premia (ties) un verdor placiente (pleasing) e flores de jazmines; quiso desir que la crespina (hairnet) suya era de seda verde e perlas.*

Non es el rayo del Febo° luciente, — Apollo
nin los filos de Arabia más fermosos
que los vuestros cabellos luminosos,
nin gemma° de topaza tan fulgente.° — jewel, shiny

Eran ligados° de un verdor plaziente — tied
e flores de jazmín los ornava,° — adorned
e su perfecta belleza mostrava° — shone
qual viva flamma o estrella d'Oriente.

Loó mi lengua, maguer sea indigna,
aquel buen punto que primero vi
la vuestra ymagen e forma divina,

tal commo perla e claro rubí,
e vuestra vista társica° e benigna, — penetrating
a cuyo esguarde e merçed me di.

XIV

Cuando yo soy delante

*En este catorcésimo soneto el actor muestra que él, quando es delante aquella su señora, le paresçe que es en el monte Tabor, en el qual Nuestro Señor aparesçió a los tres discípulos suyos e por quanto la historia es muy vulgar (known), non cura de la escribir.*

Cuando yo soy delante aquella dona
a cuyo mando° me sojuzgó° Amor, — command, subjugated

cuido ser uno de los que en Tabor[5]
vieron la gran claror° que se razona,° — light, is spoken of

o que ella sea fija de Latona,° — Diana, moon goddess
según su aspecto e grande resplandor:
así que punto° yo no he vigor — not any
de mirar fijo su deal° persona. — divine

El su grato° fablar dulce, amoroso, — pleasing
es una maravilla ciertamente,
e modo nuevo en humanidad:

el andar suyo es con tal reposo,° — calm
honesto° e manso, e su continente, — chaste
que, libre, vivo en cautividad.

*Serranillas*

These are short poems in arte mayor that deal with the encounter between a knight and a country girl in imitation of the French pastourelle but inspired by Spanish popular tradition.

Serranilla I

Serranilla° de Moncayo, — mountain girl
Dios vos dé buen año entero,
ca de muy torpe° lacayo — unskilled
faríades cavallero.

Ya se pasava el verano,
al tiempo que onbre° se apaña° — **=hombre,** dresses
con la ropa á la tajaña,° — shoulder
encima de Oxmediano[6]
ví serrana sin argayo° — cape
andar al pie del otero,° — hill

[5] **Tabor** mountain in the Holy Land where Jesus was transfigured.
[6] **Vozmediano** a town in the province of Zaragoza.

| | |
|---|---|
| más clara que sale en mayo, | |
| ell alva,° nin su luzero.° | dawn, morning star |
| | |
| Díxele: "Dios os mantenga,° | keep |
| serrana de buen donayre."° | witty |
| Respondió como 'en desgayre:° | scornfully |
| ¡Ay!, que en hora buena venga | |
| aquel que para Sanct Payo° | San Pelayo |
| desta yrá mi prisionero." | |
| | |
| E vino a mí como un rayo | |
| diziendo: "Preso, montero." | |
| | |
| Díxele: "Non me matedes, | |
| serrana, sin ser oído, | |
| ca yo non soy del partido,° | type |
| desos por quien vos lo avedes.° | think |
| | |
| Aunque me vedes 'tal sayo° | dressed in this cloak |
| en Agreda soy frontero,° | frontier soldier |
| e non me llaman Pelayo, | |
| magüer me vedes señero."° | alone |
| | |
| Desque oyó lo que dezía, | |
| dixo: "Perdonad, amigo, | |
| mas folgad ora comigo, | |
| e dexad la montería.° | hunting |
| | |
| A este çurrón° que trayo | shepherd's pouch |
| quered ser mi parcionero,° | share with me |
| pues me falleció° Mingayo | died |
| que era comigo ovejero.° | shepherd |
| | |
| Entre Torellas y el Fayo | |
| pasaremos el febrero." | |
| | |
| Díxele: "De tal ensayo,° | trial |
| serrana, soy placentero."° | pleased |

Serranilla III

Después que nací,
no ví tal serrana
como esta mañana.

Allá en la vegüela° — fertile valley
a Mata'l Espino,
en ese camino
que va a Loçoyuela,
de guissa la vy
que me fizo gana
la fruta tenprana.[7]

Garnacha° traía — full-length dress
de oro, presada° — sleeves; tied
con broncha° dorada, — pin
que bien parecía.

A ella volví
diziendo: "Loçana,° — spritely lass
¿e soys vos villana?"° — peasant

"Sí soy, cavallero;
si por mí lo avedes,
decit ¿qué queredes?,
fablat verdadero."

Yo le dixe assí:
"Juro por Santana° — **=Santa Ana**
que no soys villana."

Serranilla VI

---

[7] **Que me fizo...** I desired the early fruit.

Moça tan fermosa
non ví en la frontera,
como una vaquera° — cowherder
de la Finojosa.

Faziendo la vía
del Calatraveño
a Santa María,
vençido del sueño,
por tierra fragosa° — full of brambles
perdí la carrera,
do ví la vaquera
de la Finojosa.

En un verde prado
de rosas e flores,
guardando ganado
con otros pastores,
la ví tan graciosa,
que apenas creyera
que fuese vaquera
de la Finojosa.

Non creo las rosas
de la primavera
sean tan fermosas
nin de tal manera;
fablando 'sin glosa,° — simply
si antes supiera
de aquella vaquera
de la Finojosa.

Non tanto mirara
su mucha beldad,
porque me dexara
en mi libertad.

Mas dixe: "Donosa° — graceful
(por saber quién era),
¿aquella vaquera
de la Finojosa?..."

Bien como riendo,
dixo: "Bien vengades,
que ya bien entiendo
lo que demandades:
non es desseosa
de amar, nin lo espera,
aquessa vaquera
de la Finojosa.

Serranilla IX

Moçuela de Bores
allá do la Lama
'púsom'en amores.° — made me fall in love

Cuydé que olvidado
Amor me tenía,
como quien s'avía
grand tiempo dexado
de tales dolores,
que más que la llama° — flame
queman amadores.

Mas ví la fermosa
de buen continente,° — countenance
la cara plaçiente,
fresca como rosa,
de tales colores
qual nunca vi dama
nin otra, señores.

Por lo qual: "Señora

(le dixe), en verdat
la vuestra beldat
saldrá desd'agora
dentre estos alcores,° hills
pues meresçe fama
de grandes loores."

Dixo: "Cavallero,
'tiratvos á fuera:° go away
dexat la vaquera
passar al otero;
ca dos labradores
me piden de Frama,
entrambos° pastores." both

"Señora, pastor
seré si queredes:
mandarme podedes,
como a servidor:
mayores dulçores
será a mí la brama° lowing
que oyr ruyseñores."

Asy concluymos
el nuestro proçesso° discussion
sin facer exçesso,
é nos avenimos.° came to an agreement

E fueron las flores
de cabe Espinama
los encobridores.° covered us

Serranilla X

De Vytoria me partía
un día desta semana,
por me passar a Alegría,

do ví moça lepuzcana.° — Guipuzcoan

Entre Gaona e Salvatierra,
en esse valle arbolado° — filled with trees
donde s'aparta la sierra,
la ví guardando ganado,
tal como el alvor del día,
en un cargante° de grana,° — surcoat, scarlet
qual tod'ome la querría,
non vos digo por hermana.

Yo loé las de Moncayo
e sus gestos e colores,
de lo qual non me retrayo,° — go back on my word
e la moçuela de Bores;
pero tal fisonomía
en toda la su montaña
çierto non se fallaría,
nin fué tan fermosa Yllana.

De la moça de Bedmar,
a fablarvos çiertamente,
raçón ove de loar
su grand e buen continente;
mas tampoco negaría,
la verdat, que tan loçana,
aprés la señora mía,
non ví doña nin serrana.

Serranilla (Villancico) que hizo el Marqués a tres hijas suyas

Por una gentil floresta° — wood, glade
de lindas flores e rosas,
vide tres damas fermosas
que de amores 'han requesta.° — made a petition

Yo, con voluntad muy presta

me llegué a conoscellas.
Començó la una dellas
esta canción tan honesta:

Aguardan° a mí:                wait
nunca tales guardas vi.

Por mirar su fermosura
destas tres gentiles damas,
yo cobríme con las ramas,
metíme so la verdura.°                greenery

La otra con gran tristura
començó de sospirar
[e] dezir este cantar
con muy honesta mesura:°                rhythm

La niña que los amores ha
sola, ¿cómo dormirá?

Por no les fazer turbança
non quise yr más adelante
a las que con ordenanza°                measure
cantaban tan consonante.°                harmony

La otra con buen semblante
dixo: "Señoras de estado,
pues las dos aveys cantado,
a mí conviene que cante:

Dexadlo al villano pene:°                suffer
véngueme° Dios dele."                avenge

Desque huvieron cantado
estas señoras que digo,
yo salí desconsolado,
como hombre sin abrigo.

Ellas dixeron: "Amigo,
non soys vos el que buscamos,
mas cantad, pues que cantamos."
Dixe este cantar antiguo:

Sospirando yva la niña
e non por mí,
que yo bien ge° lo entendí. =se

Canción

(Que fizo el Marqués de Santillana a sus fijas loando la su fermosura)

Dos serranas° he trovado° mountain girl, fo
a pié de áspera montaña,
segund es su gesto e maña° habits
non vezadas° de ganado. accustomed

De espinas trahen los velos° veils
e de oro las crespinas,° hairnets
senbradas° de perlas finas, decorated
que le aprietan° sus cabellos; hold in place
e las trufas° bien posadas,° accessories, plac
a más, de oro arracadas,° pendant earring
rruvios, largos cabellos
segund doncellas d'estado.

Fruentes claras e luzientes,
las çejas en arco alçadas,
las narizes afiladas,° elegant
chica boca e blancos dientes,
ojos prietos e rientes,
las mexillas como rosas,
gargantas maravillosas,
altas, lindas al mi grado.

Carnoso,° blanco e liso — full
cada cual en los sus pechos,
porque Dios todos sus fechos
dexó quando fer las quiso;
dos pumas° de paraíso — apples
las sus tetas ygualadas,
en la su çinta delgadas
con aseo° adonado.° — appearance, graceful

Blancas manos e pulidas,° — smooth
e los dedos no espigados,° — pointy
a las juntas no afeados,° — ugly
uñas de argent guarnidas,° — decorated
rrubíes e margaridas,° — pearls
çafires e diamantes,
axorcas° ricas, sonantes, — bracelets
todas de oro labrado.

Ropas trahen a sus guisas
todas fendidas° por rrayas,° — cut, pleats
do les paresçen sus sayas° — skirts
forradas en peñas° grisas;° — fur, gray
sus ropas bien asentadas,
de azeytuní° quartonadas,° — rich oriental cloth, divided; thread
de filo° de oro brocado.

Yo las vi, si Dios me vala,
posadas en sus tapetes,° — carpets
en sus faldas los blanchetes,° — lapdogs
que demuestran mayor gala.° — elegance

Los finojos he fincado,
segund es acostumbrado
a dueñas de grand altura:
ellas por la su mesura
en los pies m'an levantado.

Dezir

1
Yo, mirando una ribera,
ví venir por [u]n grant llano
un hombre, que cortesano
pareçía en su manera:

vestía ropa estrangera,
fecha al modo de Bravante,° — place in Belgium
bordada, bien roçegante,° — showy
pas[s]ante° del estribera.° — beyond, stirrup

2
Traía al su diestro lado
una muy fermosa dama,
de las que toca la fama
en superlativo grado:
un capirote° charpado° — cape, of elegant mat
a manera bien estraña
a fuer del alta Alimaña° — Germany
donosamente° ligado. — artfully

3
De gentil seda amarilla
eran aquestas dos hopas,° — tunics
tales, que nunca ví ropas
tan lindas a maravilla:

el guarnimento° e la silla — adornment
d'aquesta linda señora,
çertas después nin agora
non lo vy tal en Castilla.

4
Por música maestría° — artistry
cantava esta cançión,
que fizo a mi coraçón

perder el pavor que avía:

"Bien debo loar amor
pues toda vía
quiso tornar mi tristor° — sadness
en alegría."

## Comedieta de Ponza

This poem is written in *arte mayor*, allegorical in approach, and modeled after Dante. It deals with the capture of Alfonso V of Aragon by the Genoese, the author's exposition of the shifts of fortune, and the dreams of the wives of the captured princes and of the king

Oh vos, dubitantes,° creed las historias — doubters
e los infortunios° de los humanales,° — misfortunes, humans
e ved si los triunfos, honores e glorias
e grandes poderes son perpetüales.
¡Mirad los imperios e casas reales 5
e cómo Fortuna es superïora:
revuelve lo alto en bajo 'a deshora° — unexpectedly
e face a los ricos e pobres iguales!

II
Invocación
¡Oh lúcido Jove,° la mi mano guía, — Jupiter
despierta el ingenio,° aviva la mente, 10 — wit
el rústico modo aparta° e desvía,° — put aside, turn away
e torna mi lengua, de ruda, elocuente!
E vos, las hermanas,° que cabe° la fuente — muses, near
de Helicón° facedes continua morada, — home of the muses
sed todas comigo en esta jornada, 15
porqu'°el triste caso denuncie e recuente. — **=para que**

III
Descripción del tiempo
Los campos e mieses° ya descoloraban — grainfields
e los deseados tributos rendían;
los vientos pluviosos las nubes bogaban,° — pushing away
e las verdes frondes el aire tremían.° 20 — moved
Dejado° el stilo de los que fingían — abandoned
metáforas vanas con dulce locuela,° — elocuence
diré lo que priso mi última cela;° — memory cell
e cómicos° oyan si bien los oían. — authors of plays

IV
Al tiempo que salen al pasto° o guarida° 25 — pasture, cave
las fieras silvestres e humanidad
descansa o reposa, e la fembra ardida° — valiant (Judith)
libró de Oloferne° la sacra cibdad,[8] — Holofernes
forzada del sueño la mi libertad,
diálogo triste e fabla llorosa° 30 — tearful
firió° mis orejas, e tan pavorosa° — struck, frightening
ca solo en pensarlo me vence piedad.

V
Así recordado,° miré do sonaba — awakened
el clamoso° duelo,° e vi cuatro donas [9] — painful, lament
cuyo aspecto e fabla muy bien denotaba 35
ser cuasi deesas° o magnas° personas, — goddesses, great
vestidas de negro e, a las tres, coronas,
llamando a la muerte con tantas querellas° — laments
que dubdo si fueron tan grandes aquellas
que Ovidio toca° de las tres Gorgonas. [10] 40 — wrote about

---

[8] **La sacra cibdad...** is Bethulia and not Jerusalem. Judith freed Bethulia from the siege of the Assyrians led by Holofernes.
[9] **Cuatro donas** are the following three queens: Maria de Aragon, Blanca of Navarra and Leonor of Aragon and the infanta Catalina.
[10] **Gorgonas** In Greek mythology three monstrous sisters. Their hair was of snakes and their faces were so hideous that those who looked at them were turned to stone.

XIV
Fabla la señora infante doña Catalina quejándose de la Fortuna e loa° los oficios bajos e serviles — praises

Non menos fermosa e más dolorida 105
que la Tiriana,° cuando al despedir — Dido
de los ilioneos° e vio recogida — Trojans
la gente a las naves en son de partir,
la lengua despierta la cuarta a decir
comenzó: Poeta, mi mala fortuna 110
non pienses 'de agora,° mas desde la cuna — only now
jamás ha cesado de me perseguir.

XV
Humanas son tigres e fieras leonas
con nuevos cadillos,° e virgo piadosa — cubs
aquella Elenesa° que a las amazonas 115 — queen of Amazons
pensó facer libres por lid sanguinosa;
tractable° es Caribdi[11] e non espantosa, — benevolent
segund me contracta° esta adversa rueda,° — proves, fortune
a quien non sé fuerza nin saber que pueda
foir° al su curso e saña rabiosa. 120 — **=huir**

XVI
¡Benditos aquellos que con el azada° — hoe
sustentan su vida e viven contentos,
e, de cuando en cuando conocen morada° — dwelling
e sufren pascientes las lluvias e vientos!
Ca estos non temen los sus movimientos, 125
nin saben las cosas del tiempo pasado,
nin de las presentes se facen cuidado,
nin las venideras 'do han nascimientos.° — are to come

XVII
¡Benditos aquellos que siguen las fieras

[11] Charybdis was transformed by Zeus into one of the rocks bordering the Strait of Messina where many shipwrecks occurred in mythololgy.

con las gruesas redes e canes ardidos, 130
e saben las 'trochas e las delanteras° — shortcuts
e fieren del arco en tiempos debidos!° — appropriate
Ca estos por saña non son comovidos,
nin vana cobdicia los tiene° subjectos; — hold
nin quieren tesoros nin sienten defectos,° 135 — any lack
nin turban temores sus libres sentidos.

XVIII
¡Benditos aquellos que cuando las flores
se muestran al mundo deciben° las aves, — deceive
e fuyen las pompas e vanos honores,
e ledos escuchan sus cantos süaves! 140
¡Benditos aquellos qu'en pequeñas naves
siguen los pescados con pobres traínas!,° — small nets
ca estos non temen las lides marinas,
nin cierra sobr'ellos Fortuna sus llaves.° — hold

## Juan de Mena (1411-1456)

Juan de Mena cultivated the Dantesque style of poetry and showed a definite aspiration to enrich the Spanish language with Latinisms, to create a poetic language for the erudite. His best known work is the *Laberinto de fortuna*, known also as *Las trescientas* from the approximate number of its strophes. The *Laberinto* shows that Mena imitated Dante, Virgil, Lucan, and others. It is a long allegorical poem which even has the general idea of the *Paradiso* of Dante. Perhaps its greatest value lies not in the poetry itself or in the symbols called into play, but in historical episodes treated with patriotic sentiments and vision.

The poem is dated 1444 and dedicated to King Juan II. In it the poet is transported in the chariot of Belona, goddess of war, to the palace of Fortune where Providence appears to serve as his guide. In the palace he sees three wheels, two stationary representing the past and the future, and a third in constant motion representing the present.

Each wheel contains seven circles, symbolic of the seven planets known at that time. In each of these circles, the various episodes of the work take place, for on the wheels of Fortune mortals receive their rewards and punishment. Each wheel is presided over by goddesses of classic mythology. On the wheel of the past, one sees mythological and historical figures, on the wheel of the present, heroic or legendary men and women of Spain; and on the wheel of the future, the poet reads signs of coming triumphs of the king, Juan II. It is written in 8 line stanzas of 12 syllable lines of arte mayor divided into two hemistichs. (Schwartz, p. 285).

*Las CCC. De Juã de Mena*

Comiença el laberinto de Juan de Mena poeta castellano:
ntitulado Al muy esclarecido° — illustrious
y poderoso príncipe don Juan el segundo
Rey de Castilla y de León

Al muy prepotente° don Juan el segundo — all powerful
aquel con quien Júpiter tuvo tal zelo° — zeal
que tanta de parte le haze en el mundo.[12]
quanta a sí mesmo se haze en el çielo;
al gran rey de España, al Çésar novelo;° — young
aquél con Fortuna es bien afortunado,
aquél en quien caben virtud y reinado;° — governance
a él, las rodillas hincadas por suelo.

2

Propone

Tus casos falaçes,° Fortuna, cantamos. — false deeds
estados de gentes que giras° y trocas,° — turn, change
tus grandes discordias, tus firmezas° pocas, — steadfastness
y los que en rueda quexosos hallamos;
hasta que al tiempo de agora vengamos:
de fechos pasados cobdicia mi pluma.
y de los presentes hazer breve suma:
dé fin Apolo: pues nos començamos.

[12] **Que tanta de...**had him do so much in the world

3
Invoca
Tú, Calíöpe,° me sey favorable, — muse of epic poetry
dándome alas de don virtuoso;
por que discurra° por donde non oso. — discourse
Convida mi lengua con algo que hable;
levante la fama tu boz inefable,
porque los hechos que son al presente.
vayan de gente sabidos en gente:
olvido no prive[13] lo que es memorable.

4
Cuenta
Como no creo que fuessen menores
que los Africanos[14] los hechos del Çid,
ni que feroces menos en la lid
entrasen los nuestros que los agenores° — foreigners
las grandes hazañas de nuestros señores° — ancestors
la mucha constancia de quien los más ama
yaze en tinieblas,° dormida su fama, — darkness
dañada de olvido por falta de auctores.° — **=autores**

5
Ejemplefica
La gran Babilonia, que ovo cercado° — surrounded
'a madre de Nino° de 'tierra cocida,° — Semiramis, bricks
si ya por el suelo nos es destruida,
¡cuánto más presto 'lo mal fabricado!° — something badly bui
E si los muros que Febo° ha travado — Apollo
'argólica fuerça° pudo subverter, — the Greeks
¿qué fábrica pueden mis manos hazer:
que no 'haga curso° según lo passado? — procede

6

[13] **Olvido no prive...** let forgetfulness not take away.
[14] **Africanos** can refer to Hanibal and Scipio Africanus who were famous generals.

Otra vez invoca.
Ya pues desrama de tus nuevas fuentes
'Pierio subsidio,° inmortal Apolo; help from Muses
Epira° en mi boca por que pueda sólo breathe
virtudes e viçios narrar de potentes.
A estos mis dichos° mostrad vos presentes, words
'hijas de Tespis,° con vuestro tesoro, muses
con harmonía de aquel dulçe coro:
Suplid cobdiçiando mis inconvenientes.

7

Disputa con la Fortuna
Dame licençia mudable Fortuna,
porque blasme° de ti como debo: curse
lo que a los sabios no debe ser nuevo:
Ignoto a persona podrá ser alguna.
pues tu hecho así contrapugna:° is contradictory
haz a tus cosas como se concorden.
que todas las cosas regidas por orden
son amigables 'de forma más una.° in a united way

8

La orden del cielo exemplo te sea:
guarda la mucha constançia del Norte;
mira el Trión,° que ha deporte° big dipper, pleasure
ser muy inconstante, que siempre rodea;
y las siete Pleyas° quien las otea:° Pleaides, looks
que juntas pareçen 'en muy chica suma:° small
siempre se asconden después de la bruma.° mist
cada cual guarda qualquier ley que sea.

9

¿Pues cómo, Fortuna, regir todas las cosas
con ley absoluta, sin orden, te plaze?
¿Tú no harías lo que el ciclo haze,
y hacen los tiempos, las plantas y rosas?
O muestra tus obras ser siempre dañosas,
o prósperas, buenas, durables, eternas:

No nos fatigues con 'vezes alternas,° — changes
Alegres agora, agora enojosas.

10
Más bien acatada° tu varia mudança, — watched
por ley te gobiernas, maguer discrepante:
que tu firmeza es no ser constante.
tu temperamento es destemplança,
tu más cierta orden es desordenança,
es la tu regla ser muy enorme.
tu conformidad es no ser conforme
tú desesperas a toda esperança.

11
Comparación
Como las nautas° que van en poniente° — sailors, west
se hallan en Calez° la mar sin repunta,° — Cadiz, waves
Europa por pocas con Libia do junta,
quando Boreas° se muestra valiente, — northern wind
pero si el Austro° conmueve al tridente, — southern wind
corren° en contra de como vinieron — return
las aguas, que nunca ternán nin tuvieron
allí, donde digo, reposo paçiente,

12
así fluctuosa, Fortuna aborrida,° — hated
tus casos inçiertos semejan, y tales
que corren por ondas de bienes y males,
haciendo no cierta ninguna corrida.
Más ya porque vea la tu 'sin medida° — lack of moderation
la casa me muestra do anda tu rueda
por que vista dezir çierto pueda
el modo que tratas allí nuestra vida.

13
Ficción
No bien formadas mis voces serían
quando robada sentí mi persona,

y llena de furia la madre Belona° — godess of war
me toma en su carro que dragos° traían, — dragons
y quando las alas non bien remecían° — move
feríalos ésta con duro flagelo,° — whip
tanto que hizo hazerles tal buelo
Que presto me dexan a donde querían.

14
Comparación
Así me soltaron en medio de un llano
desque había dado conmigo una buelta,
como a las vezes el águila suelta
la presa que bien no le hinche° de la mano; — fill
yo de tal caso mirable,° inhumano, — wondrous
halléme espantado en un gran desierto,
do vi multitud no número çierto.
'en son° religioso y en modo profano. — both

15
Descripción
Y toda la otra vezina planura
estava çercada de nítido° muro, — resplendent
así transparente, clarífico,° puro, — resplendent
que mármol de Paro[15] semeja en albura,° — whiteness
tanto qu'el viso° de la criatura, — sight
por la diáfana claror° de los cantos,° — brightness, rocks
pudiera traer objectos atantos
quantos çelava° so sí la clausura.° — hidden, enclosure

16
Mas ya porque en otros algunos lugares
mi vista, bien antes que yo lo demande,
me hace grand cuerpo de cuerpo no grande
quando 'los medios son especulares,° — magnifying glass
dixe: "Si formas tan mucho dispares
bien no reguardo, jamás seré ledo° — happy

[15] **Paro** the island of Paros in the Aegean Sea

si de más cerca mirar bien no puedo
sus grandes misterios y muy singulares."

17
Comparación
Como el que tiene el espejo delante,
maguer que se mire derecho en derecho
se parte pagado, mas no satisfecho
como si viese su mesmo semblante,
tal me sentía por el semejante,
que nunca así pude hallarme contento
que no desease mirar más atento,
mi vista culpando por no ser bastante.

18
Prosigue
Estando yo allí con este deseo,
abaxa una nube muy grande y escura
el aire fuscando° con mucha presura, darkening
me çiega y me ciñe° que nada no veo; binds
ya me temía, hallándome reo,° prisoner
no me aconteciese como a Polifemo[16]
que desque çiego venido 'en extremo° totally
ovo lugar el engaño ulixeo.° of Ulysses

159
La muerte del conde de Niebla
Baxé más mis ojos, mirando las gentes
que vi sublimadas del trono mavorçio,° of Mars
dignas del mucho famoso consorçio
donde hallamos los muy prepotentes;
e yo que mirava los tan inoçentes
en un cavallero 'tardança más fiz,° I focused
del qual preguntada por mí la doctriz° guide
respuso dictando los metros siguientes:

---

[16] **Polifemo** a one-eyed Cyclops who lived in a cave in Sicily and ate human flesh.

160
«Aquel que en la barca paresçe asentado,
vestido de engaño de las bravas ondas,
en aguas crueles ya más que no hondas
con una gran gente en la mar anegado,° drowned
es el valiente, no bien fortunado,
muy virtüoso, perínclito° conde very illustrious
de Niebla, que todos sabéis bien adónde
dio fin, el día del 'curso fadado.° unhappy life

161
»Y los que lo çercan por alderredor,
puesto que fuesen magníficos hombres,
los títulos todos de todos sus nombres,
el nombre los cubre de aquel su señor;
que todos los hechos que son de valor
para mostrarse por sí cada uno,
quando se juntan y van 'de consuno,° together
pierden su nombre delante el mayor.

162
Comparación
»Arlança, Pisuerga y aun Carrión[17]
gozan de nombres de ríos; empero,° however
después que juntados, llamámoslos Duero:
hazemos de muchos una relaçión;
oye por ende, pues, la perdiçión
de sólo el buen conde sobre Gibraltar;
su muerte, llorada de digno llorar,
provoquen tus ojos a lamentaçión.

163
»En la su triste hadada partida
muchas señales° que los marineros signs
han por auspiçios y malos agüeros° omens

---

[17] **Arlança, Pisuerga, Carrión** are three small rivers that come together and join the Duero near Valladolid, thereby losing their individual identity.

fue denegada negar su venida;
las quales veyendo, con boz dolorida,
el cauto° maestro de toda su flota° — wary, fleet
al conde amonesta° del mal 'que denota,° — warns, indicated
por que la vía fuesse resistida.° — refused

164
Señales de Fortuna
»'Ca he visto', dize, 'señor, nuevos yerros° — disturbances
la noche passada hazer las planetas;
con crines° tendidas° arder las cometas, — tails, long
dar nueva lumbre las armas y fierros,° — blades
ladrar° sin heridas° los canes y perros, — bark, injuries
triste presagio° hazer de peleas — omen
las aves noturnas y las funereas° — evil omened ones
por los collados,° alturas y çerros.° — mountains, hills

165
»'Vi que las lágrimas[18] gruesas quebravan
quando las áncoras° quis levantar; — anchors
e vi las antenas° por medio quebrar, — crossbars
aunque los cárbasos° no desplegavan;° — sails, unfurled
los másteles° fuertes en calma temblavan; — masts
los flacos triquetes° con la su mezana° — small sails, medium s
vi levantarse de non buena gana
quando los vientos se no conbidavan.° — were not favorable

166
»'En la partida del 'resto troyano° — Trojan survivors
de aquella Cartago del bírseo muro,[19]
el voto° prudente del buen Palinuro[20] — decsion
toda la flota loó de más sano,
tanto que quiso el rey muy humano,

[18] **Lágrimas,** in other editions the word is *gúminas* which means the ropes that are tied to the anchors.
[19] **Bírseo muro** refers to Birsa, the fortress in Carthage.
[20] **Palinuro** was the captain of the fleet

desque° lo vido, pasado Acheronte[21] — when
con Leucaspis açerca de Oronte,[22]
en el Averno[23] tocarle la mano.

167
»Ya pues, si deve en este grand lago
guiarse la flota por dicho del sage,
vos dexaredes aqueste vïage
fasta ver día non tan azïago;° — ill-fated
las deidades levar° por halago° — deter, flattery
devedes, veyendo señal de plaga;° — affliction
non dedes causa a Gibraltar que haga
en sangre de reyes dos vezes estrago.° — destruction

168
»El conde, que nunca de las abusiones° — superstitions
creyera, ni menos de tales señales,
dixo: 'Non pruevo° por muy naturales, — approve
maestro, ninguna de aquestas razones;
las que me dizes ni bien perfecçiones° — prophecies
ni veras prenósticas° son de verdad, — predictions
ni los indiçios de la tempestad
no vemos 'fuera de° sus opiniones. — except for

169
»Aun si yo viera la mestrua° luna — monthly
con cuernos escuros mostrarse fuscada,° — blurred
muy rubicunda° o muy colorada,° — red, red
temiera° que vientos nos diera Fortuna; — suspect
si Febo, dexada la delia cuna,[24]
ígneo° viéramos o turbolento, — fiery
temiera yo pluvia mezclada con viento:
en otra manera non sé que repuna.

[21] **Acheronte** river in Hades
[22] **Leocaspis acerca de...** both Leocaspis and Oronte are Trojan sailors.
[23] **Averno** lagoon in the Underworld
[24] **La delia cuna** refers to Apollo's birthplace on the island of Delos.

170
»'Ni veo tampoco que vientos delgados
muevan los ramos de nuestra montaña,
ni hieren las ondas con su nueva saña
la playa con golpes más demasiados;
ni veo delphines° de fuera mostrados, dolphins
ni los merinos° bolar a lo seco, sea crows
ni los caístros° hazer nuevo trueco,[25] seabird
dexar las lagunas por ir a los prados.

171
»'Ni baten las alas ya los alçïones,° kingfishers
ni tientan jugando de se roçiar,° get wet
los quales amansan la furia del mar
con sus cantares y lánguidos sones,
e dan a sus fijos contrarias sazones,
nido en invierno con nueva pruína,° frost
do puestos,° açerca la costa marina laid (eggs)
en un semilunio° les dan perfeçiones. half-moon

172
»Ni la corneja non anda señera
por el arena seca paseando,
con su cabeça su cuerpo bañando
por preocupar la lluvia que espera;° is coming
ni buela la garça° por alta manera, heron
ni sale la fúlica° de la marina bird
contra los prados, ni va, ni declina° descend
como en los tiempos° adversos hiziera. weather

173
»Desplega las velas, pues, ¿ya qué tardamos?
e los de los bancos° levanten los remos,° benches, oars
'a bueltas del° viento mejor que perdemos; with
non los agüeros, los hechos sigamos,
pues una empresa tan santa levamos

[25] **Hazer nuevo trueco** to change direction

que más non podría ser otra ninguna;
presuma° de vos y de mí la Fortuna — boast
no que nos fuerça, mas que la forçamos'.

174
»Tales palabras el conde dezía
que obedesçieron el su mandamiento
e dieron las velas infladas al viento,
no padesçiendo tardança la vía;° — course
según la Fortuna lo ya desponía,° — as determined
llegaron açerca de la fuerte villa
el conde con toda la rica quadrilla,° — retinue
que por el agua su flota seguía.

175
»Con la bandera del conde tendida
ya por la tierra su fijo viniera
con mucha más gente qu'el padre le diera,
bien a cavallo y 'a punto guarnida,° — perfectly outfitted
por que a la hora que fuese la grida,° — battle cry
súpitamente, en el mesmo deslate,° — attack
por çiertos lugares oviese combate
la villa que estava desaperçebida.° — unprepared

176
»El conde y los suyos tomaron la tierra
que está entre el agua y el borde del muro,
lugar con menguante° seco y seguro, — tide ebbs
mas con la creciente° del todo se çierra; — growing tide
quien llega más tarde presume que yerra,
la pavesada[26] ya juntas sus alas,
levantan los troços,° crecen° las escalas, — sails, raised
cresçen las 'artes mañosas° de guerra. — machines

177
»Los moros, veyendo cresçer los engaños,

[26] **Pavesada** is a kind of protection or defense made of nets.

y viéndose todos çercados por artes
e combatidos por tantas de partes,
allí socorrieron° do ivan más daños, helped
e con nesçesarios dolores estraños
resisten sus sañas las fuerças agenas;
e lançan los cantos° desde las almenas,° boulders, towers
e botan los otros que non son tamaños.° so large

178
Comparación
»Bien como médico mucho famoso
que trae el estilo por mano seguido,
en cuerpo de golpes diversos herido
luego socorre a lo más peligroso,
así aquel pueblo maldito, sañoso,
sintiendo más daños de parte del conde,
con todas las fuerças juntado, responde
allí do el peligro más era dañoso.

179
»Allí desparavan° bombardas° y truenos° were shooting, g
e los trabucos° tiravan ya luego noise; catapults
piedras y dardos y hachas° de fuego torches
con que los nuestros hazían ser menos;
algunos de moros tenidos por buenos
lançan temblando las sus azagayas,° darts
pasan las lindes,° palenques° e rayas,° borders, staked f
doblan sus fuerças con miedos agenos. boundaries

180
»Mientra murían e mientra matavan,
de parte del agua ya cresçen las ondas,
y cubren las mares sobervias y hondas
los campos que ante los muros estavan,
tanto que los que de allí peleavan
a los navíos si se retraían,

las aguas cresçidas les ya defendían
tornar a las fustas° que dentro dexavan. boats

181
»Con peligrosa y vana fatiga
pudo una barca tomar a su conde,
la qual le levava seguro, si donde
estava bondad no le fuera enemiga:
padesçe tardança, si quieres que lo diga;
de los que quedavan e ir lo veían,
e otros que ir con él no podían
¡presume° qué boz dolorosa se siga! imagine

182
»Entrando tras él por el agua, dezían:
'Magnánimo conde, ¿ya cómo nos dexas?,
nuestras finales e últimas quexas
en tu presençia favor nos serían;
las aguas la vida nos ya desafían:
si tú no nos puedes prestar el bivir,
danos linaje mejor de morir:
daremos las manos a más que devían,

183
»o bolveremos a ser sometidos
a aquellos adarves,° maguer non devamos, paths
por que los tuyos moriendo podamos
ser dichos muertos mas nunca vençidos;
sólo podremos ser redargüidos° accused
de temeraria,° loca, osadía,° rash, daring
mas tal infamia mejor nos sería
que so las aguas morir sepelidos.° buried

184
»Hizieron las bozes al conde 'a desora° too late
bolver la su barca contra las saetas

e contra las armas de los mahometas,
ca fue de temor piedat vençedora.
Avía Fortuna dispuesta la ora,
e como los suyos comiençan a entrar,
la barca con todos se ovo anegar
de peso tamaño non sostenedora.

185
»Los míseros cuerpos ya no respiravan,
mas so las aguas andavan ocultos,
dando y trayendo 'mortales singultos° — death rattles
de aguas, la ora que más anhelavan;
las vidas de todos ansí litigavan° — in contention
que aguas entravan do almas salían;
la pérfida° entrada las aguas querían, — perfidious
la dura salida las almas negavan».

186
¡O pïedat fuera de medida!
¡O ínclito conde!, quisiste tan fuerte
tomar con los tuyos enantes° la muerte — **=antes**
que no con tu hijo gozar de la vida.
Si fe a mis versos es atribuida,
Jamás° la tu fama, jamás la tu gloria — always
darán a los siglos eterna memoria:
será muchas vezes tu muerte plañida.° — lamented

187
Después que yo vi que mi guiadora
avía ya dado su fin a la ystoria,
yo le suplico me haga memoria
la vida de otros que allí son agora;
la qual, mis plegarias oídas, implora
el divino nombre con muy sumo grado,
el qual humilmente por ella invocado,
respóndeme breve como sabidora:° — wise person

Tornándose contra el cuerpo mesquino,
quando su forma vido seer inmota,° immobile
con biva culebra lo fiere° e açota° strikes, beats
por que el espíritu traiga maligno;
el qual quiçá teme de entrar, aunque vino,
en las entrañas eladas,° sin vida, cold
o, si viene el alma que dél fue partida,
quiçá se detarda más en el camino.

250
La maga, veyendo cresçer la tardança,
por una abertura que fizo en la tierra:
dixo «¿Hécate° non te hagan guerra goddess of witches
más las palabras que mi boca lança?;
si no obedesçes la mi ordenança,
la cara que muestras a los del infierno,
haré que la buelvas al cielo superno,
tábida° aborrida° e sin alabança. corrupted, hated

251
»¿E sabes, tú triste Plutón,° que haré? god of Hades
Abriré las bocas por do te goviernas,
e con mis palabras tus hondas cavernas
de luz subitánea te las heriré;
pues ven y obedesçe, si no llamaré
a Demogorgón,[27] el qual invocado,
treme° la tierra, que tiene tal hado° trembles, fate
que a las Estigias[28] non mantiene fe».

252
Los miembros ya tiemblan del cuerpo muy fríos,
medrosos de oír el canto segundo;
ya forma bozes el pecho iracundo,
temiendo la maga e sus poderíos;
la qual se le llega con sones impíos

---

[27] **Demogorgón** is the father of all the gods, companion of Chaos and Eternity.
[28] **Estigias** is the river Styx which is crossed before entering hell.

e haze preguntas por modo callado
al cuerpo ya vivo, después de finado,
por que sus actos non salgan vazíos.

253
Con una manera de bozes estraña
el cuerpo comiença palabras atales:
«Irados y mucho son los infernales
contra los grandes del reino de España,
porque les hazen injuria tamaña
dando las treguas° a los infieles, truces
ca mientra les fueron mortales, crueles,
nunca tovieron con ninguno saña.

254
»Ánimas muchas fazen que non ayan
en hazer pazes con aquella seta,° Muslims
mas ellas ya buelven por arte secreta
otros lugares por donde les vayan;
e porque hizieron las pazes, ensayan
Bolver° tal discordia entre castellanos cause
que fe non se guarden hermanos a hermanos,
por donde los tristes fenescan° y cayan perish

255
»E quedarán d'estas indignidades,
sobre partir tales discordanças,
que por los puños° rompan muchas lanças blows
veréis rebuelta de muchas çibdades;
por ende, vosotros, esos que mandades,
la ira, la ira bolved en los moros;
no se consuman ansí los thesoros
en causas no justas como las hedades.

256
»E del condestable juzgando su hecho,
ansí determino su hado y pregono:
será retraído del sublime trono

e aun a la fin del todo desfecho;
pues sy viniere en un tal estrecho,° difficulty
según lo que hallo, forçado conviene,
finja color el que la no tiene,
e busque cada uno temprano provecho».

257
¡Quántas licencias° y despedimientos° permissions, leaves
al buen condestable fueron demandadas!
¡Quántos fizieron palabras osadas,
con vana sobervia de los mudamientos!
Fortuna, que nunca nos tovo contentos,
haze a muchos partirse, dexando
al su señor propio, non bien acatando° heeding
qué fin avrían sus meresçimientos.° merits

258
Los que se parten por tal novedad
liçençia por muchas razones pretenden:° claim
unas alegan, mas otras entienden,
e cubren con falsa color de verdad;
pues ya detenedvos, siquier esperad,
porque entre buenos° razón no admite good men
causas que ponga ninguno ni quite,
quando el señor es en nesçesidad.

259
Al camaleón° que en el aire se cría chameleon
son semejantes los tales efectos,
que tantos y quantos tocare de objectos
de tantas colores se buelv'en el día.
O rica nobleza, o gran hidalguía,
o ínclita sangre y ¿cómo sostienes
por vana coddiçia de mundanos bienes
tocar los umanos tal vil villanía?

260
Fama vos mueva de justo deseo

Pues 'tanto que° a Çésar siguió Labïeno[29] — while
siempre le dieron el nombre de bueno,
hasta que tovo señor a Pompeo;
así los señores, segunt lo que veo,
los que a dos partes ansí prevarican° — betray trust
menos los precian si más los platican;
danles partido,° mas non buen arreo.° — portion, situation

261
Comparación
Como los árboles presto se secan
que muy a menudo las gentes remudan,° — transplant
así los que a muchos señores ayudan
en vicio semblante presumo que pecan;
e como las peñas° que de alto derruecan° — rocks, tumble down
hasta lo fondo no son detenidas,
así acaesçe a los que sus vidas
con muchos señores descojen° e truecan. — choose

262
¡O vil cobdiçia, de todos errores
madre y carrera de todos los males,
que çiegas los ojos así de mortales
y las condiçiones de los servidores;
tú que endureces° así los señores, — harden
tú que los méritos tanto fatigas
de vana esperança que a muchos obligas
tales miserias fazer o mayores!

263
Después ya del caso del todo pasado,
los ya nuevamente hechos adversarios,
veyendo los fines del todo contrarios
al triste juizio que estava hadado,

[29] **César siguió Labieno** Labieno was a legate of Julius Cesar and his good friend in the wars against the Gauls. Later in the wars between Cesar and Pompey he joined Pompey's forces.

buelven aquella que les avía dado
las inevitables y duras respuestas,
diziéndole cómo no fueran aquéstas
las grandes fortunas que havía memorado.

264
«Si las palabras», mirastes por fuero
«sobre el condestable y bien acatastes,
e las fortunas venidas mirastes,
veréis que ha salido todo verdadero:
ca si le fuera hadado primero
que presto desfecho sería del todo,
mirad en Toledo, que por este modo
le ya desfizieron con armas de azero.

265
»Que a un condestable armado, que sobre
un gran vulto de oro estava asentado,
con manos sañosas vimos derribado° — knocked down
e, todo desfecho fue tornado cobre.
¿Pues cómo queredes que otra vez obre
Fortuna, tentando lo que es importuno?° — ill-timed
Basta que pudo derribar el uno,
que al otro más duro lo falla que robre». ° — oak tree

266
Comparación
Ansí como hazen los bravos leones
quando el ayuno les da grandes hambres,
comen las carnes eladas, fiambres,° — cold meat
porque las bivas les dan evasiones,
bien así hazen las costellaçiones
quando su hado hallan un obstante:° — hindrance
hartan° sus iras en forma semblante — satisfy
donde executan las sus impresiones.° — wills

267
Por ende, magnífico, gran condestable,

la çiega Fortuna, que avía de vos fambre,
harta la dexa la forma de arambre:° — copper
de aquí adelante vos es favorable;
pues todos notemos un caso mirable° — marvelous
e nótenlo quantos vinieren de nos:
que de vos y d'ella, y d'ella y de vos
nunca se parte ya paz amigable.

## Gómez Manrique (1412?-1490?)

The poet, dramatist, warrior and statesman was born in Amusco, Spain. He was a nephew to the Marqués de Santillana and brother to Maestre don Rodrigo about whom his own nephew, Jorge Manrique, wrote his famous *Coplas*. He is a member of the most important Medieval Spanish literary family. His poetry includes didactic-religious works as well as courtly poetry which is graceful and intellectually stimulating.

### A una dama que iba cubierta

El corazón se me fue
donde vuestro vulto° vi, — face
e luego vos conocí
'al punto que° vos miré; — as soon as
que no pudo facer tanto,
por mucho que vos cubriese
aquel vuestro negro manto,
que no vos reconosciese.
Que debajo se mostraba
vuestra gracia y 'gentil aire,° — noble bearing
y el cubrir 'con buen donaire° — gracefully
todo lo manifestaba;
así que con mis enojos° — annoyance
e muy grande turbación° — confusion
allá se fueron mis ojos
do tenía el corazón.

Coplas

¡Ay dolor, dolor,
por mi fijo y mi Señor!
Yo soy aquella María
del linaje de David.
Oíd, señores, oíd,
la gran desventura mía.

¡Ay dolor!
A mí dixo Gabriel
qu'el Señor era conmigo,
y dexóme sin abrigo,° — protection
amarga más que la hiel.° — bile
Díxome qu'era bendita
entre todas las nacidas
y soy de las afligidas
la más triste y más aflicta.

¡Ay dolor!
¡O vos, hombres que transistes° — pass by
por la 'vía mundanal,° — worldly path
decidme si jamás vistes
igual dolor de mi mal!
Y vosotras que tenéis
padre, fijos y maridos,
acorredme° con gemidos,° — help me, moans
si con llantos no podéis.

¡Ay dolor!
Llorad conmigo, casadas;
llorad conmigo, doncellas,
pues que vedes las estrellas
escuras y demudadas,° — changed
vedes el templo rompido,
la luna sin claridad.
Llorad conmigo, llorad
un dolor tan dolorido.

¡Ay dolor!
Llore conmigo la gente
de todos los tres estados,° nobles, clergy, comm
por lavar cuyos pecados folk
mataron al inocente,
a mi fijo y mi señor,
mi redentor verdadero.
¡Cuitada!° ¿Cómo no muero afflicted as I am
con tan estremo dolor?

¡Ay dolor!
¡Ay dolor, dolor,
por mi primo y mi Señor!
Yo soy aquel que dormí
en el regazo sagrado,
y grandes secretos vi
en los cielos sublimado.

Yo soy Juan,° aquel privado° John the Baptist,
de mi Señor y mi primo; confidant
yo soy el triste que gimo
con un dolor estremado.

¡Ay dolor!
Yo soy el 'primo hermano° first cousin
del facedor de la luz,
que por el linage humano
quiso subir en la cruz.
¡O, pues, ombres pecadores,
rompamos° nuestros vestidos! tear
¡Con dolorosos clamores° cries
demos grandes alaridos!° shouts

¡Ay dolor!
Lloremos al 'compañero
traidor° porque le vendió. Judas

Lloremos aquel cordero° — lamb
que sin culpa padesció.
Luego me matara yo,
cuitado, cuando lo vi,
si no confiara de mí
la madre que confió.

¡Ay dolor!
Estando en el agonía
me dijo con gran afán:° — concern
"Por madre ternás° tú, Juan,° — =**tendrás**, the Evangelist
a la Santa Madre mía."
¡Ved qué troque° tan amargo — exchange
para mí de grande cargo!° — charge

¡Ay dolor!
¡O hermana Madalena,° — Mary Magdalene
amada del Redentor!
¿Quién podrá con tal dolor
remediar tan grave pena?
¿Cómo podrá dar consuelo
el triste desconsolado
que vido crucificado
al muy alto rey del cielo?

¡Ay dolor!
¡O Virgen Santa María,
Madre de mi Salvador!
¡Qué nuevas de gran dolor
si podiese vos diría!
mas, ¿quién las podrá decir,
quién las podrá recontar,
sin gemir, sin sollozar,
sin prestamente° morir? — quickly

¡Ay dolor!
Vós, mi fijo adotivo,° — adopted
no me fagáis más penar.° — suffer

Decidme sin dilatar° — delay
si mi redentor es vivo,
que las noches y los días,
si d'Él otra cosa sé,
nunca jamás cesaré
de llorar con Jeremías.

Señora, pues 'de razón° — truly
conviene que lo sepáis,
es menester° que tengáis — necessary
un muy fuerte corazón,
y vamos, vamos al huerto,° — garden
do veredes sepultado
    vuestro fijo muy preciado
    de muy cruda muerte muerto.

## JORGE MANRIQUE (1440?-1479)

The *Coplas* is an elegy written on the death of Jorge Manrique's father, don Rodrigo Manrique, Maestre de Santiago, the perfect knight and valiant soldier in the fight against the Moors. It consists of 40 strophes of *pie quebrado* verse (two 8 syllable lines followed by a half line of 4 syllables). Most of the themes of the poem were known and used by others such as the *ubi sunt?* (where are they?), *vanitas vanitatum* (the fleetingness of worldly goods and pleasures) and death as the great equalizer. Manrique divides life into three categories: the human and mortal, the life of fame and eternal life.

The death of don Rodrigo leaves his family, friends and members of his household consoled by the virtuous life he led, his heroic deeds and his acceptance of God's will in the face of death. Among the influences in the poem are the Book of Ecclesiastes, the *Moral Commentaries on the Book of Job* by St. Gregory and François Villon's famous *Ballade des Dames du Temps Jadis* where similar themes are treated.

### *Coplas por la muerte de su padre*

Recuerde° el alma dormida, — awaken

| | | |
|---|---|---|
| | Avive° el seso y despierte | sharpen |
| | contemplando | |
| | cómo se pasa la vida, | |
| 5 | cómo se viene la muerte | |
| | tan callando, | quietly |
| | cuán presto° se va el placer, | quickly |
| | cómo, después de acordado,° | being remembered |
| | da dolor; | |
| 10 | cómo, a nuestro parecer,° | opinion |
| | cualquiera tiempo pasado | |
| | fue mejor. | |
| | | |
| | Pues si vemos lo presente | |
| | cómo en un punto° 'se es ido° | second, it is gone |
| 15 | y acabado, | |
| | si juzgamos° sabiamente, | consider |
| | daremos° 'lo no venido° | consider, what has not |
| | por pasado. | come |
| | No se engañe nadie, no, | |
| 20 | pensando que 'ha de durar° | will last |
| | lo que espera, | |
| | más que duró lo que vio | |
| | porque todo ha de pasar | |
| | 'por tal manera.° | in similar fashion |
| | | |
| 25 | Nuestras vidas son los ríos | |
| | que van a dar° en la mar, | flow |
| | que es el morir;° | death |
| | allí van los señoríos° | largest rivers |
| | derechos° 'a se acabar° | straight, to end up |
| 30 | y consumir; | |
| | allí los ríos caudales,° | large |
| | allí los otros medianos | |
| | y más chicos, | |
| | y llegados,° son iguales | having arrived |
| 35 | los que viven por sus manos | |
| | y los ricos. | |

INVOCACIÓN:
Dejo las invocaciones<br>
de los famosos poetas<br>
40 y oradores;<br>
no 'curo de° sus ficciones, — care about<br>
que traen° 'yerbas secretas° — carry, poisons<br>
sus sabores;° — pleasures<br>
A aquél sólo me encomiendo,<br>
45 aquél sólo invoco yo<br>
de verdad,<br>
que en este mundo viviendo<br>
el mundo no conoció° — recognize<br>
su deidad.

50 Este mundo es el camino<br>
para el otro, que es morada° — dwelling<br>
sin pesar;° — grief<br>
mas cumple° tener buen tino° — it is necessary, judgment;<br>
para andar esta jornada° — journey<br>
55 sin errar.° — going astray<br>
Partimos cuando nacemos,<br>
andamos mientras vivimos,<br>
y llegamos<br>
al tiempo que fenecemos;° — die<br>
60 así que cuando morimos<br>
descansamos.

Este mundo bueno fue° — =**fuera**<br>
si bien usáramos de él<br>
como debemos,<br>
65 porque, según nuestra fe,<br>
es para ganar aquél° — heaven<br>
que atendemos.° — wait for<br>
Aun aquel hijo de Dios,<br>
para subirnos al cielo<br>
70 descendió<br>
a nacer acá entre nos,° — =**nosotros**<br>
y a vivir en este suelo

| | | |
|---|---|---|
| | do murió. | |
| | | |
| | Ved de cuán poco valor | |
| 75 | son las cosas tras° que andamos | after |
| | y corremos, | |
| | que en este mundo traidor,° | traitorous |
| | aun 'primero que° muramos | before |
| | las perdemos: | |
| 80 | 'de ellas° deshace° la edad,° | some of them, destroys, time; |
| | de ellas 'casos desastrados° | accidents of fortune; |
| | que acaecen,° | happen |
| | de ellas, por su calidad, | |
| | en 'los más altos estados° | highest social standing |
| 85 | desfallecen.° | fail |
| | | |
| | Decidme: la hermosura, | |
| | la 'gentil frescura y tez° | exquisitely smooth complexion |
| | de la cara, | |
| | el color y la blancura, | |
| 90 | cuando viene la vejez, | |
| | '¿cuál se para?° | what remains |
| | Las mañas° y ligereza° | skills, agility |
| | y la fuerza corporal | |
| | de juventud, | |
| 95 | todo se torna graveza° | burdensome |
| | cuando llega al arrabal° | threshold |
| | de senectud. | |
| | | |
| | Pues la sangre de los godos,[30] | |
| | y el linaje y la nobleza | |
| 100 | tan crecida,° | important |
| | ¡por cuántas vías y modos | |
| | se pierde su gran alteza° | nobility |
| | en esta vida! | |
| | Unos, por poco valer,° | worth |

[30] **Godos** The Visigoths invaded Spain in the 5th century and the most noble Spanish families claim to be their descendents.

105 ¡por cuán bajos y abatidos° — spiritless
que los tienen!
otros que, por no tener,
con oficios° 'no debidos° — jobs, inappropriate
se mantienen.

110 Los estados y riqueza
que nos dejan 'a deshora,° — unexpectedly
¿quién lo duda?
no les pidamos firmeza,° — constancy
pues son de una señora
115 que se muda.° — changes
Que bienes son de Fortuna
que revuelve con su rueda
presurosa,° — quick
la cual no puede ser una° — unchangeable
120 ni estar estable ni queda° — quiet
en una cosa.

Pero digo que acompañen
y lleguen hasta la huesa° — grave
con su dueño:
125 por eso nos engañen,
pues se va la vida apriesa° — quickly
como sueño;
y los deleites° de acá — pleasures
son, en que nos deleitamos,
130 temporales,
y los tormentos de allá,° — in the beyond
que por ellos esperamos,
eternales.

Los placeres y dulzores° — sweetness
135 de esta vida trabajada° — harsh
que tenemos,
no son sino corredores,° — scouts
y la muerte, la celada° — ambush
en que caemos.

No mirando nuestro daño,° — harm
corremos 'a rienda suelta° — swiftly
sin parar;
desque° vemos el engaño — when
y queremos 'dar la vuelta,° — turn back
no hay lugar.° — chance

Si fuese en nuestro poder
hacer la cara hermosa
corporal,
como podemos hacer
el alma tan gloriosa,
angelical,
¡qué diligencia tan viva° — constant
tuviéramos 'toda hora,° — at every moment
y tan presta,
en componer 'la cativa,° — the vile one (here face)
dejándonos 'la señora° — the soul
descompuesta!° — neglected

Esos reyes poderosos
que vemos por escrituras° — writings
ya pasadas,
por casos° tristes, llorosos,° — events, lamented
fueron sus buenas venturas° — fortunes
trastornadas;° — undone
así que no hay cosa fuerte,
que a papas y emperadores
y prelados,° — prelates
así los trata la muerte
como a los pobres pastores° — shepherds
de ganados. — cattle

Dejemos a los troyanos,° — Trojans
que sus males no los vimos
ni sus glorias;
dejemos a los romanos,
aunque oímos y leímos

175 sus historias.
No curemos de saber
'lo de° aquel siglo pasado — the matters of
qué fue de ello;
vengamos a lo de ayer,
180 que también es olvidado
como aquello.

¿Qué 'se hizo° el rey don Juan?[31] — became of
Los infantes de Aragón[32]
¿qué se hicieron?
185 ¿Qué fue de tanto galán,° — courtier
qué fue de tanta invención° — undertaking
como trajeron?
Las justas° y los torneos,° — jousts, tourname
paramentos,° bordaduras° — accoutrements fo
190 y cimeras,° — ses, embroideri
¿fueron sino devaneos?° — helmet decorati
¿qué fueron sino verduras° — fantasies; plant
de las eras?° — fields

¿Qué se hicieron las damas,
195 sus tocados,° sus vestidos, — headdresses
sus olores?° — perfumes
¿Qué se hicieron las llamas° — flames
de los fuegos encendidos
de amadores?° — lovers
200 ¿Qué se hizo aquel trovar,° — poetry
las músicas acordadas° — harmonious
que tañían?° — played
¿Qué se hizo aquel danzar,° — dance
aquellas ropas chapadas° — elegantly embroi
205 que traían?

[31] **Juan...** King Juan II of Castile whose reign (1406-1454) was one of knightly and literary brilliance as well as deep political and social crises.
[32] **Infantes de Aragón...** Sons of Fernando de Antequera who was the uncle and tutor of Juan II and later became king of Aragon.

Pues el otro, su heredero,
don Enrique,[33] ¡qué poderes
alcanzaba!° attain
¡Cuán blando,° cuán halaguero° sweet, flattering
210 el mundo con sus placeres
se le daba!
Mas verás cuán enemigo,
cuán contrario, cuán cruel
se le mostró;
215 habiéndole sido amigo,
¡cuán poco° duró con él short time
lo que le dio!

Las dádivas° desmedidas,° gifts, beyond measure
los edificios reales
220 llenos de oro,
las vajillas° tan febridas,° dishes, so elaborate
los 'enriques y reales° coins
del tesoro;
los jaeces,° los caballos horse trappings
225 de sus gentes y atavíos° finery
tan sobrados,° abundant
¿dónde iremos a buscallos?
¿qué fueron sino rocíos° dew
de los prados?° meadows

230 Pues su hermano el inocente,[34]
que en su vida sucesor
se llamó,
¡qué corte tan excelente
tuvo y cuánto gran señor
235 le siguió!
Mas, como fuese mortal,
metióle la muerte luego° early

---

[33] **Enrique...** Enrique IV, reigned 1454-1474, was the son and heir of Juan II.
[34] **Su hermano el...** Prince Alfonso proclaimed king by the nobility died 1468 and never reigned.

en su fragua.° — forge
¡Oh, juïcio° divinal, — judgment
240 cuando más ardía el fuego,
echaste° agua! — poured

Pues aquel gran Condestable,[35]
maestre que conocimos
tan privado,
245 no cumple° que de él se hable, — necessary
sino sólo que lo vimos
degollado.° — decapitated
Sus infinitos tesoros,
sus villas y sus lugares,
250 su mandar,° — authority
¿qué le fueron sino lloros?
¿Qué fueron sino pesares
al dejar?

Y los otros dos hermanos,[36]
255 maestres tan prosperados
como reyes,
que a los grandes y medianos° — lesser nobles
trajeron tan sojuzgados° — subjected
a sus leyes;
260 aquella prosperidad
que tan alta fue subida
y ensalzada,° — exalted
¿qué fue sino claridad° — brightness
que cuando más encendida° — ardent
265 fue amatada?° — extinguished

Tantos duques excelentes,
tantos marqueses y condes
y varones° — barons

---

[35] **Gran Condestable…** Alvaro de Luna, Master of the Order of Santiago, the favorite of Juan II. Don Alvaro was decapitated in Valladolid in 1453.
[36] **Otros dos hermanos** These are Juan Pacheco and Pedro Girón favorites of Enrique IV, enemies of the Manriques.

| | | |
|---|---|---|
| | como vimos tan potentes,° | powerful |
| 270 | di, muerte, ¿dó los escondes | |
| | y traspones?° | move |
| | Y las sus claras° hazañas° | brilliant, deeds |
| | que hicieron en las guerras | |
| | y en las paces, | |
| 275 | cuando tú, cruda,° te ensañas, | cruel |
| | con tu fuerza las atierras° | knock down |
| | y deshaces. | |
| | | |
| | Las huestes° innumerables, | armies |
| | los pendones,° estandartes | penants |
| 280 | y banderas, | |
| | los castillos impugnables,° | invincible |
| | los muros y baluartes° | bulwarks |
| | y barreras,° | parapets |
| | la 'cava honda,° chapada,° | moat, fortified |
| 285 | o cualquier otro reparo,° | defense |
| | ¿qué aprovecha?° | benefit |
| | que si tú vienes airada,° | angered |
| | todo lo pasas 'de claro° | right through |
| | con tu flecha.° | arrow |
| | | |
| 90 | Aquél de buenos abrigo,° | protector |
| | amado por virtuoso | |
| | de la gente, | |
| | el maestre don Rodrigo | |
| | Manrique,[37] tanto famoso | |
| 95 | y tan valiente; | |
| | sus hechos grandes y claros° | excellent |
| | no cumple que los alabe, | |
| | pues los vieron, | |
| | ni los quiero 'hacer caros° | exagerate |
| 00 | pues que el mundo todo sabe | |
| | cuáles fueron. | |

[37] **Rodrigo...** Jorge Manrique's father and the subject of this magnificent elegy.

Amigo de sus amigos,<br>
¡qué señor para criados<br>
y parientes!<br>
305 ¡Qué enemigo de enemigos!<br>
¡Qué maestro de esforzados° — the courageous<br>
y valientes!<br>
¡Qué seso° para discretos! — good judgment<br>
¡Qué gracia° para donosos!° — wit, witty<br>
310 ¡Qué razón!° — prudence<br>
¡Cuán benigno° a los sujetos! — kind<br>
¡A los bravos° y dañosos,° — fierce, (those who) do harm<br>
qué león!

'En ventura° Octaviano;[38] — good fortune<br>
315 Julio César en vencer<br>
y batallar;<br>
en la virtud, Africano;<br>
Aníbal en el saber<br>
y trabajar;<br>
320 en la bondad, un Trajano;<br>
Tito en liberalidad° — generosity<br>
con alegría;<br>
en su brazo,° Aureliano; — (strong) arm<br>
Marco Tulio en la verdad<br>
325 que prometía.

---

[38] **Octaviano...** The list of names from Octaviano until Camilo are all historically important figures of Antiquity. Octaviano ( 83 B.C.-14 A.D.) was first emperor of Rome. Julio Cesar (100-44 B.C.) famous Roman general; Africano, i.e. Escipion Africano (235-183 B.C.), fought in Spain during the Second Punic War; Aníbal (248-193 B.C.), famous Carthaginian general; Trajano (53-117 A.D.), Roman emperor born in Spain; Tito (39-91 A.D), Roman emperor; Aureliano ( A. D.), Roman emperor; Marco Atilio (d. ca. 250 B.C.), consul who participated in the Punic Wars; Antonio Pio (86-161 A.D.), Roman emperor; Marco Aurelio (121-180 A.D.) Roman emperor; Adriano (76-138 A.D.), Roman emperor; Teodosio (346-395 A.D.), Roman emperor, Aurelio Alejandro (208-235 A.D.), Roman emperor; Constantino (272-337 A.D.), Roman emperor who made Christianity the official religion of the empire. Camilo (446 -365 B.C.), Roman tribune and dictator.

Antonio Pío en clemencia;
Marco Aurelio en igualdad° — eveness
del semblante;° — temperament
Adriano en elocuencia;
Teodosio en humanidad° — humility
y buen talante;° — will
Aurelio Alejandro fue
en disciplina y rigor
de la guerra;
un Constantino en la fe,
Camilo en el gran amor
de su tierra.

No dejó grandes tesoros,° — wealth
ni alcanzó° muchas riquezas — attain
ni vajillas;
mas hizo guerra a los moros,
ganando sus fortalezas
y sus villas;
y en las lides que venció,
muchos moros y caballos
se perdieron;
y en este oficio° ganó — work
las rentas° y los vasallos — income
que le dieron.

Pues por su honra y estado,
en otros tiempos pasados,
¿cómo 'se hubo? — conduct himself
Quedando desamparado,° — abandoned
con hermanos y criados
se sostuvo.
Después que hechos famosos
hizo en esta misma guerra
que hacía,
hizo tratos° tan honrosos — treaties
que le dieron aún más tierra
que tenía.

Estas sus viejas historias° deeds
que con su brazo pintó° accomplished
en juventud,
365 con otras nuevas victorias
ahora las renovó° repeated
en senectud.° old age
Por su grande habilidad,
por méritos y ancianía° old age
370 bien gastada,
alcanzó la dignidad
de la gran Caballería
de la Espada.[39]

Y sus villas y sus tierras
375 ocupadas de tiranos
las halló;
mas por cercos° y por guerras sieges
y por fuerza de sus manos
las cobró.° recovered
380 Pues nuestro 'rey natural,° Enrique IV
si de las obras que obró
fue servido,
dígalo el de Portugal[40]
y en Castilla quien siguió
385 su partido.° Alfonso V's par

Después de puesta la vida[41]
tantas veces por su ley° religion
al tablero;
390 después de tan bien servida
la corona de su rey
verdadero:

---

[39] **Caballería de la...** Master of the Order of Santiago, whose insignia is a red cross in the form of a sword, awarded to Rodrigo Manrique in 1474.
[40] **El de Portugal** was Alfonso V of Portugal who lost his claim to the throne of Castilla in part due to the valiant efforts of Rodrigo Manrique.
[41] **Puesta la vida...** *risked his life*. The whole expression is **ponerse la vida al tablero.**

después de tanta hazaña
a que no puede bastar
395 cuenta cierta,[42]
en la su villa de Ocaña
vino la muerte a llamar
a su puerta,

diciendo: «Buen caballero,
400 dejad el mundo engañoso
y su halago;
vuestro corazón de acero,
muestre su esfuerzo famoso
en este trago;° — difficult time
405 y pues de vida y salud
hicisteis tan poca cuenta
por la fama,
esfuércese la virtud° — courage
para sufrir esta afrenta
410 que os llama.

No se os haga tan amarga
la batalla temerosa
que esperáis,
pues otra vida más larga
415 de la fama gloriosa
acá dejáis,
(aunque esta vida de honor
tampoco no es eternal
ni verdadera);
420 mas, con todo,° es muy mejor — nevertheless
que la otra temporal
perecedera.

El vivir que es perdurable
no se gana con estados
425 mundanales,

[42] **A que no...** *too numerous to count*

ni con vida deleitable
en que moran los pecados
infernales;
mas los buenos religiosos° (members of religious orders)
430 gánanlo con oraciones
y con lloros;
los caballeros famosos,
con trabajos y aflicciones
contra moros.

435 Y pues vos, claro varón,
tanta sangre derramasteis
de paganos,
esperad el galardón
que en este mundo ganasteis
440 por las manos;
y con esta confianza
y con la fe tan entera
que tenéis,
partid con buena esperanza,
445 que esta otra vida tercera
ganaréis.»

«No tengamos tiempo ya
en esta vida mezquina
por tal modo,
450 que mi voluntad está
conforme con la divina
para todo;
y consiento en mi morir
con voluntad placentera,
455 clara y pura,
que querer hombre vivir
cuando Dios quiere que muera
es locura.

Oración:
460 Tú, que por nuestra maldad,

tomaste forma servil
y bajo nombre;
tú, que a tu divinidad
juntaste cosa tan vil
465 como es el hombre;
tú, que tan grandes tormentos
sufriste sin resistencia
en tu persona,
no por mis merecimientos,
470 mas por tu sola clemencia
me perdona.»

Fin:
Así, con tal entender,
todos sentidos humanos
475 conservados,
cercado de su mujer
y de sus hijos y hermanos
y criados,
dio el alma a quien se la dio
480 (el cual la ponga en el cielo
en su gloria),
que aunque la vida perdió
dejónos harto° consuelo — a great deal
su memoria.

## Narrative Poetry

### *Romances*

The *romance* or ballad forms the major part of narrative poetry in Spain, and the origin of the *romance* has been the subject of endless discussion. Some think the ballads were the more memorable sections of epics that were sung after the longer epic poem died; others hold that ballads were written to commemorate some event, character, or ideal; folklorists believe that *romances* are produced by the folk, that is, by unprofessional poets of the people. While students of literature may admit this for some ballads, they insist upon erudite authorship for others. Any or all of these theories can be accepted, and indeed a combination of theories may best explain how ballads were produced. The earliest mention of *romances* is in Santillana's *Prohemio y carta* (written ca. 1445). The Marqués did not hold *romances* in high esteem and thought they were written for the common people only.

In a sense he was right, for the ballad as a poetic form has never died, and is, indeed, to this day, the most frequently used of all verse forms. There is nothing more typically Spanish than a *romance*. Perhaps the first ballads were actually songs, but later ballads to be read or recited without music became extremely popular.

### *Romances*

The ballad or *romance* is a narrative poem, epic-lyric in character; its line was originally sixteen syllables long, divided into two eight-syllable, assonant-rhyming hemistichs, with a stress on the next to the last syllable of each hemistich. Eventually the lines were simply written as eight-syllable couplets. *Romances* did not appear in collections called *romanceros* until the mid-sixteenth century, but they were part of the oral tradition at least as early as the twelfth century. The first *romanceros* were the *Cancionero de romances* (1547-1549), the *Silva de varios romances* (1550-1551), and the *Romancero general* (Madrid, 1600).

Ramón Menéndez Pidal has advanced the *cantilena* theory which proposed that the *romances* were fragments of *cantares de gesta*, which were narrative epics like the *Cantar de Mio Cid*. He classified *romances* according to theme: historical ballads about Spanish heroes, events, and legends; the Carolingian and Breton cycles dealing with Charlemagne and King Arthur; novelistic ballads of chivalry and courtly love; lyrical ballads, briefer poems dealing with nature and love; frontier ballads concerning the struggle between Spaniards and Moors during the Reconquest. (Willis Barnstone, *Spanish Poetry: from its Beginnings through the Nineteenth Century*. New York: Oxford University Press, 1970, p. 190).

## ROMANCES DEL CID

*En que Jimena pide de nuevo justicia al rey*

| | |
|---|---|
| En Burgos está el buen rey | |
| asentado a su yantar,° | supper |
| cuando la Jimena Gómez | |
| se le vino a querellar;° | complain |
| 'cubierta paños de luto,° | dressed in mourning |
| tocas° de negro cendal; | headdress |
| las rodillas por el suelo, | |
| comenzara de fablar: | |
| Con mancilla° vivo, rey; | stain |
| con ella vive mi madre; | |
| cada día que amanece | |
| veo quien mató mi padre | |
| caballero en un caballo | |
| y en su mano un gavilán;° | hawk |
| por hacerme más enojo, | |
| cébalo en mi palomar;° | dovecote |
| con sangre de mis palomas | |
| ensangrentó° mi brial | he bloodied, tunic |
| ¡Hacedme, buen rey, justicia, | |
| no me la queráis negar! | |
| Rey que non face justicia | |
| non debía de reinar, | |
| ni comer pan 'a manteles,° | at table |
| ni con la reina folgar.° | have sport |

El rey cuando aquesto oyera
comenzara de pensar:
"Si yo prendo o mato al Cid,
mis cortes revolverse° han; rebel
pues, si lo dejo de hacer,
Dios me lo demandara".
Allí habló doña Jimena
palabras bien de notar:
Yo te lo diría, rey,
cómo lo has de remediar.
Mantén tú bien las tus cortes,
no te las revuelva nadie,
y al que mi padre mató
dámelo para casar,
que quien tanto mal me hizo
sé que algún bien me fará.
Siempre lo he oído decir,
y ahora veo que es verdad,
que el seso° de las mujeres reason
no era cosa natural:
hasta aquí pidió justicia,
ya quiere con él casar.
Mandaré una carta al Cid,
mandarle quiero llamar.
Las palabras 'no son dichas,° scarcely said
la carta camino va;
mensajero que la lleva
dado la había a su padre.

*De cómo el Cid fue al palacio del rey la primera vez*

Cabalga Diego Laínez
al buen rey besar la mano,
consigo se los llevaba
los trescientos hijosdalgo;° nobles
entre ellos iba Rodrigo,
el soberbio castellano.
Todos cabalgan a mula,
sólo Rodrigo a caballo;

todos visten oro y seda,
Rodrigo va bien armado;
todos guantes° olorosos,° — gloves, perfumed
Rodrigo guante mallado;° — mail
todos con sendas varicas,° — staff
Rodrigo estoque° dorado; — sword
todos sombreros muy ricos,
Rodrigo casco° afinado,° — helmet, polished
y encima del casco lleva
un 'bonete colorado.° — red cap
Andando por su camino,
unos con otros hablando,
allegados son a Burgos,
con el rey han encontrado.
Los que vienen con el rey
entre sí van razonando;° — talking
unos lo dicen de quedo,
otros lo van publicando:
Aquí viene entre esta gente
quien mató al conde Lozano.
Como lo oyera Rodrigo, 'en hito los ha mirado:° — stared at them
Si hay alguno entre vosotros,
su pariente o adeudado,° — vassal
que le pese de su muerte,
salga luego a demandallo;° — protest it
yo se lo defenderé,
quiera a pie, quiera a caballo.
Todos dicen para sí:
"Que te lo demande el diablo". 'Se apean° los de Vivar — dismount
para al rey besar la mano;
Rodrigo se quedó solo
encima de su caballo.
Entonces habló su padre,
bien oiréis lo que le ha hablado:
Apeaos vos, mi hijo,
besaréis al rey la mano,
porque él es vuestro señor,
vos, hijo, sois su vasallo.

Si otro me dijera eso,
ya me lo hubiera pagado,
mas por mandarlo vos, padre,
lo haré, aunque no de buen grado.
Ya se apeaba Rodrigo
para al rey besar la mano;
al hincar de la rodilla
el estoque se ha arrancado.° — jutted out
Espantóse de esto el rey
y dijo como turbado:° — frightened
¡Quítate, Rodrigo, allá,
quita, quítate allá, diablo,
que el gesto° tienes de hombre — face
los hechos de león bravo!° — fierce
Como Rodrigo esto oyó,
apriesa° pide el caballo; — quickly
con una voz alterada,° — angry
contra el rey así ha hablado:
Por besar mano de rey
no me tengo por honrado;
porque la besó mi padre
me tengo por afrentado.° — offended
En diciendo estas palabras,
salido se ha del palacio;
consigo se los tornaba
los trescientos hijosdalgo.
Si bien vinieron vestidos,
volvieron mejor armados,
y si vinieron en mulas,
todos vuelven a caballo.

*Dice el cuento que el rey don Fernando, preciando mucho el fuerte corazón del mozo Rodrigo, le mandó de nuevo llamar, pero asegurándole por sus cartas que no quería castigarle, pues doña Jimena le perdonaba, y diciéndole que tenía que hablar con él cosas que eran a gran honra suya y mucho servicio de Dios y de la paz del reino. Rodrigo volvió a Burgos, llevando consigo doscientos pares de lanzas enhiestas; y desque habló con el rey y vio en el palacio a la antes enemiga doña Jimena, avino de muy buen corazón en el casamiento que el rey le proponía.*

*Es el de la jura en Santa Gadea*
En Santa Gadea de Burgos
do juran los hijosdalgo,
allí toma juramento° — oath
el Cid al rey castellano,
sobre un cerrojo° de hierro — bolt
y una ballesta° de palo. — crossbow
Las juras eran tan recias° — strong
que al buen rey ponen espanto.
Villanos te maten, rey,
villanos, que no hidalgos;
abarcas° traigan calzadas, — sandals
que no zapatos con lazo;° — tie
traigan capas aguaderas,° — for rain
no capuces° ni tabardos;° — cloaks, short coats
con camisones° de estopa,° — smocks, burlap
no de holanda° ni labrados;° — linen, worked
cabalguen en sendas burras,
que no en mulas ni en caballos,
las riendas traigan de cuerda,° — cord
no de cueros fogueados;° — hardened
mátente por las aradas,° — fields
no en camino ni en poblado;
con 'cuchillos cachicuernos,° — horn-handled knife
no con puñales° dorados; — daggers
sáquente el corazón vivo,
por el derecho costado,
si no dices la verdad
de lo que te es preguntado:
si tú fuiste o consentiste
en la muerte de tu hermano.
Las juras eran tan fuertes
que el rey no las ha otorgado.° — sworn
Allí habló un caballero
de los suyos más privado:
Haced la jura, buen rey,

no tengáis de eso cuidado,
que nunca fue rey traidor,
ni Papa descomulgado.° — excommunicated
Jura entonces el buen rey,
que en tal nunca se ha hallado.
Después habla contra el Cid
malamente y enojado:
—Mucho me aprietas,° Rodrigo, — pressure
Cid, muy mal me has conjurado,
mas si hoy me tomas la jura,
después besarás mi mano.
—Aqueso será, buen rey,
como fuer galardonado,
porque allá en cualquier tierra
'dan sueldo° a los hijosdalgo. — pay
—¡Vete de mis tierras, Cid,
mal caballero probado,
y no me entres más en ellas
desde este día en un año!
—Que me place -dijo el Cid-,
que me place de buen grado,
por ser la primera cosa
que mandas en tu reinado.
Tú me destierras° por uno, — exile
yo me destierro por cuatro.
Ya se partía el buen Cid
sin al rey besar la mano;
ya se parte de sus tierras,
de Vivar y sus palacios:
las puertas deja cerradas,
los 'alamudes echados,° — bolts thrown
las cadenas deja llenas
de podencos° y de galgos;° — hunting dogs, greyhounds
sólo lleva sus halcones,
los pollos y los mudados.° — molting hawks
Con él iban los trescientos
caballeros hijosdalgo;
los unos iban a mula

y los otros a caballo;
todos llevan lanza en puño,° fist
con el hierro acicalado,° polished
y llevan sendas adargas° shields
con bordas° de colorado. edges
Por una ribera arriba
al Cid van acompañando;
acompañándolo iban
mientras él iba cazando.

ABENÁMAR[43]

«Abenámar, Abenámar,
moro de la morería,° Moorish quarter
el día que tú naciste
grandes señales° había. signs
Estaba la mar en calma,
la luna estaba crecida;° full
moro que en tal signo nace,
no debe decir mentira.»
Allí respondiera el moro,
bien oiréis lo que decía:
«No te la diré, señor,
aunque me cueste la vida,
porque soy hijo de un moro
y una cristiana cautiva;
siendo yo niño y muchacho
mi madre me lo decía:
que mentira no dijese,
que era grande villanía:° villany
por tanto pregunta, rey,
que la verdad te diría.
«Yo te agradezco, Abenámar,
aquesta tu cortesía.
¿Qué castillos son aquéllos?
¡Altos son y relucían!»° shine

[43] **Abenámar** (Yusuf Ibn-Alahmar) was pretender to the throne of Granada and supported by the Christians.

«El Alhambra era, señor,
y la otra la mezquita;° — mosque
los otros los Alijares,° — palace
labrados° a maravilla. — wrought
El moro que los labraba
cien doblas° ganaba al día — money
y el día que no los labra
otras tantas se perdía.
El otro es Generalife,° — summer palace
huerta° que par no tenía; — garden
el otro Torres Bermejas,
castillo de gran valía.»
Allí habló el rey don Juan,
bien oiréis lo que decía:
«Si tú quisieras, Granada,
contigo me casaría;
daréte en 'arras y dote° — dowry
a Córdoba y a Sevilla.» — Granada la ciudad está hablando
«Casada soy, rey don Juan,
casada soy, que no viuda;
el moro que a mí me tiene
muy grande bien me quería.»

LA BELLA MAL MARIDADA

La bella 'mal maridada,° — ill-married
de las lindas que yo vi,
véote tan triste enojada;
la verdad dila tú a mí.
Si has de tomar amores
por otro, no dejes a mí,
que a tu marido, señora,
con otras dueñas lo vi,
besando y retozando:° — frolicking
mucho mal dice de ti;
juraba° y perjuraba — swore
que te había de ferir.
Allí habló la señora,
allí habló, y dijo así:

Sácame tú, el caballero,
tú sacásesme de aquí;
por las tierras donde fueres
bien te sabría yo servir:
yo te haría bien la cama
en que hayamos de dormir,
yo te guisaré° la cena — prepare
como a caballero gentil,
de gallinas y capones
y otras cosas más de mil;
que a éste mi marido
ya no le puedo sufrir,
que me da muy mala vida
cual vos bien podéis oír.
Ellos en aquesto estando
su marido hélo aquí:
—¿Qué hacéis mala traidora?
¡Hoy habedes de morir!
—¿Y por qué, señor, por qué?
Que nunca os lo merecí.
Nunca besé a hombre,
mas hombre besó a mí;
las penas que él merecía,
señor, daldas vos a mí;
con riendas de tu caballo,
señor, azotes a mí;
con cordones de oro y sirgo
viva ahorques° a mí. — hang
En la huerta de los naranjos
viva entierres a mí,
en sepoltura de oro
y labrada de marfil;
y pongas encima un mote,° — inscription
señor, que diga así:
«Aquí está la flor de las flores,
por amores murió aquí;
cualquier que muere de amores
mándese enterrar aquí.

que así hice yo, mezquina,
que por amar me perdí.»

LA MORA MORAIMA
Yo me era mora Moraima
morilla 'de un bel catar.° — good looking
Cristiano vino a mi puerta
cuitada,° por me engañar: — wretched
hablóme en algarabía° — Arabic
como quien la sabe hablar:
«ábrasme las puertas, mora,
sí, Alá te guarde de mal.»
«¿Cómo te abriré, mezquina,
que no sé quién te serás?»
«Yo soy el moro Mazote
hermano de la tu madre,
que un cristiano dejo muerto
y tras mí viene el alcalde:
si no me abres tú, mi vida,
aquí me verás matar.»
Cuando esto oí, cuitada,
comencéme a levantar,
vistiérame un almejía° — Moorish cloak
no hallando mi brial
fuérame para la puerta
y abríla 'de par en par.° — wide

ROMANCE DE DOÑA ALDA
En Paris está doña Alda,° — Roland's betrothed
la esposa de don Roldán,° — Roland
trescientas damas con ella
para bien la acompañar;
todas visten un vestido,
todas calzan un calzar,
todas comen a una mesa,
todas comían de un pan.
Las ciento hilaban el oro,
las ciento tejen cendal,° — fine cloth

ciento tañen instrumentos,
para a doña Alda alegrar.
Al son de los instrumentos
doña Alda adormido se ha;
ensoñado había un sueño,
un sueño de gran pesar.
Despertó despavorida° — frightened
con un dolor sin igual,
los gritos daba tan grandes
se oían en la ciudad.
¿Qué es aquesto, mi señora,
qué es lo que os hizo mal?
Un sueño soñé, doncellas,
que me ha dado gran pesar:
que me veía en un monte,
en un desierto lugar,
y de so los montes altos
un azor° vide volar; — hawk
tras dél viene una aguililla° — little eagle
que lo 'ahincaba muy mal.° — pursued
El azor con grande cuita
metióse so mi brial;
el águila con gran ira
de allí lo iba a sacar;
con las uñas lo despluma,
con el pico lo deshace.
Allí habló su camarera,
bien oiréis lo que dirá:

Aqueste sueño, señora,
bien os lo entiendo soltar:° — interpret
el azor es vuestro esposo,
que de España viene ya;
el águila sodes vos,
con la cual ha de casar,
y aquel monte era la iglesia
donde 'os han de velar.° — they will marry you
—Si es así mi camarera,

bien te lo entiendo pagar.—
Otro día de mañana
cartas de lejos le traen;
tintas venían de fuera,
de dentro escritas con sangre,
que su Roldán era muerto
en la caza de Roncesvalles.
Cuando tal oyó doña Alda
muerta en el suelo se cae.

ROMANCE DE FONTE FRIDA Y CON AMOR

Fonte° frida,° fonte frida
fountain, cold
fonte frida y con amor,
do todas las avecicas°
little birds
van tomar consolación,
sino es la tortolica,°
turtledove
que está viuda y con dolor.
Por ahí fuera a pasar
el traidor del ruiseñor;°
nightingale
las palabras que le dice
llenas son de traición:
«Si tú quisieses, señora,
yo sería tu servidor.»
«Vete de ahí, enemigo,
malo, falso, engañador,
que ni poso° en ramo° verde
perch, branch
ni en ramo que tenga flor,
que si el agua hallo clara
turbia la bebiera yo;
que no quiero haber marido
porque hijos no haya, no;
no quiero placer con ellos
ni menos consolación.
¡Déjame triste, enemigo,
malo, falso, mal traidor;
que no quiero ser tu amiga
ni casar contigo, no!»

ROMANCE DE ROSAFLORIDA

En Castilla está un castillo,
que se llama Rocafrida;
al castillo llaman Roca,
y a la fonte llaman Frida.
El pie tenía de oro
y almenas de plata fina;
entre almena y almena
está una piedra zafira;° saphire
tanto relumbra de noche
como el sol a mediodía.
Dentro estaba una doncella
que llaman Rosaflorida;
siete condes la demandan,
tres duques de Lombardía;
a todos les desdeñaba,
tanta es su lozanía.° hautiness
Enamoróse de Montesinos
'de oídas,° que no de vista. hearsay
Una noche estando así,
gritos da Rosaflorida;
oyérala un camarero,° chamberlain
que en su cámara dormía.
"¿Qu'es aquesto, mi señora?
¿Qu'es esto, Rosaflorida?
"O tenedes mal de amores,
o estáis 'loca sandía."° totally mad
"Ni yo tengo mal de amores,
ni estoy loca sandía,
"mas llevásesme estas cartas
a Francia la bien guarnida;° rich
"diéseslas a Montesinos,
la cosa que yo más quería;
"dile que me venga a ver
para la 'Pascua Florida;° Easter
"darle he siete castillos
los mejores que hay en Castilla;
"y si de mí más quisiere
yo mucho más le daría:

"darle he yo este mi cuerpo,
el más lindo que hay en Castilla,
"si no es el de mi hermana,
'que de fuego sea ardida."°     damn her

ROMANCE DE ROSA FRESCA

¡Rosa fresca, rosa fresca,
tan garrida° y 'con amor,°     beautiful, in love
cuando yo os tuve en mis brazos,
non vos supe servir, non:
y agora que vos servía
non vos puedo yo haber, non!
—Vuestra fue la culpa, amigo,
vuestra fue, que mía non;
enviásteme una carta
con un vuestro servidor,
y, en lugar de recaudar
él dijera 'otra razón:°     something else
que érades casado amigo,
allá en tierras de León;
que tenéis mujer hermosa
e hijos como una flor.
—Quien vos lo dijo, señora,
non vos dijo verdad, non;
que yo nunca entré en Castilla
ni allá en tierras de León,
sino cuando era pequeño,
que non sabía de amor.

ROMANCE DEL INFANTE ARNALDOS

¡Quién hubiera tal ventura
sobre las aguas del mar
como hubo el infante Arnaldos
la mañana de San Juan!°     magical time
Andando a buscar la caza°     meat
para su falcón cebar,°     feed
vio venir una galera
que a tierra quiere llegar;

las velas° trae de sedas,
la ejarcia° de oro torzal,°
áncoras° tiene de plata,
tablas° de fino coral.
Marinero que la guía,
diciendo viene un cantar,
que la mar ponía en calma,
los vientos hace amainar;°
los peces que andan al hondo,
arriba los hace andar;
las aves que van volando,
al mástil° vienen posar.
Allí habló el infante Arnaldos,
bien oiréis lo que dirá:
Por tu vida, el marinero,
dígasme ora ese cantar.
Respondióle el marinero,
tal respuesta le fue a dar:
Yo no digo mi canción
sino a quien conmigo va.

sails
rigging, wrought
anchors
planks
calm down
mast

ROMANCE DEL PRISIONERO

Que por mayo era por mayo,
cuando hace la calor,
cuando los trigos encañan°
y están los campos en flor,
cuando canta la calandria°
y responde el ruiseñor,°
cuando los enamorados
van a servir al amor;
sino yo, triste, cuitado,
que vivo en esta prisión;
que ni sé cuando es de día
ni cuando las noches son,
sino por una avecilla
que me cantaba al albor.°
Matómela un ballestero;°
déle Dios mal galardón.°

grow tall
lark
nightingale
dawn
crossbowman
reward

ROMANCE DEL REY DON SANCHO

¡Rey don Sancho, rey don Sancho! no digas que no te aviso,° — warn<br>
que de dentro de Zamora un alevoso° ha salido; — traitor<br>
llámase Vellido Dolfos, hijo de Dolfos Vellido,<br>
cuatro traiciones ha hecho, y con esta serán cinco.<br>
Si gran traidor fue el padre, mayor traidor es el hijo.<br>
Gritos dan en el real:° -¡A don Sancho han mal herido! — royal camp<br>
Muerto le ha Vellido Dolfos, ¡gran traición ha cometido!<br>
Desque le tuviera muerto, metióse por un postigo,° — back gate<br>
por las calles de Zamora va dando voces y gritos:<br>
Tiempo era, doña Urraca, de cumplir lo prometido.

## Satirical Narrative Verse

The *Danza de la muerte* or *Danza general*, as it is sometimes called, is a Spanish version of the well known theme of the dance of death in which all mortals take part, for all must die. Versions appear in Latin, German, French, etc., but the Spanish rendition is one of the best. In the 79 *coplas* the poem presents a mighty satire on society at various levels and reveals many of the vices and the virtues of the age.

The Spanish version of this poem is written in *arte mayor* (stanzas of 8 lines of 12 syllables) and is considered the best example of this verse form. The pattern is one of death calling members of all walks of life, lay and cleric, nobles and commoners, to come to the dance. Each one protests and tries to excuse himself, but Death insists on each one's sins and shortcomings, letting no one escape. In the 79 stanzas we meet 33 victims: an emperor, a pope, an abbot, a sacristan, a lawyer, a farmer, a merchant, and a squire among others. Written in dialogue, it seems to have a dramatic quality and could have been theatrically represented. According to J. D. M. Ford in his book, *Old Spanish Readings* (1906), "the Spanish piece is far superior to the others in literary merit, excelling them in liveliness of spirit, in characterization and in the keenness of its satire." (pps. 172-73).

## *Danza de la muerte*

Aquí comiença la dança general, en la qual tracta cómo la Muerte avisa a todas las criaturas que paren mientes en[a] la breviedad de su vida e que della mayor cabdal[b] non sea fecho que ella meresce. E asimesmo les dize e requiere que vean e oyan bien lo que los sabios pedricadores[c] les dizen e amonestan[d] de cada día, dándoles bueno e sano consejo que pugnien en[e] fazer buenas obras porque hayan complido[f] perdón de sus pecados. E luego siguiente mostrando por espiriencia lo que dize, llama e requiere a todos los estados del mundo[g] que vengan de su buen grado o contra su voluntad. Començando dize ansí:

LA MUERTE:
Yo so la Muerte cierta a todas criaturas
que son y serán en el mundo durante;
demando y digo: «O homne, ¿por qué curas
de vida tan breve 'en punto° pasante? — in a moment
Pues non hay tan fuerte nin rezio° gigante — robust
que deste mi arco° se pueda anparar, — bow
conviene que mueras quando lo tirar
con esta mi frecha° cruel traspasante. — **=flecha**, piercing
¿Qué locura es ésta tan magnifiesta,
que piensas tú, homne, que el otro morrá,° — will die
e tú quedarás, por ser bien compuesta° — strong
la tu complisión° e que durará? — constitution
Non eres cierto si en punto verná
sobre ti a desshora alguna corrupción
de landre° o carbonco,° o tal inplisión° — tumor, boil, swelling
porque el tu vil cuerpo se dessatará.° — disintegrate
¿O piensas por ser mancebo valiente

[a] consider
[b] importance
[c] **= predicadores**
[d] admonish
[e] strive
[f] complete
[g] levels of society

o niño de días que 'a lueñe° estaré — distant
e fasta que liegues° a viejo impotente — **=llegues**
la mi venida me detardaré?
Avísate° bien que yo llegaré — be advised
a ti 'a deshora,° que non he cuydado — unexpectedly
que tú seas mancebo o viejo cansado,
que qual te fallare,° tal te levaré. — I may find you
La plática° muestra seer pura verdat — speech
aquesto que digo sin otra fallencia;° — fail
la sancta escriptura con certenidad
da sobre todo su firme sentencia° — teaching
a todos diziendo: «Fazed penitencia,
que a morir habedes non sabedes cuándo;
si non, ved el frayre que está pedricando,
mirad lo que dize de su grand sabiencia».

EL PREDICADOR:
Señores honrrados, la sancta escriptura
demuestra e dize que todo homne nado° — born
gostará° la muerte maguer sea dura, — taste
ca traxo° al mundo un solo bocado;° — =**trajo**, bite
ca papa o rey o obispo sagrado,
cardenal o duque e conde excelente,
el emperador con toda su gente
que son en el mundo morir 'han forçado.° — have to
Señores, punad en fazer buenas obras,
non vos fiedes en altos estados,
que non vos valdrán thesoros nin doblas° — money
a la Muerte que tiene sus 'laços parados.° — traps set
Gemid°vuestras culpas,° dezid los pecados — bemoan, guilt
en quanto podades con satisfación,° — penance
si queredes haver complido perdón
de aquel que perdona los yerros pasados.
Fazed lo que digo, non vos detardedes,
que ya la Muerte encomiença a ordenar
una dança esquiva,° de que non podedes — dangerous
por cosa ninguna que sea escapar,
a la qual dize que quiere levar

a todos nosotros lançando sus redes.
Abrid las orejas que agora oiredes
de su charambela° un triste cantar. rustic flute

LA MUERTE:
A la dança mortal venit los nascidos
que en el mundo soes° de cualquiera estado, =**sois**
el que non quisiere a fuerça e amidos° unwillingly
fazerle he venir muy toste° parado:° quickly, stopped
pues que ya el frayre vos ha pedricado
que todos vayaes a fazer penitencia,
el que non quisiere poner diligencia,
por mí non puede ser más esperado.
Primeramente
llama a su dança a dos donzellas.
A esta mi dança traxe de presente
estas dos donzellas que vedes fermosas.
Ellas vinieron de muy malamente
oír mis canciones, que son dolorosas,
mas no les valdrán flores e rosas
nin las composturas° que poner solían: make-up
de mí si pudiesen partirse querrían,
mas non puede ser, que son mis esposas.
A estas e a todos por las aposturas° beauty
daré fealdad, la vida partida,
e desnudedad° por las vestiduras; nakedness
por siempre jamás muy triste aborrida,° hated
e por los palacios daré 'por medida° made to measure
sepulcros escuros de dentro fedientes,° reeking
e por los manjares° gusanos royentes° food, gnawing
que coman de dentro su carne podrida.° rotten
E porque el sancto padre es muy alto señor
que en todo el mundo non ay su par,
desta mi dança será guiador,
desnude su capa, comience a sotar;° dance
non es ya tiempo de perdones dar
nin de celebrar en grande aparato,° pomp
que yo le daré en breve mal rato:

dançad, padre sancto, sin más detardar.

EL PADRE SANCTO:
¡Ay de mí, triste, qué cosa tan fuerte!° terrible
¡Y yo que 'tractava tan grand perlazía,° naming prelates
haver de pasar agora la muerte
e non me valer lo que dar solía
Beneficios° e honrras e grand señoría, church benefices
tove en el mundo pensando vevir;
pues de ti, Muerte, non puedo fuir,
valme Ihesuchristo, e tu Virgen María!

LA MUERTE:
Non vos enojedes, señor padre sancto,
de andar en mi dança que tengo ordenada;
non vos valdrá el bermejo manto,
de lo que fezistes habredes soldada.° payment
Non vos aprovecha echar° la cruzada, begin
proveer de obispados nin dar beneficios:
aquí moriredes sin fer más bollicios.° fuss
Dançad imperante con cara pagada.

EL EMPERADOR:
¿Qué cosa es ésta que a tan sin pavor
me lleva a su dança a fuerça sin grado?
Creo que es la Muerte, que non ha dolor° pity
de homne que sea grande o cuitado.° needy
Non ay ningund rey nin duque esforçado
que della me pueda agora defender.
¡Acorredme todos! Mas non puede ser,
que yo tengo della todo el seso° turbado.° mind, muddled

LA MUERTE:
Emperador muy grande en el mundo potente,
Non vos cuitedes, ca non es tiempo tal
que librar vos pueda imperio nin gente,
oro nin plata, nin otro metal.
Aquí perderedes el vuestro cabdal

que atesoraste° con grand tiranía, — gathered
faciendo batallas de noche e de día:
morid, non curedes,° venga el cardenal. — worry

EL CARDENAL:
¡Ay, madre de Dios, nunca pensé ver
tal dança como ésta a que me fazen ir!
Querría si pudiese la muerte estorcer,° — turn away
non sé dónde vaya, comienzo a thremer.° — tremble

Siempre trabajé notar y escrevir
por dar beneficios a los mis criados,
agora mis miembros son todos torvados° — disturbed
que pierdo la vista e non puedo oír.

LA MUERTE:
Reverendo padre, bien vos avisé
que aquí habríades por fuerça llegar
en esta mi dança en que vos faré
agora aína un poco sudar.
Pensastes el mundo por vos trastornar,° — change the order
por llegar a papa e ser soberano,
mas non lo seredes aqueste verano.
Vos, rey poderoso, venid a dançar.

EL REY:
¡Valía,° valía, los mis cavalleros, — help
yo non querría ir a tan baja dança!
Llegar vos con los ballesteros,° — crossbowmen
amparadme todos por fuerça de lança!
Mas ¿qué es aquesto que veo en balança?
Acortarse mi vida e perder los sentidos,
el cor° se me quexa con grandes gemidos. — heart
Adiós, mis vasallos que muerte me tranza.° — destroying

LA MUERTE:
¡Rey fuerte, tirano, que siempre robastes
todo vuestro reyno o fenchistes° el arca! — swelled

De fazer justicia muy poco curastes
segunt es notorio por vuestra comarca.
Venit para mí, que yo so monarca,
que prenderé a vos e a otro más alto,
llegad a la dança cortés en un salto.
'En pos de° vos venga luego el patriarca. after

EL PATRIARCA:
Yo nunca pensé venir a tal punto
nin estar en dança tan sin piedad.
Ya me han privado, segunt que barrunto,° sense
de beneficios e de dignidad.
¡Oh, homne mezquino que en grand ceguedad
andove en el mundo no parando mientes,
como la Muerte en sus duros dientes
roba a todo homne a qualquier edad!

LA MUERTE:
Señor patriarca, yo nunca robé
en alguna parte cosa que non deba;
de matar a todos costumbre lo he,
de escapar alguno de mí non se atreva.
Esto vos ganó vuestra madre Eva
por querer gostar fructa devedada.° forbidden
'Poned en recabdo° vuestra cruz dorada. hide
Sígase con vos el duque antes que más veva.

EL DUQUE:
¡O qué malas nuevas son éstas sin falla
que agora me traen que vaya a tal juego!
Yo tenía pensado de fazer batalla,
espérame un poco, Muerte, yo te ruego.
Si non te detienes, miedo he que luego
me prendas o mates: habré de dexar°
todos mis deleites, ca non puede estar
que mi alma escape de aquel duro fuego.

LA MUERTE:

Duque poderoso, ardit° e valiente, brave
non es ya tiempo de 'dar dilaciones,° hesitate
andad en la dança con buen continente,° face
dexad a los otros vuestras guarniciones.° arms
Jamás non podredes cebar° los alcones, feed
ordenar las justas nin fazer torneos:
aquí habrán fin los vuestros deseos.
Venid, arçobispo, dexad los sermones.

EL ARÇOBISPO:
¡Ay Muerte cruel! ¿Qué te merescí
o por qué me llievas tan arrebatado?° suddenly
Viviendo en deleites nunca te temí,
fiando en la vida quedé engañado.
Mas si yo bien rigera° mi arçobispado, ruled
de ti non oviera tan fuerte temor,
mas siempre del mundo fui amador,
bien sé que el infierno tengo aparejado.

LA MUERTE:
Señor arçobispo, pues tan mal registes
vuestros subdictos° e clerezía, =**sujetos**
gostad amargura por lo que comistes
manjares diversos con grand golosía.° gluttony
Estar non podredes en Sancta María
con 'palo romano° en pontifical:° crozier, vestments
venit a mi dança pues soes mortal.
Pase el condestable por otra tal vía.

EL CONDESTABLE:
Yo vi muchas danças de lindas donzellas,
de dueñas fermosas de alto linaje,
mas segunt me paresce no es ésta dellas,
ca el tañedor° trae feo visaje. musician
Venit, camarero, dezid a mi paje
que traiga el cavallo, que quiero fuir,
que es ésta la dança que dizen morir:
si della me escapo, tener me han por saje.° clever

LA MUERTE:
Fuir non conviene al que ha de estar quedo;° — still
estad, condestable, dexat el cavallo,
andad en la dança alegre muy ledo,° — happily
sin fazer ruido, ca yo bien me callo.
Mas verdad vos digo que al cantar del gallo
seredes tornado de otra figura:
allí perderedes vuestra fermosura.
Venit, vos, obispo, a ser mi vasallo.

EL OBISPO:
Mis manos aprieto, de mis ojos lloro
porque soy venido a tanta tristura.
Yo era abastado° de plata y de oro, — supplied
de nobles palacios e mucha folgura.° — pleasures
Agora la Muerte con su mano dura
trae me en su dança medroso° sobejo:° — frightened, very
parientes, amigos, poned me consejo,
que pueda salir de tal angostura.° — tight spot

LA MUERTE:
Obispo sagrado que fuestes pastor
de ánimas muchas, por vuestro pecado
a juicio iredes ante el Redemptor
e daredes quenta° de vuestro obispado. — **=cuenta**
Siempre anduvistes de gentes cargado,
en corte de rey y fuera de igreja,
mas yo gorciré[43] la vuestra pelleja.
Venit, cavallero que estades armado.

[43] **Gorciré** is read by several editors as **(s)sorzir** and seems to mean mend or fix up according to J. Gulsoy of the University of Toronto who has reviewed the Morreale edition of this work. *Romance Philolgy*, v. 26, 1 (1972) pp.199-200. Other editors say it means to tan referring to animal hides.

EL CABALLERO:
A mí non paresce ser cosa guisada° — appropriate
que dexa mis armas e vaya a dançar
a tal dança negra de llanto poblada
que contra los vivos quisiste ordenar.
Segunt estas nuevas, conviene dexar
mercedes e tierras que gané del rey:
pero a la fin sin dubda non sey
quál es la carretera que habré de levar.

LA MUERTE:
Cavallero noble, ardit e ligero,
fazed buen semblante en vuestra persona,
non es aquí tiempo de contar dinero,
oíd mi canción por que de modo entona.° — sung
Aquí vos faré correr la atahona,° — mill
e después veredes como ponen freno
a los de la banda que roban lo ageno.° — that of others
Dançad, abad gordo, con vuestra corona.° — tonsure

EL ABAD:
Maguer provechoso° so a los relijiosos, — generous
de tal dança, amigos, yo no me contento.
En mi celda havía manjares sabrosos,
de ir non curava comer a convento.
Dar me hedes signado° como non consiento — order
de andar en ella, ca he grand recelo,° — fear
e si tengo tiempo, provoco e apelo:[44]
mas non puede ser que ya desatiento.° — don't pay attention

LA MUERTE:
Don abad bendito, folgado,° vicioso, — pleasure-seeking
que poco curastes de vestir celicio.° — hairshirt
Abrazadme agora, seredes mi esposo,
pues que deseastes plazeres e vicio.
Ca yo so bien presta° a vuestro servicio, — quick

[44] Standard legal formula for "I appeal."

haved me por vuestra, quitad de vos saña,
que mucho me place con vuestra compaña.
E vos, escudero, venid al oficio.

EL ESCUDERO:
Dueñas e donzellas, haved de mí duelo,
fazen me por fuerça dexar los amores,
echó me la Muerte su sotil anzuelo,° — hook
fazen me dançar dança de dolores.
Non traen por cierto firmalles° nin flores — brooch
los que en ella dançan, más grand fealdad.
¡Ay de mí, cuitado, que en gran vanidat
andove en el mundo sirviendo señores!

LA MUERTE:
Escudero polido,° de amor sirviente, — courteous
dexad los amores de toda persona,
venit ver mi dança e cómo se adona,° — one is adorned
e a los que dançan acompañaredes.
Mirad su figura, tal vos tornaredes° — change
que vuestras amadas non vos querrán veer:
habed buen conhorte, que así ha de ser.
Venit, vos deán, non vos corrocedes.° — be angry

EL DEÁN:
¿Quí es aquesto que 'yo de mi seso salgo?° — I am losing my s
Pensé de fuir e non fallo carrera;° — escape
grand renta° tenía e buen deanazgo,° — income, deanshi
e mucho trigo en la mi panera.° — granery
Allende de aquesto estava en espera
de ser proveído de algún obispado.
Agora la Muerte envió me mandado:
mala señal veo, pues fazen la cera.

LA MUERTE:
Don rico avariento, deán muy ufano° — haughty
que vuestros dineros trocastes en oro;
a pobres e a viudas cerrastes la mano

e mal despendistes el vuestro thesoro.
Non quiero que estedes ya más en el coro, — dance
salid luego fuera sin otra pereza,
yo vos mostraré venir la pobreza.
Venit, mercadero, a la dança del lloro.

EL MERCADERO:
¿A quién dexaré todas mis riquezas
e mercadurías° que traigo en la mar? — merchandise
Con muchos traspasos° e más sutilezas° — sales, guile
gané lo que tengo en cada lugar.
Agora la Muerte vino me llamar.
¿Qué será de mí? Non sé qué me faga,
o, Muerte, tu sierra° a mí es grand plaga.° — saw, calamity
Adiós, mercaderos, que voime a finar.

LA MUERTE:
De hoy más non curedes de pasar en Flandes,° — Flanders—center of trade
estad aquí quedo e iredes a ver
la tienda que traigo de bubas° e landres: — tumorS
'de gracia° las do, non quiero vender. — gratis
Una sola dellas vos fará caer
'de palmas en tierra° dentro mi botica, — flat on your face
e en ella entraredes maguer sea chica.
E vos, arcediano,° venid al tañer. — archdeacon

EL ARCEDIANO:
¡O, mundo vil, malo e fallescedero,° — errant
que me engañaste con tu promisión!
Prometiste me vida, de ti non la espero,
siempre me mentiste en toda sazón.
Faga quien quisiere la vesitación° — visit
de mi arcedianasto por que trabajé.
¡Ay de mí, cuitado, grand cargo tomé!
Ahora lo siento, que hasta aquí non.

LA MUERTE:
Arcediano amigo, quitad el bonete,° — cap

venit a la dança suave e honesto,
ca quien en el mundo sus amores mete,
el mesmo le faze venir a todo esto.
Vuestra dignidad, segunt dice el testo,° — text
es cura° de ánimas e daredes cuenta: — care
si mal las registes° habredes afruenta.° — cared, judgment
Dançad, abogado, dexad el Digesto.° — law book

EL ABOGADO:
¿Qué 'fue hora,° mezquino, de quanto aprendí, — has happened
de mi saber todo e mi libelar?° — legal writing
Quando estar° pensé, entonces caí, — I had arrived
cegóme la Muerte non puedo estudiar.
Recelo he grande de ir al lugar
do non valdrá libelo° nin fuero,° — petition, local law
peor amigo es que sin lengua muero.
Abarcóme° la Muerte, non puedo fablar. — seized me

LA MUERTE:
Don falso abogado, prevalicador,° — liar
que de ambas las partes levaste salario,[45]
'véngasevos miente° cómo sin temor — remember
bolvistes la foja° por otro contrario.° — page, side
El Chino e el Bártolo e el Coletario[46]
no vos librarán de mi poder mero:° — great
aquí pagaredes como buen romero.
E vos, canónigo, dexad el breviario.

EL CANÓNIGO:
Vete ahora, Muerte, non quiero ir contigo,
déxame ir al coro ganar la ración,° — benefice
non quiero tu dança nin ser tu amigo.
En folgura vivo, non he turbación.
'Aun este otro día° hove provisión — just the other day

---

[45] **que de ambas...** you took money from both parties
[46] **El Chino e...** Reference to commentaries of Cino de Pistoia, jurist from Bologna, Bártolo de Sassoferrato and the Coletario, a work of canon law attributed to San Isidoro.

desta calongia° que me dio el perlado: canonry
desto que tengo soy bien pagado.
Vaya quien quisiere a tu vocación. invitation

LA MUERTE:
Canónigo amigo, non es el camino
ese que pensades, dad acá la mano,
el sobrepeliz° delgado de lino surplice
quitadlo de vos e irás más liviano.° quickly
Darvos he un consejo que vos será sano:° helpful
tornad vos a Dios e fazed penitencia,
ca sobre vos cierto es dada sentencia.
Llegad acá, físico,° que estades ufano. doctor

EL FÍSICO:
Mintióme sin duda el Fen de Abicena[47]
que me prometió muy luengo bevir
rigiéndome° bien a yantar e cena, advising me
dexando el bever después de dormir.
Con esta esperanza pensé conquerir° earning
dineros e plata enfermos curando;
mas agora veo que me va llevando
la Muerte consigo: conviene sofrir.

LA MUERTE:
Pensastes vos, físico, que por Galeno
o por don Ipocras° con sus aforismos Hipocrates
seríades librado de comer del feno,° straw
que otros gastaron de más sologismos.° **=silogismos**
Non vos valdrá 'fazer gargarismos,° gargle
componer xaropes° nin tener diecta.° syrups, **=dieta**
Venit vos, don cura, dexad los bautismos.

[47] **Fen de Abicena** is a famous book of medicine by Avicena studied as the canon of medicine in medieval universities and was the translation into Latin by Gerardo de Cremona.

EL CURA:
Non quiero exenciones nin conjugaciones,[48]
con mis perrochianos° quiero ir folgar; parishoners
ellos me dan pollos e lechones° suckling pigs
e muchas obladas° 'con el pie° de altar. offerings, at the foot
Locura sería mis diezmos° dexar tithes
e ir a tu dança de que non se parte,
pero a la fin non sé por qual arte
desta tu dança pudiese escapar.

LA MUERTE:
Ya non es tiempo de yazer al sol
con los perrochianos beviendo el vino.
Yo vos mostraré un 're mi fa sol° musical notes
que agora compuse de canto muy fino.
Tal como a vos quiero haber por vezino,
que muchas ánimas tovistes en gremio,° flock
segunt las registes° habredes el premio. ruled
Dance el labrador que vien del molino.° mill

EL LABRADOR:
¿Cómo conviene dançar al villano
que nunca la mano sacó de la reja?° plow
Busca, si te place, quien dance liviano,
déxame, Muerte, con otro trebeja,° frolic
ca yo como tocino e a vezes obeja,° mutton
e es el mi oficio trabajo e afán° toil
arando° las tierras para sembrar° pan: plowing, sow
por ende non curo de oír tu conseja.

LA MUERTE:
Si vuestro trabajo fue siempre sin arte° trickery
non faziendo° fruto de la tierra ajena, taking
en gloria eternal habredes grand parte,
e por el contrario sufriredes pena.

---

[48] **Exenciones nin conjugaciones** seems to refer to the difficulty in learning Latin grammar with its rules and exceptions.

Pero con todo eso, poned la melena,° yoke
allegad vos a mí, yo vos uniré,
lo que a otros fize a vos lo faré.
E vos, monje negro, 'tomad buena estrena.° make an entrance

EL MONJE
Loor e alabanza sea para siempre
al alto Señor que con piedat me lieva
a su santo reyno a donde contenple
'por siempre jamás° la su magestad. for ever and ever
De cárcel escura vengo a claridad
do habré alegría sin otra tristura,
por poco trabajo habré grand folgura.
Muerte, no me espanto de tu fealdad.

LA MUERTE:
Si la regla sancta del monje bendicto° Benedictine
guardastes del todo sin otro deseo,
sin dubda tened° que soes° escripto know, are
en libro de vida segunt que yo creo.
Pero, si fezistes lo que fazer veo
a otros que andan fuera de la regla,° rule
vida vos darán que sea más negra.
Dançad, usurero,° dexad el correo.° usurer, running around

EL USURERO:
Non quiero tu dança nin tu canto negro,
mas quiero prestando doblar mi moneda.
Con pocos dineros que me dio mi suegro
otras obras fago que non fizo Beda.° Venerable Bede
Cada año los doblo, demás está queda
la prenda° en mi casa, que está por el todo. security
Allego° riquezas yaziendo 'de codo,° accumulate, on my side
por ende tu dança a mí non es leda.° happy

LA MUERTE:
Traidor usurario de mala concencia,° conscience
agora veredes lo que fazer suelo:

en fuego infernal 'sin más detenencia° — without delay
porné° vuestra alma cubierta de duelo. — =**pondré**
Allá estaredes, do está vuestro abuelo,
que quiso usar segunt vos usastes:
por poca ganancia mal siglo ganastes.
E vos, frayre° menor, venit a señuello.° — =**fraile**, lure

EL FRAYRE:
Dançar non conviene a maestro famoso,
segunt que yo so en la religión,
maguer mendigante° vivo visioso° — mendicant, at ea
e muchos desean oír mi sermón.
Decídesme agora que 'vaya a tal son,° — dance to your tu
dançar non querría si me das lugar.
¡Ay de mí, cuitado, que habré de dexar
las honrras e grado° que quiera o que non! — pleasure

LA MUERTE:
Maestro famoso, sotil e capaz,
que en todas las artes fuestes sabidor,
non vos acuitedes, limpiad vuestra faz,
que a pasar habredes por este dolor.
Yo vos levaré ante un sabidor
que sabe las artes sin ningunt defeto:
sabredes leer por otro decreto.
Portero 'de maza,° venit al tenor.° — with a mace, orc

EL PORTERO:
¡Ay del rey barones, acorredme agora!
Lévame sin grado esta Muerte brava!
Non me guardé della, tomóme 'a deshora,° — early
a puerta del rey guardando estava.
Hoy en este día el conde esperava
que me diese algo porque 'le di puerta:° — let him in
guarde quien quisiere o fínquese abierta,
que ya la mi guarda non vale una fava.° — bean

LA MUERTE:
Dexad esas voces, llevadvos corriendo,°
que non es ya tiempo de 'estar en la vela.° watching
Las vuestras baratas° yo bien las entiendo, deceits
e vuestra cobdicia por qué modo suena.° works
Cerrades la puerta de más quando yela° it is cold
al homne mezquino que 'bien a librar:° comes to get out of the cold
lo que dél levastes habrés de pagar.
E vos, ermitaño, salit de la celda.

EL ERMITAÑO:
La muerte recelo maguer que so viejo,
Señor Iesuchristo, a ti me encomiendo;
de los que sirven tú eres espejo,
pues yo te serví, la tu gloria atiendo.° await
Sabes que sofrí laceria viviendo
en este desierto de contemplación,
de noche e de día faziendo oración,
e por más abstinencia las yerbas comiendo.

LA MUERTE:
Fazes grand cordura, llamar te ha el Señor
que con diligencia pugnaste servir.
Si bien le servistes habredes honor
en su sancto reyno do haves a venir.
Pero con todo esto habredes a ir
en esta mi dança con vuestra barbaza: long beard
de matar a todos aquesta es mi caça.° hunt
Dançad, contador,° después de dormir. accountant

EL CONTADOR:
¿Quién podría pensar que tan sin disanto° holy day
había de dexar mi contaduría?
Llegué a la muerte e vi desbarato destruction
que fazía en los homnes con grand osadía.
Allí perderé toda mi valía,° worth
haberes e joyas e mi gran poder:

faza libramientos de hoy más 'quien quisier,° — whoever wishes
ca cercan dolores el ánima mía.

LA MUERTE:
Contador amigo, si bien vos catades
como por favor e a veces por don
librastes° las cuentas, razón es que hayades — exempted
dolor e quebranto° por tal ocasión. — suffering
Cuento° de alguarismo° nin su división — account, number
non vos ternán pro° e iredes conmigo: — benefit
andad acá luego, así vos lo digo.
E vos, diácono, venit a licción.

EL DIÁCONO:
Non veo que tienes gesto° de lector — appearance
tú que me convidas que vaya a leer.
Non vi en Salamanca maestro nin doctor
que tal gesto tenga nin tal parescer.
Bien sé que con arte me quieres fazer
que vaya a tu dança para me matar.
Si esto así es, venga administrar
otro por mí, que yo vome° a caer. — =me voy

LA MUERTE
Maravillo me mucho de vos, clerizón,
pues que bien sabedes que es mi doctrina
matar a todos por justa razón,
e vos esquivades oír mi bocina.° — call
Yo vos vestiré almática° fina — deacon's vestment
labrada de pino° en que ministredes: — pine (coffin)
fasta que vos llamen, en ella iredes.
Venga el que recabda° e dance aína. — collects

EL RECAUDADOR:° — collector
Asad 'he que faga° en recabdar — have to do
lo que por el rey me fue encomendado,
por ende non puedo nin debo dançar
en esta tu dança que non he acostumbrado.

Quiero ir agora 'apriessa priado° — very quickly
por unos dineros que me han prometido,
ca he esperado e el plazo° es venido. — deadline
Mas veo el camino del todo cerrado.

LA MUERTE:
Andad acá luego sin más tardar,
pagad los cohechos° que haves levado,° — bribes, taken
pues que vuestra vida fue en trabajar
como rabariedes° al homne cuitado. — cause suffering
Dar vos he un poyo° en que estéis sentado — bench
e fagades las rentas que tenga dos pasos:° — steps
allí darés cuenta de vuestros traspasos.° — transgressions
Venit, subdiácono, alegre e pagado.

EL SUBDIÁCONO:
Non he menester de ir a trocar
como fazen esos que traes a tu mando;
antes de evangelio me quiero tornar
estas cuatro temporas° que se van llegando. — days of fasting
En lugar de tanto veo que llorando
andan todos esos, non fallan abrigo,° — protection
non quiero tu dança, así te lo digo,
mas quiero pasar el salterio rezando.

LA MUERTE:
Mucho es superfluo el vuestro alegar,° — protests
por ende dexad aquesos sermones,
non tenés maña° de andar a dançar, — cleverness
nin comer obleas° cerca los tizones.° — wafers, embers
Non iredes más en las procisiones° — **=procesiones**
do 'davades vozes muy altas en grito,° — shouted loudly
como por enero fazía el cabrito.° — kid (goat)
Venit, sacristán, dexad las razones.

EL SACRISTÁN:
Muerte, yo te ruego que hayas piadad° — **=piedad**
de mí que so 'moço de pocos días,° — young lad

non conoscí a Dios en mi moçedad
nin quise tomar nin siguir sus vías.
Fía de mi, amiga, como de otros fías,
por que satisfaga del mal que he fecho,
a ti non se pierde jamás tu derecho,° justice
ca yo iré si tú por mí envías.

LA MUERTE:
Don sacristanejo 'de mala picaña,° full of deceit
ya non tenés tiempo de saltar paredes
nin de andar de noche con los de la caña° jousters
faziendo las obras que vos bien sabiedes.
Andar a rondar vos ya non podredes,
nin presentar joyas a vuestra señora,
si bien vos quiere, quite vos agora.
Venit vos, rabí, acá meldaredes.° read religious texts

EL RABÍ:
¡Oh Helohim° e Dios de Abrahám God
que prometistes la redempción!
Non sé qué me faga con tan grand afán,° worry
mandad me que dance, non entiendo° el son. hear
Non ha homne en el mundo de quantos hi son
que pueda fuir de su mandamiento.
Veladme,° dayanes,° que mi entendimiento watch over me, jud
se pierde del todo con grand aflición.° anxiety

LA MUERTE:
Don rabí barbudo que siempre estudiastes
en el Talmud e en los sus doctores,
e de la verdat jamás non curastes,
por lo qual habredes penas e dolores.
Llegad vos acá con los dançadores
e diredes por canto vuestra baraha:° blessing
dar vos han posada con rabí Aza.
Venit, alfaquí,° dexad los sabores. wise man

EL ALFAQUÍ:
Si Alah me vala, es fuerte cosa
esto que me mandas agora fazer;
yo tengo mujer, discreta, graciosa,
de que he gasajado° e asaz plazer. — joy
Todo quanto tengo quiero perder,
déxame con ella solamente estar,
'de que fuere viejo,° manda me levar, — when I am old
e a ella con migo si a ti ploguier.

LA MUERTE:
Venit vos, amigo, dexad el zalá[49]
ca el gameño° pedricaredes, — hell
a los veinte e siete[50] vuestro capellá, — Moorish cape
nin vuestra camisa non la vestiredes.
En Meca nin en Layda° y non estaredes — Leyden (Holland)
comiendo buñuelos en alegría:
busque otro alfaquí vuestra morería.° — Moorish quarter
Pasad vos, santero, veré qué diredes.

EL SANTERO:[51]
Por cierto más quiero mi ermita servir
que non ir allá donde tú me dices.
Tengo buena vida aunque ando a pedir,
e como 'a las veses° pollos e perdices;° — sometimes, partridges
sé tomar al campo bien las codornices° — quail
e tengo en mi campo asaz de repollos.° — cabbages
Vete, que non quiero tu gato con pollos:
a Dios me encomiendo y a señor san Helices.° — **=Félix**

---

[49] Some editions have **zalá** meaning prayer and others **rallar** meaning to talk.
[50] According to the edition of the **Danza** by Haydee Bermejo Hurtado and Dinko Cvitanovic p. 42, note 593 **los veinte y siete** refers to the 27th day in the month of Ramadan, the Muslim month of fasting, this is the night that God listens to all the faithful.
[51] **Santero** is the person who cared for an image in a hermitage and traveled with a replica of the image to collect alms and oil for the lamp at the shrine.

LA MUERTE:
Non vos vale nada vuestro recelar,° fear
andad acá luego, vos, don taleguero,° provisioner
que non quisistes la ermita adobar,° supply
fezistes alcuza° de vuestro garguero.° jar, throat
Non vesitaredes° la 'bota de cuero° visit, wineskin
con que a menudo solíades beber,
zurrón[52] nin talega° non podredes traer, pouch
nin pedir gallofas° como de primero. rolls

LA MUERTE A LOS QUE NON NOMBRÓ:
A todos los que aquí non he nombrado
de qualquier ley e estado o condición,
les mando que vengan muy 'toste priado° very quickly
a entrar en mi dança sin escusación.
Non rescibiré jamás exebción
nin otro libelo° nin declinatoria:[53] petition
los que bien fizieron habrán siempre gloria,
los que lo contrario, habrán dapnación.

LOS QUE HAN DE PASAR POR LA MUERTE:
Pues que así es que a morir habemos
de nescesidad sin otro remedio,
con pura conciencia todos trabajemos
en servir a Dios sin otro comedio.° concern
Ca él es principio, fin e medio
por do si le plaze habremos folgura,
aunque la Muerte con dança muy dura
nos meta en su corro 'con qualquier comedio.° at any time

## Theater

Very little drama has survived from the 15th century. The *Danza de la muerte* may conceivably have been dramatic; but plays as such are limited to only a few writers. Gómez Manrique wrote a

[52] **Zurrón** large, leather, shepherd's pouch
[53] **Declinatoria,** questioning the authority of a judge

play called *Representación del Nasçimiento de Nuestro Señor* for the monastery of Calabazanos, near Palencia. He depicted the birth of Jesus and the adoration of the shepherds in simple language in a play that is certainly drawn from the liturgical dramas handed down from the Middle Ages.

## *La Representaçión del Nasçimiento de Nuestro Señor*

A instançia de doña María Manrique, vicaria en el monasterio de Calabaçanos, hermana suya.

Lo que dize JOSEPE,° sospechando de Nuestra Señora: José

¡Oh viejo desventurado!° unlucky
Negra dicha° fue la mía fate
en casarme con María
por quien fuesse deshonrado.
Ya la veo bien preñada,° pregnant
no sé de quién, nin de cuánto° how long.
Dizen que d'Espíritu Santo,
mas yo d'esto non sé nada.

La oraçión que faze la GLORIOSA:
¡Mi solo Dios verdadero,
cuyo ser es inamovible,° immutable
a quien es todo posible,
fáçil e 'bien fazedero!° possible to do
Tú que sabes la pureza
de la mi virginidad,
alumbra la çeguedad° blindness
de Josep, e su simpleza.

El ÁNGEL a JOSEPE:
¡Oh viejo de muchos días,
en el seso° de muy pocos; intelligence
el principal de los locos!
¿Tú no sabes que Isaías

dixo: «Virgen parirá»;
lo cual escribió por esta
doncella gentil, honesta,
cuyo par° nunca será? equal

La que representa a la GLORIOSA,
cuando le dieren° el Niño: give
Adórote, rey del cielo,
verdadero Dios e Hombre;
adoro tu santo nombre,
mi salvación e consuelo.
Adórote, fijo e padre,
a quien sin dolor parí,° gave birth
porque quesiste° de mí wanted
fazer de sierva tu madre.
Bien podré decir aquí
aquel salmo gloriöso,
que dixe, fijo preçioso,
cuando yo te conçebí;
que mi ánima engrandeçe° magnifies
a ti, mi solo Señor,
y en ti, mi Salvador,
mi spíritu floreçe.
Mas éste mi gran plazer
en dolor será tornado,
pues tú eres envïado
para muerte padeçer
por salvar los pecadores,
en la cual yo pasaré,
non menguándome° la fe, diminishing
innumerables dolores.
Pero mi precioso prez,° honor
fijo mío muy querido,
dame tu claro sentido
para tratar tu niñez
con debida reverençia,
e para que tu pasión
mi femenil coraçón

sufra con mucha paciençia.

La denunçiaçión° del ÁNGEL a los pastores: — annunciation
Yo vos denunçio, pastores,
qu'en Bellén° es hoy naçido — Bethlehem
el Señor de los señores,
sin pecado conçebido.
E porque non lo dudedes° — doubt
id al 'pesebre del buey,° — manger of the ox
donde çierto fallaredes
al prometido en la Ley.

El UN PASTOR:
Dime tú, ermano, di,
si oíste alguna cosa,
e si viste lo que vi.

El SEGUNDO:
Una gran voz me semeja
de un Ángel reluziente° — shining
que sonó en mi oreja.

El TERCERO:
Mis oídos han oído
en Bellén ser esta noche
nuestro Salvador naçido.
Por ende dexar debemos
nuestros ganados° e ir — cattle
por ver si lo fallaremos.

Los PASTORES veyendo al glorioso Niño:
Este es el Niño eçelente
que nos tiene de salvar.
Hermanos, muy omilmente° — =humildemente
le lleguemos a adorar.

La adoraçión del PRIMERO:
Dios te salve, gloriöso

infante santificado,
por redemir envïado
este mundo trabajoso° of suffering
Damos te grandes loores
por te querer demostrar
a nós, míseros pastores.

Del SEGUNDO:
Salve te Dios, Niño santo,
envïado por Dios Padre,
conçebido por tu madre
con amor e con espanto.° amazement
Alabamos tu grandeza
qu'en el pueblo d'Israel
escogió nuestra simpleza.

Del TERCERO:
Dios te salve, Salvador,
hombre que ser Dios creemos.
Muchas graçias te facemos
porque quisiste, Señor,
la nuestra carne vestir,
en la cual muy cruda muerte
has por nós de reçebir.

Los ÁNGELES:
Gloria al Dios soberano
que reina sobre los çielos,
e paz al linaje humano.

SAN GABRIEL:
Dios te salve, glorïosa
'de los maitines estrella,° morning star
después de madre donzella,
e antes que fija, esposa.
Yo soy venido, señora,
tu leal ambaxador,
para ser tu servidor

en aquesta santa hora.

SAN MIGUEL:
Yo, Micael, que vençí
'las huestes luçiferales,° — Lucifer's hosts
con los coros° çelestiales — choirs
que son en torno de mí,
por mandato de Dios padre
vengo tener compañía
a ti, beata° María, — blessed
de tan santo Niño madre.

SAN RAFAEL:
Yo, el ángel Rafael,
capitán d'estas cuadrillas,° — bands
dexando las altas sillas,
vengo a ser tu donzel;° — servant
e por fazerte plazeres,
pues tan bien los mereçiste,
¡oh María, 'Mater Criste,° — Mother of Christ
bendicha° entre las mujeres! — blessed

Los martirios° que presentan al Niño: — sufferings

El CÁLIZ:° — chalice
¡Oh santo Niño naçido
para nuestra redençión!
Este cáliz dolorido
de la tu cruda° pasión — cruel
es neçesario que beba
tu sagrada majestad,
por salvar la humanidad
que fue perdida por Eva.

El ASTELO° e la SOGA:° — column, rope
E será en este astelo
tu cuerpo glorificado,
poderoso rey del çielo,

con esas sogas atado.

Los AÇOTES:° lashes
Con estos açotes crudos
romperán los tus costados
los sayones° muy sañudos° ministers of jus
por lavar nuestros pecados. angry

LA CORONA:
E después de tu persona
ferida con deçeplinas° whips
te pornán esta corona
de dolorosas espinas.

La CRUZ:
En aquesta santa cruz
el tu cuerpo se porná;° **=pondrá**
a la hora no habrá luz
y el templo caerá.

Los CLAVOS:° nails
Con estos clavos, Señor,
te clavarán pies e manos;
grande pasarás dolor
por los míseros humanos.

LA LANÇA:° spear
Con esta lança tan cruda
foradarán° tu costado, pierce
e será claro, sin duda,
lo que fue profetizado.

Cançión para callar al Niño:

Callad, fijo mío
chiquito.
Callad vos, Señor,
nuestro Redentor,° redeemer

que vuestro dolor
durará poquito.
Ángeles del cielo,
venid, dar consuelo
a este moçuelo° — little boy
Jesús tan bonito.
Este fue reparo,° — remedy
aunqu'el costo caro,
d'aquel pueblo amaro
cativo en Egito.
Este santo dino,° — worthy
Niño tan benino° — good
por redemir vino
el linaje aflito.° — afflicted
Cantemos gozosas,
hermanas graciosas,
pues somos esposas
del Jesús bendito.

# Glossary

**a cabo de** at the edge of, at the end of, next to
**a pos** next to
**a razón** right size
**abadón** fat abbot
**aballar** to pin down
**abarcar** to seize
**abarcas** sandals
**abastado** supplied
**abastar** to provide, supply, be supplied
**abatido** spiritless
**abatir** to strike down
**abaxado** lowered
**abaxar** to come down, lower
**abbat** abbot
**abbatissa** abbess
**abenençia** settlement
**abertura** opening
**abiltar** to be shamed
**ábito reglar** religious order
**abivarse** to strive
**ablentado** soft
**abondar** to grant
**aborrido** hated
**abrasado** aflame
**abreuiar** to shorten
**abrigo** protection
**abtarda** buzzard
**abtezas** jewels
**abusión** superstition
**acabado** great, perfect
**acabamiento** outcome
**acabar más de preçio** to earn more
**acabar** to enjoy, win
**acabdillar** to lead
**acabesçer** to get, obtain
**acaecer** to happen
**acarrear** to bring, transport
**acatar** to heed, to watch
**acayaz** title of respect
**açechar** to stalk
**acero** steel
**açi = aquí** here
**aciclado** polished
**açitara** tapestry
**acoger** to come, take refuge
**açomar** to propose
**acomendado** ordered
**acomendar** to commend
**acometer** to accomplish, attack
**aconseyar** to advise
**açor** hawk
**acordado** agreed, harmonious, prudent, remembered
**acordar** to be in agreement, wake up
**acorre** relief
**acorrer** to help
**acorro** help
**açotar** to strike, beat
**açote** lash
**acreçentar** to make bigger, increase, make more important
**acuitar** to pursue, attack
**adalid** scout
**adarga** shield
**adarve** path
**adebdado** obligated
**adelante: en —** from this point on
**adeliñar** to go directly, go on, head for, go straight for, toward
**aderedor** from there
**adestrar** to lead
**adeudado** vassal
**adevinar** to predict
**adó** where
**adobado** dressed, outfitted, prepared
**adobar** to prepare, restore, supply
**adobo** bed linen, garment
**adonado** blessed, gifted, graceful
**adonar** to adorn
**adormecerse** to fall asleep

**adotivo** adopted
**adtor mudado** molting hawk
**aducir** to bring
**adugamos** we will bring
**adurar** to bring
**aduzir** to bring, lead
**afán** affliction, toil, worry
**afanar** to toil
**afé** behold
**afeado** ugly
**afemencer** to look intently
**afeytado** adorned
**afijado** child
**afilado** elegant, thin
**afinado** polished
**afincadamente** earnestly
**afincanças** effort
**afincar** to insist, urge
**afirmar** to declare
**aflición** anxiety
**aflito** afflicted
**afogar** to drown
**afontado** offended
**aforgar** to drown
**aforzado** heartened
**aforzar** to take courage
**afrenta** insult
**afrentado** offended
**afruenta** battle, contest
**afruento** danger
**agenor** foreign
**agitado** stormy
**agotar** to use up
**agradar** to be pleased
**agrado** pleasure
**agradoso** pleased
**agranizar** to hail
**agraz** sour grape
**aguadera** raincoat
**aguadero** for rain
**aguardador** escort
**aguardar** to accompany, wait for, watch
**agudeza** intelligence, wit
**agudo** sharp
**agüero** omen
**aguijar** to spur on
**aguijón** spur
**águila** eagle
**aguililla** little eagle
**aguisado** certain, proper, raised, set, **bien —** elegantly
**aguissar** to chastise
**ahincar** to pursue
**ahondar** to be sufficient
**ahontado** shamed
**aí = allí** there
**aína** quickly
**airado** angered
**aírar** to anger
**aire** bearing
**ajeno** of another
**ajuntar** to meet
**al** the other, something else
**alá** ho there
**alabar** to praise
**alabar** to praise
**alamud** bolt
**alana** mastiff
**alançador** lance thrower
**alarido** shout
**alauut** my soul
**alba** dawn
**albardón** packsaddle
**albergada** army, encampment
**albergar** to spend, stay
**albo** (adj) white
**albor** dawn
**alborada** dawn
**albricia** rejoice
**albuerguía** lodging
**albura** whiteness
**alcaide** first lieutenant, judge
**alcaldía** jurisdiction
**alcançar** to reach, to catch up
**alcançe** pursuit
**alcándara** hook
**alcanzar** to attain, reach
**alçar** to hide, raise
**alción** kingfisher
**alcor** hill
**alcuza** jar
**alderredor** around
**alegar** to protest
**aleuoso** treacherous
**alevoso** traitor, treacherous

**alexado** distanced
**alfaquí** wise man
**alfaya** gift, **de alfaya** valued
**alfoz** district, region, territory
**algarabía** Arabic
**algarivo** grieved
**algo** value
**alguaçil** sheriff
**alguandre** nothing, not a thing
**alhaonar** to bother
**alimosna** alms
**aljama** quarter (Moorish)
**allegar** to accumulate
**allende** beyond
**alleviado** alleviated
**alma** soul, spirit
**almádana** sledgehammer
**almática** deacon's vestment
**almejía** Moorish cloak
**almena** tower
**almofalla** carpet
**alongar** to make longer
**alterado** angry
**alteza** nobility
**alto** lofty, noble
**altura** merit
**aluen** further on
**alunbrar** to enlighten
**aluo** white
**alva** dawn
**alvergar** to protect
**amador** lover
**amainar** to calm down
**amanca** love
**amanecer** to dawn
**amansado** tamed
**amansar** to tame
**amanzellado** dishonored
**amar** to love
**amargores** bitterness
**amargura** bitterness
**amariello** yellow
**amaro** bitter
**amatado** extinguished
**amatar** to end
**ambaxador** embassador
**amenazar** to threaten
**amidos** unwillingly
**amo** protector, tutor
**amodorrido** asleep
**amonestar** to admonish, indicate
**amor, con amor** in love
**amortecido** fainted away
**amos en par** both of us
**amos = ambos** both
**amparar** to help
**añader** to add
**añal** yearling
**anchura** wide plain
**ancianía** old age
**ançilla** handmaiden
**áncora** anchor
**andadas** travels
**andidiste = anduviste** walked, went
**andodieron** went
**anegar** to drown
**angosto** narrow
**angostura** narrow place, tight spot
**anhelar** to long for
**aniello** ring
**ánima** soul
**anochecer** to grow dark
**anparar = amparar** to help
**ante** first
**antenna** crossbar
**antes** rather
**anyal** yearly
**anzuelo** hook
**apagar** to cool down
**apaladinar** to explain
**apañarse** to dress
**aparato** pomp
**aparellado** available
**apartado** retreat, wide-set
**apartamiento** place apart
**apearse** to dismount
**apedreado** stoned
**apedrear** to stone
**apeonado** on foot
**apesgado** very grieved
**apetito** desire
**aplanado** even
**aponer** to accuse
**aportar** to arrive (at port)
**apostado** delicate
**apostura** beauty, quality

**apremiar** to be strict
**apremido** disciplined
**apreso** informed
**apretar** to hold in place, press, pressure
**apriesa** quickly
**apriso** 3rd per sing. pret. learned
**apuestamiente** courteously
**apuesto** convenient, elegant, fine
**aquijoso** prickly
**aquilón** north
**aquisado** caulked
**arado** field
**arambre** copper
**arbitrio** reason
**arbolado** filled with trees, grove
**arca** chest
**arcediano** archdeacon
**archa** chest
**arco** bow
**arder** to burn, shine
**ardido** brave
**ardit** bold, brave
**ardor** heat
**ardudo** burned
**ardura** concern
**arena** sand
**arenga** harangue
**argayo** cape
**argento** silver
**armargura** sadness
**armiña** ermine
**arqueta** chest
**arrabal** threshold
**arracada** pendant earring
**arrancada** rout
**arrancar** to defeat, to jut out
**arrar** to plow
**arras** marriage gift of groom to bride
**arrastrar** to drag
**arrebatado** suddenly
**arredrado** at a distance, separated
**arredrar** to distance, separate
**arrematar** to finish
**arrendar** to rein in (a horse)
**arreo** situation
**arrepentir** to repent
**arrevatimiento** impetus, ecstasy, seizure
**arroyo** stream
**arrugado** wrinkled
**arte** deceit, trick, trickery
**artero** artful
**artorgar = ortorgar** to grant
**arveja** bean
**asado** roasted
**asanar** to get angry
**asar** to burn, roast
**asaz** clearly
**ascendente** rising star
**asconas** throwing weapons
**asconder = esconder** to hide
**ascoroso** bothered
**asechar** to lurk, stalk
**asegurar** to trust one's safety
**aseo** appearance
**asmado** imagined
**asmar** to consider, imagine, judge reasonably, plot, think
**asnudo** donkey-like
**áspero** difficult, harsh
**assaz** enough
**assentado** seated
**assenter** to sit up
**assomar** to appear
**asta** lance
**astelo** column
**astil** shaft
**astinençia** abstinence
**astragado** laid waste
**astrolabio** astrolabe (instrument to measure positions of heavenly bodies)
**astrosía** evil
**astroso** vile, vile one
**asustar** to frighten
**ata** across
**atahona** mill
**atamaño** great
**atambor** Moorish battle drum
**atán por arte** without great astuteness
**atán** such
**ataúd** casket
**atavío** finery
**atender** to wait for

**atenençia** friendship
**aterrar** to knock down
**atesorar** to gather
**atizar** to stir
**atomar** to arrest
**atorgar** to agree to
**atravesado** pierced through
**atreguar el cuerpo** to guarantee safety
**atreguar** to arrange a truce
**atrevido** daring
**atrevudo** daring
**atributado** one who pays tribute
**aturdido** flustered
**auctoridat** authority
**aue** bird
**auenir** to agree
**auer** thing, wealth
**aueziella** little bird
**auino = avino** happened
**aun de cabo** furthermore
**auze** good luck
**avariento** greedy
**avecica** little bird
**avenençia** agreement
**avenir** to agree, be able to, get along
**aver** wealth, possession, worth
**avés** hardly, scarcely
**aviltar** to insult
**avisar** to warn
**avitamiento** house
**avivar** to sharpen
**avolverse** to get involved with
**avoroz** celebration
**avuero** omen
**axaraf** plain
**axenuz** fennel seed
**axorca** bracelet
**axuvar** dowry
**ayna** quickly, sooner
**ayuno** fasting
**ayuntamiento** meeting
**ayuntar** to gather, meet
**az** line of warriors
**azagaya** dart
**azcona** dart
**azeite** oil
**azemila** pack mule
**azes** face
**azeytuní** rich oriental cloth
**aziago** ill-fated

**baço** dark-skinned
**báculo** stick
**baldón, a gran baldón** free
**baldonar** to be generous
**ballesta** crossbow
**ballestero** crossbowman
**baluarte** bulwark
**banco** bench
**baraia** struggle
**barata** deceit, value
**barbaza** long beard
**barbiella** chin
**barqua** ship
**barragán** valiant
**barragana** concubine
**barraganía** bravery
**barrera** parapet
**barruntar** to sense, suspect, sniff
**barua = barba** beard
**baruj rapado** beardless
**barva** whisker
**barvapuñient** young
**bastar** to be enough
**bastecido** prepared
**bastido** supplied
**bastir** to arrange
**batallador** warrior, soldier
**batallar** to do battle
**batir** to beat
**batuda** trace
**bautizar** to baptise
**bavequía** foolishness
**bavieca** stupid person
**beato** blessed
**bel catar** good looking
**beldad** beauty
**Belleem = Belén** Bethlehem
**bellido** beautiful
**bendiçión** blessing
**bendixieron** pret. of bendecir to bless
**benedicto** blessed
**beneficio** church benefice
**benigno** kind

**beodo** drunk
**bermejo** red
**bestido = vestido** clothes
**Betlem** Bethlehem
**betume** tar
**beudo** drunkard
**bevedor** drinker
**bevir, bivir, vevir** to live
**bezerro** calf
**bibda = viuda** widow
**bien ante** long ago
**bien lieve** apparently
**bien** rather, truly, well-mannered
**bienfaziente** well behaved
**bienquerencia** good will
**biltança** humiliation
**bispado** bishopric
**blago** staff (of religious authority)
**blanchete** lapdog
**blando** sweet
**blasmar** to curse
**blasmo** balm
**bloca** center of the shield
**bocado** bite, morsel
**bocina** call
**bodega** wine cellar
**bofordar** to joust
**bolar = volar** to fly
**bollicio** fuss
**bombarda** gun
**bondad** goodness
**bonete** cap
**boquita** little (dear) mouth
**borda** edge
**bordadura** embroidery
**bordón** staff
**bota de cuero** wineskin
**botica** pharmacy, drugstore
**botín** booty
**boz = voz** voice
**braça** measurement (length of an arm)
**braçale** arm bracket
**braçero** arm
**bragas** underwear
**brama** lowing
**bravo** fierce
**brevïario** breviary, story
**brial** tunic, underclothing
**broncha** pin
**buba** tumor, sore
**buelo = vuelo** flight
**buelta = vuelta** turn
**buen amar** wonderful love
**buenas, a buenas** happily
**buey** ox
**bufón** peddler
**buhón** peddler
**burcés** citizen
**burgalés** from city of Burgos
**burzes** townspeople
**busca** search
**butor** vulture
**ca** because, but
**cabalgar** to ride (on a horse)
**caballero** knight
**cabalmente** perfectly
**cabdal** importance
**cabdal** large, wealth
**cabdellar** to carry
**cabdiello** leader
**caber** to fit
**cabez** head
**cabezal** pillow
**cabezprieto** black-haired
**cabillo** meeting
**cabo adelante** ahead
**cabo** next to, **de —** again
**caboso** perfect, virtuous
**cabrito** kid (goat)
**caça** game, hunt, hunting
**caçador** hunter
**cachicuerno** horn-handled
**cadena** chain
**cadió** 3rd per. pret. caer fell
**cadría = caería** would fall
**caer en alcaz** to pursue, **caer en pesar** to worry
**caer** to happen
**çaga** rearguard
**caístro** seabird
**cal** street
**calabrina** mortal condition
**calandre** lark
**calandria** lark
**calanna** the like

**calat = callad** be quiet
**calçado** provided
**calçado** shod, have on, provided, wearing
**calçado** shoes
**calçar** shoes, to wear shoes
**calças** trousers
**caldera** kettle, pot
**caleja** alley way
**calentura** fever, heat
**cáliz** chalice
**callar** to quiet, be still, maintain silence
**calongia** canonery
**calor** heat
**calze** chalice
**camaleón** chameleon
**cámara** room
**camarero** chamberlain
**camenna** bed
**camiar = cambiar** to change, exchange
**camisón** smock
**campo** battlefield
**can** dog
**cañado** lock
**cañavera** sugar cane
**çanca** thigh
**caño** cave
**cansedat** weariness
**canssado** tired
**canto** boulder, rock, stone
**çapata** shoe
**capiello** hat
**capilla** chapel
**capirote** cape
**captado** selected
**captenençia** behavior
**capuz** cloak
**cara** face, head
**çarapico** sea bird
**çaratón** mask
**cárbaso** sail
**carboncla** red gemstone
**carbonco** boil
**cárcel** prison, den (of an animal)
**carga** weight, influence
**cargado** heavy, laden
**cargante** surcoat
**cargar** to load
**cargo** charge
**carne** flesh
**carnoso** full
**carradas** cartloads
**carrera** escape, journey, path, road, street, trip, way
**carta** degree
**cartas por ABC** copies of same
**casamentera** matchmaker
**cascavielo** bell
**casco** helmet
**casiella** cell
**caso** event
**castaña** chestnut
**castidat** chastity
**castigamiento** counsel
**castigar** to advise, charge, instruct
**castigo** penance
**casulla** chasuble
**catadura** look
**catar** appearance, to look, observe, read, search, wait
**catar mesura** to practice moderation
**catina** wicked one
**cativado** captive
**cativo** captive
**caualgar** to ride
**caudal** important, large
**cauto** wary
**cava honda** moat
**cavadura** crevice
**cavar** to dig, pawing
**cavelero** knight
**cavero** horse, knight
**cayan = caían** they fell
**cebar** to feed (animals)
**çebo** bait, food
**çegar** to blind
**ceguedad** blindness
**çeio** face
**celada** ambush
**çelar** to hide
**celicio, çeliçio** hairshirt
**cellarero** mayordomo
**çellero** coffer
**cenado** eaten

**çenar** to sup
**çencerro** cow bell
**cendal** fine cloth, **çendal** fine silk
**çeñiglo** white goosefoot bush
**ceñir** to bind, gird on
**çentura** waist
**çepa** vine
**çepos** stocks
**çera** wax
**cercado** surrounded
**çercar** to lay siege, surround
**cerco** siege
**çerneia** hairline
**çerrenícolo** kestrel
**çerro** hill
**cerrojo** bolt
**çertera** certain
**çessar** to stop
**chapado** elegantly embroidered, fortified
**charambela** rustic flute
**charpado** elegant material
**chufa** joke
**çiclatón** garment, silk, undergarment
**çiego** blind
**ciertas** surely
**çierva montesina** mountain deer
**cima** top
**çimas** top branches
**cimera** helmet decoration
**çimiento** foundation
**çincha** cinch belt
**çinquaesma** Pentecost
**çinta** waist
**çintura** waist
**çinxó** 3rd per. pret. of çeñir girded on
**çipdad = ciudad** city
**çítula** string instrument
**clamado** called
**clamor** cry
**claridad** brightness
**claro** bright, brilliant, excellent
**claror** brightness, light
**clausura** enclosure
**clavo** nail
**clemencia** mercy
**clerezía** learning
**clérigo** scholar
**cobarde** coward
**cobdicia** greed
**cobdiçiar** to desire, long for
**cobdo = codo** elbow
**cobertura** protection
**coberturas villutadas** plush clothing
**cobrante** conqueror
**cobrar** to claim, pay, recover
**cobro** remedy
**coçeado** trodden
**cochillo** knife
**cochura** displeasure
**codar** to think, believe
**codiçia** greed
**codo, de codo** on one's side
**codorniz** quail
**codrado** red
**cofradría** companions
**coger** to gather, go, welcome, strike (camp, take down)
**cogido** taken down
**cogulla** habit
**cohecho** bribe
**coidar** to think
**coita** distress, care, worry
**colcha** blanket, mattress
**colgado** suspended
**colgar** to hang
**collación** meal
**collado** mountainous hill
**collar** necklace (white pearls)
**colonge** canon
**coloradita** red
**colorado** red, rosy
**colpada** blow
**colpe, primer colpe** immediately
**colpes** blows
**comarca** area
**combidar** to invite
**comedio** concern
**comedir** to reflect
**comendaçión** committal prayer
**cometer** to attack, commit
**comidir** to consider, think long about, plan
**compaña** men, company
**companas** soldiers

**compasado** well formed
**complido** ended, excellent
**complimiento** respect
**complir** to permit
**complir: mal —** not to keep one's word
**complisión** constitution
**compostura** make-up
**comprar** to pay
**compriso** possessed
**compuesto** strong
**con todo** nevertheless
**conbater = combatir** to fight
**conbidar** to invite
**concordarse** to agree
**condado** countship, county
**condepnar = condenar** to condemn
**condesa** countess
**condesado** kept
**condesiguo** hiding place
**condir** to embalm, annoint
**condonar** to grant
**conducho** food, provisions
**coñecer** to recognize
**confiar** to trust
**confita** cell
**confuerto** consolation, **= conforto** comfort
**confundido** ashamed
**congrueca** mistress
**conhuerto** encouragement
**conjurar** to beg
**conmover** to move
**connusco** with us
**conocer** to recognize
**conortar** to comfort
**conorte** comfort
**conpeçar = comenzar** to begin
**conplido** filled, full
**conplir** to fulfill
**conptar** to tell
**conquerir** to conquer
**conquerir** to earn
**conseia** story
**conseio** council
**consejador** counselor
**consejar** to consult, to plot
**consejo** decision, help
**consenter** indulge
**consistorio** assembly
**consonante** harmony
**consorçio** assembly
**consuelo** consolation
**consuno, de consuno** together
**contador** accountant
**conteçer = acontecer** to happen
**contender** to insist
**contido** happened
**contienda** battle, disagreement, problem
**continente** face
**contir** to happen
**contra** compared, toward
**contrallo** against it
**contrapugnar** to be contradictory, to contradict
**contrario** side
**contrubar** to compose
**conuiniente** appropriately
**conveniente** good
**convent** population
**conventos, a conventos** in groups
**convido** invitation
**conviento** gathering
**copençar = comenzar** to begin
**cor** heart
**coraçón loçano** valiant
**coraçón** valor
**corada** entrails
**coral** of the heart
**corças** coat of arms
**corderino** wool
**cordero** lamb
**cordón** rope
**cordouán** Cordovan leather
**cordura** sanity
**cormano** cousin
**cornadura** horns
**corneja** crow
**coro** choir
**coro** chorus, dance
**corona** tonsure of a priest
**coronado** tonsured
**corpus domini** Eucharist
**corredor** scout
**correntero** in a hurry

**correo** leather pouch, running
**correr** to run, be widespread
**corrida** path, way
**corridor** shamed
**corroceder** to be angry
**corte** court
**cortejar** to court, woo
**cortes, de cortes** courtly
**cortesa** generous
**cortesía** courtly behavior
**cortina** veil
**cosimente** conscious
**costado** side
**costilla** rib
**cotayfesa** girlfriend of a lowly soldier
**coxo** lame
**coyta** haste
**cozer** to cook
**cras** tomorrow
**crebantar** to break
**creçer** to grow
**crecido** full, important
**creío** believed
**crespina** hairnet
**criado** reared
**criar** to create, rear
**criazón** child, group, servants
**crin** mane
**crines** hair
**crismar** to anoint
**crispal** glass
**crovo = creyó** believed
**crudo** cruel, harsh
**cruenza** cruelty
**cuadrilla** band
**cuál** what
**cuba** chest, wine barrel
**cubierta** horse blanket
**cubierto** covered, protected
**cuchiello** knife
**cudado = cuidado** care, careful
**cudar** to believe
**cueba = cueva** cave
**cuello** neck
**cuempadre fontano** baptismal godfather
**cuenta** account
**cuer, de cuer** truly
**cuerda** cord, tie
**cuerdo** obedient
**cuerno** horn
**cuerpo** body
**cueta** tight spot, difficulty
**cueva** cave
**cuidado** worry
**cuidar** to intend, think
**cuita** distress, worry
**cuitado** needy, suffering soul, wretched
**culpa** blame, guilt
**culpar de** to sin against
**cumple** it is necessary
**cumplido** complete
**cumplimiento** fulfillment
**cuño** wedge
**cunplir** to suffice
**cuntado** counted
**cuntir** to happen
**cura** care, worry
**curar** to worry, to care about
**cúrcuma** saffron
**curia** interest
**curiar** to safeguard, keep, suspect
**çurrón** leather sack, shepherd's sack
**curso** life
**curso rimado** poem
**cutiano** daily
**cuyta** cruelty

**d'aquent** from here
**dado** gift
**damas** both
**dañado** harmed
**daño** harm
**danzar** to dance
**dapñar** to harm
**daquend** from here
**dar: — dilación** to hesítate; **— salto**, to assault, rush out; **— sueldo** to pay; **— la vuelta** to turn back
**dávida** gift
**dayán** judge
**de allén** beyond
**de buenas yentes** of a good family

**de claro** right through
**de iusso** under
**de que** since
**de valde** without cause
**deal** divine
**debatas** defeat
**debatirse** to prostrate oneself
**debdo** duty, **en** — as a promise
**deçebido** deceived
**deçeplina** whip
**decir loor** to tell the praises
**declarer** to tell
**decliner** to descend
**decorar** to memorize
**decretal** decree
**defensión = defensa** defense
**degollado** decapitated
**degollar** to slit someone's throat
**deidad** diety
**delante** first
**delantera** front rank
**delantrera** front row
**delegar** to leave
**deleite** delight, pleasure
**delfín** dolphin
**delibrar** to empty
**delicado** thin
**deliçio** delight
**della e della parte** on all sides
**demanda** riddle
**demandar** to ask for, look for
**demás** also, **aun demás** in addition
**demasiado** too much
**demora** delay
**demudado** angry, changed
**demudar** to change
**denegrido** blackened
**dennesti, denesti** you deigned
**denostar** to challenge, insult, scorn
**denosteste** you scorn, belittle
**dentre** within
**denunçiaçión** annunciation
**departiçión** parting
**departir** to explain, render (an opinion), speak
**depassada** step
**deportar** to entertain, have a good time, sport, take pleasure
**deporte** sport, pleasure
**deprender** to spend
**depué = después** afterward, then
**depuerto** game
**derechero** honored
**derecho** justice, righteous, straight
**derechura, en derechura** straight
**derramar** to spill
**derranchar** to leave the field
**derredor de** around
**derredor** place
**derribar** to destroy, knock down
**derrocar** to knock down, tumble down
**desafiar** to challenge
**desagradar** to displease
**desagradesçer** to be ungrateful
**desaliñar** to ruin
**desamparado** abandoned
**desamparar** to abandon
**desanparar** to spare
**desaperçibido** unprepared
**desarrado** forlorn, helpless
**desarramiento** confusion
**desatar** to get loose
**desatentar** not to pay attention
**desavenido** disconcerted
**desayre** anger
**desbaldir** to waste
**desbaratado** impoverished
**desbarato** destruction
**desberconçado** shameful
**desbolver** to wave
**descabeçar** to behead
**descansar** to rest
**descavalgar** to get off a horse
**descoger** to choose **(descojer)**
**descomponer** to spoil
**descompuesto** neglected
**descomulgado** excommunicated
**desconortado** disconsolate
**desconsseiado** helpless
**desconveniente** improper
**descorazonado** unfeeling
**descreença** disbelief
**descubrir** to tell
**descuentra** toward
**desdecir** to scorn

**desdeñar** to scorn
**desdonado** unpleasant
**desechar** to fight against
**desende** from then on, then
**desent** later
**deseredado** defenseless
**deserrado** afflicted, confused
**desfallecer** to fail
**desfazer** to vanish
**desfriado** bored
**deshacer** to destroy
**deshora** early, **a deshora** unexpectedly
**deslate** attack
**deslizar** to slip
**desmayado** fainted
**desmedido** beyond measure
**desmedrido** frightened
**desmentir** to belie
**desnudar** to take off one's clothes
**desnudedad** nakedness
**desnudo** bare, nude, unsheathed
**desollar** to flay, to strip off
**desordenança** disorder
**desparar** to shoot
**despartir** to go away from
**despavorido** frightened
**despedaçar** to tear to pieces
**despedazado** torn to pieces
**despedimiento** leave
**despeñar** to get off, hurl from a cliff
**despender** to pay for one's sins, spend
**despenssa** amount
**despenssar** to pay
**despertar** to wake up
**desplega** displeases
**desplegar** to unfold
**desplumar** to pluck feathers
**despossar** to marry
**despreçiado** dishonored
**despugado** condemned
**despuiar** to take off
**desque** when
**desramar** to pour, to flow
**dessarrado** disturbed
**dessatar** to disintegrate
**destaiar** to cut short
**destajado** apart, destined
**desterrar** to exile, leave
**destetar** to cut off the breast
**desventura** misfortune
**desventurado** unlucky
**desvergonzante** shameless
**detardado** tarried
**detardar** to delay
**detardarse** to delay
**detenencia** delay
**devaneo** fantasy, **de devaneo** frivolous
**devedado** forbidden
**dexar** to tell
**dezer** to say
**diablado** devilish
**días chicos** young
**dicha** fate
**dicho** word
**dictado** story
**diecta** diet
**diestro** right
**diezmo** tithe
**digades** tell
**dilatar** to delay
**dinarada: al menos —** the least amount
**dinidad = dignidad** high honor
**dinno = digno = dino** worthy
**dirruye** destroys
**disantero** feast day
**disanto** holy day
**discordança** discord, disagreement
**discrepante** disagreeing
**discurrir** to discourse
**dispar** different
**ditado** poem, writing
**diversorio** common room
**divinidad** religion
**do** where
**dobla** money
**doblado** folded, two part
**doblar** to double, do the same
**dobro** small coin
**doctriz** guide
**dolioso** grievous
**dolor** pity
**domar** to tame

**domno** man
**don** gift
**dona** gift
**donaire** grace
**donar** to give
**donayre** gracefulness
**donayre: de buen —** witty
**doncel** servant
**doncella** maiden
**donçelleta** maiden
**doñeador** suitor
**doñeo** flattery
**dono** taint
**donosamente** artfully
**donoso** graceful, witty
**dorado** golden, guilded
**drago** dragon
**dreito** straight
**drumón** ship
**dubdado** fearsome
**dubdar** to be afraid, to fear
**ducho** skilled
**dudado** feared
**duelo** grief
**dueña** lady
**dueño** lord, owner
**dulçora** sweetness
**dulzor** sweetness
**durador** sturdy
**durament** really
**duro, de duro** difficult

**e = he** I have
**echado** lying down, thrown
**echar** to begin, lie down, put, throw out; **echarse** to lay down
**edad** time
**edat** generation
**eglera** open space
**eglesia = iglesia** church
**egual** proportioned
**eio** I knock kown
**ejarcia** rigging
**elado = helado** frozen, cold
**elli** he
**elogio** praise
**embargada** pregnant
**embargado** bewildered, frightened
**embargo** obstacle
**embebdarse** to get drunk
**embergonzado** embarassed
**embraçar** to seize
**emendar** to correct
**ementar** to mention, speak, talk about
**emfermar** to become sick, sicken
**emparar** to protect
**emparedaçión** cell
**emparedado** recluse
**empedeçir** to harm
**empenar** to pawn
**empeñar** to pawn
**emperante** emperor
**emperecer** to be lazy
**empero** however
**empreñar** to become pregnant
**empresa** undertaking
**emtrambos** both
**en cabo** after all, in the end
**en nombre de** as
**en somo de** on top of
**enantes = antes** before
**enartado** deceived
**enbaído** shamed
**enbargado** overwhelmed
**enbiar = enviar** to send
**enboluer** to wrap
**encamar** to unseat (a horseman)
**encañar** to grow tall
**encara** still
**encaualgado** mounted
**encender** to stir up
**encendido** ardent
**ençerrado** cloistered, wrapped
**encerrar** to close; to enclose
**ençiua** gum
**enclaveado** nailed shut
**enclinar** to reach down
**encobrir** to cover up
**enconado** poisoned, poisonous
**encontrado** encounter
**encordar** to ring bells
**encubierta** deceit
**end** from it
**endurecer** to harden
**endurido** afflicted

**enemiztad** enmity
**enervolar** to poison
**enfermar** to get sick, become ill
**enfestado** raised, unfurled
**enfiesto** erect, steep, tall
**enfiuzante** trusting
**enflaquesçer** to weaken
**enflaquido** weak
**enfogar** to choke, to repress
**enformar** to teach
**enfurecido** stormy
**engañador** deceiver
**engannar = engañar** ro deceive
**enganno** = **engaño** deceit , trick
**engastonado** incrusted
**engendrar** to sire, engender
**engramear** to shake
**engrandecer** to magnify
**enjugar** to dry
**enjuto** dry
**enlazado** tied together
**enloquecido** crazed, crazy, mad
**enmienda** amends
**ennartar** to deceive
**enogo = enojo** anger, annoyance
**enpeleçido** hairy
**enpenado** lined
**enplasto** bandage
**enredar** to trap
**enrizar** to urge on
**ensalzado** exalted
**ensanchar** to increase, make larger
**ensangrentar** to bleed, bloody
**ensayar** to attack, try, try out
**ensayo** trial
**ensellar** to saddle up
**ensoma** on high
**ensoñar** to dream
**enssenyado** experienced
**enssienplo = ejemplo** example
**ent** about this
**entecado** sick
**entecar** to bother
**entençia** discussion
**entençión** case, contention
**entender** to hear
**entendera** lady love
**entendido** intelligent
**entenebrado** without sparkle
**entero** whole, entire
**entonar** to sing
**entorreado** turreted
**entrar** to understand
**entre dientes** mumbling
**envergonçar** to become abashed, embarrassed
**enviar** to order
**enxemplo: de tal —** like
**era** field
**ergudo** pursued
**ermita** hermitage
**errado** mistaken, wayward person
**erranza** error
**errar** to err, make a mistake
**erveia** bean
**es = ese** that
**esa ora** then
**escala** ladder
**escalentado** raging
**escalentar** to warm
**escalera** ladder
**escalón** stair
**escaño** bench
**escantador** enchanter, sorcerer
**escanto** magic
**escapulado** monk
**escaque** chess
**escarmentar** to learn a lesson
**escarnir** criticize, mock, scorn
**escarno** doubt
**escarvar** to dig
**esclarecido** illustrious
**escolar** scholar
**escontra** toward
**escopir** to spit
**escribano** scribe
**escritura** writing
**escrivano** writer
**escudero** squire
**escudo** shield
**escueso** frog
**escuro** dark
**escurrir** to accompany, escort
**esflaqueçer** to weaken
**esforçado** determined, expert, strong

**esforçar** to strengthen
**esforçio** courage
**esforzado** courageous
**esfriado** cooled off
**esguarde** look
**esmerado** precious
**esmortecer** to faint
**espaçio** situation
**espadada** sword blow
**españon = español** Spanish, Spaniard
**espantada** fright
**espanto** amazement
**especular** magnifying glass
**espedir = despedir** to say good-bye, take leave of
**espejo** mirror
**espender** to spend
**espertar = despertar** to awaken, wake up
**espesura** thickness
**espeto** spit
**espigado** gleaned, pointy
**espina** thorn
**espinazo** back
**espirar** to breathe
**espolonear** to spur on
**espresso** thick
**espuera** spur
**espulgar** to delice
**esquivar** to avoid
**esquivo** dangerous, illusive
**essas oras** then
**essora** at that time
**establía** stable
**establo** stable
**estaca** stake (tent)
**estado** level of society, social standing
**estados** estates (nobles, clergy, commonfolk)
**estança** condition
**estemado** cut off
**estido** was
**estilo** scalpel
**esto = estoy**
**estopa** burlap
**estoque** sword
**estorçer** to deviate, turn away
**estordido** dazed
**estoria = historia** story
**estornino** starling
**estoz = entonces** then, later
**estrago** destruction
**estranno = estraño** strange, special
**estrecho** difficulty
**estrella** star
**estrellero** astrologer
**estremar** to decide
**estrena** entrance, gift
**estribera** stirrup
**estromento = instrumento** musical instrument
**estropeçer** to trip
**estudieron = estuvieron** they were
**evades** behold
**exida, a la exida de** on leaving
**exir** to go out
**eya** behold

**fabla** ficticious story, speech
**fablar** to compose
**fabliella** fabled
**fabrar = hablar** to speak
**fabró = habló** 3per. pret. hablar to speak
**fabular** to speak
**facienda = façienda** deeds, business, event, story
**fadar** to predict a fate
**fado** fate
**falago** compliment
**falaguero** flatterer
**falar = hallar** to find
**falaz** false
**faldrido** valiant
**falesçer** to fail
**falla** doubt
**fallecer** to be lacking
**fallencia** fail
**fallescedero** errant
**fallesçer** to fail
**fallido** false, lacking
**fallir** to be discourteous
**falsedat** lies, untrue things, charge
**falssar** to penetrate, break through

**fambre = hambre** hunger
**fanbre = hambre** hunger
**farina = harina** flour
**farre** giddyup
**fartar = hartar** to be sated, have one's fill
**fascas** almost
**fasta = hasta** until
**fata** until
**fatila** bandage
**fava** bean
**favló = habló**
**fazaña = fazanna** event, fact
**fazer todo recabdo** to take good care
**fazienda** deeds
**fazimiento** friendship
**fe** faith, word; **— que devedes** by the faith you owe
**feble** weak
**febrido** elaborate
**fecho** deed
**fediente** reeking
**felix = feliz** happy
**fellón** violent
**fellonía** anger
**felón** cruel
**fembra** woman
**femençia** effort
**femenil** of a woman
**fenbra = hembra** female, woman
**fenchir** to swell
**fender** to split or is it fendir?
**fendido** cut
**fenecer** to die
**fenescer** to perish
**feno** straw
**fer** to carry out, do, make
**fereza** ferocity
**ferida** blow, kick, wound
**feridor** striker, wielder
**ferir = herir** wounding, to strike, wound
**fermoso** handsome
**feroz** ferocious, fierce
**ferrero** blacksmith, color of iron
**festino** quickly
**fetillado** grieving
**fi** son
**fiador** guarantor
**fiambre** cold meat
**fianza** pledge
**fiar** to trust
**fiebre** fever
**fierga** wound
**fiero** great, strong
**fiero** wild
**fierro = hierro** iron, blade
**figo = higo** something of little worth
**figura** face, form
**fijarse** to notice
**fijo/a dalgo** nobleman/woman
**fillo = hijo** son
**filo = hilo** thread
**fin** courtly
**finar** to die
**finare** death
**fincar** to lean, leave, set up (tents); **— los inojos** to kneel
**finear** to stay
**finiestra** window
**finir** to end
**firgir** to strike, wound
**firmalles** brooch
**firmeza** constancy, steadfastness
**físico** doctor
**fixa = fija** daughter
**flaco** weak
**flagelo** whip
**flamma** flame
**flecha** arrow
**florecer** to flourish
**floresta** wood, glade
**florido** white
**flota** fleet
**floxo** closed
**fluctuoso** fluctuating
**flumen** river
**foir = huir** to flee
**foja** page
**folgado** at peace, recovered, pleasure-seeking
**folgar** to rest, take one's ease
**folgura** ease, luxury, pleasure, rest
**follía, folía** folly, sadness

**fondo = hondo** deep
**fondón** below
**fonsado** army
**fonsario** burial place
**fonte** fountain
**foradado** opened
**foradar** to make a hole, pierce
**forado** entrance
**forçar** to force, have to
**forniçio** fornication
**foya = hoja** leaf
**fragoso** brambled
**fragua** forge
**fraire = fraile** friar
**franco** French money lender, generous
**franquear** to be generous
**frecha = flecha** arrow
**freira** anchoress
**freno** bit, stop
**fresco** young
**friçio** fruit
**frido** cold
**fridor** cold
**frisa** cloth
**friura** cold
**fromera** den
**frontero** frontier soldier
**fruente** forehead
**fuelgo** I relax
**fuent, fuente** fountain, stream, source of water
**fuera de** except for
**fuerça, por fuerça** with force
**fuero** law, customary privilege, custom
**fuerte** fierce, terrible
**fuessa** grave
**fulán** so and so
**fulgente** shiny
**fulgor** brilliance
**fundar** to base
**fundir** to sink
**furçudo** strong
**furtar** to steal
**fuscar** to darken, blurr
**fusó** he fled
**fusta** boat
**fuxó** 3rd per. pret. **fuir = huir** to flee

**gabar** to joke
**gafo** leper
**gala** elegance
**galán** courtier
**galardón** reward
**galea** galley (ship)
**galera** galley ship
**galeya** galley
**galgo** greyhound
**gallarín doblado** doubling geometrically
**gallo** rooster
**gallofa** rolls
**gana, de non buena gana** unwillingly
**ganado** cattle
**gañar = ganar** to earn, win
**gangoso** nasal
**garça** heron
**garçon** lad
**gargarismo** gargle
**garguero** throat
**garnacha** blouse, full-length dress with sleeves
**garrido** beautiful, elegant
**gasiado** company
**gastar** to waste
**gauilán** sparrowhawk
**gavilán** hawk
**gaya** magpie
**gayo** crow
**gemido** moan
**gemir** bemoan, moan
**gemma** jewel
**genta** kind
**gentil** graceful, noble
**gesta** story of deeds
**gesto** appearance, face
**girar** to turn
**girgonça** gemstone
**glera** sandy area (near a river)
**glosa, sin glosa** simply
**gobernó** rudder
**godos** Goths
**golosía** gluttony
**gordo** fat, thick

**gostar** to taste
**gozo** joy
**gozoso** joyous
**gracia** blessing, wit
**gracia, de** gratis, free
**grada** step
**gradar** to be glad
**gradecer** to thank
**grado** pleasure, step
**grado, de** willingly
**gradoso** joyful
**gramtago** grammarian
**gran cuita** great sorrow
**grana** scarlet
**grana** seed (for dyeing)
**granado** big, flowered
**granar** to bear fruit
**grande** long
**grannado** large
**grant contrario** ill-tempered
**grato** pleasing
**grave** hard
**graveza** burdensome
**gremio** flock
**grida** battlecry
**grinyón** facial hair
**gritador** warbler
**gruillos** shackles
**guadalmeçi** tooled leather
**guante** glove
**guarda** guardian
**guardar** to attend, keep, look at
**guarida** cure, remedy
**guarido** cured, protected
**guarimiento** salvation
**guarir** to cure, heal
**guarnición** adornment, arm, weapon
**guarnido** decorated, rich
**guarnimente** accessory
**guarnimento** adornment, trapping, armor
**guarnizón** armor
**guarrir** to cure
**guedejuela** long hair
**guerreador** warrior
**guiñar** to wink
**guión** guide
**guisa** way
**guisado = guissado** appropriate, just, opportune
**guisar** to prepare
**guise** quality
**gusano** worm

**haber de** to have to, be supposed to, be to
**hacer caro** to exaggerate; **hacer curso** to procede; **—se** to become
**hacha** torch
**hadar** to fate
**hado** fate
**hal** all the rest
**halago** flattery
**halaguero** flattering
**halcón** falcon
**hartar** to satisfy
**harto** a great deal
**hascas** almost
**haver** money
**hazaña** deed
**hechicero** enchanter
**hechos** deeds
**hechura** guise
**hedat = edad** age
**hembra** woman
**henchir** to fill
**heredad** inheritance, promised place
**herejía** heresy
**herida** wound, injury
**hermitannía** hermitage
**herrar = errar** to err
**hi** there
**hiel** bile
**hierro** iron
**hilar** to sew
**hincar** to bend
**hinchar** to fill
**hirsse = irse** to leave
**hito, en hito** stare
**hiuan = iban** were going
**ho = o** or
**hobo = hubo** 3rd per. pret. **haber**
**holanda** linen
**homen** no one

**homenaj** promise
**homildat** homage
**hondo** deep, depths
**honesto** chaste
**hopa** tunic
**hora, en poca hora** in a short time
**huebos** need
**huebra** adornment
**huerta** orchard, garden
**huerto** garden
**huesa** grave
**huésped** guest
**hueste** army
**huir** to flee
**humanidad** humility
**huviar** to help
**ieiunio** fasting
**ierro** error
**ígneo** fiery
**igualdad** evenness
**ijada** side
**implisión** swelling
**importuno** ill-timed
**impresión** will
**impugnable** invincible
**inamovible** immutable
**incalar** to matter, be of importance
**incar** to fill
**inconveniente** hardship
**increpar** to rebuke
**infançón** noble, knight
**inmoto** immobile
**instancia** request
**invención** undertaking
**iogó** he lay
**ir a la zaga** to go backwards
**iracundo** angry
**irado** swift
**irse** to escape
**iudgado** judged
**iurar = jurar** to swear
**iusto = justo** just
**ixcades** get you out
**jaez** horse trapping
**jantar** to eat
**jazer** to lie down
**jogar las tabras** to joust
**jogar** to gamble
**joglaría** work of minstrels
**jogral = juglar** minstrel
**jogrería** entertainment
**jornada** day's journey, journey
**judgar** to do justice
**judicio, judizio** judgment
**juego** fun, joking; **por —** in jest
**jugador de tablas** jouster
**juicio** judgment
**julgar** to judge
**juñir** to join
**juntado** gathered
**juntar** to join up
**jura** oath
**juramento** oath
**jurar** to swear, take an oath
**jusgar = juzgar** to judge
**juuenta** youth
**juyzio** judgment, opinion
**juzgar** to consider, to judge

**labrado** worked, wrought
**labrar** to weave
**labriellos** little lips
**labro** lip
**lacayo** lackey
**laço** trap
**ladrar** to bark
**ladronciello** thief
**lagar** winepress
**lagremal** tear
**lana** wool
**lança** lance, spear, warrior
**lançar** to hurl, throw, set (a trap)
**landre** tumor
**lanzada** lance thrust
**lápida** tombstone
**largo** wide
**laso** tired
**latinado** Spanish-speaking
**laudar** to praise
**lauor** work
**lazar** to entangle
**lazdrado** suffering
**lazo** tie, trap
**lazrado** harsh, martyred
**lechiga** bed
**lecho** bed

**lechón** pig
**lectión** reading
**ledanía** story
**ledo** happy
**leer** to teach
**lego** layman
**lejado** left
**lençuelo** shroud
**lengulado** wryneck (bird)
**lenno = leno = lleno** full
**leticia** happiness, joy
**letrado** learned, educated
**levar** to take
**lexer = dejar** to allow
**ley** religion
**leyenda** story
**libelar** legal writing
**libelo** petition
**liberalidad** generosity
**librado** completed, unencumbered
**librar** to clear, exempt, free, give
**libre** book
**licencia** permission; **liçençia soltada** permission granted
**lid** battle
**lidiar** to fight, do battle
**liegues = llegues** you come, arrive
**liesen** they read
**ligado** tied
**ligereza** agility, skillful act
**ligero** light
**lilio** lilly
**limosna** alms, charity
**limpio** clear, clean
**linatge** lineage, family
**linde** border
**lino** linen
**lirio** lily
**liuyano** happy
**liviandad** folly
**liviano** loose, quickly
**lixo** dirty place
**lixoso** filthy
**liz veçera** arduous battle
**llaçio** flat
**llaga** wound
**llagado** wounded
**llagua** wound
**llama** flame
**llano** flat, unworthy; plain
**llegar** to come
**llenero** abundant
**lloroso** lamented, sad
**lo de** matter(s) of
**loar** to praise
**lobo** wolf
**loca sandía** totally mad
**loçano** beautiful, delightedly, happily, smooth, spritely
**locura** madness
**lodo** mud
**logar = lugar** place
**logareio** little place
**lograr** to achieve, attain, succeed in
**logrero** money lender
**logro** payment
**loguer** earnings
**loor** praise
**lóriga** mail armor cover
**lozanía** hautiness
**lozano** haughty one
**luchar** to fight for, strive, wrestle
**luçir** to shine
**luego** here, immediately
**lueñe, a lueñe** distant
**luengo** distant, long, tall
**lujuria** lust
**lumbre** light, torch
**lumen** light
**luva** glove
**luzero** morning star
**luziello** grave

**maçana** apple
**madrina** godmother
**madrugar** to get up early
**madurguada = madrugada** early morning
**maestrar** to confess
**maestría** artistry, mastery, skill
**maestro** doctor
**maga** witch
**magado** beaten
**mager** although
**maguer** although, in spite of
**mahometa** Muslim

**majar** to beat
**mal achaque** sad reason; — **acordado** foolish; — **levar** to quarrel; **por su** — sadly; — **prez** dishonor; — **pro** no benefit; — **sen** foolishness; — **trecho** ill-treated
**mal** disease, suffering
**mala mana** bad manners
**malandanza** disgrace
**malatía** malady
**malato** leper
**maldad** stupidity
**maldecir = maldezir** to curse
**malfadado** ill-fated, unhappy
**malgranar** pomegranate
**malincónico** angry
**malos sabores** troubles
**malquerençia** ill will
**maltraer** to mistreat
**malueztat** wickedness
**malvado** bad
**malveztat** evil deed
**man a mano** immediately
**man** morning
**maña** great, habits, morning, skill, virtue
**mana** trait
**manar** to flow
**mançanar** apple grove
**mançebez** youth
**mancebía** as a young woman
**mancebo** young man
**mançibiello** young
**mancilla** stain
**mandadero** emissary
**mandado** command, message
**mandados** news
**mandamiento** commandment, orders
**mandar** authority, to discipline
**mando** command, rule
**manefestar** to confess
**manjar** food
**manso** gentle, tame
**manta** blanket, cloth
**mantel** tablecloth, **a —es** at table
**mantenencia** dealings, sustenance
**mantener** to indulge
**manto** cloak, shield
**mantón** cape
**manya** practice
**marfil** ivory
**margarida** pearl
**marido** afflicted
**marinero** sailor
**marrar** to lack
**marrido** sad
**martiriar** to martyr
**martirio** suffering
**masa** stuff
**masiella** cheek
**massa** dough
**mástel** mast
**mástil** mast
**mata** tree
**material** subject
**matines** morning prayers, matins
**matino** morning
**mayo** may song
**mayor** greater, ruler; — **medida** utmost
**mays alto** the better one
**mays = mas** but
**maza** mace
**maziella** cheek
**meatat** half
**mecer** to shrug
**medida** measure, moderation
**medio** middle
**medroso** afraid to, fearful, frightened
**meetad = mitad** half
**meiorar = mejorar** to improve
**meldar** to read religious texts
**melecina, melezina** medicine
**melena** yoke
**membrar** to think
**menazar** to threaten
**menbrar** to remind
**mencoios** eyelashes
**mendigante** mendicant (order of friars)
**mendigo** beggar
**menear** to lead, shake
**menester** necessary, need, work

**mengua** lack
**menguado** lacking, wanting
**menguar** to diminish, need
**menos** unless
**mensajes** news
**mensaz** message
**mentira** lie
**menudo** small
**merca** matter
**mercado** abundance, business, trade
**mercaduría** merchandise
**merçet** mercy, famous
**merecer** to deserve
**mereçimiento** merit
**meresçer** to deserve
**meresçiente** deserving
**meretriz** prostitute
**merezría = merecería** would deserve
**meridiana** siesta
**merino** judge
**merlino** sea crow
**mero** great
**mesagería** letter
**mesajero** messenger
**mesarse las barvas** to regret
**mesclado** in turmoil, mixed
**mesiello** wretchd one
**mesnada** men, entourage, troops
**mesquino** bad tasting, miserable one, wretched
**messar** to pull (one's beard)
**mester** need, task, work
**mestruo** monthly
**mesturero** gossipy, liar, slanderer
**mesura** moderation, pleasure, position, rhythm, size
**mesurado** prudently
**mesurar** to behave, cut short, measure
**meter** to put, **— apellido** to complain; **— coraçón** to encourage; **—se** to enter
**metré = meteré** I will put
**Mexía** messiah
**meyor = mejor** better
**mezana** medium sail
**mezquino** wrteched
**mezquita** mosque
**miedo** fear
**miel** honey
**mienbro** body part
**mientre** while
**migero** mile
**mijor = mejor** better
**minera** mines
**ministerio** duties, service for the dead
**mintroso** lying
**mío serviçio prender** to accept my work
**mira** amazement
**mirable** marvelous, wondrous
**miraclo = milagro** miracle
**mirarse** to be amazed
**mirra** myrrh
**mísero** poor
**misión** reason
**moçuelo** little boy
**moguer** but
**moguer = mujer** wife, woman
**mojado** wet
**mojón** border
**molaziello** altar boy
**molino** mil
**mollera** head
**mollido** moldy
**mollura** softness
**molsa** down
**mondado** cleaned
**mondar** to clean
**monedado** money
**monge = monje** monk
**mongía** convent
**monja** nun
**monje** monk
**mont, monte** forest
**montería** hunting
**montero** huntsman, one who flushes out game
**montesa** mountain goat
**morada** dwelling
**morare = morar** to dwell, live
**morder** to bite
**morería** Moorish quarter
**morir** death

**morrá = morirá** will die
**mortaldade** slaughter
**mortandat** killing
**mostrar** to shine
**mote** inscription
**moxmordo** protruding
**moyar** to weep
**mudado** molting
**mudar** to change, lose, molt
**mudas e dones** gift exchanges
**muio** a lot
**mundanal** worldly
**muñeca** wrist
**muro** wall
**musar** to wait
**muzo** seam

**nacençia** birth
**nadi = nadie** no one
**nado = nacido** born
**narices** nose
**nasco** 3rd per. pret. of **nacer** to be born
**Natal** Christmas
**natura** kind, lineage
**natural** faithful, liege, man, native
**nauta** sailor
**nave** ship
**navío** boat, ship
**negar** to deny
**negro** bad
**nemiga** evil deed
**niev = nieve** snow
**ninna = niña** girl, maiden
**ninnes** youth
**nítido** resplendent

**no ...maes** never
**nobleza** honor, riches
**novas** news
**novelo** young
**nublo** cloud
**nue = nube** cloud
**nuevas** news
**nul** nothing
**nunqua = nunca** never
**nuve = nube** cloud

**o = ó** where
**oblada** offering
**oblea** wafer
**oblidar** to forget
**obrir** to open
**obstante** hindrance, obstacle
**octavario plenero** a whole week
**odrá = oirá** 3rd sing. fut. oír to hear
**odredes** fut. of oír you will hear
**offiçio = oficio** duty, job, undertakings, work
**ofrenda** offering
**oi = hoy** today
**oídas, de oídas** hearsay
**ojeriza** grudge
**ojos del mar** sea of tears
**ola** wave
**olbidado = olvidado** forgotten
**oler** to smell
**olivar** olive trees
**olor** perfume
**oloroso** perfumed
**ombro = hombro** shoulder
**ome despensero** steward
**omenaje** sworn promise
**omiçero** murdered
**omildoso** humble
**omillarse** to kneel
**omilmente** humbly
**omne** man
**on** where
**onçeno** eleventh
**onda** wave, whence
**ondrar** to honor
**onestat** chastity
**onores** property
**ora** time; **al ora** immediately
**orador** one who prays
**oral** veil
**orar** to pray
**oras** sometimes
**oratge** storm, wind
**orça** honey jar
**orden** religious order
**ordenado** clergy
**ordenança** order
**ordenanza** measure
**ordio** barley, barley flour

**oreja** ear
**orejudo** big eared
**organar** to sing
**orior** oriole
**ornar** to adorn
**oruela** wind
**osadas, a** boldly
**osadía** daring
**osar** to dare, dare to
**oso** bear
**ospedado** hospitality
**ossado** emboldened
**ostal** common room, lodging
**otear** to look around, look at, watch
**otero** hill
**otorgado** sworn
**otorgar** to base
**otra razón** something else
**otramiente** otherwise
**otro tal** also
**otrosí** also, likewise
**oueia, oveja** sheep, mutton
**ovejero** shepherd
**ovi = tuve** I had

**pace** peace
**padescer** to suffer
**padir** to do
**pagado** grateful, happy,satisfied
**pagamento** contentment
**pagar** to be pleased
**paja** straw, something of little worth
**palabrera** talkative
**paladinamiente** clearly
**palafrés** palfrey
**palanca** lever
**palancada** blow with a stick
**palenque** staked fence
**palero** gallows
**palmas, de —** face down
**palo** stick, wood; **— romano** crozier
**palomar** dovecote
**palomba = paloma** dove
**palombar** dovecote
**palomela** dove
**palonbo torcado** white-necked dove
**palparse** to touch oneself
**panera** granary
**paneziello** bread
**pánicos** underwear
**pannos** clothes
**paños de luto** mourning attire
**panza** stomach
**papagayo** parrot
**par en par** wide
**par** equal, **pares** peers
**parado** set
**parage** noble
**paramento** accoutrement for horses, oath
**parar mientes** to consider, notice, set eyes on
**parar(se)** to stop; **pararse** to remain
**paraula = palabra** word
**parçir** to pardon
**parecer** opinion
**parejo** alike
**pargamino** parchment
**parias** tribute, tribute payments
**parida** new mother
**pariente** relative
**parir** to give birth
**parrado** arranged
**parte** side
**partiçión** division of spoils
**partida** departure, share
**partido** partisan, portion, type
**partir de** to avoid, take off
**parua** heap of grain
**pasada** pace, step
**pasamiento** death
**pascua** great feast
**paso** quickly, step
**passante** beyond
**passar** to die, cross
**pastor** shepherd
**patada** footprint
**Paternóster** Our Father
**patz = paz** peace
**pauón = pavón** peacock
**pavor** fear
**pavoroso** frightening
**pavura** fear
**paxarillo** bird
**peannos** garments
**pecado** devil

**pecador** sinner
**pecadriz** sinner
**pecar** to err
**pecca** freckle
**pecha** tribute
**pechar** to make up
**pedrán = perderán** they will lose
**pedricador** preacher
**pegado** like pitch
**pelegrino = peregrino** pilgrim
**peligrar** to venture
**pelisco** partridge
**pelliçón** fur
**peña** fortification, fur, rock
**pena** punishment, Purgatory
**penar** to suffer
**peñavera** ermine
**pendón** pennant
**pendones** knights
**penitençia** absolution
**pénnola** feather
**peorar** to get worse
**pepión** worthless thing
**perdición** damnation
**pérdida** loss
**perdiz** partridge
**perdonança** pardon for
**perenal** perennial
**pereza** laziness, delay
**perfeçión** prophecy
**pérfido** perfidious
**periglo = peligro** danger
**perigloso = peligroso** dangerous
**perínclito** very illustrious
**perjurado** perjured
**perlazía** prelate
**permanecer** to stay, remain
**pero** although
**peroque** although
**perro marino** sailor
**perrochiano** parishoner
**pesado** heavy, threatening
**pesar** to displease
**pescado** fish
**pescoçudo** thick-necked
**pescueço** neck
**pesebre** stable
**peso igual** even handed
**pessar** grief
**pesso** weight
**pestiello** door lock
**petrina** bosom, chest
**peyón** highwayman
**peyor = peor** worse
**pez** pitch
**piadoso** merciful
**picaça** magpie
**picaña** deceit
**pico** beak
**pieça** while
**piedra** stone, rock
**piel** surcoat
**pielles** skins
**pierna** leg
**pilare** large stone
**pino** pine
**pintura** color
**pisar** to step
**plaça** battlefield
**placentero** pleased
**placer** favor
**plaga** affliction, calamity
**plagado** wounded
**plango** I weep
**plañido** lamented
**plañir** to bemoan, grieve, lament
**plano** simple
**planto** complaint, lament
**planura** plain
**plática** speech
**plazo** deadline
**plega** pres. subj. of placer to please
**plegadizo** beggar
**plegado** bound
**plegar = llegar** to arrive, draw near
**plegaria** prayer, request
**pleito** contract, demand, thing
**pleno de** full of
**pletesía** business
**pliego** rope
**plogo** pret. of placer to please
**plomaças** bedding
**plorar = llorar** to cry
**pluvial = lluvia** rain
**poblado** full, town
**poblar** to populate

**poble = pobre** poor
**pobleza = pobreza** poverty
**poco, por poco** almost
**podenco** hunting dog
**poderes** armies
**poderío** power
**podestad** magistrate
**podrido** rotten
**polido** courteous
**pollo** chicken, young fowl
**polvo** dust
**poner a letras** to study; **— en recabdo** to hide; **— en somo** to lift
**poniente** west
**ponte = puente** bridge
**pontifical** vestment [bishop]
**poquellejo** very few
**por do** everywhere; **— onde** wherever; **— ver** truly
**pora** equal
**pora = para** for
**porfazado** censured, harshly accused
**porfazo** disgrace
**porfía** struggle, stubbornness; **a porfía** diligently
**porfiar** to insist
**porfidioso** stubborn
**porfiosa** persistent person
**poridad** secret
**portaleyo** door
**porter** door keeper
**pos, en pos de** after
**posada** camp, lodging, place to stay
**posar** placed, to land, perch, rest, sit
**posas** handcuffs
**posiesta: a la —** late
**postigo** back gate
**postremería: a la —** finally
**postremero** last
**potente** powerful
**potestad** power
**poyal** high bench
**poyo** bench
**prado** meadow
**preciado** valuable
**preçiar** to consider, value
**precio** honor
**preçioso** important, precious
**predicaçión** preaching
**predicar** to preach
**pregar** to pray
**pregón** call to arms
**prelado** superior (ecclesiastical)
**premiar** to lower
**premir** to close
**preñada** pregnant
**prenda** security for a loan
**prender** to capture, receive, take; **— lengua** to get news; **— martirio** to be martyred
**prendudo** taken
**prennedat** pregnancy
**prenóstica** prediction
**prepotente** all powerful
**presa** prey
**presado** tied
**presagio** omen
**preso** held, prisoner
**presón** prison
**prestar** to help, to lend, minister to; **de —** noble, worthy
**presto** quick
**presumir** to boast, imagine
**presura** haste
**presurado** in a hurry
**presuroso** quick
**pretender** to claim
**prevalicador** liar
**prevaricar** to betray trust
**prez** honor, reputation, value
**priado** ready
**priesa** stress
**primençias** first fruits
**primería** start
**primeriza** first pregnancy
**primero hermano** first cousin; **primero que** before
**primir** to lower
**primo** cousin
**priso** pret. of prender, to take
**privado** confidant, fast, hurry, quickly, son
**pro** advantage, something good; **de pro** noble
**probar** to attempt, prove

**profecía** prophecy
**prohío** I believe
**pronunçiador** secret
**pronunciamiento** tidings
**prosa** story
**provar** to approve
**provechoso** generous
**pudrir** to rot
**pueent = puente** bridge
**puerco espín** porcupine
**puerco** pig, boar
**puerto** (mountain) pass
**pugnar por** to strive for
**pujar** touch, push to
**pulgar** thumb
**pulido** smooth
**puma** apple
**puñal** dagger
**punar** to strive
**puño** blow with fist, fist
**punto** moment, second, time; **al — que** as soon as; **en buen —** at a propitious time
**punto** in a moment
**qua** because
**quadrilla** retinue
**quam** how
**quand** how
**quartonado** divided
**quebraçado** cracked
**quebrantado** exhausted
**quebrantar** to break, defeat
**quebranto** afflicted, punishment, suffering
**quebrar albores** to dawn
**quedar de** to cease; **—se** to stay
**quedo** quiet, quietly, still
**quemar** to burn
**quento = cuento** story
**queque** as son as
**quequiere** whatever
**querellar** to complain
**querimonia** distress
**quessa** complaint
**quexado** sick
**quexar** to complain
**quexoso** complaining, lamenting
**qui** who, whom
**quier** whether
**quilma** sack
**quinto** fifth part of booty of a battle
**quinze días** two weeks
**quisquiere** everyone
**quisto** beloved
**quitar** to avoid, leave, go out, take away

**rabia** distress
**rabo** tail of an animal
**raça** tatter
**raçión** alms, benefice, part, ration
**raçonar** to speak
**rafez** easy, vile
**raído** smooth
**ramo** branch
**rancado** conquered
**rançal** linen
**rancura** resentment
**rapagón** stableboy
**rastrar** to be left
**rastro** trail
**raya** boundary, pleat
**rayar** to dawn
**rayo** lightning bolt, ray
**raýzes** land
**razón** discourse, prudence, reason, speech, story, tales, thing; **de —** truly
**razonar** to talk, speak of
**real** royal camp
**rebata** fright
**rebatado** dark
**reboltor** conspirator
**rebtar** to challenge
**rebuelta = revuelta** revolt
**recabdar** to collect, execute, get, state
**recabdo** caution, help, judgment, message, problem, prudence, warning
**recaudar** message
**recelar** to fear
**recelo** fear
**reçibir** to hold
**recio** insistently, strong
**reclamar** to invoke

**recluso** recluse
**recombrar** to recover, get back, take back
**recordar** to awaken, regain consciousness, remember
**recudir** to come back, come to, return, respond
**red** cage, net
**redargüido** accused
**redondo** round
**redor** around
**refecho** enriched
**referir** to keep away
**refertero** quarrelsome
**refez** easy, easily,vile
**refuyr** to flee
**regannado** bared
**regir** to advise, to rule
**regla** rule
**regnado** kingdom
**regocijar** to be overjoyed
**rehezmientre** easily
**reinado** kingdom, governance
**reja** plow
**relaçión** account, tale
**relampagar** to shine
**reluciente** shining
**reluçir** to shine
**relumbor** light
**remander** to remain
**remecer** to move
**remellado** wide open
**remo** oar
**remudar** to transplant
**rencón** cell
**rencón = rincón** corner
**rencura** anxiety, resentment, suffering
**rendar** to give
**render** to give, render
**rendir** to give, make
**reninchar** to neigh
**reñir** to quarrel
**renovar** to repeat
**renta** income
**reo** prisoner
**reparo** defense, remedy
**repentir = arrepentir** to go back, repent, renege
**repicar** to ring bells
**repinteçia** repentance
**repoiado** refused
**repollo** cabbage
**reponer** to reply
**reposo** calm, rest
**repoyado** rejected, turned away
**requesto** looked for
**requexo** corner
**requiem eternam** mass for the dead
**res** anything
**resina** resin
**resistir** to refuse, reject
**resollo** blow (of breath)
**responder** to answer
**responsión** response
**respuso** pret. 3rd sing of responder, to answer, respond
**resto** survivors
**retebdar** to blame
**retenir** to jingle
**retórico** rhetorician
**retovo** pret. of retener to retain, keep
**retozar** to frolic
**retraer** to go back on one's word, to recount
**retraer** to reproach, tell; **retraerse** to withdraw
**retraído** criticized
**retrecha** fault
**reverdido** very green
**reviver** to revive
**revolver mala çeia** to frown; **— se** to rebel
**reyal** encampment
**rezar** to pray
**reziente** fresh, new born
**rezio** robust
**riba** shore
**ribar** to arrive
**ribera** coastline
**riberar** to hunt along a river bank
**rictat** wealth
**ridiendo** laughing
**ridiente** smiling
**riedro, a riedro** back
**rienda** reins; **rienda suelta** swiftly

**rimar** to row
**rimo** oar
**rioaduchos mescladizos** mixture of flotsam
**riso sobeio** laughing stock
**risueño** smiling
**robí = rubí** ruby
**robre = roble** oak tree
**robredo** oak grove
**roçegante** showy
**roçiarse** to get wet
**roçín** nag (dilapidated horse)
**rocío** dew
**rogar** to pray
**roído** noise
**romanzar** to tell in Spanish
**romeatge** pilgrimage
**romería** pilgrimage
**romero** pilgrim
**romper** to tear
**rovar = robar** to rob, steal
**rraviar** to go crazy
**rrebatar** to take
**rrecabdar** to respond
**rren** thing
**rrependerse** to regret
**rrequerido** sought
**rrevolvedor** disrupter
**rromanze** vernacular language
**rruiseñor** nightingale
**rubicundo** ruddy, redish (face)
**rubita** blond
**ruçiadas** dew
**rudo** coarse
**rueda** wheel
**ruego** prayer, request
**ruiseñor** nightingale
**ruuio** blond
**ruysennor** nightingale

**saber** to be able, to know
**sabido** crafty
**sabidor** informed, wise, wise person
**sabiençia** wise saying
**sabor** pleasure
**saborgado** pleased
**sabroso** delightful
**sacar** to gamble, go out of one's mind, remove, take out
**saeta** arrow
**sage** wise man
**sagrado** shrine
**saia** skirt
**saje** clever
**salado** salted
**salló = salió** 3rd per. pret. left
**salmo** psalm
**salsa** sauce
**salterio** psalter
**salud** greeting
**saludar** to kiss
**salutaçión** greeting
**salva** except
**salvar** to greet
**salvo** care, innocent
**sana = saña** anger
**sancto = santo** holy
**sangriento** bloody
**sano** healthy, helpful, whole, well
**santiguarse** to make the sign of the cross
**sañudamiente** angrily
**sañudo** angry
**sanya** quarrel
**sarna** itch
**savanna = sabana** sheet
**saya** habit
**sayón** minister of justice
**sazón** time
**scoria** slag
**scripto** scriptures
**se** if
**se quier** not even
**seda** cloth
**sedía** was seated
**seellado** sealed
**seglar** worldly
**segudado** driven away
**segudar** pursuit, to pursue
**seguida, en —** at once
**sellado** sealed
**semblante** appearance, image, temperament
**semblar** to recognize
**sembrar** to sow
**semejança** example

**semejar** to look, to seem
**semilunio** half-moon
**sen** mind
**sen pecado** perfect
**senado** rational
**señal** sign, omen; **de —** emblazoned
**senall** sign
**señas** two
**senbrado** decorated
**senectud** old age
**señero** alone, individually
**senes** without
**sennera** characteristic
**seno** breasts, heart
**señor** my lady (courtly language)
**señoría** power
**señorío** dominion
**sentençia** destiny; **sentencia** example, teaching
**sentido** sense, understanding
**señuelo** lure
**seny** good sense
**sepelido** buried
**sereno** evening
**sermonario** sermon
**seror** sister
**serraniella** peasant
**seso** good judgment, intelligence, mind, prudently, reason
**sesso** judgment; **in —** immature
**seta** sect
**seteno** seventh
**seyes = seis** six
**si non** except
**sieglo** world
**siegro** world
**siella** saddle, throne
**siempre jamás** ever and ever
**sierpe** serpent, snake
**sierra** saw (tool)
**sierraniella** mountain girl
**siervo** servant
**siglo** world
**signado** order
**sigro = siglo** world
**silla** saddle
**síllava** syllable
**sin art** loyally, without deception; **— embargo** unblemished; **— par** peerless; **— sazón** not aged
**siniestro** left
**siquier** neither
**siquiera** even
**sirguera** goldfinch
**so** under, beneath; **so su mano** in his power
**sobeio, sobejo** extreme, very
**soberano** very
**soberbia** pride
**soberbio** proud
**sobollir** tu bury
**sobrado** abundant
**sobreçeia** eyebrow
**sobrelecho** bedspread
**sobrepeliz** surplice
**sobresennado** inscribed
**sobreventar** to surprise
**sobrino** nephew
**sobrio** very much
**soçietad** order
**socorrer** to help
**sofrir = sufrir** to endure
**soga** rope
**sojuzgado** subjected
**sojuzgar** to subjugate
**sol** even; **sol que** as long as
**solar** place
**solaz** comfort, entertainment, ease
**solda** salary
**soldada** money, income, pay, reward, salary, wages
**soldado** paid
**solepnidat = solemnidad** solemnity
**soler** to be accustomed to
**sollozar** to sob
**sologismo** syllogism
**soltar** to interpret, let go, let loose, loosen
**somero** highest
**somirse** to die
**son** song, tone, tune
**sonar** to dream, work
**soñar** to sleep
**sonnoso** in sleep
**sonreír** to smile
**sonsanar** to rebuff

**sopieron = supieron** pret. of saber to know
**soportar** to endure, tolerate
**sorienda** lower
**sorostrado** insulted
**sorrer** to take the reins
**sosañar** to mock
**sosanno = sosaño** reproach, anger
**sossacado** lured
**sotar** to dance
**soterrado** buried
**soterramiento** tomb, burial place
**soterrar** to bury
**sovado** beaten
**soverviar** to humiliate
**ssobollir** to bury
**ssoterrar** to bury
**subdicto** subject
**subejano** abundant
**subitáneo** sudden
**suegro/a** father/mother-in-law
**suelo** earth, floor
**sueño** dream
**suerte, de suerte** so that
**sufrir** to endure
**superbio** proud
**superno** lofty
**súpitamente = súbitamente** suddenly
**susso** above
**sutileza** guile
**suzio = sucio** dirty

**tabardo** cloak, tabard
**tábido** corrupted
**tabla** plank
**tablado** jousting target
**tablas** backgammon
**tacha** defect, stain
**taiado** carved, shaped
**tajador** sharp
**tajaña, a la tajaña** on the shoulder
**tajar** to cut off, strike up
**tálamo** marriage bed
**talega** pouch
**taleguero** provisioner
**talente** will
**taliento** satisfaction
**tallado** with design
**tamaño** great, so large
**tandar** to ring
**tañedor** musician
**tañer** to play (musical instrument)
**tanido** ill
**tañir** to play, ring bells
**tanner** to touch
**tanso** touched
**tanta bona manera** so many good qualities
**tanto que** while
**tapete** carpet
**tardança** delay
**tardío** slow
**társico** penetrating
**távano** horsefly
**techado** disguised
**tejer** to weave
**tela** string
**temer** to fear
**temerario** rash
**temeroso** fearful
**tempora** day of fasting
**temporal** weather
**temprado** temperate, tuned
**tendal** tent
**tendejón** tent
**tender** to lay out
**tendir** to open
**tenebroso** dark
**tener** to stand, **tener —** to intend
**tenido** close
**tenor** order
**tenprado** fine (weather), temperate
**tenprar** to make moderate
**tentar** to tempt
**terminado** dead
**término** time
**terniellas** breasts
**tesoro** wealth
**testo** story
**teta** breast
**tetiella** breast
**tez** complexion
**thremer** to tremble
**tiempos derechos** fair weather
**tienda** tent

**tiento, de buen tiento** prudent
**tierno** young
**tierra cocida** brick
**tiesta** head
**timón** rudder
**tiña** mange
**tiniebla** darkness
**tiniebra** darkness
**tino** judgment
**tinta** ink
**tirar** to cast away, pull, pull out, take away, tear apart; **—se** to go away
**tizón** coal, soot
**tizón** ember
**to** tuyo
**tobaja** napkin
**toca** headdress, nun's habit, wimple
**tocado** headdress
**tocar** to touch
**toçino = tocino** bacon
**toda hora** at every moment
**todas sazones** always
**todo fecho** anything; **todo so sabor** completely
**toldría = tollería** would take away
**toller** to take away, take off
**topar** to meet
**tordo** starling, thrush
**tornar** to change, repeat, return, turn
**torneo** tournament
**torpe** awkward, dull-witted, slow person, stupid, unskilled
**torre** tower
**tortolica** turtledove
**torvado** disturbed
**torzal** wrought
**toste** quickly
**toyente** gnawing
**trabajado** harsh
**trabajoso** suffering
**trabar** to grab
**trabuco** catapult
**traer** to shake
**trago** difficult time
**traidor** traitor
**trança** beam
**transido** died
**tranzar** to destroy
**tras** after
**trasnieto** great grandchild
**traspasante** piercing
**traspasar** to torment
**traspaso** sale, transgression
**trasponer** to move
**trasposar** to sleep
**traspuesto** weakened
**trastornado** silly fool, undone
**trastornar** to change the order
**trato** treaty
**traydor** traitor
**trebeja** frolic, sporting
**tregua** truce
**tremer** to tremble
**trenzado** braided
**trever** to dare
**trianza** courtships
**trifudo** large, muscular
**trigo** wheat
**triquete** small sail
**trisca** dance
**tristicia = tristeza** sadness
**tristor** sadness
**tristura** sadness
**trocar** to change, exchange
**troçido** passed through
**trocir** to be left, cross
**troço** sail
**tronpas** horns
**troque** exchange
**trova** verse
**trovado** found, told
**trovar** poetry, to find
**trueno** nose
**trufa** accessory
**tuelle (toller)** to take away
**tuero** share
**tuerta** twist
**tuerto** wrong
**tunbal** hollow
**turbación** confusion
**turbado** frightened, muddled
**turbar** to befuddle, disturb
**turbio** angry, dark, murky
**turbulento** turbulent
**tus** incense

**uço** door
**uerto** orchard
**ueste** host, army
**ufano** haughty
**uña** finger nail
**unirse** to merge
**uno, en uno** together
**untar** to wet
**usado** usual
**usar** to purge
**usurero** usurer
**uviado** arrived

**vado** ford
**vagar** respite
**vaias = vayas** go
**vajillas** dishes
**valer** to be worth, help; **valer un figo** to be worth very little
**valía** power, worth
**vallitanía** lie
**vando** company
**vanidat** illusion
**vaquero** cowherder
**vara** javelin
**varica** staff
**varón** baron, man
**vaso** vessel
**vassalo = vasallo** vassal
**vazío** empty, **en vazío** miss the mark
**vedar** to forbid, prevent, refuse, stop
**vegada** time (instance)
**vegedat** old age
**vegez = vejez** old age
**vegitar** to dress
**vegüela** fertile valley
**veído** seen
**vela** sail
**velar** to be watchful
**velido** beautiful
**velloso** hairy
**velludo** hairy
**veluntad = voluntad** will
**venado** deer
**vençer** to conquer
**vençido** convicted
**vençudo** conquered
**vendríe = vendería** would sell
**vengar** to take revenge, avenge
**ventado** discovered
**ventura** chance, good fortune, luck
**verdor** greenery
**verdura** plant
**verga** staff
**vergel** clearing
**vergüença** shame
**vermeión** red
**vermejo** red
**versificador** poet
**versificar** to tell in verse
**verter** to spill
**vertido** spilled
**vesitación** visit
**vestidura** clothing
**vestiglo** monster
**vestimenta** church vestment
**vevir** to live
**vez** chance
**vezado** accustomed
**vía** path
**viage = viaje** voyage
**vianda** meat
**viçio = vicio** comfort, delights, pleasure
**viçioso** at ease
**vieiio** old
**ventar** to smell
**viento** adversity, empty air
**vieso** song, verse
**viésperas** vespers
**viga** post of wood, **— lagar** wine press
**vigor, a vigor** quickly
**vilano** peasant
**villanía** coarse remarks
**villano** peasant
**viña** vineyard
**viola** lute, violet
**violar** to play the lute
**violero** lute player
**vira** dart, arrow
**virtud** courage, test
**visioso** at ease
**viso** face
**visquiessen** imp. subj. of vivir
**vistía = vestía** was dressed, wore

**viudo/a** widower, widow
**vocación** dedicated, invitation
**volar** to fly
**voluntad** mind
**volver** to wage
**voto** decision
**voz** call
**vueitre carniçero** meat-eating vulture
**vuelto** covered, done
**vulto** face
**xamet** rich silk cloth
**xarope** syrup
**ximio** monkey
**xpiano** Christian neighbor

**y** there
**yacer** to be
**yagar** to rest
**yamás = jamás** ever, never
**yantar** supper
**yazer** to lie, sleep
**yedra** ivy
**yeguariza** mare herder
**yelmo** helmet
**yentes = gentes** people
**yer = ayer** yesterday
**yerba** grass, herb, weed
**yermo** desert, unpopulated place, wilderness
**yerno** son-in-law
**yerro** disturbance, error
**yjada** thigh
**ylada** cold
**yrado = irado** angry
**yuierno = invierno** winter
**zafira** sapphire
**zaga** rearguard
**zancajada, poner —** to trip
**zelo** zeal